The Making of a Modern Saint

A Biographical Study of Thérèse Lisieux

by

Barry Ulanov

Templegate Publishers
Springfield, Illinois

This edition published in 2004 by Templegate Publishers

Templegate Publishers
302 East Adams Street
Post Office Box 5152
Springfield, Illinois
62705-5152
217-522-3353
templegate.com

Excerpts from *The Collected Letters of Saint Thérèse of Lisieux* edited by
the Abbé Combes, translated by F.J. Sheed. Copyright 1949 by Sheed &
Ward, Inc. Reprinted by permission of the publisher.

For Margaret O'Brian

and John C. H. Wu

PREFACE

IT'S the little things that count—how often have we heard that bromide? Or its corollary—*I can put up with the great crises; they don't come very often and when they do I can manage them. It's the little ones, the ones that come all the time, that are so unnerving.* These are commonplace expressions, bromides, clichés—whatever disparaging name seems to fit. They are also fair readings of the experience of large numbers of people who do not have a particularly fresh or engaging way in which to express that experience. Perhaps the fundamental genius of Thérèse Martin, St. Thérèse of Lisieux, was her ability to see the truth in these commonplace observations and to find fresh and engaging ways to say the same things, and then to discover out of her own experience of the tyranny of trivia ways of dealing with the unnerving little crises of everyday life.

That genius of Thérèse's for accurate observation of the world around her and all the people in it was, I think, what first attracted me to her rather than the multitude of miracles—large miracles as well as small miracles—attributed to her. I found myself marveling over her realism, marveling all the more as her true words surfaced from under the sea of sentiment in which it had been drowned for so long, some of it of her own making, but all of it more sticky than it would have been if her sister Pauline and some of her translators had not felt compelled to make *little* emendations, thousands of little emendations, in her writings. It was not merely a recognition of the tyrannous power of little things, I soon discovered, that gave Thérèse great power. It was also a profound understanding of the graces of little things, an understanding which she rarely couched in a saccharine rhetoric. On the contrary, this understanding more often drew from her a remarkably plain and forthright speech in which she asserted the beauty to be found amid pain, the wisdom in suffering, the strengthening power of ordinariness. If one read hastily through the passages in her autobiography or her letters in which she asserted these things, one could easily mistake the assertions for commonplaces, stoical commonplaces, even stuffy commonplaces. But if, I found, one read these passages quite slowly, in French and in context, there was no mistaking the wit, the charm, or the wisdom for anything less than those things. This was a large person, of large resources, whose special miracle was to have found a way of transforming the bedevilments of daily life into joys, and a guide to the many wonders that the bedevilments so often keep us from seeing. No small part of that miracle was that it was accomplished in a very short life in a small Carmelite convent in a comparatively small town in Normandy in the late years of the nineteenth century. There, living at a prodigious pace, Thérèse somehow anticipated most of the textures of modern life, both pleasing and disturbing, and so proved herself at the very least a prophet.

Prophets, as has been remarked before, are rarely also redeemers. In St. Thérèse, however, the two functions seem to have been combined. This book is to some extent an attempt to show her as both prophet and redeemer, without claiming extravagant feats for her in either role. In both, her performances were small-scale, yet important. She made no sweeping predictions, but she did, I think, work remarkably well in the role of mediator between the divine and the human, the ancient role of the prophet, the *nabi* of the Old Testament. However diffident she was about her own contribution—and she really was quite modest about it—she did fully trust her own resources and those of other little people, of all childlike little people, to understand and to judge events and to gather great mercies from them or to keep from being badly buffeted by them. Her observation was too precise and her mind too tough to permit her to think anyone could altogether avoid suffering or that the world could ever find sufficiently strong assuagements to banish pain or to make it inconsequential, any more than it could outlaw death. But though she welcomed the beauty and wisdom she was able to extract from pain and suffering, she was far from taking masochistic delight in her own pain or callous pleasure in the suffering of others. That, however, is a discussion for another place—it is a large part of the burden of this book. If

I have been successful in conveying the wisdom and the beauty of Thérèse Martin's way of living with suffering and dealing with suffering and transcending suffering and finding ways and words for others to do the same, then some of her redemptive power will be clear.

It seems to me that it is almost impossible to examine Thérèse at any great length without finding something large and moving and valuable to one's own life in her littleness, that extraordinarily endowed littleness, that elegantly exhibited littleness, that sweetly gifted littleness. My confidence in her paradoxically large stature has grown exceedingly in the course of my long examination of her life and works; that will be clear to anyone who reads these pages. What may not be so clear is the variousness of the ways in which I came to examine Thérèse and the largesse of the people I met in each of the ways I took. I should like, just like Thérèse, to have been able to say, "I choose all," and then, again like her, to show that I chose all—to cite all the techniques of analysis, all the books, all the documents, all the people without which and without whom I should not have been able to produce these pages. That I cannot do, not only because of lack of space, but also because to attempt to recall all the aids in the making of a book such as this one would be to try to list almost every significant experience in half a lifetime. Perhaps it will be enough to call attention to some of the sources, a few of the people, and to send all those who find themselves deeply interested in and very much moved by Thérèse to the most logical place for all who are touched by her, to Lisieux.

In Lisieux, one has, of course, the physical background of Thérèse's life. But one has more. There, a large number of periodicals centering on Thérèse's life are published. There, the enormous literature that has gathered round her is kept, distributed, and when necessary printed or reprinted. One can have only the deepest respect for the way the community of nuns at the Carmel in Lisieux has supported every sort of Thérèsian literature, from the simplest sort of popularization to scholarly editings of the basic texts. The production of the Thérèsian manuscripts and those of the rest of her family came late, but when they came, they came well edited, free of pockmarks of any kind. There is more to come, perhaps only small pieces which will give us a little bit more of the lives and works and words of the remarkable sisters of Thérèse and her even more remarkable parents. As will be clear enough in this book, I have the strongest possible conviction of the quality of the entire Martin family, a family of large gifts, a family more subtle and more sensitive and more sensible than the beefy burghers of Normandy that too many accounts of Thérèse describe, whether on purpose or not, a family graced as a family with a large religious imagination and with the necessary wit to use it well.

The community at Lisieux was very kind to me, gracious in showing to me, without bars or glass or any other obstacle, the rooms and the furniture and the books and toys and other possessions of Thérèse and the rest of her family, both in Lisieux and Alençon. Much of the kindness was, I am sure, the natural kindness of the Carmel. But much again was extended to me, I know, because of my very dear friend Margaret O'Brian, one of the two people to whom this book is dedicated. She was herself so good a friend of Céline Martin, and remains so close to the present community, that any friend of hers is bound to benefit in making approaches to the Lisieux Carmel. It would be hard to find a more discerning guide to Thérèse and her family, or one more generous in sharing her discernments.

One must say many of the same things for John C. H. Wu, another old friend of the Carmel at Lisieux and of the Martin sisters who survived Thérèse. No dedication, no words in a preface can properly acknowledge how much I have learned over the years from John Wu's writings, from his talk, from his friendship. It may be enough to say that he lives *The Interior Carmel*, that splendid way he chose to describe the spirituality of Thérèse and of Teresa of Avila in the book so titled.

Everyone with special Thérèsian material whom I approached proved generous. Typical of the kind of sharing of the fruits of thought and meditation and scholarship I was privileged to have in the making of this book was the time Monsignor Vernon Johnson gave me and the almost complete back file of his magazine, *Sicut Parvuli*, which he presented to me in England in 1963. One could thank Monsignor Johnson, not only for these considerable gifts, but for all he has done to promote interest in and understanding of Thérèse, to bring discussions of her spirituality to a level of theological seriousness and psychological depth, especially among priests. The thanks would, in a sense, be uncalled for. For those who are as much caught up in the theology and psychology of Thérèse as Monsignor Johnson quite clearly cannot pass up any opportunity, no matter how slight, to discuss both. That must, to some extent anyway, account for the enormous and steadfast interest in this manuscript displayed, from opening discussions to closing paragraphs, by my editor and friend Naomi Burton and by my wife. I am deeply grateful for their interest and for their aid, as I am for that one indispensable translation of Thérèse, of her letters, so accurately and so handsomely turned into English by Frank Sheed.

Barry Ulanov

THE MAKING OF A MODERN SAINT

A Biographical Study of Thérèse of Lisieux

ONE

*I*F, as Pius X said of her, Thérèse of Lisieux was the greatest saint of her century, it was not because of any outward grandeur. She did not do any heroic deeds, as the world rates these things. Her struggles were small-scale. She left a happy home to go to another happy home. All her life she was surrounded by love, and if her life was short and filled with pain, she was never without the constant assurance that those around her to some extent measured the substance of their lives by the part she played in them. With the exception of a pilgrimage to Rome and some seaside jaunts as a child, her adventures were confined to home and cloister. Her geography was of the spirit, her history was of the soul. But they were enough. Within herself, moving always shorter distances, from cell to garden, from bed to chair, from one side of the bed to the other, she was able to do mortal combat against suffering, and to leave such an imperishable and moving record of her warfare of the spirit, that all over the world thousands of others, no larger in worldly achievement than she and as unmistakably afflicted with suffering, have been able to take courage from her example and to find dignity in the smallness and pain of their lives. The drama is indeed a small and an ordinary one, but it is everybody's drama, and it has with Thérèse a dimension that quite justifies Pius X's superlative, the dimension of love.

"My vocation," Thérèse said, "is love," and to it she dedicated her very short life, her death, and her influence after death. Everything in her was drawn to love, that she might herself be a passionate lover and that she might make others equally passionate. Even the vision of eternal beatitude, in the heightened language of most descriptions of the face-to-face encounter with God, was not enough.

"It is not that which attracts me," she told her sister Céline, two months before she died.

"What then?"

"Oh," she replied, "it is love! To love, to be loved and to come back to earth to make Love loved!"

However one translates the phrase—*revenir sur la terre pour faire aimer l'Amour*—the words are awkward in English: "To make Love loved" or, in an agony of infinitives, "to make Love to be loved." But that is the aim of Thérèse and it is her achievement, no matter what the awkwardness of the English or the original French, no matter what artificialities must be resorted to, on her part or ours, to make some sense out of the tangled mysteries of love, to make an endurable life out of them and to make death itself endurable as a result.

Simply to commend love, with a lower-case "l" or a capital, is not enough to make a saint. It is certainly far from enough to make even the most impeccable of saints—one who has filled in the table of virtues with a vengeance—attractive to others not so insistently heaven-bent. The passionate utterance of the name of Jesus has been heard before. The deep desire to be one with him is not unknown among religious, especially female religious. Most of the language in which that particular cry of love has been raised has, in fact, become dulled to our ears by repetition. The girl who cries lamb, like the boy who cries wolf, even when she is crying "Lamb of God!", can only lose conviction with constant reiteration. We may not cease to believe her, but there is a very good chance that we will cease to be interested. And yet with Thérèse, the more we hear her and the more we know her, the more we are convinced, the more we are moved, the more we are caught, caught up in her, caught up in her love, perhaps even caught up in her lover.

There are all sorts of reasons that can be advanced for Thérèse's appeal, all sorts of facile explanations and all sorts of explanations marvelously intricate and contrived. Even the facile explanations require a small book. The intricate ones take many more pages. None, long or short, are altogether satisfying if they attempt to satisfy all, to ask all the questions and to give all the answers. By the sense she made out of love in general and her own love in particular, Thérèse did not take the mystery out of love. Rather, she enlarged it. She made the mystery of love more mysterious, and gave it more grandeur. And yet, at the same time, she made love more accessible to our understanding because she made it more available to our experience. To know Thérèse is to feel Thérèse and to feel her love, to feel it in every way, to feel it psychologically, to feel it theologically, yes even perhaps to feel it physically.

The love that is in Thérèse's life and in her words is not at all remote or academic. It has a desperate reality about it at all times, even before she or anybody else knows her life is to come to a quick and shattering conclusion. Love is all to her. She feels about it, at all times, in all circumstances, what Kierkegaard says about it at the beginning of his *Works of Love*, "To cheat oneself out of love is the most terrible deception; it is an eternal loss for which there is no reparation, either in time or in eternity." What is more, she satisfies exquisitely all the demands of abasement in the eyes of men that Kierkegaard makes for those who go beyond the "half measures" of those for whom love has nothing of the divine in it. He speculates—

> I wonder if anyone has ever been more gossiped about for his self-love than one who has really held fast to the God-requirement and, faithful to this, has loved men and because of this has continued to love them in spite of persecution and misjudgment. Is it not natural, too, that the world is enraged because there is One whom such a man loves more than he loves the world, because there is One towards whom the love of such a man is expressed in love to men?

—he speculates and he describes and what he speculates about and what he describes is Thérèse's kind of love, a love which she will not cheat herself out of nor allow others to steal from her, a love which seems to consume all her days, all her energies, all of her, and yet at the same time grows and grows, and grows all the more as a love of others the more it concentrates on the One.

It is easy to misjudge Thérèse and many have not hesitated to misjudge her. Her stance often seems to be that of a nun concerned only with her own sanctification. She is so Other-directed —with the largest of capital O's—that at times creatures don't seem to be in her life or prayers or thoughts at all. Her prose often seems to dissolve into warm treacle, and when it hasn't suffered from its own embarrassments, it has been deformed by the mutilations of others—her first editor, who was her sister Pauline, and almost all her translators. She has been the victim of the worst art in the Church since sculptors first began to hack away at images of the Virgin Mary and painters first began to deface our conception of that great lady with pictures slobbery with their own sentimentality. She has been misjudged and she has been persecuted by her own admirers, who have insisted upon the sentimental images of Thérèse. And not only have they insisted upon them for themselves, but they have foisted them upon others, in churches, in their homes, everywhere they could thrust the brown and white plastercast of the Carmelite saint, bedecked in roses and a simpering expression selected from the large reservoir of simpering expressions kept by those for whom the seasick look signifies high spirituality. And besides all this, who is she, what is she, but a cloistered religious of the late nineteenth century, dying of tuberculosis and lost in romantic reveries about herself and her God, a poor sick Sister who, as even her venerators admit, was neurotic.

Poor sick Sister she may be, but Thérèse of Lisieux—Saint Thérèse of the Child Jesus and the Holy Face—is also the preeminent saint of the twentieth century, *the* modern saint, canonized as much for her doctrine as for her heroic virtue. The many who misjudge her are matched by as many more who do not. For every intellectual who cannot stand her style and insists upon confusing the real saint with the plaster saint there is at least one corresponding intellectual who has broken through the plaster to find the real Thérèse and has come away with profound admiration for her depth of insight into the nature of love and her prodigious skill in translating her perceptions into actions. She is, in fact, beyond everything else a translator of doctrine into life. Hallowed words, honeyed words leap high over their hallowings and their honeyings in her performance; they leap into life; they do not remain stuck in their own rhetoric, no matter how sticky that rhetoric may appear to be or may really be. The imitation of Thérèse, as her most intense followers have all learned by now, cannot be merely verbal. She is much too possessed by the need for action, she has much too sharp a sense of reality for that.

The imitation of Thérèse is of course the imitation of Christ and that is never meant to be merely verbal. But in the imitation of Christ, whether one follows the counselings of Thomas à Kempis, with whom the majestic phrase itself is irrevocably as-

4

sociated, or anyone else, one tends to get bogged down in words, words which for all their majesty also suffer from an unfortunate obscurity. Thérèse's words are not obscure. Especially now that they have been restored to their original bluntness, with all the false mediating sweetness and moderation removed, they speak to us—of us—with a splendid directness. The only mediation that remains is the mediation of Jesus Christ. This will always remain. This there is no escaping. For Thérèse's passionate love of Jesus is all to her. It is the violent center of her life. It makes her words. It shapes her actions. It sustains her. It sustains all who follow her. It is strangely enough what makes her so unmistakably the most modern of saints, the special saint and the saint in ordinary to this century.

One wonders, even when one has been fully caught by Thérèse, how a doctrine that is in so many ways so traditional and so familiar can be so modern. How, one asks oneself—and how often I have done it!—how does this particular love of Christ, this particular lover, differ from any other? What makes hers a modern love? What makes her seem so distinctly of our time? How does she differ from St. Bernard of Clairvaux? From St. Margaret Mary Alacoque? From Joan of Arc? From Thomas à Kempis and his fellow Brethren of the Common Life? From the troubadours and the minnesingers? From the hermits of the desert? These are not insignificant musings. They are at the center of Christianity; and in the multiple meditations that they set forth and in the answers to questions, however awkwardly phrased and incomplete, that they elicit lies not only the secret of St. Thérèse, but also, I think, the special wisdom of Christianity for our time, its striking relevance, its modernity.

Certainly Thérèse is not the saint most people expected when they began to cast about in their minds for a saint for the times, for a thoroughly modern and up-to-date saint. The saint needed, the saint prayed for, was a contemporary Summist, a systematic debunker and rebuilder, who by masterly classification and arrangement—not to speak of arraignment—would expose the thousand weaknesses and incompletenesses of modern thought, the hollowness of so much science, the vanity of so many scientists, and show by contrast the wisdom of the Christian ages. A new methodology and methodologist were expected, or at least a modern demonstration of the genius of the old. St. Thomas Aquinas

Redivivus was the saint called for, and if not Thomas, why then at least a Bonaventure or an Albertus Magnus, even if he had to be an Albertus Minimus. The age demanded somebody who could deal with modernity on its own terms, and dealing with it, could deliver us from it. And what did we get, whom did we get? What a farce, what a folly, what a wildly improbable set of answers to these prayers!

Seek and ye shall find. Ask and it shall be given you. Oh, yes, ye shall find; it shall be given you. Ask for an Albertus and you get a Saint Bernadette. Ask for a Bonaventure and you get Saint Joan of Arc. Ask for a Thomas Aquinas, even, if need be, a Sister Thomas Aquinas, and what do you get? A Saint Margaret Mary, a Saint Thomas More, a Saint Thérèse of Lisieux. These are the saints who have been canonized in the twentieth century, not a Summist, not a methodologist, not a fine systematic mind among them. Not one a canny confronter of the hollows and vanities of modern science. Not one a good thumping debunker. What we have instead is a moving defender of the faith in Thomas More, but not such a defender as was ever asked for by the admirers of Summas and Summists. For all his noble learning and endless fertile wit, he never perpetrated a systematic treatise in his life. His *Utopia* is a brilliant ironic jest, to show not the marvels of Christians, but their poor employment of their enormous gifts when compared with the judicious use of their resources by the Gentiles to whom no revelation had been given. What's more, Sir Thomas is so humane a humanist that he doesn't demand that anyone else emulate his example in refusing to accept Henry VIII's usurpation of papal authority, but expressly leaves all others, and with genuine compassion and respect, to their own consciences.

As with Thomas More, so with the others. Joan of Arc fought for her king, for her voices, for her conscience—for her several lords, in sum. What's more, she fought against the Church itself, took bishops and inquisitors in stride, in womanly stride, for all the fact that her legs were clad in the trousers of a soldier's uniform. As for the breadth of her wit, the depth of her wisdom, both were there, palpable to the mind spry enough to spot them, but hardly exposed in the language of a Summa or system of any kind. She didn't have the learning, she didn't have the language; she barely had the words to refuse to abandon her conscience, to deny her voices, to desert her king. Another defender of the faith, Joan of Arc, the simplest and the most convincing; like Thomas More, she was canonized in the twentieth century, but not, surely not, to convince anyone, in any learned detail, of the truths of a methodical theology or philosophy.

Bernadette Soubirous was a visionary to whom the most magnetic apparitions of our time were granted. What she saw of the Mother of God at Lourdes others hoped also to see and came—and still come—by the thousands, hoping for some express intervention in the misery of their lives, a healing touch, an explicit remission of suffering, an end to a crippling deformity, an extension of life. Not many have seen what she saw, perhaps none. The interventions do come, the remissions are effected, life is extended, but only now and then, on no regular schedule, and with nothing like a certainty which can be systematized and programmed. What Bernadette's example demands—and receives—is the emulation of stubborn silence against mockery and unbelief, the willingness to be, or to appear to be, unlettered, and to be so openly, avidly, if need be, the mutest of witnesses, the most willingly mute of witnesses. As Bernadette said to one scoffer, "I have to tell you what I saw; but I don't have to make you believe it." In sum, another twentieth-century saint.

Margaret Mary Alacoque is still another saint of this century. Though, like Thomas More and Joan of Arc, her sanctity had been long praised and her support equally long petitioned, it was not until 1920, two hundred and thirty years after her death, that she was canonized. And why? For her elucidations of the doctrine of the Sacred Heart, the doctrine which teaches that the infinite love of God was made manifest in Jesus's heart? Hardly. Neither in her letters nor in her autobiography can any large clarity about the doctrine be found. Then for the revelation about the Sacred Heart devotion that was made through her, for the famous nine promises that brought about the universal institution in the Church of receiving Communion on First Fridays? Perhaps so. But this devotion did not start with Margaret Mary's revelations, however much it may have been popularized by them, nor was she expressly canonized for her support or explication of the devotion. It was the intensity of her love for her Lord, in and out of the Sacred Heart, that raised her to the altars. It was her dedication, from infancy, to a service that was as unswerving and passionate as it was mysterious and inexplicable, that made her so unmistakable a saint that she could survive the tortures of the canonizing process and could continue to survive the contempt of those who see in so long-lasting a dedication and so violent a one little more than the exaggerations and distortions of a neurotic disposition. For Margaret Mary has won the indulgence and even the affection of twentieth-century minds who would normally not be able to stomach the religiosity of a person who insists upon proclaiming herself "a she-ass" and "the vilest and most miserable of all sinners," and what's more uses such language, such self-opprobrium, to promote devotion to her lover. Still another saint of our time, acknowledged as such in our time, and warmly received as such in our time!

One need not, one should not, stop with Thomas More and Joan and Bernadette and Margaret Mary. There is also Maria Goretti, a twelve-year-old girl killed by a nineteen-year-old boy whose importunings to sexual intercourse she constantly and successfully refused. Held up as a model of the "holy purity" whose victim she was, her appeal to the twentieth-century imagination is surely much larger than that. It must come from her demonstration of a delicacy of temperament so precise and insistent, that in support of it she could forget the most fundamental urges to self-preservation and then prove that this was no accident by lovingly forgiving her murderer. No one is for a moment tempted to find in such a saint any exploration of doctrine, much less a learned explication of it. One could, perhaps, find doctrinal matters at the center of the life of Pius X, who became Pope the year after Maria Goretti's death, and who entered the select lists of the blessed with her a half century later. He was a stern opponent of what the theologians of his pontificate called "modernism," and on that perilous issue he caused a small number of documents to be issued and a substantial number of minds to be troubled. But it was not modernism that made little children pray to him and adults so thankful to him. It was rather his fervent promotion of frequent Communion and early Communion. It was the fact that Saint Pius X, like all the other notable saints of this century, made his appeal to human experience. It was his insistence at all times and in all things upon the accessibility of God to human experience, to anybody's experience and not simply to rarefied souls, who by special gifts of intelligence or particular breeding could

8

discover what the common people could not. In this context, with this emphasis, one can understand his zeal for liturgical music that has some inner depths of its own and does not sink into sentimentality and one can perhaps even respect his crusade against those whose infatuation with modern scholarly techniques had made them scornful of experiences and perceptions that go beyond techniques of any kind.

Defenders of the faith, visionaries, a self-styled "she-ass," a murdered twelve-year-old girl who willingly and happily pardons her murderer, a Pope intent on bringing little children to the altar rail as early in their lives as possible and all to the same place as often as possible—these are Thérèse's contemporaries in the lists. This is her world. This is the texture of her spirituality. Each of these saints of this century was dedicated, like her, to love itself and to making love better loved. Each was determined in his own way, with all the special accents of devotion and temperament and environment that make every one of the saints so unmistakably singular, to make God more accessible to human experience.

What gives Thérèse her singularity, what makes her stand out even in such company, is that her defense of the faith, her vision, her pardonings and pleadings, are worked so ingeniously into a pattern, and from a pattern into a spirituality, and that the spirituality has such fullness and such depth that with her the expectations and the prayers for a systematic thinker seem in some way to have been answered. The three parts of her autobiography and her letters do not take on the shape or structure of a *Summa Contra Gentiles* or a *Summa Theologica*. Even when one adds the reminiscences of her sisters, with their recording of some of her most significant words, and her Act of Oblation, and the testimony of witnesses at the proceedings which led to her beatification and canonization, and the expert certifications of all the others who knew her and admired her and kept something like an accurate register of her thought, even then one does not have anything like a fine clean scholastic structure, arranged in a neat chain of cause and effect. Except for the continuity given her autobiographical pages by the narrative of her life, her writings are more like the *Pensées* of Pascal than any systematic structure. They are the random impressions of a soul almost preternaturally gifted with the ability to lift any event, no matter how commonplace, into an anticipation of the eternal, or still more startlingly, into a direct experience of eternity. Almost every encounter with another person, no matter how trivial, becomes some sort of encounter with God.

Thérèse's life was filled with trivia. She knew more than her share of the asininities and the disturbances that human beings make for each other. Even in the convent—some might say, especially in the convent—she had ample opportunity to experience the intrusions of the addleheaded and the impertinences of the small-minded and the self-centered. She had in addition a large share of the ills that the flesh is heir to, ending with the torments of a case of tuberculosis so severe and so poorly ministered to that gangrene settled in her lungs, and with the physical miseries she had an equally large portion of the ills of the soul that the Lord seems to reserve for his best friends, including the tortures of a case of temptations against faith so severe and so poorly understood that she was, right up to her last moments, plagued with terrible doubts. It was these experiences, large and small, mildly disturbing and terrifying, that equipped her so well to become everybody's saint, the saint of those afflicted with nervous little headaches that buzz around the skull like myopic mosquitoes, the saint of the cancerous, the saint of the grievously insulted and injured, the saint of those afflicted with caviling friends and captious enemies, the saint of those doomed to a life of nagging, nattering, carping, grumbling, whining, and sniffling, their own or other people's.

The greatness of Thérèse's little way is that there is no misery too small to be accommodated by it, nor any distress too large to be comprehended by it. With her, one knows that every illness, from leukemia to housemaid's knee, can be understood and not only can be understood but can be given unction and not only can be given unction but can be raised to the highest power. For what Thérèse did with her own life, with life itself, was to make all of it a part of an all-embracing theology and psychology of love. This is what makes a close inspection of her life so useful, so satisfying, and even, I would say, so necessary; yes, still another close inspection, after so many others have looked, and looked closely, for there is so much worth looking at, so much revealed in it, perhaps even love itself.

TWO

*T*HE piety of Thérèse's parents has been much commented upon, much praised, and not a little scorned. From the pages of Father Stéphane-Joseph Piat's *Story of a Family*, and all those who follow his enthusiastic lead, emerges a glowing portrait of "A Vocation to Home-Making" and "The Greatness of Family Life," to quote two of Father Piat's chapter titles. Dickens at his most sentimental was never stickier than this. Everything attached to the Martin family, everything in its background, has express divine sanction: "Preparing the way . . . there was, providentially arranged, a whole family heritage of courage, soldierly honor and faith."

For the opposite point of view, the most articulate presentation is Ida Goerres's, in *The Hidden Face*. Here one may find described the "puritanical atmosphere" of the Martin household, "the sharp separation between occupation and the private religious world which was so typical of the Catholics of the period," reflecting an unfortunate nineteenth-century atmosphere, as Mrs. Goerres chronicles it, in which "the very secularization of life which [Catholics] were condemning and rejecting penetrated, in the methods which were used to combat it, through all back doors into the heart of the Church." And so the Martins rejected the world, wanting absolutely "no part of it," and were, both Mama and Papa, "veritable models of the respectable rising bourgeoisie who were beginning a tremendous economic and social upsurge in the second half of the nineteenth century." Under the heading of "bourgeois," then, almost every activity of the family can be catalogued: their home comforts, their vacation trips to the country; boarding-school provision for some of the girls, private tuition for the others; painting instruction; maids; the requirement that the children always go to school in two's and three's, or with a

11

maid. "The family had become bourgeois, outwardly and inwardly."

It is not important to quarrel in detail over either approach to the Martin family, for there is truth in both. There was a glow to the household, in Alençon, where Thérèse was born, and in Lisieux, where the Martins moved when Mme. Martin died. The sweetness may not have been quite so unvarying as the sisters remembered it decades later—one rather hopes it was not. The light was surely more diffused. But an intense and well-instructed faith did order things in the home, in school, on the streets, in the garden, at the seashore, wherever the Martins spent their time. Similarly, there is no question about the secularization of life among Catholics in the nineteenth century in France. History is very precise on this point. Every turn of the French economy and the French polity made itself felt in the social life of the French people. It was a century of revolutions, from Robespierre's to Adolphe Thiers's, with every stop on the way—the first Napoleon's, the third Napoleon's, Charles X's, Louis-Philippe's, the Commune's—reinforcing the power of the government or of business or of both in the lives of ordinary men and women, and with each time of change an increase in awareness on the part of ordinary men and women of the kind of world in which they lived, its politics, its economics, its social strictures, its opportunities for advancement, its possibilities for downfall. But that awareness, which was borne in upon the Martins very sharply with the Franco-Prussian War and the events of the Commune, did not necessarily create a corollary acceptance. The Martins never altogether rejected the world, never altogether accepted it. They did have their puritan prejudices—"biases" may be a better word; they were very much a part of their rising class, a mixed bag of artisans and managers; they were also the inheritors of a royalist-military tradition, on both sides; they had, too, their own tonality, their own personalities, their own individualities. One cannot, either in the interests of sweet ancient piety or of sour modern hagiography, make *vrais types* of the Martins. They were in the lovely tradition of the little Vermont boy protesting to a visiting city child who had insisted that a croaking animal belonged to him: "He doesn't belong to anyone," the Vermont boy said, "he's his own toad!" They were themselves before they were anything else, as singular in their own way as their sainted daughter, as full of irregularities, contradictions, paradoxes.

Louis Martin's background was a pious one and a romantic one. It was also in some ways a gloomy one, constantly bedecked in black crepe and mortuary cards. Martin *grandpère*, Louis's father, was a captain in Napoleon's army who married the daughter of another captain, one who had at least twice left military service because of incidents not clearly specified in the records, but ugly enough to demand his retirement and apparently unwarranted enough to gain him the warm support of good and articulate priests. Louis's one brother and three sisters all died young: the boy in a shipwreck, one girl at twenty-six, another at twenty-seven, the last at the age of nine. Louis's mother was what was described in the language of the time as a gentlewoman, but not so much of one that she could or would hesitate to press her thirty-five-year-old son into marriage when Zélie Guérin turned up in his life. Louis's father was, in the language of a later time, a character, openly pious in his habits, openly royalist in his affections. And Louis, what was he like? Much like what might have been expected of the son of a Napoleonic soldier with strong religious attachments; much like what might have been expected of an inadequately educated boy with fingers skillful enough to become learned in clockmaking and the jeweler's craft; and something very different indeed, neither Napoleonic in origin nor out of the clock trade, a man with a meditative gift, a natural contemplative. He required the country as some men require a particular kind of food or drink; he lived on its peace, drawing constant recollection from it. But then he drew constant recollection from many sources. A scriptural text, a homely motto, the poems of the romantics, the bewilderments and frustrations of business, the satisfactions of family life—from all these things, he gathered the great warmth of his days, the soft flow of his conversation, the calm restful atmosphere he carried always with him, like a retreat.

Louis's view of events was from above, from an isolation romantic and religious. His taste in literature was very firmly romantic: Alphonse de Lamartine, François-René de Chateaubriand, and François de Salignac de la Mothe-Fénelon. He undoubtedly admired the fine round sound of their names as he did the fine round sound of their writing. In them, his isolation could find solid support. For there they were, great names holding noble views, and holding them with the times, against the times, into that eternity which is the constant object of their invocations and the glorious subject of their supplications. For Louis, there would be no hollows in Lamartine, no corniness, no objectionable sentimentality. Neither would there be much that was superficial. His favorite verses, his daughter Céline tells us, were those which made little of time and everything of eternity—

Time is your sailing ship and not your home.

"Jealous time," as Lamartine called it, did not trouble Louis. He was glad to summon it to justice in the familiar accents of the romantics—"Hé quoi!" "What about it?" And he unquestionably revelled in the not-so-familiar sweetness of sound of the romantics; not so familiar, at least, in the towns in which he had grown up, Strasbourg and Alençon—

Éternité, néant, passé, sombres abîmes,
Que faites-vous des jours que vous engloutissez?
Parlez: nous rendrez-vous ces extases sublimes
Que vous nous ravissez?

Eternity, Death, Past, gloomy depths,
What do you do with the days that you swallow?
Speak: will you give us back those glorious ecstasies
That you tear away from us?

Lamartine's isolation in the French legislature—eighteen years alone, without friends, without enemies, in the Chamber of Deputies—would have appealed to Louis Martin. The poet's idealism in politics, like his idealist aesthetic, would have had large resonances for Louis, who was, in his wanderings through nature, in his travels, in his early ambition, to dedicate himself to the most romantic service in the priesthood, at the great St. Bernard monastery in Switzerland, so much like a figure out of Goethe, out of Chateaubriand, out of all the romantics who associated nature and God and man's vagrant journeys through the one to find the other. As far as we know, Louis never lost his faith, as Chateaubriand did, and did not have to recover it, but he was moved by the writer's sonorous testament to his own recovery of faith, Le Génie du Christianisme—The Spirit of Christianity—as he must have been again by Chateaubriand's brightly polished portraits of The Martyrs and his Itinerary from Paris to

Jerusalem, a record of a trip that all his life Louis eagerly wanted to take, over and over again ardently hoped for, and never was able to accomplish. How much Chateaubriand's sounding phrases appealed to him! When the writer praised Homer for his sound —"Thus does the voice of heaven, in a tempest, alternately rise and fall in the recesses of the forests"—Louis could hear all at once the marvels of the past and the present, of nature and supernature. He himself knew the voice of heaven in a tempest. He heard—he saw—he felt—he tasted supernature in the midst of nature. That was the texture of his contemplative exercises, conducted while fishing, which he did well and often, on walking tours, on pilgrimages, on retreats, or in his many hours at the Pavilion, outside of Alençon, which he bought in 1857, the year before his marriage.

The Pavilion is still a handsome retreat, though now it survives only as a monument to the Martins, and though today the city of Alençon, small as it is, has crept right up to its borders. But its hexagonal shape, its three stories, its several openings to the countryside around it, all still suggest that kind of withdrawal which Louis found in his favorite writers, in his favorite sports, in his favorite religious texts. Each time he entered the Pavilion, the framed texts greeted him, hung next to hunting and fishing implements, on the walls of the tower. When they were not enough for him, he had recourse to a small library of spiritual reading. Even here, his taste was not without its romantic overtones. In Fénelon he found a congenial advisor, a chivalrous nature, repelled by the indifference to the great Christian truths at the court of Louis XIV, one that was uneasy with the systematic and rationalistic philosophical exercises of his contemporaries and that was inclined to the warmest confidence in human resources for good, to the point of accepting all he could find that was positive in the Quietist doctrines of Mme. Guyon. If the word did not still upset heresy hunters, who would be quick to jump to an unwarranted conclusion, one could say with some justice that Louis Martin was himself something of a Quietist, in the sense that his quiet faith was constantly supported by both the hidden and the open voices in nature. For Louis, communion with God was as easily entertained in the casual encounters of the day as in the liturgical solemnities which he sought so frequently and so eagerly. Like Fénelon's *Télémaque*—Ulysses's son Telemachus—

Louis was on pilgrimage in a hostile and artificial world. As Telemachus had Mentor to guide and counsel him, Louis had Lamartine and Chateaubriand and Fénelon. His adventures were not so dramatic as Telemachus's, on the surface at least, but they reached as far into history for their points of reference and dipped as deep into mystery for their points of celebration.

If it is easy to misjudge Thérèse, it is just as easy to misjudge her father. He can seem a soft, sentimental man, made fearful and retiring by the world. He can seem prematurely fixed in his timid ways. One might think, as Ida Goerres does, that "there had developed" in his "family a tacit agreement to treat Papa as a peculiarly fragile treasure. A veritable conspiracy of tenderness spread protective wings over his life." But this "fragile treasure" was famous for saving a drowning friend, with whom he had been on a walking tour, and, according to Céline, for rescuing several others who were about to go under rough waters. He rose at the ring of fire bells like a Dalmatian and rushed to the scene of a conflagration with the determination of a Fiorello LaGuardia, to see whom or what he could save. At least once he put out a fire all by himself, in a shack opposite his home, rescuing the old Irish woman who lived in it. There *was* fear for him in the family, a "veritable conspiracy of tenderness," elicited time and again when he stepped in to separate two street fighters, boys or men. The fear was that he would get badly beaten himself. He once took on a wild bull, who was tearing up his box of fishing gear, with nothing more formidable as weapons than his fishing rods, and managed to save everything, gear, rods, himself.

One never knew whom Louis might bring home. He lifted an old drunk out of the muddy streets of Lisieux and brought him back to the house for repairs. His particular solicitude for drunkards was commented on by several of his children. He took in an entire family when it was evicted. When the destitute aged were his companions, on the street or at home, he had his daughters kneel down to them for their blessings. He befriended tramps, the poor, the sick. Several sources speak of the speed with which he responded, not simply to the appeal, but to the mere sight of the rejected and despised of this world. When he found an epileptic at the railway station without enough money for his fare, Louis took up a collection in his own hat, starting with what money he had of his own. It is not enough to say, as Mrs. Goerres does, that "The traditional charities of the wealthy bourgeois household were practised as a matter of course." No actions in this man's life, and especially not his acts of charity, were merely a matter of course.

It would be silly to pretend that Louis Martin had an extraordinary intellectual reach. But he did have a sensibility that was all feeling—not sentimentality but feeling, a delicate compound of emotion and ratiocination, which responded quickly and sensitively to people and things, to poetry, to spiritual writing, to the visible things of this world and to the invisible. He was, like Ignatius Loyola and Teresa of Avila, a lover of chivalric romances who delighted in the high-flown language associated with those tales. He had himself, according to a contemporary, "the air of a cavalier," and he constantly assured his daughters of their equal and opposite virtues by calling them "the dauntless one" (Céline), "the good-hearted" (Léonie), "the diamond" or "the gypsy" (Marie), "the fine pearl" (Pauline). Then, in a rash of such rhetoric, freshly or not so freshly coined for his youngest, he dubbed Thérèse "little queen," and not only "little queen," but "Little Queen of France and Navarre," or "the bouquet," or "little blond May-beetle," or, in memory of those children who were victimized by the terrible losses in a famous battle during Napoleon's retreat from Moscow, "the orphan of the Berezina." As for himself, he liked the name of "Xavier," and used to sign himself that way, in a kind of fantasy of association with St. Francis Xavier, whose title and performance as Apostle to the Indies must have had for Louis delightful overtones of chivalry and knight-errantry. He and his wife both hoped eagerly for a son who could become such a missionary and, with their two boys, that was the image that came to them with each birth, and disappeared with the death of each, each as an infant.

Religion and romance were indissolubly linked for Louis Martin, but not in any merely crude or fulsome display. When he signs his letters to his children with a thousand kisses or a fervent embrace, he does so out of a full heart which has never been closed to the joy and tenderness of paternal love, not to any of it. When he closes a letter to his wife, reporting on his successes in selling the lace she has been producing in her workrooms, with the customary embrace and the promise that he is "your husband and true friend who loves you forever," he is not simply echoing copybook gentility. The love is real and so is the respect. He *is* her true friend, who had thought, at first, that his union with her would be only in God, without any overt sexuality. Like the hero of Lamartine's *Jocelyn,* soon to be ordained a priest, who loved a girl whom he had saved from death with the love of a brother for a sister, Louis thought such a relationship perfectly reasonable. We have no reports from the marriage bed of the Martins, but clearly, once the confessor of the couple had followed Mme. Martin's lead in explaining to Louis that brother and sister relationships were generally destined for brothers and sisters, Louis was determined to have as many children as his late marriage would permit and, after nearly a year of celibate marriage, he fell to his new purpose with exemplary vigor, producing nine children, five of whom survived.

Louis had been frustrated in his ambitions to the religious life. His attempt to join the Augustinian Canons of St. Bernard in the Swiss Valais, in their work of ministering to the bodies of lost travelers with the aid of the great dogs named after their monastery and attending to their own and other souls with vocal and contemplative prayer, was apparently doomed when the Prior required that he fill in some of the gaps with which his poor education had left him, and especially that he learn Latin. Louis tried. He bought the necessary books, Greek as well as Latin, and enrolled with a Latin master in Alençon. But his zeal to become a monk was not enough. He was not a natural student. He became sick. The signs were clear. He quit. But he did not stop thinking in terms of a resolute asceticism, as the way he began his marriage makes clear enough. And he obviously had a large contemplative gift, which was fed by the simple blunt sentences with which he placarded his walls at the Pavilion—"God is all"; "God above all"; "*Ad majorem dei gloriam.*" Ignatius's motto, which Catholic boys and girls have been printing in initials above their homework and exams for several centuries now, was not beyond his Latin—everything "For the greater glory of God."

If the contemplation had never reached beyond the sententious, Louis would have been an ordinary enough devout man. But he saw in the sentences from poets and saints and philosophers and historians, which he collected into a special book, a multiplicity of meanings, a constant counsel to go well above and beyond appearances, like the sacramentality of the things of nature, which reveal to those who look closely enough design, purpose, nothing less than adumbrations of eternity. To a modern man, a more skeptical man, Louis must seem hopelessly naïve, trusting, simple-minded. He brings home moss and shells for Pauline to make into ornamental collages. He plays King to his subject-children, to reward them for good work in school or to frown at poor work. He encourages his youngest daughter to make toy altars in the garden. He constantly takes the children, all of them, to Masses, Benedictions, or visits to the Sacrament. He demands custody of the eyes when they pass bathing places or the unshaded windows of those less self-consciously modest than he. He will not tolerate strong language. And yet he never seems a tyrant, never—if we can trust his daughters' accounts—evokes the rebellion so essential to the children of our century. He remains, in fact, such a repository of the virtues and so benevolent a figure that Thérèse sees God the Father in his image—*Papa le bon dieu* she calls the Creator.

The point is that Louis Martin *was* hopelessly naïve and trusting and simple-minded, even by the standards of his own time. People wrote poems to him to praise him for his charity, as full of aphorisms as this great keeper of pithy sayings could have wished. He had made the tired old statements believable again, as perhaps every really good person does at some time or another, but not by any merely epicene performance of moral duties or any nagging, smirking goodness of the kind which quite properly draws echoing smirks and sniggers and snipes from those who mock it. There was about him always, apparently, an unmistakable virility, of the kind which, for example, allowed him, simply by walking at the head of a group of pilgrims returning from Lourdes, with an oversized wooden rosary thrust round his neck, to stop the jeers of an unfriendly crowd. His faith was great, his hope was great, his trust was great, but he was not without fears. He did not move easily with the times, with its language or with its customs, with its changing standards of dress or undress. He was sorely tempted by some woman or women at least once in Paris, so sorely, as he told it later on to his wife, that she used the intensity of his response as a basis for warning her brother to remain vigilant against such temptations when he went to the big city to train as a pharmacist. Louis was not without his reluctances and regrets, too, as he saw each of his daughters take off for the convent or plan to do so, even though four of the five were to remain at hand, just around the corner and down the street at the Carmel in Lisieux. But there was in him at all times a remarkable serenity. If it was not always his first resource, his inevitable response to tension and anxiety, it was there, not far from the surface, accessible even in such terrible stress as his last lingering illness provided.

For seven years Louis suffered from strokes and paralysis and a series of fluctuating mental disorders, the result, it is fairly clear, of cerebral arteriosclerosis. As Thomas Verner Moore, who makes this diagnosis, points out, this "last illness of Louis Martin is not only an illustration of the development of mental symptoms in arteriosclerosis but also a beautiful picture of sanctity at its therapeutic level." For Louis still had hold of his serenity. Ultimately both his legs were paralyzed. He spoke with difficulty. His memory came and went. But when he could, he followed the prescriptions and proscriptions of the Church, observing what his mental state permitted of Lenten regulations, going, when he could, to daily Mass and Communion. Most significantly, as is pointed out by Céline, who along with Léonie took care of him at home the last two years of his life, "even in his attacks of nervousness or of sadness, he never showed signs of revolt, nor of any violent or unbecoming behavior." This, she says, "explains . . . what made him seem so touching in the midst of his infirmities. . . ." Thus, comments Father Moore, the psychiatrist doubling as spiritual writer, "Thus did great holiness show its power to maintain the vigor of the personality in spite of ever increasing damage to the brain."

Unless there is enormous exaggeration and distortion in the accounts of Louis given by his daughters and his and their contemporaries, and nothing has been brought forward by anyone to suggest that this is so, he must be accepted as a personality of extraordinary gifts, perhaps as so generously endowed with faith that he must be denominated a genius in this area. He did not live with verbal fictions; what he said he believed, he truly believed, he entirely believed, and when he should have been most delusive and his faith most attenuated, he remained firm enough, clear enough, directed enough in his beliefs to accept his trials as a necessary humiliation, sent to him to chasten his pride and to provide others with an opportunity for understanding and, it might even be, for conversion. "I was always accustomed to command," he lamented to his doctor at the hospital to which he was first sent, "and here I must obey; it is hard! But I know why God has sent me this trial. I never had any humiliations in my life; I needed one." His life had style right to the very end.

Style may also be an appropriate word for the life of Zélie Guérin, but it is a different style, I think, closer to stoicism and the product of greater, or at least more protracted, agonies than Louis's. She also was the child of a professional soldier of some real military and human distinction. Her mother, on the other hand, was a stiff-lipped, stiff-necked person, indulgent to her one son, Isidore, severe in her treatment of her two daughters, Marie-Louise and Zélie, and unbending enough in her disposition generally to make her no success at all in her attempt to run a café when the family moved to Alençon from the small village where Zélie was born in 1831. Mme. Guérin was a pious woman, indeed a preacher of pieties to anyone who could be persuaded to listen. Remarkably enough, in spite of a personality that did not please her daughters much more than it did other people, she did not blunt the religious fervor of either girl. The older, Marie-Louise, after several rejections, became a Visitation nun. The younger, Zélie, made application to the Sisters of Charity, and though she was refused, with a flat denial by the religious superior of even the possibility of her having a vocation, she remained dedicated to some form of direct service that could be interpreted as doing her Lord's will in the married state.

Zélie Guérin's life followed a pattern of denials and deprivations. Education was for Isidore. The religious life was for Marie-Louise. She, Zélie, had no dowry, and little hope of one. She could only hope that the voice she heard one day, a few weeks before her twentieth birthday, was not an illusion but a useful and trustworthy counsel to become a maker of *Point d'Alençon*. At least once again, when she first saw Louis Martin, she seems to have heard an interior voice identifying Louis as the man for her —"This is he," she heard, after she passed Louis on the bridge of St. Léonard, "he whom I have selected for you." Delusion? Authentic experience? Who could possibly know? The sequels are simple and clear enough, however. She married Louis. She became an expert maker of the *Point*, that is, of the Alençon stitch, a lacy linen delicacy reaching back to the fifteenth century for its origin, and an exquisite edging for almost any purpose for which a lace border might be appropriate. I have held her work in my hands and examined and admired its handsome involutions, picked out so carefully, first in vellum and then in linen; leaves, buds, flowers, hanging from a net border at the top, falling to a subtle and tender silhouette, formed at the bottom by the outline of each of the constituent elements of the lace design. It is not hard to see why her work prospered. Her performance, or that of the other makers of *Point d'Alençon* whom she directed, was both skilled and imaginative.

Zélie had been making her lace for almost seven years, as student and professional, when she married Louis on July 13, 1858. She had a small but substantial establishment in her own home, to which workers in the Alençon specialty brought their pieces to be assembled. She had, finally, a small dowry and her own savings, about half again as large as her dowry. With Louis's monies, gathered from his jewelry and clock business, and his house in Alençon, just around the corner from hers, and the Pavilion, the couple started married life in some comfort. They needed it, Zélie particularly. There was no great consolation in the vow of celibacy which Louis had taken and Zélie had, she thought, fully accepted. But she cried bitter tears when she went, shortly after their wedding day, to visit her sister at the convent in Le Mans, partly, it appears, tears of frustrated motherhood, partly tears of frustration of that ancient ambition to the religious life which Marie-Louise was fulfilling as Sister Marie-Dosithée of the Visitation.

Zélie never reproached Louis for the difficult ten months with which their marriage began. When, in 1877, she recalled for Pauline her visit to her sister at the Le Mans convent on the day of her marriage, she explained that their feelings were always the same, that Louis was always her comfort and her support. But she also said that on that day she "cried all my tears, more than I had ever cried in my life before, more than I was ever to cry again. My poor sister didn't know how to console me." She was crying for her loss of vocation, that seems clear—all vocation, as it must have seemed to her then. Seeing her sister ensconced in the convent reminded her of how much she wanted to be there—that she tells Pauline. Feeling that unhappiness must also have reminded her of the emptiness of her marriage, an incomplete comradeship, a desolate future—that she does not tell Pauline. But the coming of children changed everything: "We lived only for them. They were all our happiness and we never found any except in them. Nothing troubled us anymore; the world was no longer all on our shoulders. It was a great recompense for me. I wanted lots of children, to prepare for eternity."

The French is clear enough: Zélie wanted to raise her children for their heavenly destination. But the preparation was her own as well, in some ways almost as hard and bitter as the years of suspended vocation. The preparation entailed years of children's illnesses and deaths, years of her own growing weakness and approaching death. All the pictures we have of her show a long sad face, the eyes almost on the edge of tears. The sorrow is not only intelligible in this face, it is also intelligent. Even in the somewhat fuzzy old photographs, even in Céline's rather rhapsodized drawings, Zélie looks as if she has moderated her misery with careful thought and meditation. In most women, of her time or any other, the plain high-necked dress and severely drawn hair, pinned behind her head into a tight bun, would produce an appearance of primness, of unhappy or critical withdrawal from the world, of harshness. Not so in Zélie, I think. Brooding, yes; deep concern; the scars of difficult childbirths and uncertain infancies; finally, those terrible years, from 1867 to 1870, when one after another, her two boys died, one under five months, the other nine months old, and then Hélène, suddenly, at the age of five, and once more, Mélanie Thérèse, after only six and a half weeks—all this seems to show on her sorrowful face, but so does a lively wisdom. If this is reading too much into her face, we have the confirmation of wisdom in her letters, 217 of them, from the first of January, 1863, the year her third child, Léonie, was born, to the sixteenth of August, 1877, twelve days before her own death. It is sometimes a folk wisdom, steeped in the difficulties of sustaining a complex family life, with her father-in-law and mother-in-law in the house, her own family just across the road, her brother delighting her and worrying her as he grows into manhood, her sister in the convent engaging her deepest sympathies, and more, what is usually called *holy* envy, to baptize a not quite consolable ache. It is a wisdom always pungent with a sharp self-consciousness, best exhibited in the letters to her sister-in-law, a woman more than good enough for her brother Isidore, she thought, a woman close enough in temperament to her to draw, along with Isidore, her most candid confidences, her most detailed narratives, her fairly frequent admission of her defenselessness in the face of mortality.

When her father-in-law died on June 26, 1865, she wrote her brother the next day the clearest avowal: "I confess to you that death scares me. I have just come from seeing my father-in-law, his arms so stiff and his face so cold! And to think that I shall see my own loved ones like that or that they will see me! If you are used to looking at death . . . as for me, I have never seen it so close up." It wasn't long before she was to see it with a stunning regularity, and to face it with a remarkable strength. She saw with joy the first of her two Josephs dressed up in princely clothing to celebrate New Year's Day in 1867. Louis said she was "exhibiting him like a wood carving of a saint." The little baby laughed with "a full heart," she wrote her sister-in-law. And so she returned from the home of the wet nurse, just outside Alençon, where the boy was being looked after. But what brief joy, she laments. At three o'clock the next morning, a knock at the door; the boy is very sick; he may die. He did die, probably of the infection which had caused the three-A.M. knock at the door. They called it erysipelas or St. Anthony's Fire; we now know it to be caused by several varieties of streptococcus.

The second Joseph lasted a little longer than the first. He too was left with the wet nurse, Rose Taille. He was always sick, with bronchial disorders, with intestinal trouble; he was wasting away. At nine months, his arms and legs were no bigger than they had been at three. Zélie tells her brother how pleased she is to see his wife and little girl look well. But this makes her sigh, not, she assures him because of any jealousy, that he must understand—

> because I should be terribly hurt to see you as unhappy as I am, weighed down with a difficult business and five children to bring up. But God, who is a good father and who never asks more of creatures than they can take, has lightened the burden—the *Point d'Alençon* is slowing down. This is a relief for me, I tell you; I don't know how I could take it if I were to get a rush of orders right now.

No medicine worked. Zélie admitted to being thoroughly discouraged, with no more strength to look after him, with her heart anguished "to see so small a child suffer so much." What was left was a small melancholy cry, wide-open eyes without sleep, death, which Zélie had prayed for: "My heart was relieved when I saw him give up his last breath."

On and on the illnesses and deaths came. Ten days after the death of the second Joseph, Zélie's father died. There was some comfort in the fact that she had been able to persuade him to live his last few years with her, in her house, in spite of his own objections. There was a certain consolation in the old man's fortitude in the face of death, his openness to it, with much making of the sign of the Cross—"I hope my death will be like his." She invites her sister-in-law to come and see her, "It would be a great treat . . . but what shall I say, I am so used to sorrow."

She was nearly deranged from sorrow. "I preach to others," she tells her sister-in-law, unhappy with a sick husband, "and I am hardly reasonable myself. Saturday, I looked all over for my father; I was sure I would find him; I couldn't understand that I was separated from him forever. Yesterday, I went to the cemetery. Seeing me, anyone would have said, 'There is the coldest woman in the world.' I was on my knees at my father's grave, but I could not pray. A few steps away, I knelt at the tomb of my two little angels; again, the same apparent lack of feeling." She tried to assuage her sorrow and to deepen her feeling with the offering of all the good works she should be able to do in her life, and with the good works, the pains as well; all her suffering, everything, to be offered up for her father. And she suffered! All these deaths and a violent toothache, too. "My God!" she exclaims to her brother, "how bored I am with suffering! I haven't a penny's worth of courage."

A year later, she was restored to something like full peace and happiness. Her oldest child, Marie, had had a gala first Communion. After some months of intense prayer for Sister Marie-Dosithée, in which Marie Martin had led the way, the family's own nun seemed to be recovering from the latest of her attacks of tuberculosis. Zélie's seventh child, Céline—or rather, Marie-Céline, for like all the children, boys as well as girls, she bore the name of Marie first—was doing well with the wet nurse, the same everblooming Rose. Zélie tells her brother she will have another child, though she assures her husband she will not. She wants a son, but she wants no more heartache. By the fall of 1869 she can announce a hard-won equanimity: "neither on one side nor on the other do I have any worries. My business goes neither well nor badly; that's the way I'd like it to stay. For the moment, I've got everything except trouble!"

The calm did not last. Old Grandpère Guérin's favorite child, Hélène, sickened and died. Zélie bitterly mourned the loss of a girl who had proved more than even compensation for the two boys, a girl who had been a constant source of happiness, one who had pleased everyone, at home, at school, wherever she went. Zélie was once again thoroughly mixed up about her children. The blows had been too many. She had become used to childhood illnesses with her first girls, but now what to do with a sick Léonie? Her brother told her to change medicines, but change to which one? With her others, one docter had prescribed nothing; another had a new remedy every day. Now Léonie was still sick with an affliction of the eyes which she had been bothered with for five years, since she was two. Please, Zélie implores her brother, if you know any cure for this, let me know. "This poor child worries me," she explained, and on many counts: "she has an undisciplined character and a poorly developed mind." She had some consolations. Céline eagerly turned to her father, and Louis responded just as eagerly. And worrying once about Hélène in purgatory, thinking about how an inconsequential lie might have destined the child to great suffering, she heard again her interior voice, this one seeming to come from a statue of the Virgin, announcing with solemn assurance that Marie-Hélène was with her, in heaven.

Zélie Martin's difficulties never drove her to despair, as far as one can discover from her letters and such testimony as her adoring children offer, but she did succumb often enough to an alternative frustration and bewilderment. Amidst the horrors of the Franco-Prussian War, which involved the occupation of Alençon by the Germans and the billeting of nine enemy troops on the Martin household, came the short life of Marie-Mélanie-Thérèse. Zélie's eighth child lived from August 16, 1870, to October 8, less than three months. The Martins tried to find a wet nurse who would live with them, when it became clear that once again Zélie could not herself nurse her child. That proved impossible. The nurse they did find proved fatal. Her negligence was almost certainly the cause of Mélanie's quick decline and death. She allowed the baby to starve and by the time the parents discovered what was happening it was too late to get enough nourishment back into her. Once again Zélie is sick with grief. Each death is a little worse than the others. To each new child, she feels a deeper attachment than to the others—not a difficult feeling to understand. When she speaks in her inevitable record of pain, her customary mortuary letter to her sister-in-law, of Mélanie's "agony," the word has some of its stark Greek character. It was once more a convulsive struggle, a conflict between death and life, in which Zélie lost some of her own life along with the child's, and we must recognize the terror of the experience in all its intensity, in spite of the conventional phrases in which she records it. She really is desolate, that is to say, stripped, wretched, alone. She really does want to die herself. She cannot eat. She is worn out after two days of her vigil, the last entirely without food. This really is, as her familiar phrase has it, "mortal anguish."

What comfort was there for Zélie? What consolation was there for Louis, for the remaining children? What kind of life could they wrest from such a constant struggle with death? They had the war to occupy their thoughts. They were not as overrun with soldiers as many others in Alençon, but they had to make some provision for their nine, let them have the entire second floor of their house, supply them with food, or have the food they brought in cooked for them. Louis fought with a soldier who tried to steal a watch from his shop, and succeeded in getting rid of him. He complained to the German authorities right after it happened, but the next day he went to plead for the man's life when he discovered that another soldier who had been caught stealing eggs had been shot to discourage any further theft. These things did concern them, did fill their time; Zélie's letters in 1870 and 1871 bear abundant witness to the catastrophe which had hit France. The horror of the events of the Paris Commune for a zealous Catholic can also be gleaned from her correspondence. She is "bowled over," she writes her sister-in-law in Lisieux, by the death of the Archbishop of Paris and the killing of sixty-four priests by the Communards. She is worried about her brother, about his attempt to expand his business in such miserable times, about business generally. She has begun to work again at her lace in an atmosphere of doom. But no matter how terrible things become, she is capable of just the necessary amount of resignation to sustain herself and her family through the terror. And again, the phrases are not merely conventional with her any more than they are with her husband. When she writes to console her sister-in-law, whose infant son died even more quickly than her two, she writes with the fullest awareness of what such an experience means. She *is* "sorely afflicted" by Mme. Guérin's misfortune, by this terrible "trial" of her "poor, dear sister." She *does* very much want to see her resigned to the Lord's "holy will." She *is* herself certain that the little boy is "with Him," and that "he sees you, he loves you, and one day you will find him again." That was the basis of her own reconciliation with such misery and it still is.

> When I closed the eyes of my dear little children and buried them, I felt the sorrow through and through, but I was resigned to it always. I did not regret the pain and the care I had undergone for them. People said to me, "It would have been better never to have had them." I couldn't stand such language. I couldn't believe that the pains and the cares could ever be balanced against the eternal happiness of my children. Furthermore, they were not lost forever; life is short and full of miseries, and we shall find them again up above.

It was the first death that was the most instructive, she explains; it was then that she was most "vividly aware of having a child in heaven." She learned to make direct appeals to her own holy innocents, and she firmly believed that one of those petitions to her "little Joseph" cured Hélène of an illness for which medicine had been unable to find a remedy. This happy reminiscence will not lead her to sanctimonious reassurances. "You see, dear sister, how very good it is to have little angels in heaven," she sums up, "but it is no less painful to our nature to lose them; these are the great sufferings of our life."

These were the great sufferings of her life, greater than her own physical pain, of which she had been more and more aware since the spring of 1865, when she first felt the pain in her breast which a more alert medicine would have been able to trace to a potentially dangerous tumor. These sufferings eclipsed the turmoil of war and the chaos of occupation; they chased away the melancholy occasioned by financial disorder and the frightening news from Italy, where the Pope seemed to be the victim of a virulent anti-Catholicism, which, not content with imprisoning him, might seek the abolition of the Papacy as a logical fruit of the Risorgimento and union of all Italians. A child's illness was far more serious than anything else. It took precedence over national and international disturbances, over financial reverses, over personal illness. The insistent witness of the older Martin children to Zélie's tranquility in the face of great difficulties does not adequately record her concern for them and for their sisters, which to some extent underlay the sale of Louis's business and the house in the Rue du Pont Neuf, the move to the Guérin house in Rue Saint Blaise, and the consolidation of all the Martin life in that one environment.

It was in the new house that Thérèse was born, on January 2, 1873, and where she too quickly seemed ready to give up food, to give up life, and to die, like her short-lived sister, after whom she was named, and like her brothers. It was in the new house, just as some balance was achieved in the baby Thérèse's life by sending her to board with the family's reliable old wet nurse, Rose Taille, that another crisis quickly developed. Marie had been sent home from the convent at Le Mans, where she and Pauline were boarding students. She had a bad case of typhoid fever and had immediately to be isolated. Excellent baptism, all of this, for a new home, the inevitable kind of sanctification in suffering which the Martins brought with them wherever they went. If this sort of life can be accounted typical of "the respectable rising bourgeoisie who were beginning a tremendous economic and social upsurge in the second half of the nineteenth century," what an enormously underrated class that class must be! If these are the signs of a family that was "outwardly and inwardly" bourgeois, what a treasured classification that classification must become!

It is hard to believe that anybody would be content with easy generalizations about such a family, whether they are directed toward social and economic categories or a strenuous piosity of a quite different kind. The conventional phrases of the Martins, *Père et Mère*, can lead one to glib acceptances or rejections or to some alternately tender and harsh analysis which (one thinks) will prove one free of the sticky susceptibilities of traditional hagiography. None of this is fair, however, to the accepter or the rejecter or the schizophrenic analyst who moves busily back and forth among the familiar attitudes, and certainly not to the family. It is a saint's family, and perhaps, as its great enthusiasts in and out of Carmel suggest, a family of saints, like that of Gregory the Great in which, in addition to a canonized mother, there were two sainted aunts, or like the remarkable troupe of Spanish *santos*, Isidore of Seville, his brothers Leander and Fulgentius, and his sister Florentina. It is best understood, I think, as one of a kind, admirable, emulable, but most interesting, most engaging, for its own ways of life and death, and especially those ways that helped to shape and give persuasive force to Thérèse's little way.

THREE

*W*HEN Zélie Martin returned home from her pilgrimage to Lourdes, two months before her death, she wrote to Pauline, "I want to know what shape you're in and if you're still angry with the Holy Virgin because she didn't want to make you jump with joy . . . she said to all of us what she did to Bernadette: 'I will make you happy, not in this world but in the next.'" That was Zélie's considered philosophy, as she said in her next few lines to her daughter: "Do not look for much joy on earth; you will be very much disappointed. As for me, I know by experience how much to rely on the joys of earth. If I did not have such hope in the joys of heaven, I would be terribly unhappy." So above all, she tells Pauline, "Above all, courage and confidence!"

It was an old story with Zélie, a constant refrain. To her brother in 1864, she wrote a lengthy gloss on the text of a wealthy woman of Alençon who was full of self-congratulations on her new home, on her money, on everything in her splendid life. "My God! How happy am I!" Zélie quotes the woman. "I lack nothing. I have health, I have wealth; I can buy anything I want. I have no children to bother me. I know no one as well off as I am." Zélie quotes a proverb: "Thrice unhappy is he who speaks in this way!" She is so convinced that this is so, she tells Isidore, that whenever she has been happy, she has been unable to face her happiness without trembling. "No, happiness is not found here below; it is, in fact, a bad sign when everything goes well. In his wisdom, God has wanted things this way to make us remember that the earth is not our true home."

When her brother's warehouse, with a large supply of drugs in it, was burned down, Zélie wrote to her sister-in-law of her own sense of loss, of how she had tried to communicate as much to her children—"What I have written them will hardly make them rejoice"—and how much aware she was of the trial for Isidore, who had worked so hard to organize and develop his business in drugs, and now must see all that work lost in one blow. "One must have great faith and resignation to accept such a reverse without a murmur. . . ." Remember, she counsels, "that everyone has his cross to carry, but some find theirs heavier than others. You have now begun to see, dear sister, that all is not roses in this life. God sends us such burdens to detach us from earth and to draw our thoughts toward heaven."

There is a kind of delicate irony in Zélie's cautionary words, "all is not roses in this life," in the light of her daughter Thérèse's association with the same flowers. If one understands Zélie well, I think, one must see that she was not unaware of the irony of such words—not, of course, with any presentiment of Thérèse's spiritual gardening. But Zélie was not without her own wit, her own flickering acerbities. She looked at her own limitations with a sense of humor. Writing to her sister-in-law to comfort her on her constant minor illnesses, on being confined so much to bed and the consequent "mortal boredom," she recalled her own impatience with life and its difficulties. Once, she remembers, "I said to God, 'You know well enough that I have no time to be sick.' My prayer was heard beyond my deepest expectations and I began to glory in it just a little bit. Whereupon He seemed to answer me, 'Since you have no time to be sick, perhaps you'll have time for other trouble?' And I assure you, I wasn't spared!" The point is, she concludes her entertaining but quite serious reflections, "That's the way it is in this world, you must carry your cross one way or another. You say to God, 'I'll have none of that.' And often, you're answered, but to your unhappiness. It's better to take what comes patiently. There's always joy alongside the pain. And that's what you will discover, you'll see, my dear sister."

Zélie found constant delight in the little things of life, especially in the antics of her children, which many of her letters describe, and sometimes mimic, with great charm and gaiety. She was fascinated by their individuality, and observed and described it with intelligent and affectionate detail. Her admiration and love for all her children did not prevent her from being objective about their small faults, but neither did her realization of their faults cause her to exaggerate difficulties or to spoil her pleasure in their developing personalities.

She was particularly delighted with the baby Thérèse. She found her, at various times, beautiful, darling, gracious, and astonishingly intelligent. At one, Thérèse was, her mother said, "as gentle and sweet as a little angel. She has a charming character . . . she has such a sweet smile!" At two, she was "very intelligent and we have very amusing conversations." The two-year-old's mispronunciation of *Messe* (Mass) as *Mette* delighted Zélie, who was also very very pleased that Thérèse seemed already to know how to pray. Just before Thérèse's third birthday Zélie boasted that her smartest child was already learning to read, a fact confirmed by Marie in a letter of the same time. At three, Thérèse was talking about assuring herself of heaven: she said she was going to throw herself into the arms of her mother —who would already be there—and make it impossible for God to pry her loose. Thus did Thérèse conceive her doctrine of the little way, at the age of three, and announce it to her mother. In the midst of Zélie's miseries, the four-year-old Thérèse continued to bring her mother great joy, because of her "angelic little nature," like that of her sister Céline, and because of her precocious wisdom which, according to Zélie, was more than equal to that of Céline, although Céline was twice her age.

The language of Zélie's letters remains conventional, but the attitudes and events do not. She constantly sees joy alongside suffering with a certitude that reaches far beyond the kind of self-assurance which is merely wishful thinking or the use of consoling phrases for the purposes of self-hypnosis or the easy assuagement of others, worried about their own griefs or her extra-heavy load. There was in her that rare degree of consciousness that indicates spiritual maturity. Physical suffering inevitably is raised, in her conscious mind, to the level of spiritual suffering. It takes an act of consciousness to do this which only a well-trained and courageous will could manage. The exposure to the preliminary exercises of such consciousness is universal, but only a very few souls are capable of sustaining the experience. We all must face suffering, our own and others', again and again, but most of us turn away from it, eager for any appeasement of the pain. To face it, to accept it, and even more, to dwell on it with meditative fervor—that's more than any of us needs to take. But only by welcoming ardors like Zélie's, only by a total surrender of consciousness to the several states of being involved in suffering, can we possibly achieve a balance like hers. Only then, at the far edge of a meditation conceived in physical pain and developed in spiritual suffering, can we find the appeasement which we think to discover in the normal channels of escape.

Obviously, there is no deliverance from pain except in pain. Joy in suffering, self-evidently, depends upon a sufficient amount of suffering, both in length of time and intensity, to permit the joy to develop. Not everyone has this opportunity, a fact that delights most people and for which they offer up fervent thanks. But it is a considerable opportunity, which some strange souls, like Zélie Martin and her youngest daughter, seem to regard as a great grace and to give their equal and opposite thanks for receiving. Zélie offered what was called in her time the "heroic vow" for the remission of her father's purgatorial suffering. Thérèse offered herself as a victim to assuage the sufferings of others and translated that offering into the chilling language of an act of oblation, which to somebody without any understanding of, or sympathy for, this kind of attitude must seem a supreme act of masochism. The most skillful performers of India and Southeast Asia are no more adept at sticking pins and steel shafts into their bodies or of burning their flesh than Zélie and Thérèse and people like them are in plaguing their bodies and minds and souls together. And, just like the masters of Yoga, they regard their ability to torture themselves as a special gift.

Special gift? Did the Martins have any alternative? Death called on them with such regularity that they had to become affable in the face of its visits or go out of their minds. Suffering was so much their lot that any kindness that may seem to grow out of it, any ease that they may seem to show under it, is simply the most elementary kind of facing of facts, the most simple sort of self-preservation. But this facing of facts, this self-preservation of theirs, is also remarkably eloquent of their constant awareness of what they are doing, a rich evidence of that total consciousness of the spiritually alert that confers meaning on the most trivial event and turns every unpleasant experience, from a pinprick in the ego to gangrene of the lung, into a significant event, which is to say one that really signifies.

Most of us, I suspect, would at the very least find the constant search for significance boring and, at worst, terribly upsetting, but not because there is anything instrinsically dull or irritating about

34

this sort of interior pursuit. We are not used to so dogged an interiority. If we use phrases like Zélie's, or their later equivalents, they tend to be merely conventional for us, to express no greater upset than a minor headache or a nagging uncertainty as to a social or business procedure. If we suffer from a more serious physical ailment or some form of depression or anxiety that will not let up, we rarely turn to our own resources. We go, as we certainly should go, to some well-accounted physician of body or soul, to find a remedy in medication or surgery or to talk therapy of some kind. We are much too unlearned in the arts of interior conversation to canvass the possibilities for relief right there, within ourselves, if not in place of the medicine or the knife or the help of clinically trained counsel, at least as a corollary to it. But the Martins did have something else, always had something else; they had themselves.

Zélie's letters are the best records we have of her research into herself. The memoirs of her children are good supplementary records. From both we learn the same thing over and over again. She had developed, like her husband before her and her daughters after her, especially Thérèse, a positive liturgy of self-examination. It was as much a human as a divine office. It was prayed with regularity. And it was contagious. Her children picked it up from her, as from her husband, from *Papa-Maman* or *Maman-Papa*, as Marie and Pauline called that strange and wonderful phenomenon that more and more they looked upon as one person, and from whom they parted with "abysses," as Marie calls them, of tenderness and of grief. The letters of Zélie to Pauline are particularly rich in the witness they give to the communication from parent to child of interior exercises. They ramble; they move helter-skelter, in a jerky sort of motion, over the events of the household, the joys provided by the baby Thérèse, the doubts and difficulties offered in such perplexing abundance by Léonie. Zélie does not hesitate to share her innermost thoughts with Pauline when her second daughter is only twelve or thirteen—she was not yet sixteen when Zélie died. She tells Pauline how smart Thérèse is—with an intelligence "I did not see in any of you." She tells her how stubborn Thérèse is, with nothing like Céline's sweetness, and a will that is unbreakable: "When she has said 'No,' nothing will make her change her mind; one could put her in the cellar for the whole day; she would rather sleep there than say 'Yes.'" She doesn't make clear whether or not Thérèse actually spent any time in the cellar, but it is clear enough that she was a perplexing and difficult mixture of obstinacy and candor, of toughness and love. For along with her stubbornness, Zélie tells Pauline, the little girl has a good heart, marvelously open and affectionate. "It is something to see her run after me to make her confession: 'Mama, I pushed Céline just once, I hit her once, but I won't do it again.'" When she broke a vase, one about as "big as a thumb," that Zélie had given her the same morning, she ran to her mother to show it to her and to ask her not to be unhappy: "When I am making money, I promise you I will buy you another."

In the same very long letter—Pauline demanded a regular newspaper-length missive of news from home—Zélie tells of dispatching Thérèse, in the midst of gathering flowers in celebration of Marie's month of May, to give a small offering to a poor old man whom they had seen together. "He seemed so touched and thanked us so much that I could see how really miserable he was. I told him to follow us, that I would give him some shoes. . . . We gave him a good dinner—he was dying of hunger." Then follow reflections on the old man's life, on the freezing cold to which he had been exposed in winter in an abandoned shack, the inadequate food on which he subsisted, the need to get him into a home, a task with which she presented her husband. And then, after various small episodes and some congratulations to Pauline for many good marks—for "many decorations and the *Croix d'Excellence*"—she recommends to her prayers, to her aunt's prayers and to those of another "good Sister" at the Visitation, a "poor old man who is about to die." He hasn't been to confession in forty years, but in spite of all of Louis's efforts to bring him back to the sacraments, he remains intransigent. He is a good man; that's clear. But it is more difficult to convert a good one than a bad. "Only a miracle of grace can tear away the heavy veil that he has before his eyes."

Zélie discussed her pleasures, her pains, all her children, and most of her thoughts, with Pauline. Zélie filled her letters to Pauline with her experiences and asked for her prayers and hopeful comments. There was, for example, the grueling time she spent watching a poor old woman's last moments, a woman whose particular misery at the end was that she could not rest in bed for more than a few minutes at a time, and who for two weeks had stayed up every night. But worse still, the woman's two youngest children seemed altogether unconcerned by her approaching death, a response that amazed Marie as much as Zélie. But that's the way of children, Zélie muses, especially ones so poorly brought up. "My God," she says, "how sad a house is without religion! How frightening death is there! In the sick woman's room, not a single image on which she could rest her sight. Lots of images, there were, but none of anything like a religious kind!" God will take pity on her, she thinks; she herself was so poorly brought up. A few days later, Zélie ends another letter with ardent thanks to Pauline: "you are my true friend; you give me courage to sustain life with patience." And a few days after that she begins another letter with thanks for Pauline's last letter and gratitude as well for all the good news she has of her from her aunt, Sister Marie-Dosithée: "I thank you Pauline for giving us all such joy. God will reward you both in this world and in the next. . . ."

She tells Pauline in an affecting paragraph of how she prayed for her on the feast of the Immaculate Conception in 1860, exactly nine months before Pauline was born, of how she prayed to be given "a little Pauline":

> but I can't think of it without laughing, for I was just like a child who asks for a doll from its mother and I behaved in exactly that way. I wanted a Pauline like the one I have and I dotted the *i*'s, for fear the Blessed Virgin would not understand just what I wanted. Of course, first and foremost she must have a beautiful little soul, capable of becoming a saint, but I also wanted her to be very attractive. As for that, she is hardly pretty, but I think she's beautiful, very beautiful, just as I wanted her to be!
> . . . I'm not going to pray to the Virgin for any more little daughters. I'll pray only that those she has already given me will all become saints and that I may follow close behind—but they must be better than I.

She tells Pauline of reading the life of St. Jeanne de Chantal; she's within a couple of hours of finishing the first volume of the biography after two weeks of hard reading. Oh, how the Visitation stays with her as a way of life! How she loves everything and everybody connected with it, now (with Pauline and Marie boarding there, with their aunt) more than ever! She can speak of nothing else, so much so that Louise, the maid, gets angry about

37

it—"For two weeks I've heard nothing else but St. Chantal and St. Francis [de Sales]!"

Everything finds its way to Pauline. Sad reflections on Léonie —on her eczema, on her sluggishness, on her general dull-wittedness: "the things of this world do not get to her any more quickly than those of the spirit. . . ." Poor thing, she even forgets that she has left a dishcloth in the soup tureen, which gives the soup a remarkable texture. Happy thoughts about Céline: "everything in her makes for virtue, it is the very fiber of her being; she has a most open soul and a horror of evil." And as for Thérèse, from the very beginning she brings joy; she is anticipated with pleasure, her every moment is chronicled as a step toward perfection, and she doesn't hesitate to compare her so favorably with all the others that only the most preternaturally unselfish of children could bear the comparison. To contrast with the happiness the children provide, there are an unusual number of dead bodies in these letters, even for a woman so generously open to others' misfortunes. A poor woman—they are always "poor" women, "poor" old men; the adjective is direct or the tone implies it—a "poor" woman is glimpsed by Zélie, who is out walking with her oldest daughter, a "poor" woman with a maddened look, staring out of her open window: her husband has just "fallen to earth, dead." "Poor" old "V., my assembler of the *Point d'Alençon* for fifteen years—you'll remember her well, she used to come to us often enough with her little dog. *Eh bien!* Monday evening, after she had set her table for supper, her neighbors heard the noise of a heavy fall. . . . they found the poor old lady stretched out on the ground, lifeless, the dog licking her hands and face."

In the last year of her life, she confides things in even greater detail to Pauline. When Sister Marie-Dosithée finally succumbs to the tuberculosis that made her nineteen years in the Visitation convent such a symphony of manic-depressive ups and downs, Zélie prays to her for special help with Léonie, and in less than three weeks, her prayers are answered. "You know what she was like, your sister," she reminds Pauline: "the spirit of insubordination, never wanting to obey me except by force, always, with her contrariness, doing the opposite of what I wanted, even when she herself had the same desire, obeying only the maid." Marie had noted with growing unhappiness the close relationship between Léonie and Louise, the maid, who had worked over the child a power that once would have been called magical, that today we should insist had at the least a questionable perversity, and perhaps worse, a hint of perversion in it. Léonie was hers to do with as she wished. But no longer, after the nun's death. Zélie asked for help, asked for her daughter's obedience, for Léonie's "heart." Suddenly, on Sunday morning, "I was heard. . . . Now she doesn't want to leave me for a minute; she kisses me until she nearly asphyxiates me, does everything I tell her without an argument, works side by side with me all day long." It is for Léonie that Zélie wants to live as she has not wanted to ever before. "I am really necessary to this child. After I'm gone, she will be miserable and no one will be able to make her obey except the woman who persecuted her—but no, not that, for as soon as I am dead, she must go at once. I'm sure that they will not refuse to carry out my last wishes."

It is to Pauline that she entrusts all her hopes and fears and uncertainties in the pilgrimage to Lourdes, on the journey as well as before and after, filling her not only with brave thoughts, battered feelings, rebounding strength, faltering energies, but with her last meditations about Léonie as well. Here she reads like an instructor in Thérèse's little way. The seeds of the great spirituality to come out of this family are planted in Léonie's garden. Let me live, Zélie prays the Almighty; let me live a few more years, she asks, pleading for the intercession of the Virgin—"not because I ask to have my illness taken from me, but only . . . to have time to raise my children, and especially poor Léonie, who needs me so much and for whom I am so sorry." Léonie has fewer gifts than the others, but she, like everybody else, is eager "to love and to be loved," and only a mother can give her enough love and stay close enough to her to give her what she deserves. Zélie is full of Léonie's "unbroken tenderness," her anticipation of her mother's desires, her anxiety to do anything, to do everything for her, though not, she reports sadly, for anybody else. But this too is changing slowly. Léonie can be brought to love the Lord without reservation and then everybody else as well.

A few weeks later, Zélie is reporting Léonie's last-ditch effort to save her mother. She had read in *La Semaine Catholique* (*The Catholic Weekly*) of a "saintly soul who had offered her life for the Pope and who had been heard." Léonie thought a great deal about this startling idea. She would do the same thing. One morning she sought out Marie and said to her, "I am going to die! God has heard me; I feel sick." Marie broke up with laughter. Léonie was "mortified"; she had spoken very seriously. She began to cry. Fifteen minutes later, when her tears were all dry and she felt better, "something else entered her head: she needed carpet slippers." But, Zélie quotes herself as saying to Léonie, "since you are going to die, that would just be money thrown out." Léonie didn't say a word, according to her mother, "undoubtedly hoping to have enough time left to her to use the slippers."

In the same letter, a handsome compound of misery and mirth, Zélie scolds Pauline for her offer to suffer in place of her mother. "I should be really angry," she tells her. "You don't want me to get to heaven. You want everything for yourself. . . . Don't trouble yourself so much, my dear Pauline! As for me, I will have maybe a hundred years of Purgatory to do! Do you want to do those for me also?" She has reassurances for Pauline: she is really much better; since yesterday her neck hasn't bothered her; there is only a small swelling. And she is looking forward to the long vacation —Pauline is awaited with impatience. "We propose to welcome you as never before!"

Lourdes was a failure for Zélie, but it was a great success for the family, and even for Zélie it had the salutary effect of preparing her for her death with a certainty that was at once doomful and happily clarifying. Man's fate and her own future were very much on her mind at the end of her life. In the same letter in which she announces to Pauline the forthcoming pilgrimage to Lourdes, she jokes about a good man, a prayerful one, who never missed an opportunity to pray, even while at work, but who had had some strange visions and a very odd prediction to make. On Wednesday of Holy Week, he climbed up a roof just in time to see in the sky a great luminous cross mounted over the sun. Besides such shining sights, the man is very specially gifted; "he knows what the angels of God do not know: the week when the world will come to an end (it will be the first week of January 1880). So now he has the missionary duty to find all the bishops in the world and tell them. He has already placed his house on sale. . . ." Marie was delighted with the story. Zélie saw that the man was "touched," but also that, in spite of his "singular madness," he was a good man. What startled her beyond anything else was the way his wife believed in him and his visions and

40

predictions, "like the Gospels!" Now they are off together to effect some cures. "As you can see, the nuttiness of good people. . . ." And then she breaks off her letter, because "your father has asked me to go out walking with him, and since I am really obedient, I haven't even finished my sentence!"

Lourdes, she told Pauline, absorbed all her attention. She is confident that she will recover, as she has been for the last ten or fifteen days, ever since the death of her sister. Everybody must prepare, however, with all their resources, for this pilgrimage, she tells her second daughter in her next letter to her: "I count on you more than the others for this. I don't know why I have this feeling, since Marie prays so much for me, with all of her heart, too." Pauline took this request very seriously indeed. She believed her mother was already cured, even before the pilgrimage, Zélie explained to her brother, "because when the sick have a great deal of hope, that is an absolute sign of a cure." But, says Zélie, I can't take much joy in that, "because my hope doesn't go as far as absolute certainty." And the surrounding signs were not good. A doctor's examination just before she left for Lourdes confirmed the fact that it was much too late for an operation. Yes, a cure was not impossible, it certainly wasn't. . . . "One never knows how things will go." At Lourdes, the usual crush; they were with strangers, from Angers; there was the not unfamiliar mix-up over lodgings; Sister Marie-Dosithée's rosary, a precious relic to the Martins, was lost by Marie; Pauline lost her rosary, to which two medals of her aunt's were attached; Zélie's spirits sank lower and lower. The waters looked frightfully cold. Zélie plunged in and jumped right out again. Four times she made the plunge, the last time just two hours before leaving Lourdes. While she was in the water, immersed up to her neck, she felt no pain, but afterwards the agonies returned, as usual.

She was not the only one tested in this way. She saw many others as miserable on leaving as on coming to the grotto where Bernardette had seen the Virgin, as sick after bathing in the pool or drinking the waters as before. Zélie was particularly saddened by a thirteen-year-old girl who was being carried on her mother's shoulders in the processions, in fact all day long. The girl's legs were shriveled, "dead," Zélie called them; her back was covered with such sores that Zélie could only look at her from a distance. Others, who had come to Lourdes before, left again, uncured.

41

Zélie watched the burial of a seventy-two-year-old man who had died suddenly, after having drunk, in an agony of perspiration, too much water from the grotto.

Zélie worried more about the effect of this on Pauline than upon herself. The day after getting home she wrote her daughter, whom she had left at the Le Mans academy again, on the way back. She had been troubled as soon as she had put Pauline on the bus, she tells the girl, though she knew there was no need to torment herself so about the child: she would have her good friends to console her and the peace she would need after the pilgrimage. I still have all my confidence, she assures her daughter, in spite of what I see on the faces of those I tell about the trip to Lourdes. She says her novena prayers again; she puts Lourdes water on her wounds. And she puts up with her neighbors, those only too anxious to tell her how inevitable her failure was; for example, "Mlle. X, who told me—what I certainly knew already—that she didn't believe in miracles. I told her that, nevertheless, my hope remained . . . I saw the depth of her thinking. . . ."

Who can understand the "divine dynamics," as Huysmans describes the actions of God in his last book, *The Crowds of Lourdes?* Lourdes is, as he says several times in that book, "a place both repulsive and divine," but it is also "only right," as his book goes to some length to insist, "to make trial of it by personal experience." When science admits it can do nothing more for the relief of the sick, just at that point they would "do well" to go to Lourdes, "for if the Virgin does not hearken to their prayers, she will repay them for the toil and the fatigue of their journey by bestowing upon them the blessings of resignation and comfort. . . ." Lourdes promises much, says this zealous convert—visions of moral beauty, of spiritual beauty, of human generosity, the poor well treated as almost nowhere else on earth, and, in all the misery, the stink of decay, the tortures of the afflicted, the examples of saintliness, if nobody else's, then Bernadette's. Huysmans's meditations are like many others occasioned by Lourdes, occasioned by Bernadette, occasioned by the example of saintliness. His resistance to the distorted image of Bernadette—"an angel and a plaster saint fit for a niche"—is perhaps a little stronger than most. His defense of the little girl—"of a lymphatic nature, nervous, puny and small . . . her face . . . pleasing and her make delicate"—is possibly more convincing than most: "what a singular case of hallucination was this little girl who only suffered from it long enough to reveal and to establish the Virgin's work, and never showed any signs of hallucination before or since!"

Lourdes was Zélie's last test of faith and as much confirmation of her own faith as she needed. She had to put up with stares of "incredulity," she reports, from the very same people who had advised the trip to Lourdes, who, she now saw, never believed in the faintest possibility of a miracle, who now took pleasure in the triumph of their faithlessness—"not that they wish me any evil, of course." She had to put up with her own increasing torments, in the neck, in the breast, in her whole being, and, according to those who examined her body after death, without any pain reliever of any enduring strength—no aspirin, even. She had to narcotize the pain of her husband, of her children, and to make plans for their future. Her brother had warned her that her time was short and begged her to get her husband to promise to bring his family to Lisieux, where the Guérins could look after them. Her sister-in-law and her brother both repeated the request in the middle of July, a few weeks after Zélie's return from Lourdes. Zélie is touched, she answers, but Louis can't or won't make up his mind. And anyway, what can one say about something necessarily in the future and obscured as a result? "Man proposes but God disposes."

Zélie's disposition was to pray for an old friend who was offering up three months of her own misery for her, all her aches and pains, and they were considerable, not only those of a seriously ailing foot but of a heavy and inconsolable heart, presented to the Sacred Heart for Zélie's sake. "I am going to send her some Lourdes water and make a novena for her. God must cure one of us. I will be nearly as pleased if it is she rather than I, though I haven't got her disinterestedness and I don't think I have decided to make the sacrifice of my life for hers." Zélie's sister-in-law has asked for details of her illness; she gives them to her—her general weakness, her fever, her inability to dress herself, her inability to stand up for any time; crises at night, a few nights of sleep, many more of agitation. "You tell me not to lose confidence, but that's just what I do. I know very well that the Virgin can cure me, but I can't stop myself from fearing that she doesn't want to and I tell you in all candor that a miracle now appears to me very doubtful." She says she must act as if she were going to die. She must not lose any of the small amount of time that remains to her: "these are days of salvation that will never come again; I want to profit from them."

Zélie meant what she said. She thought seriously that some of her purgatory could thus be accomplished on earth. She knew she suffered less—as she had told others again and again, when counseling them in their troubles—when she resigned herself to her shortening days and took full advantage of them, as much to comfort others as to put her own house in order. She made wry noises about her inability to offer her life for another, but she continued to think about the suffering of her sacrificial old friend, about her niece Jeanne Guérin, and especially about Léonie— "who wants to die in my place, who prays every day for that, but begins to lose courage because the illness [that she longs for] doesn't come." Almost up to the end she made plans for others, she looked after her business, she concerned herself for her suffering children: "That poor Marie really has a lot of trouble over me and she is as good as can be imagined. Every day she explains that she cannot go to Lisieux, and go about places, while I am sick. But I will do as I did with Pauline at the Visitation . . . I will write that I am well and thus they will not torment themselves. . . ."

She insisted upon going to Mass on Sunday, July 22, with Marie. Every step she took, Marie writes to the Guérins, she felt in her neck. And with every step she thought the pain would disappear, but of course it didn't, and of course she wouldn't hear of returning home. She stopped again and again, gathered her small strength together, and went on again. Sunday Mass should not be missed; she was not quite that ill. But she was so weak, Marie also reports, that she did not take care of her business. She just lay in bed, or better, sat in her armchair, where the pressure on her neck was not so great. She couldn't quite suppress all her groans, because the slightest movement caused her terrible pain. But in all of this, says Marie, "with what patience and with what resignation she bears her illness! She doesn't stop saying her rosary; she prays all the time, in spite of her pain. We are all rapt in admiration, for she has a courage and an energy that nothing can equal. Just two weeks ago, she said a full rosary on her knees at the feet of the Blessed Virgin in my room, the one she likes so much. Seeing her so sick, I wanted to make her sit down, but it was useless."

Once again, on August 3, she insisted upon going to Mass, because it was First Friday. And so she went to the seven o'clock, supported by Louis, and was so spent by the time she arrived at the church that, Marie writes her uncle and aunt, in Zélie's own words, if there had not been someone there to push open the doors for her, she could not have entered! By August 16, when she wrote her last letter, she could no longer stand. She moved only from her bed to her armchair and from her armchair to her bed. Her nights were "cruel," she told her brother. And when she washed herself in water of Lourdes, she suffered all the more: "Really and truly, the Holy Virgin does not want to cure me." That's the way it is, she sighs, almost audibly from the paper: "If Our Lady does not cure me, it is because my time has come and God wants me to rest elsewhere than on earth. . . ." Her last ten days were made agony by swellings in her legs and arms; her last few days, she was reduced to sign language. Two days before the end, Marie mourns, "if she were left alone in her room, she would die rather than call for help." She was spared nothing in the calendar of suffering: hemorrhages, total enfeeblement, a ravaged face, a body shockingly emaciated where it was not swollen. A biographer attempting to avoid the melodrama of sentimental hagiology is stuck here: he must run through all the clichés of the last moments of long-suffering saints, or suppress the truth.

Zélie's brother and sister-in-law arrived in time for her last moments, for Extreme Unction, for a last moving look by Zélie at Céline Guérin, her beloved correspondent, and for Zélie's death at half past midnight, in the first hour of August 28. All five children gathered around for the last sacraments, "arranged according to age," Thérèse remembers, "and poor dear Father was there also, sobbing."

Thérèse's memories of Zélie's death are quite precise. Now she and Céline could come in from the exile in which they had languished in the last days of their mother's life, banished to the outer precincts of family life, with Louis's niece by marriage, Mme. Leriche, in charge. But first Thérèse came to look at her mother in her coffin, so large that she had to raise herself up to see it at full length, and, from her father's arms, to kiss her mother for the last time. "I don't remember crying very much; I spoke to no one of the deep feelings I felt. I looked and I listened in silence. Nobody had any time to bother with me."

A little later, on the day of the funeral, the five girls were gathered together, intensely aware of each other and their collective sorrow. The maid who, by Zélie's express order, was about to be dismissed, was there too, and at the sight of the two small girls, Céline and Thérèse, she burst out, "Poor little things, you have no mother now." At this, Thérèse says, "Céline threw herself into the arms of Marie, saying, 'All right, then you must be Mama.'" Whereupon, Thérèse threw herself with equal force into Pauline's arms, crying, "Right! For me, Pauline will be Mama."

We have to depend upon the memories of Zélie's daughters for a record of her last days, and though the miseries of those anguish-filled moments are well preserved, something is missing. Zélie's sense of humor is not there to balance the torture with her characteristic wry delight, with a self-deprecating comment, a reassertion of balances in that entertaining way of hers to which the letters have accustomed us. Marie is full of sorrow; she is writing to her aunt and uncle, who will soon enough come to share the sorrow. Thérèse is terse; she is writing her memoirs directly to Mother Agnès of Jesus, at the time of writing her prioress in Carmel, but also still, for all the formality of the relationship in religion, her sister Pauline, who will remember well enough the sadness all the girls shared together. For one reason or another, the death of Zélie falls deader than any other event in her life. Zélie is dead and we need Zélie to tell us about Zélie. That totality of being which makes her so satisfactory a chronicler of herself and her family is from now on fragmented, to be collected, incompletely, from the bits and pieces of her that remain in others, in their memories, in their habits of thought, in their persons. It is not hard to make out her influence, even in Thérèse, who of all the girls necessarily knew her least well. One sees her toughness, her wit, her enormous openness to the sufferings of others, her determination to make sense of suffering, her own or other people's, and to make sense of it in terms of the divine will which she regularly confessed she found inscrutable and then, just as regularly, did her best to scrutinize. Not unlike the Buddhists who echo their master in rejecting as beyond analysis those things on which no edification is necessary but go on speculating about them just as if they could discover more and more about them,

Zélie was an eager conductor of colloquies with a God whose distance from her was unmistakable, but whose immediate presence she felt just as surely.

There was no easy boundary for Zélie Martin between the natural and the supernatural. Though her style was, as I have said, very different from her husband's, she shared with him a constant urge to some kind of interior conversation. She never found, as far as any of the available evidence suggests, any release in nature. She did not accompany Louis when he went fishing or on long walks into the country, as her children did so often after her death. Her flowers were those she, or others working for her, picked out so meticulously in vellum and lace. But she always translated events that occurred in human time into the chronology of eternity, and what is more, did it without pretentiousness of any kind, but not, as one might be tempted to say, unself-consciously. For her awareness of herself was very strong, very clear, direct, and unembarrassed. She practiced the presence of God in the only way she could possibly do so, by first practicing the presence of Zélie. Never in doing so, however, did she separate the two presences completely, even in her bursts of cauterizing humbleness. Her humility was really not hers alone, it was man's, though she probably would not have confessed it in such global terms. Where she failed, she failed because she was human. Where she succeeded, she succeeded because she was human and because to be human is also to be divine, wildly, improbably, wonderfully divine. Wildly, improbably, wonderfully? Yes, all these. For such a balancing sense of proportion as Zélie possessed, such a sense of humor in the face of unrelenting illness, death, and torment, was not the result of good breeding, good reasoning, sound morality or the constant practice of the virtues, however much these things may have been involved. It was a gift, nothing less, a great gift; even, if one insists, an undeserved gift. I prefer to say an improbable gift, as improbable, in its context, as it was a wild and a wonderful one, and one for which, no matter what name we prefer to give it, we should all, like Zélie's children, like Zélie herself, be thankful.

FOUR

*I*N the thirteenth folio of manuscript A of her autobiography, Thérèse begins what she calls the second period of her life, "the saddest" of the three epochs into which she has divided her story, *The Springlike Story of a Little White Flower, Written by Herself and Dedicated to Reverend Mother Agnès of Jesus.* Though it was only then, she tells us, that she was beginning to understand the seriousness of life, it was just at that moment that she recovered her qualities as a child. This should not surprise anyone. There is nothing more serious in Thérèse's temperament or in her spirituality than her childlike character, nor anything more childlike than her kind of seriousness, with that special intensity of concentration, that deeply searching glance, that determined sobriety which refuses to be shaken by anything, with which we associate the seriousness of children.

For a while the seriousness was all. Thérèse was moody, retiring, easily aroused to tears, she who had been so lively, so open, so confiding. Her joy was to be left alone and especially not to be disturbed by strangers. Only with her family did she still show her once characteristic gaiety. In spite of all this, everyone around her showed her the utmost compassion, especially Louis and Pauline and Marie. In this thirteenth folio, she writes, "*Le coeur si* tendre *de Papa avait joint à l'amour qu'il possédait déjà un amour vraiment maternel! . . .–Vous, ma Mère, et Marie n'étiez-vous pas pour moi les mères les plus* tendres, *les plus désinteressées?*" We have an interesting choice of translations of this simple passage. Father Taylor, in the first of the English versions, writes: "Papa's affectionate heart seemed endowed with a mother's love, while you and Marie were no less tender and devoted." John Beevers makes it, "Daddy's affection seemed enriched by a real motherly love, and I felt that both you and Marie were the most tender and self-sacrificing of mothers." Ronald Knox, working from the original manuscript, offers: "Papa's compassionate nature made him a mother as well as a father to me, and hadn't I two mothers as well in you and Marie, the best, the most unselfish mothers that ever were?" The sense of the French is in each of the translations. But none of them gets the exclamatory force of Thérèse's description of her father's heart—"*si* tendre," that is, *so* soft, sensitive, delicate, affectionate, so loving, with the degree of feeling twice underscored by the use of the adverb and the italicizing of the adjective. And not only was her father's heart, as always, *si tendre*, but in it "he had united with the love he already possessed a truly maternal love."

We all recognize the problem of the translator. It is an almost inflexible rule of the game never to use a cognate, never "tender" for *tendre*, certainly not "disinterested" for *désinteressées*. We know that wherever possible we must avoid the commonplace words of a language, such as *si* or *vraiment*, that is, "so" or "truly," especially when their force is to be felt in other words that can be more gracefully translated. Finally, a sensitive translator must not repeat the same word again and again, even if it is repeated again and again in the original. But when we do this with Thérèse, when we observe all the rules, we achieve one grace at the expense of another. She, after all, does repeat the word "love" again and again and again. It is at the center of her thought, of her feeling, of her spirituality. In Papa's loving heart, it was maternal love that was joined to paternal love. Furthermore, she is full of underlinings; she uses commonplace adverbs and many exclamation marks. Feeling tumbles through her writing, feeling that her British translators are much too reserved to allow to come through their translations. All have their moments. Father Taylor comes very close to the sense of the mottled text that was first published by the Carmel of Lisieux. Monsignor Knox has, as always in his work, some handsome phrases that are perhaps more interpretations than precise renderings, and they are very useful; like his translations of the Epistles of St. Paul, they offer us a running commentary, with some inspired glosses that help disentangle the knottier sections of the work (though—and let us be quite clear about this—there are very few knotty sections in Thérèse's book). John Beevers is a sympathetic and felicitous translator, less fearful of cognates than the others, but he too attenuates

Thérèsian feeling—there is nothing in the French about *Daddy's* feeling *seeming* to be endowed with a mother's love; Thérèse comes right out and says that her father united the two kinds of love in his loving heart. And as for *Daddy* and *Mummy*—even the most insular Briton would not be offended by *Papa* and *Mama;* some Englishmen, corrupted, perhaps, by too many trips across the Channel at an early age, have even been known to use the continental forms.

In Thérèse's manuscript there are other interesting details that cannot be reproduced in a translation, except by a literal transcription of all the emendations and erasures of the holograph copy. But these are not essential, except to the dogged pursuer of every texture of the saint's personality, no matter how light or unimportant. But the tone that her own precise choice of words establishes, her own syntax, her own punctuation—these are quite different things, and to lose as much of them as we have in English and others have in other languages is to lose a great deal of Thérèse. To some it is an insignificant loss; the vital stresses of the saint's spirituality are all there, and were, in fact, quite accurately preserved from the very beginning, in spite of Pauline's thousands of little changes in the original French, in Father Taylor's translation and everybody else's. To some, it is a loss for which to be devoutly thankful. For Thérèse's style, for these people, is an unfortunate obstacle that somehow must be overcome, or at least overlooked. Father Peter-Thomas Rohrbach, the Carmelite author of *The Search for St. Thérèse,* speaks for them: "No apology need be made for Thérèse's mincing, callow style," he says, and then forthwith offers an elaborate and, I think, unnecessary apology for her style:

> It was poor style, a product of one of the very worst artistic eras in the world's history. But through this argot Thérèse expressed herself, and we must not confine her to style and vocabulary. It is not so much *how* she said it, but rather *what* she said. Thérèse was an astonishingly honest person, and she meant every word she wrote. When she uses what we might now term a cliché (if that word has any meaning at all, since all lasting and endurable expressions must eventually become clichés) we must remember that it was not a cliché or a mere verbalism for her. Every word, every phrase, was deeply felt and experienced. Her articulation was limited to the mode of that time, but in those clumsy and awkward expressions she was trying to express the most vital truths with all the honesty, all the candor she could muster.

Thérèse did not write in an "argot," that is, in slang or a jargon. She probably used very few "argot" words even in her conversation. Her father demanded a very civil tongue and he would angrily have censured slang words or expressions if they had turned up in the family. If her "articulation was limited to the mode of that time," it was not because she was an admirer of clichés or a poor stylist but simply because, like all but the most pretentious people, the most *précieuse*, she was at ease in the language of her time. It was certainly a time in which ugly churches were being built all over France and in which a dubious spirituality was frequently marketed in an even more dubious style—but not her style, really, any more than it was her spirituality. It was also the time of the Impressionists in painting, of the resurgence of French music under the impetus of César Franck, of the growth and development of modern philosophy and psychology, of the last works of that French stylist par excellence, Gustave Flaubert. Charles Péguy was her exact contemporary; Marcel Proust was born two years before her, André Gide five years earlier. They too were products of this grim "artistic era."

Father Rohrbach quotes Jean Guitton in an effort at doing justice to Thérèse as a writer, but not enough of Guitton, who attributes the imperfections of her language to her teachers, "who transmitted a very second-rate tongue to her." But after this, which Father Rohrbach quotes, Guitton says a great deal more about Thérèse's style:

> The seventeenth and especially the eighteenth centuries had a common language, exact, austere, averse to exaggeration . . . a language spoken by woman. Renan tells us that his sister Henrietta saved him from rhetoric; whole circles were infected with romanticism; people thought that the right way to speak of religious feelings was to put into one's style all the sublime impulse in one's heart. But only the Saint can do that.
>
> As a result, wherever Thérèse followed the bad taste of her time, she alone was not in bad taste: for a style is always good when it is exact and true.

Father Rohrbach quotes only the last short paragraph, leaving out the substance of Guitton's argument, namely, that Thérèse was able to put the sublime impulse in her heart into her style. Guitton goes on at some length about Thérèse's style and her choice of words. He points to an "error of taste" which must be "admitted: the abuse of diminutives." But even though "everywhere else and in every case, we may have no use for diminutives, in her case and in hers alone we find that the diminutive suits her message, on condition that we understand the growing power of this diminishing."

Guitton's enthusiasm for Thérèse seems to me to be handsomely modulated to her skills with words, and skills they surely are. As Guitton says, "whenever she escapes from language and rediscovers the word, she attains a real style." He has in mind, he tells us, such special coinage as "melancholize"—military music *melancholizes* us, according to Thérèse—and "virginize"—St. Cecilia's resignation is able to *virginize* souls. He praises her transparency: her words require no comment. And then he pays her verse what some would think an extravagant compliment: "she has that sense of pure rhythm that Valéry admired in Racine. She needed only a good guide to show her how to avoid mawkishness."

Thérèse never found her good guide and frequently, as a result, she does not know how to avoid mawkishness, or at least what seems to be a sentimentality of phrase, if not of thought. But she does teach her way, as Guitton concludes, with a "strange" authority, a "radical" authority, "although she is so young and so untaught. . . . She is a child without childhood and outside of childhood. Childhood is usually the age when people seek the opinion of adults and copy them. Even when they say 'I,' they are remembering someone else." Not so Thérèse. She had a blessed "ignorance"—the word is Guitton's—which prepared her particularly well to speak to masses of people in our time, those people for whom an egregious culture would be an egregious nuisance.

A greater nuisance, I think, is the self-appointed tutor of Thérèse whose teaching must all be after the fact. There is the translator who constantly improves on her words, straightens them out, rearranges them in a more tasteful way, subduing the sentimental exaggerations, imposing upon the poor benighted saint the restraint and indirection—insofar as that is possible—of men of good education and subtle sensibility. Where the translator is unfortunately restricted in his operations by the text, there is the office of the good gray apologist. He or she can see to it that Thérèse's bold colors are softened, the stickiness washed away, a sensible tone of moderation infused throughout. She is really much better than she appears to be, you know. Give her a chance, or rather,

52

give us a chance and then we will be bound to give her the chance she deserves.

Perhaps Thérèse does need intermediaries, or at least can benefit from them, but not this sort, not those so intent on explaining her away, not those so eager to prove that something of quality is there in her work and in her doctrine, but that it is only to be found after the hobbling superstructure of her style has been dismantled and the saint has been revealed in all her purity. The point is that the saint is the girl—or the woman—revealed in the impurity (if that is the word) of the manuscript. There, in all the apparatus of *sentiment*, all the proliferation of diminutives, all the anatomizing of love and affection and tenderness and every related state of being, there she is fully exposed, transparent to our sight, to our taste, open to all our senses, open to all our feelings. To this extraordinary person we do not need to reconcile ourselves as if to a disagreeable medicine, which we know, in spite of its ugly taste, has great curative powers. And so when we examine her in that crucial second period of her life, stretching for ten years from the end of the summer of 1877 to the year which ended her childhood, 1887, we must take her as she sees herself, as she writes about herself, as she is. The terms are uncompromising. "Ah!" she exclaims, "if God had not lavished his bountiful sunshine on his little flower, she would never have taken root here below. She was still too weak to endure the wind and the rain. She needed warmth and dew and the spring breeze, none of which she was ever without, for Jesus gave them to her, even in the winter of her great trial."

Read hastily, this passage may seem like calendar art. Read with care, in context, one sees how solid an extension it is of Thérèse's central allegory and how very apt an illustration of this particular moment in her life. To begin with, Thérèse always keeps her allegory in mind, *The Springlike Story of a Little White Flower*, which is a story that has about it something of the quality of rebirth in nature. It is, then, in the most firmly established of Christian traditions, a resurrection story. Whose resurrection? Her own, of course; she tells us so: *The Springlike Story of a Little White Flower, Written by Herself*. There are several reasons why some people might be put off by it. We are not much used to allegories today; Ernest Hemingway's *The Old Man and the Sea* and Albert Camus's *The Plague* are rare examples in modern writing of the use of allegorical fictions. When we think of allegories, we usually think of John Bunyan's *Pilgrim's Progress* or *Grace Abounding*, that is, we think in terms of the crudest kind of personification allegory, with the crudest sort of moralizing. There are some interesting exceptions, we know, but these are safely locked away in the past, in the Middle Ages, chiefly, and between their distance, which gives them a suitable obscurity, and the intrinsic ambiguity of the craft as practiced a millennium or more ago, they are never likely to embarrass us by insisting upon awkward identifications and blunt moralizations. As for whatever modern ones may continue to claim our attention, such as Melville's *Moby Dick*, they are deliberately oblique, so in their pages too we will be spared any disconcertingly quick and simple identifications.

Thérèse liked allegories, parables, fables. As a nun, she always carried a copy of the Gospels with her; she wore it, really, next to her heart, and she wore it in her temperament, too, as she did all the parabolic episodes she knew in the Old Testament and the dialogues between the soul and Jesus in *The Imitation of Christ*. As her father drew a constant stream of contemplation from the world of nature around him and from everything he read, so did Thérèse. Fabliaux, bestiaries, exempla—she needed no training in the literature of the Middle Ages to convert the humblest experience into a signifying tale, in which, as there always must be with a Christian humanist, there is some definitive encounter between the soul and God. Of all the identifications Thérèse found for herself in her tales, she particularly treasured the one of the little white flower. Her aunt at the Visitation, in one of her consoling letters to Zélie after the death of one of her children, had described those who die very young as little flowers that God picks in the early springtime. The day Thérèse chose to tell her father of her decision to enter Carmel, the feast day of Pentecost, 1887, Louis performed, without knowing it, she says, a "symbolic action" which she never forgot. He pointed out some little white flowers, "rather like miniature lilies," picked one out for her, and as he gave it to her explained with what special attention God had nourished the flower and preserved it until that very hour. As she listened to her father, Thérèse says, she felt she was hearing the story of her own life, "so close was the analogy between what Jesus had done for the *little flower* and for *little Thérèse*. I took the flower from him as if it were the relic of a saint, and I noticed that he had pulled it out by the roots, without bruising any of it; it seemed as if it were meant to grow in more fertile soil than the soft moss in which it had spent its first days." That, she feels, is what her father had done for her in allowing her to leave the gentle valley of her childhood and to ascend Mount Carmel. She put the flower in her copy of the *Imitation*, at Chapter Seven of Book II, "On the Duty of Loving Jesus above All Things." And there, she tells us, it still remains, "only the stalk has now broken off, close to the root, as if God were telling me that he was soon going to break the ties of his little flower with the earth completely, instead of allowing it to fade away slowly." As a footnote in the French edition of the manuscripts reminds us, she wrote these words in 1895; she fell mortally ill at Easter in 1896, another fortuitous detail for her allegory, the beginning of her own resurrection following so closely upon the celebration of the resurrection of her Lord and lover. She could not have planned it better herself.

If one sees, then, how fundamental the figure of the little white flower is to Thérèse's imagination, if one understands how thoroughly she had identified herself with that figure, with the flower, then the rhetoric does not seem extravagant and the image of the small plant enduring the wind and the rain and the snow becomes not merely acceptable but handsomely apposite. Furthermore, the most casual observation of the little flowers that hang on into the winter, in Normandy, in southern England, even in some parts of the northern States, will confirm the justness of her botany. With great warmth, late dews, and soft breezes that some years seem to linger on, out of season, past summer and autumn into winter, some flowers show just the kind of stubborn resistance to the snow that Thérèse indicates.

One difficulty remains for those whose first response to Thérèse's imagery is a shudder, more or less polite—that is the figure of Jesus. Thérèse says Jesus gave "his" little flower the balm of sun and dew and soft breezes. Father Taylor and Monsignor Knox, as if to pacify the ruffled sensibilities of their English readers, say "our Lord." Even in translating the title of the chapter in the *Imitation* where Thérèse placed her keepsake flower, Knox changes the name from Jesus to God. But Thérèse is as stubborn as the flower in her allegory: she means the second person of the

Trinity, she means the man-God, she means her lover, she means Jesus. One cannot get away from him, by name and by works, in her autobiography, without getting a great distance away from her. It was his presence she felt as the presence of man and God, of God and man. There was no retreat from that presence for her; there is no retreat from that presence in her. She felt—more, she knew—that she was wooed by him, that she was won by him. From the first blind steps that she took toward him at the age of two, when in some curious, inchoate fashion she opened herself to the religious life, she was his—or at least that's the way she saw her life and her love as she looked back over both in writing her autobiographical allegory.

Thérèse did not know what it meant to be a nun, could not have known, when she first talked about becoming one, which was, as a matter of fact, not long after she first began to talk. She could not have had any very clear idea about the meaning of going to church at two and a half, but she ran off to it at that age, on a famous day in her childhood, when she had just come home with her parents, who had forgotten to close their door—ran off in the rain. At three, she had a clear enough idea of heaven to talk to her mother of wanting to go there and to promise to behave like an angel in order to achieve that goal. "Heaven," she tells us in the autobiography, is the first word she learned to read. In the Easter vacation of 1877, when Thérèse was just a few months past her third birthday, Pauline writes to her friend Louise Magdelaine about Thérèse's inordinate ambitions:

> What do you do with your days? I hope you often see Sister Marie de Sales. I want you to tell her that in a few years she will have a future novice, guess who? Like Madame de Sévigné, I give you ten guesses, thirty, even a hundred. Marie? No. . . . Léonie? No. . . . You, then? Not you either. . . . Very well, the new postulant is, is, is . . . Mademoiselle . . . Thérèse Martin. . . . Listen to the motives which will bring her. Yesterday evening she gave me her whole confidence, I could have died laughing: "I shall be a nun in a convent because Céline wants to go, and then too, Pauline, people must be taught to read, don't you see? But I won't take the class, it would be too much of a nuisance. Céline will, I will be the Mother; I shall walk round the convent all day and then I'll go with Céline, we'll play in the sand and then with our dolls." . . . I speedily brought down her castles in Spain: "Do you really think, my poor Thérèse, that you will be talking all day? Don't you know there has to be silence?"

"Has there? . . . Ah well, so much the worse, I shan't say a word." "What will you do, then?" "That's no great trouble. I shall pray to the good Jesus; but then how can I pray to Him without saying anything, I really don't know, and who will there be to show me, as I'll be the Mother, eh?" I had a frightful desire to laugh. But I kept serious. She looked at me thoughtfully. Her little face had so candid an expression; all she said to me came from so deep in her heart, that it was impossible not to be interested. At last, having reflected a few moments, she fixed her big blue eyes on me and with a mischievous smile she made gestures with her little arms like a grown-up and said: "After all, my little Pauline, it isn't worth while tormenting ourselves now. I am too little, don't you see, and when I'm big, like you and Marie, before I go into the convent, they will tell me what to do?" "That's right, baby dearest," I answered, covering her with kisses. "Now it's late, let's go to sleep; I'll undress you. . . . You can still spend a few nights before calling yourself Sister Marie Aloysia (that's the name she has chosen), you've still got time to think about it." Then we both went upstairs. I put her to bed, and with no further thought of what she had said to me, she went off to sleep in peace. . . . *How* I wish the little angel need not grow up, a little soul that has never offended the good God is so lovely. . . . I love having my Thérèse with me; I feel that, with her, no harm can touch me. . . .

It is unlikely that Thérèse's thoughts about the convent ended quite as abruptly as Pauline suggests. Certainly she lived surrounded with an unceasing awareness of the religious life. Life at home in Lisieux was a community life. When Thérèse did anything that had to be censured, that could be called naughty, she was told, by Céline, by Pauline, by someone, that she had offended Jesus. She worked "all day playing naughty tricks on my poor little sisters," she wrote Pauline's friend Louise; "in fact, I am a little imp, always laughing." Céline was a particular devotee of the chaplet of movable beads that Marie had discovered at the Visitation, a combination rosary and abacus for keeping track of acts of virtue, and even before the family had left Alençon, Thérèse had her own chaplet on which to count her successes, however small they were; they became, in time, the tiny foundation of her little way.

The community life of the Martins in Lisieux was a succession of small pleasures, most of them religious in tone, and those that were not were given some religious inflection, no matter how slight. Thérèse had her daily lessons, writing under the supervision of her godmother, Marie; all the rest were directed by her adoptive *Maman*, Pauline. She enjoyed her Catechism and Scripture history, but grammar "made the tears run": her difficulties were exactly those an English-speaking student has with French—"Remember the business about masculine and feminine!" she reminds Pauline. Afternoons, she walked round the town with Louis, pausing at each of the churches, St. Jacques, the Cathedral of St. Pierre, St. Désir, the chapel at the Carmel, to visit the Blessed Sacrament. There was play in the garden, into which she drew her father, like any little girl, feeding him her "precious *tisanes*" (herb-tea) in cups she herself had made of bark. He made an earnest pretense of drinking his tea and played ardent admirer of the altar architecture with which she busied herself in her own little corner of the garden. She went fishing with Louis, her king, her liege lord, her *"roi chéri,"* and mixed her jam sandwiches on the blissful days spent outside the city with rudimentary meditations. "My thoughts really deepened, then, and though I didn't know what it meant to meditate, my soul plunged into a true state of prayer." She listened to the soft sound of the wind, to the distant noises of marching soldiers, which "sweetly melancholized my heart. Earth seemed a place of exile and I dreamed of heaven."

Walking back to the house, if they met any poor people, Louis would send Thérèse to give them some small alms. One memorable man, pulling himself along on crutches, would take no money; he just smiled sadly at Thérèse as he refused her help. She thought how nice it would be to give him something, perhaps the cake Louis had just bought her, but she was not daring enough. Then she remembered having been told that on one's day of first Communion one could get anything one prayed for: she was only six, but she promised herself she would pray for him on that important day, and, she says, at her first Communion five years later she did so.

Small pleasures these were, for a small community, living in a small house in a small city. Les Buissonnets, as the Martins came to call their home, was derived from the ancient name of the district at the edge of town in which it was located—Les Buissons, The Bushes, we would probably say, or perhaps, The Shrubs, or The Thicket. The furnishings of the simple red-brick house were gathered together again some years after Louis's death, under the direction of Céline, who remembered each piece, each picture, each book, though some had been dispersed as far away as Paris. It is a pleasant enough house, with small rooms well filled with furniture, rather heavy but not tasteless pieces. One entered, in the time of the Martins, into a country kitchen, with rafters overhead and a large wide fireplace; this was, along with the small dining room at the right, the center of family activities. The chairs and the round table at which the Martins dined are comfortable, I can testify; I had breakfast there, a privileged as well as a comfortable spot from which to observe the curtains of *Point d'Alençon,* the gold clock made by Louis, the moralizing engravings on the wall. There are several such pictures. In one, a blind man's dog is run over by a Tilbury carriage, a desolate scene summed up in its ironic title, a quotation from Scripture, *"Qui m'aimera . . .",* that is to say, "Whoever loves me will love the least of my children." In another, entitled "Innocence and Fidelity," the central sentimental roles are played by a babe in a cradle and a dog.

Over this room is the room where Thérèse spent her tortured days of illness. It is now an oratory, with an altar where Thérèse's bed used to be and next to it a replica of the statue of the Virgin of the Smile, the statue, originally at Louis's Pavilion, to which Thérèse attributed her cure. The original pieces that remain in the room are a solid *garde-robe,* the same sort of wardrobe that one finds in every French hotel except, perhaps, the most modern, and a black and white marble fireplace, topped by a mirror. Next door, in Louis's room, the full set of furniture echoes the same wooden and marble solidity: a curtained Empire bed, very much like the bed at Alençon in which Thérèse was born, a square *secrétaire* desk, an armchair, two other chairs, a marble-topped bureau, a marble night table, and a round table of marble. One significant set of books is in evidence, the full set of Dom Guéranger's *L'Année Liturgique,* which Pauline brought back from the Visitation in 1877, and which Louis used to read from every night at Les Buissonnets, to mark each day in the liturgical year. There is no squalid spirituality or stickiness of style in these volumes by the Solesmes Benedictine who knew and admired Zélie's sister in her years at the Visitation, and who was himself so much admired by those who recognized in his work the beginning of a serious attempt to make sense of the liturgy for the laity and to encourage their taking a larger share in it.

The room that Thérèse and Céline shared still holds Thérèse's bed, a number of her toys, some of her books, the hamper in which she collected her father's fish, her garden wheelbarrow, the watch and chain Louis gave her to mark her first Communion, her crucifix, her prie-dieu. The glass screen behind which these objects rest was removed for me, and I was able to pick up and examine her doll and cradle; her skipping rope, complete with strong handles; a wooden trumpet, a kaleidoscope, a miniature stove, and a doll's tea set, exactly the same as the nineteenth-century American toys that are now beginning to fetch substantial prices in antique stores, as much, I think it can be fairly said, for their good workmanship and innate charm as for their rarity. Thérèse's geography and Cathechism and Gospels and Bible History are the usual late-nineteenth-century French texts, with worn cardboard covers on which are pasted title pages in drab colors, but inside the pages are well printed and the rather stiff paper has a good rag content. Unlike the modern French product, these books last; they are still pleasant to handle and fun to read; they must have been very satisfying to the smallest of the Martins, for whom the physical appearance of any object was always something to note.

Upstairs at Les Buissonnets is the Belvedere, that wonder room of the house, that attic palace which was Louis's retreat and Thérèse's favorite game room; where she played quietly on the floor, while her father read or thought or prayed; from which she and Céline surveyed the town by day or the stars at night. The Belvedere is small, like everything else in the house, but it oozes warmth; its eaves are just high enough to sit under with comfort, just low enough for little girls to walk under with ease. It is not hard to understand the appeal of this corner of the house for Thérèse or her sister or her father.

Les Buissonnets is itself a community, a community of corners, corners in the house, corners in the gardens, the middlingly formal little garden in front which leads to the cobblestone road that the Martins took every day to church and the large informal garden in back, with the recess in the wall where Thérèse made her altars and farther along the wall that spot where the little white flowers grew ready at hand for Louis's symbolic action when Thérèse announced her ambitions to the Carmelite life. The little summerhouse—a model of a fin-de-siècle gazebo—and the few iron pieces in the garden, the path that runs beside the wall, the trees, the lush Norman grass—all are appointed to relaxation and reflection. No member of this community had to go far to find the peace and calm necessary for meditation. The hidden life to which Thérèse found herself drawn after her mother's death was sweetly, gently, firmly solicited and supported in these gardens.

The Martins lived in seclusion in Lisieux. Their points of contact with the town were very few. Mostly, they saw the Guérins, Isidore and Céline, and their two daughters, Jeanne and Marie. On Sundays the whole family went calling on their cousins and uncle and aunt; on Thursdays, one or another girl would spend the afternoon chez les Guérins. On New Year's Day, when the Guérins had to make sixty calls to satisfy their social obligations, the Martins could almost dispense themselves from the obligation altogether: four visits and their duties were finished. They were not churlish about these things, nor was their retirement such that they found meeting people an impossible embarrassment. Louis went four times a year to Alençon, at least during the first years, to see friends as well as to conduct business. There were delighted visits to the seashore, at Deauville and Trouville, in 1878, the year after the Martins moved to Lisieux, and then a number of times again; in 1885, 1886, and 1887, it was counted upon as a regular part of family life. But Thérèse's special life was not the one that took her away from the home community; she found her extraordinary pleasures in the ordinary. She liked nothing more than her routine schoolroom engagements with Marie and Pauline at home, her walks with her father, church-going, country hikes, fishing, games up in the Belvedere and down in the kitchen and out in the garden, and if any of this palled—and nothing she or anybody else has recorded suggests that it ever did—there was always her remarkable collection of birds.

Thérèse's love for birds was extensive. It covered every species she saw. It involved looking after them, feeding them, playing with them, burying them. She would not rob a mother of its young, even when they were highly desirable little chaffinches, left alone for a moment in their nest. In her garden aviary, she had doves and parrots and canaries, brightly colored bullfinches and softly colored linnets. The linnets and bullfinches vied with the canaries in their morning arias. The parrot was briefly challenged by a magpie that Thérèse and Céline added to the collection. As might have been expected, that most quarrelsome and thieving of birds snatched at other birds' food, snapped at the two little girls, and then tried to ingratiate itself with faltering, crackling attempts at pronouncing their names, Thérèse's especially. When it finally drowned in a water trough, nobody mourned it much.

Birds figure many times in Thérèse's rhetoric, at particular length in the letter addressed to her sister Marie, which forms the second of the three parts of the autobiography. There, in a famous flight, speaking directly to Jesus, as in the *Imitation*, she compares herself to *un faible petit oiseau*, a weak little bird, a fledgling, covered only with fine soft hair. "I am not an *eagle*, but I do have an eagle's *EYES* and its *HEART*, and with them I dare to look, like an eagle, straight at the sun, the sun of divine love." The fledgling would like to sail straight ahead, like its brothers among the eagles, right to the throne of the Blessed Trinity, but all it can do is to mimic the attempt in a helpless flapping of its wings. Shall it die, then, of disappointment and shame? No, says Thérèse, "with an audacious spontaneity, it will remain fixed on the sun. Nothing will frighten it away, neither wind nor rain. . . ." If the heavenly light is lost for a moment under dark and ominous clouds, the bird will not shift its gaze. It knows that behind the clouds the brightness of the sun is never dimmed, not even for a second.

She carries the rhetorical figure as far as she can. It is the little bird that, every once in a while, finds its heart shaken by storms, so shaken that it cannot believe that anything else exists in the world but the storm clouds that envelop her. Then she knows her weakness and the "perfect joy of being weak. What happiness there is in remaining there, concentrating on the invisible light which can be seen only with the eyes of faith!" Thérèse knows, she says, how steadfast Jesus's love has been for the little bird, which has never strayed very far from him. But it is an imperfect little creature; it has allowed itself to be distracted; it has not remained fixed upon the sun, as it should. It has wandered off after food, after water to wet its half-formed wings; it has lost itself in looking at flowers. No eagle, it has been caught up time and again in the trifles of the earth. But equally often it returns to the sun, to confess its infidelities in the soft groaning song of the swallow. It is content to be weak, to remain in the cold; it rejoices in its suffering. "O Jesus! how happy your fledgling is to be little and frail! What would become of it if it were one of the great birds?" It could never, then, fall asleep in his presence, that is to say, one of the great souls of God would never dare to fall asleep over prayer, would never be able to entrust its cause to hardier representatives, to the majestic angels and saints who fly off like eagles, right to the central throne.

Thérèse sees the audacity of the eagle in the deeds of the towering saints of Christendom, the audacity and the unconquerable strength and the urge to protect the weak. In their shadow, she will come to God; borne on their wings, made bolder by their boldness. She looks to Jesus to lift her straight to the sun, to be consumed in it, to be caught up entirely in divine love. She does not use the ancient myths of Icarus or Phaëthon, but they are obviously not far behind her words. Her little bird is as poorly directed in its flight as Phaëthon, if left to its own resources; it is as waxen-winged as Icarus. But it will not fall headlong into the sea. It will not endanger the world. For it can look to extraordinary help, to divine support. And in that great sustaining hand that comes from above, that condescension beyond description, every creature, even the unlikely one more weak than she is, can look to be held and supported. Please, she begs Jesus at the end of her letter to Marie, please do it; please choose a legion of such little souls and make them worthy of your love.

Watching her birds was one of the things Thérèse liked best, one of the things she did best; for as later she found them figures as useful for her parables as her little white flower, so earlier she must have discovered in them some of that remoteness, that hidden life, which she accounted so precious. In their grace she could find ample evidence of the grace of a superior being. But most of all, it was the frailty of the young birds, their untried strength, their awkward movements toward mature flight, their helpless flapping of wings, that caught her imagination and remained imbedded in it as exquisite analogies for the poor fluttering attempts of weak souls to achieve grace of some sort, to find, in some manner or mode, peace and consolation. She knew her own weaknesses as a child, her own impetuousness, her own grand ambitions, her own awkwardness, her own status as a fledgling. The Martins went *en famille* to May devotions, but not Thérèse. Marie and Pauline went to choir practice on Wednesday evenings, but not Thérèse. She remained at home with her nurse, Victoire, and made her own May devotions with toy candlesticks and flowerpots and little wax matches which gave her improvised altar an unexpected splendor, and sometimes Victoire gave her the ends of proper wax candles to make the celebration really grand. But Victoire was not always so cooperative. When Thérèse asked her, one night during the sequence of May devotions, to begin the Memorare, because, as she said, "I'm about to light up," Victoire could only look at her and laugh. She asked her once again to start the prayer, but Victoire could only laugh, whereupon Thérèse, seeing that her wax matches were rapidly burning down, could only reply by telling "poor Victoire" that she was naughty, adding force to the epithet with a kick, into which, says Thérèse, she put all her strength. Victoire stopped laughing. She produced the endpieces of candle she had brought for Thérèse and the little girl moved from "tears of anger to tears of repentance."

Victoire's ways were strange to Thérèse. When she wanted a bottle of ink that was on a high shelf, beyond her reach, and expected Victoire to get it for her, the maid refused, telling Thérèse to find a chair and get it for herself. She did, but not without letting Victoire know what she thought of her, using the strongest words Victoire had ever used to her to do so. "Victoire," she said, just as she was jumping down from the chair, "you are a brat!" She apologized later, because Marie insisted that she do so, but not because she was genuinely sorry—"if Victoire would not stretch out her long arm to do me so small a service, she deserved the name of brat." But on other occasions, Victoire was exceedingly helpful to the little fledgling. She pulled her out of the fireplace, where there was no fire, it was true, but where the cinders were magnetic enough to stick to Thérèse and hot enough to burn her. And she rescued her from *un grand péril* which reads like a scene from a Mack Sennett comedy. Thérèse was watching Victoire walk past her with a pail of water from a precarious perch on a chair, where she was, "as usual," doing some sort of balancing act. The chair slipped. Thérèse fell, not onto the floor, but bottom first into the pail, where she remained, firmly locked in, her head touching her feet. Thérèse struggled to get out; anybody who has seen enough early film comedies will be able to imagine what she looked like. Victoire stared for a while, this time apparently without laughing, and then pulled her out, soaked, she says, like a piece of bread in a bowl of soup.

There was enough to keep Thérèse busy at Les Buissonnets, enough studying to do, enough games to play, enough songs to sing with Louis, enough walks to take with him, enough conversation with him, enough of everything to make for an exemplary fullness. There was no withdrawal from life in the isolation of the Martins. There was enough joy, enough interest in the interplay of wills, in the personal exchanges; more than enough to make up for the absence of others. Each day's exchanges brought the children closer to each other, and not simply in a physical closeness, but in a touching of souls, a mixing of interiorities. It was their interior lives that they were sharing, over games of checkers, listening to Louis recite poetry, sifting each other's accomplishments and failings, advising each other, especially the older girls, Marie and Pauline, counseling the younger, Céline and Thérèse, and, when she would listen, Léonie. This sort of discussion in the Martin community was more a chapter of virtues than a chapter of faults, and more a series of sessions of spiritual direction than either. Pauline guided Thérèse to her first confession and somehow found words to answer such extraordinary questions about the sacrament from the six-year-old as one in which the little girl tried to establish the priest's precise relation to God: "Shouldn't I tell M. Ducellier that I love him with all my heart, since it is God that I am going to speak to through him?"

First confession came years before first Communion in Thérèse's day, half a lifetime, almost five full years before. Thérèse had to stand up in the confessional; she was too short to kneel. She listened gravely to the Abbé's words about devotion to the Virgin and came out ten feet tall: "I was so pleased, so lighthearted. I had never before felt such joy in my soul. From then on, I went to Confession at all the big feasts and it was a true feast for me every time I went."

Sundays were Sabbaths in the Old Testament sense for the Martins. In Alençon, Louis would also shut his shop as tightly as he knew how on Sundays, would not even entertain a discussion of business on the holy day. If, as happened just once or twice, he

65

saw something he wanted in one of the stores, most of which were open on Sunday, he would point to it, or speak guardedly about it, reserving purchase or talk of purchase for the next day or even the day after. In Lisieux, the rhythm of the week was based on the cadence of Sundays. "And what a day it was, Sunday!" Thérèse rhapsodizes, ". . . God's own feast day, the day of rest." It was for the Martins more or less what it had been for the Israelites who first gave God's day its worshipful prominence. On that day, Thérèse was allowed to tarry in bed; there, Pauline brought her her morning chocolate, and then dressed her "like a little queen." Marie did her hair and produced a few yowls when she pulled it too tight. And then Thérèse descended, in full regalia, to take the hand of her king and to be kissed by him, "more lovingly even than usual," and off the family went to Mass.

At church, the first greeting was usually from Thérèse's uncle, sitting in his place of honor among the churchwardens. But all around people looked up, as Thérèse remembers the great occasions, "so moved to see so handsome an old man with a little girl so small" that they always moved along to make room for them, no small tribute from a Catholic congregation, which usually seems to regard its places in church as God-given, even when they have only been found and secured two seconds before. For once, Thérèse was not discomfited by the stares and the general flurry of interest. The sermon claimed her interest. Her father might be leaning over to remind her, when the preacher mentioned St. Teresa of Avila, that this was her patron saint, but even if he had nothing to say to her, she found his face uncommonly interesting, endlessly absorbing to watch, especially when his eyes filled with tears, as they did often enough at church, though he tried hard to hold them back.

Thérèse went on Sundays to Vespers and Compline with a sense of lingering sorrow. The day that was the fullest and the grandest in the week, the day for which the week existed, was coming to an end. It would be extended a little afterwards for one of the girls, the one who would be left at the Guérins' to spend Sunday evening with them; that Thérèse enjoyed enormously as long as not too much attention was paid to her and her uncle did not unnerve her by taking her on his knee and singing a song about Bluebeard in "a formidable voice." But the day, as Thérèse mused so often during Compline, was soon to end, the day of rest to be replaced by days of work, days of learning. Like Zélie so often before her, she felt that she was in exile here on earth; she "sighed for the eternal rest of heaven," for the Sundays that would never end, in her "true home." When she walked home from the Guérins' with Louis, she wanted to see nothing of "the scurvy earth." She kept her eyes fixed on the stars, like Dante emerging from one of his circlings of the afterlife, not looking to see where she was going, lost in contemplation.

It was Papa's firm hand that carried her through Sundays, from the first ceremonial descent of the narrow stairs of Les Buissonnets to the last rapturous inspection of the sky. The rest of the week she was much more on her own, and when she was not left to her own resources, she had a full schedule of duties to perform, not the least of them sudden errands across the house at night, into a devilishly dark room. Thérèse credits Pauline's inflexible will with breaking down her fear of the dark, which was considerable, and with teaching her how to take direction. Even Louis had to wait upon Pauline's permission to take Thérèse out for a walk, and if Thérèse's adoptive mother said no, then no it was, beyond argument or appeal, even from the great Louis, King of France and Navarre, as he seemed to be when he distributed prizes on the family's own prize day, when the year's schoolwork was finally adjudged.

Pauline's great skill, as Thérèse saw it in retrospect, was to make "the most sublime mysteries" somehow accessible to the little girl's approach, if not her understanding. She had become Thérèse's confidante as easily, and as thoroughly, as she had been her mother's. She guided her through her first serious doubts about God's beneficence. Why, Thérèse asked, were the degrees of glory so different from person to person? Why would they not all share the same munificence in heaven? Pauline had Thérèse bring her Louis's large drinking glass. Next to it she put Thérèse's tiny thimble. She poured water into both and then asked which was more full. Each, obviously, was as full as it could be. Thus, she explained to Thérèse, it was with souls: to each was given the amount of glory it could hold; none should be envious of any other, any more than the thimble should be jealous of the large drinking glass.

Pauline's counsels had their effect upon Thérèse's growing interiority. She provided the necessary interest, the necessary warmth, the necessary understanding; though it was older child to younger child, it was still child to child, and not simply child to child, but girl to girl, and the directing girl one who had long been accustomed to the musings and meditations and intimate confidences of a mother richly endowed with a speculative spirituality. Like Zélie, Pauline could mix religious discussions with a simple earthliness—she always had time to push Thérèse around the garden in a wheelbarrow and to help her keep her garden well stocked in plants. When Thérèse fell sick, as she did every winter, Pauline would install her in her own large bed and conduct long and serious conversations with her. They were some preparation for Thérèse's conversations with herself, that always deepening interior conversation which sprang from her growing awareness of herself. She had, in astonishing abundance, at the age of six, what the author of *The Cloud of Unknowing* understands by the words *the first fruits* in the verses from the third chapter of Proverbs that enjoin the reader to "Honor the Lord with your substance, and give him of the first of all your fruits. And your barns will be filled with abundance, and your presses will run over with wine." The fourteenth-century mystic says, "I call them your fruits with which you are bound to foster and feed in this life, both bodily and spiritually, all your brothers and sisters in nature and in grace, as well as your own proper self. The first of these gifts I call the first of your fruits." And what is that first fruit? "The first gift in each creature is the being of that creature." The writer's own deepening of his answer corresponds very well, I think, to the experience the little girl was going through: "If you spread out the curious opening of your heart to any or all the subtle qualities and worthy conditions that pertain to the being of man—the noblest being of all things made—for evermore you will find that the first point and the sharpest edge of your awareness, whatever it is, is your own naked being."

Thérèse would have had no difficulty in following this reasoning. She would have been able to say, with the author of *The Cloud of Unknowing*, this is the point at which you say, "I am, I see, and I feel that I am. And not only I am, but this is what I am, and this, and this, and this," adding up and enumerating, in so doing, all the special qualities of her being. And then she would surely have gone on to say, in the manner of the fourteenth-century mystics, "That is what I am and how I am, in nature and in

68

grace, and all I have is from you, Lord, and you are all it is. And I offer it all to you, principally to praise you, for the help of all my fellow Christians and of myself." It was not many years later that her own language was up to some such translation of inner experience into outer language. As Pauline's student, she accepted Pauline's language, Pauline's lead. But she was burgeoning with a sense of her own being, as so many little children are, and she needed some vehicle outside herself in which to carry that feeling. That is all she is doing, really, when she writes to Céline, in a booklet she herself had made out of letter paper, cutting it and folding it and sewing it so that it could contain, one word to a page, the following words:

Darling Céline,

You know I love you a lot. Goodbye, darling Céline.
Your little Thérèse who loves you with all her heart.

Thérèse Martin.

The message is unvarying. When she writes Pauline from their aunt's house, just across town, she has nothing much more to say. "I am very pleased to be writing to you," she tells her sister. "I asked my aunt if I could, I make a lot of mistakes but you know your little Thérèse, so you know I am not very clever." But she doesn't want this to be the only impression, so she boasts that she received "four good marks the first day and five the second." She distributes kisses to Papa and Pauline's godmother, explains that she is coloring "little pictures" while Marie helps her aunt with the year's accounts, and then says, "Goodbye, darling Pauline, your little *Thérèse* who loves you."

The phrases are felicitously made for a six- or seven-year-old. There is nothing pompous in Thérèse's notes, but neither is there anything profound. Many little girls her age could have written the same notes; many undoubtedly did. The insistent awareness of oneself at that age is given to all, but the encouragement of that awareness is rare. Perhaps it requires a situation as out of the way as Thérèse's to bring out in a child the inner depths which are then being sounded with such resonance; perhaps one must have such isolation as the Martin family had created for itself with a spiritual craftsmanship as precise and detailed and shrewdly husbanded as that which Louis organized and directed for himself and his daughters after his wife died. Certainly, one must have express direction to offer up, as *The Cloud of Unknowing* counsels, "your naked being, which is the first of your fruits, in continual sacrifice for the praise of God, both for yourself and for all others," as Thérèse did in such precocious fullness, even then, even at the age of six.

In his seventh year, Mozart made his first professional tour of Europe. In her seventh year, Thérèse had a prophetic vision of her father in old age, his body twisted with paralysis, his face veiled in a thick apronlike covering of an uncertain color which made it impossible to make out his features. She thought at first it was Louis walking in front of the laundry, as she looked out of an attic window, where she was standing in a kind of happy abstraction. He had been away for some days and was not expected home for several more. She thought he had come back early and was disguising himself as a trick to amuse her, but she was frightened and called out in a voice shaking with emotion, "Papa, Papa!" The figure walked on without betraying any response to her voice and disappeared into the trees.

Fifteen years after the vision, it remained as clear as on the day it happened to this Mozart of saints. She often forgets details of other significant events in her childhood and tells us as much. But this mysterious apparition, with its sad portents, was incisively etched in her memory. Marie, in the next room with Pauline, started in fright when she heard Thérèse calling; she knew something strange was happening. She ran in to Thérèse and asked her what she could have meant; Papa was in Alençon, of course. When Thérèse told her what she had seen, Marie tried to reassure her. It was Victoire, she said, trying to scare her; but Victoire insisted that she had never left the kitchen. When they looked for some sign of the man outside, they found nothing, no footprints, no marks of any kind.

Thérèse was not given to apparitions or visions of any kind. That is one reason why many people, who rest their understanding of mystical graces upon a show of extraordinary phenomena of this kind, deny that she was in fact a mystic. She did predict her own death, but she did not need any special gift of precognition to do so; in her last years, the signs of an advanced case of tuberculosis were self-evident to almost everyone except the examining doctors. She read character with extraordinary understanding. She had at a very early age a remarkable sensitivity to people—Father Piat calls it, in the context of her illness, "that acute over-sensitiveness, and that exaggerated impressionability which led her to weep floods for the most futile causes"—which was either a supernatural gift, a functional or an organic disorder, depending upon one's own reading of her character. She did spend increasingly long periods in colloquy with Jesus, but since she notes no verbal responses from him, the conversations could just as well be recorded as a series of interior monologues; they have none of the obvious marks of divine intervention. The prophetic apparition of her father, crooked with illness and age, and as Thérèse points out, veiled like the face of Jesus during his Passion, was an event by itself in her life. She did not understand what it meant when it happened; she was not prepared at the time to accept even the thought of his death. Whenever he was in a precarious position, say, poised high on a ladder, under which she stood, she had to turn away. She would say to herself, "I am not going to suffer the pain of seeing him die; I would rather die with him."

Years later, talking over the vision with her sister Marie at the convent, it all became simple enough. She saw clearly then what earlier she had only seen in the distance, "our father in his great distress," as Céline describes the apparition, "like the holy king David crushed with trials, who 'went over the brook Cedron. . . . went up by the ascent of Mount Olivet, going up and weeping, walking barefoot and with his head covered'" (2 Kg 15:23, 30). She never saw the significance of the experience as a foreshadowing of her own approaching illness, or at least she never said that she did. But it marked her as surely as her mother's death did with a further awareness of the summary partings with which our lives are inevitably afflicted, a consciousness of death as never very distant, a consciousness with which the Martins were very richly endowed. This new awareness, however opaque to precise verbalization it may have been, must have been more than merely vague and indistinct. It came at a time when Thérèse was particularly impressionable and given to prolonged meditation of a more and more serious kind. She was alert to people's responses to her—she noticed immediately what her father was doing when he signaled a man and woman who had asked whether the pretty little girl they had watched running around on the beach was his daughter; he was asking them not to pay her compliments. She was alert, too, to her own responses. When she sat on a rock at Trouville, with Pauline, watching the sun descend into an immensity of waters, she was deeply impressed by the golden track of light that it cut between the waves. It reminded her of an affecting story called "The Golden Track," out of one of her favorite collections, *La Tirelire aux histoires*, a *Treasury of Stories* compiled by Louise Swanton Belloc, Hilaire Belloc's grandmother. The story led to further reflection. She looked for a long time at the golden track of light made by the sun, for her a figure of grace illuminating the way for a little white-sailed ship, and sitting there with her sister, she determined always to stay close to her Lord until he could lead her with his *sillon d'or*, his *sillon lumineuse*, his golden track, to her heavenly destination.

Thérèse's contemplation of the sea at seven is not a child's contemplation. It has more of the anguish of adolescence about it than the small anxieties of the years before puberty. Little children may express their anxieties with piercing cries, and the piercing cries may be symptomatic of deep distress, but their distress, no matter how profoundly felt, rarely has any significant metaphysical dimension. They, all of them, begin at a very early age to fear the loss of parents, brothers, sisters, friends, but not with much, if any, prolonged speculation about the nature of death. They have not often contemplated any of those they love with the protracted gaze and inner reverie with which, regularly, Thérèse studied her father, at home, at church, on their walks together. They are not often led in their speculations into theological discussions of the kind Pauline, and others in the family, conducted with Thérèse. But even if they have such gifted collaborators as these, how often have they the inner resources to respond as Thérèse did? In a family notably set apart from others, a family just this side of eccentricity in its reclusiveness, Thérèse was remarkable for the time she spent by herself. Up in her own corner of the attic, she had constructed a small cell for herself, where she could examine her own collection of "pieties and curiosities," as she called it. "Really," she says, "that attic was a world for me, and like M. de Maistre, I could have written a book called *A Journey Around My Room*." There, in the garden, by the sea, anywhere, she could sit and contemplate. As later she did in the Carmel, she sat long hours without any necessary book or picture or object of any kind, however often she may have started with one or the other. At six, at seven, at eight, she was a natural contemplative.

Like Mozart, Thérèse was a child prodigy, and like him too she was made quickly sensitive to her art. As Leopold Mozart counseled and guided his son, so Louis Martin, with the constant help of his older daughters, advised and directed Thérèse, without embarrassment or apology when the conversation turned to fundamental theological and philosophical questions, making her from a very early age feel at ease in discussions of a fairly profound sort. Thérèse was babied some of the time. Her sisters and her nurse laughed at her pretensions to a religious life, in which she was sometimes a nun, sometimes a priest, always a theologian. But they encouraged her just enough, took her questions and reflections just seriously enough, gave her just enough of what might be called seminary training, to make it possible for her to gallop across all the preliminary encounters with God before she had ever left her house to go to school. The little girl of eight who turned up at the Benedictine abbey school in Lisieux in October of 1881 looked like a little girl of eight, but she had the religious equipment of a zealous young adult, many of the same certainties and many of the same doubts. Her feelings were intense, easily aroused, brought quickly to turmoil and confusion, or almost as quickly—if her meditations were spurred by the right object—were brought to a lengthy repose in contemplation of nothing less than eternity. Is it anything to wonder at that such a child should not have been at ease in school or should have found the departure of her dearest sister, her adoptive mother, to the convent more than she could bear?

FIVE

*L*IFE at a boarding school promised everything; the best days of one's life, the happiest, Thérèse had often heard it said. But not for her: "The five years I spent there were the saddest of my life, and if I hadn't had my dear Céline with me, I should not have been able to stay there for a month without falling sick." The little flower, she says, had been used to soil specially prepared for it. It could not settle easily into a mixed garden, with soil that had to support such a diverse collection.

There was an extraordinary variety of girls at the school that Léonie had just left and especially in Thérèse's own class. She was really too well prepared to enter the grade made up of children her own age; she was quite up to the work in the next class, where she was finally put; but there all the girls around her were larger, taller, and older than she. One of them was thirteen or fourteen and unconscionably jealous of Thérèse, whom she did her best to persecute, especially when it quickly became clear that the eight-year-old was almost always to be head of the class. Thérèse won her prizes, not only the school badges, but rewards from Papa and even from Pauline, who gave her star pupil a hoop for her star performance. But school was still a melancholy affair for Thérèse, almost all of it, even the games on Thursday afternoon, which was always a holiday for the school. She was not used to playing with strangers; her companions had always been her sister Céline and her Guérin cousins and the cousins of the Guérins, the Maudelonde girls. She did not know the games the other girls played. She tried, but she was bored, especially when she had to spend the whole afternoon dancing quadrilles. Only when they went to the star-shaped park to pick flowers was she happy and at ease: she loved doing that, and besides, she was faster at picking than anyone else and more adept at finding the prettiest ones.

With Marie Guérin, Thérèse invented a game that both enjoyed hugely—as long as they were allowed to play it: Hermits. They played at being *solitaires*, with nothing to sustain them but a wheat field and some few vegetables, with nothing to engage their time except uninterrupted contemplation. Even when there was some field work to be done, in this community one of the nuns remained absorbed in silent prayer. They kept the silence, too, whenever they were together. When Mme. Guérin sent them out to walk, they said their rosaries—on their fingers, so as not to betray themselves to the "indiscreet populace." They were perfectly matched; they enjoyed the same things, Marie and Thérèse. They found Hermits an inexhaustively fascinating game. But when, coming home from school one day, Marie refused to play seeing-eye for blind Thérèse, and both, with eyes tightly shut, crashed into a pile of boxes in front of a shop, they were separated by Marie's sister Jeanne, after a thorough scolding. Now Thérèse was linked with Jeanne, and Marie was forced to walk with Céline Maudelonde, with whom she had nothing in common except age, and with whom she argued all the time.

There was some compensation in the time she spent with her own Céline, her sister who was only four years older than she, marvelously full of imaginative mischief, and Thérèse's ardent defender at school. There they used to call her "Céline's little daughter," which Céline was quick to take advantage of—she scolded Thérèse, when she was annoyed with her, by saying, "You're no longer my little girl; that's all over with, and I'm never going to forget it!" But Thérèse would quickly win back her sympathy with her tears, "like a repentant Magdalen," pleading with Céline to become her mother again, and soon Céline would kiss her and try to comfort the little Magdalen by bringing her one of the dolls she had been instructing in a model classroom, telling it, "Darling, kiss your aunt." One of the dolls was so ardent that it caught its fingers in Thérèse's nose, from which it hung, needless to say, to Céline's great delight—though, says Thérèse, she had not intended that particular gesture of affection. When Céline went off on a three-day retreat, as preparation for her first Communion, in the May before Thérèse entered the abbey school, Thérèse was devastated. It was the first time she had been separated from her sister in all her life, and she could not believe she was gone; like Zélie looking all around the house for her father just after he had died, Thérèse saved some of her fruit for Céline on her first day away from home and was terribly gloomy when she realized she wasn't coming home, not that night or the next or the next.

The separation from Céline was terrible. It did not stop at the retreat. Pauline had told Céline that with one's first Communion one began a new life. Thérèse decided that she would share this with Céline, as she had everything else, and she felt one with her throughout the happy day, even though her own first Communion was four years off. She was not, of course, precisely Céline's twin. Though she records only her joy in the day, it marked a further isolation of Thérèse, and school coming just a few months afterwards, with all its disappointments, once more set her apart, even in her own family. Then, a few months after that, in February of 1882, Pauline made her decision to enter Carmel, and though the actual moment of departure was not to come for another eight months, the grim fact was clear enough—Pauline was going, not for three days, but for a lifetime, forever. She was not going very far, only a few hundred yards as the magpie flies, into the Carmel in Lisieux, right in their own neighborhood. But it was another world she was entering. The family community was breaking up.

Thérèse felt betrayed. She had once told Pauline that she wanted to become a *solitaire*, just as she had played at being one with Marie Guérin, and Pauline had replied that that was what she wanted too and that she would wait until Thérèse was old enough to go with her. And now Pauline was talking of going off to Carmel, whatever that was. "How can I tell you the anguish that was in my heart?" she writes to Pauline thirteen years later. "In an instant, I understood what life was all about. Until then, it had not seemed particularly bad to me, but now I saw it in all its reality. I saw that life was nothing but continual suffering, continual separation. I cried bitter tears; I did not yet understand the joy that sacrifice brings. . . ." She knew only how weak she was. It was miraculous, she thought later on, that she got through the ordeal at all, the eviscerating announcement, for which she was altogether unprepared.

Pauline did her best to assuage the bitter feelings of the would-be *solitaire* who could not bear to be left alone. She told Thérèse a great deal about Carmelite life and did so well at it that Thérèse conceived a Carmelite ambition of her own. She would not have to be separated from Pauline after all, or at least not for very long. Pauline was wise enough to give Thérèse's new ambition every sort of encouragement. She saw in it, she told the child, the will of heaven, and she promised Thérèse she would take her to see the Mother Prioress at the Carmel, to whom she was to explain exactly what had happened to her.

The solemnity of the occasion was added to when a Sunday was chosen for the visit. The special importance of Thérèse's coming conversation with the Prioress was somewhat diminished, however, when she was told that her cousin Marie would stay behind with her in the parlor; both were, after all, still young enough to see the Carmelites unveiled. But Thérèse explained that in order to show Mother Prioress the proper respect, they would have to confide all their secrets to her, which meant, reasonably enough, that each would have to speak to her alone. Marie had no secrets, but nonetheless she agreed to Thérèse's plan and so she was able to talk as candidly as she wished to Mother Marie de Gonzague, the Prioress. Mother was entirely willing to take Thérèse at her word; she believed, she told the little nine-year-old, in her vocation, but she was really too young for Carmel; she would have to wait until she was sixteen. Another, but not a crucial, disappointment. Thérèse had been planning to enter Carmel immediately and to make her first Communion on the day of Pauline's Clothing. A postponement, then, was ordained, but no more.

Carmel was auspiciously begun for Thérèse. The Mother Prioress had understood her, had believed her. And on the same remarkable visit, Sister Thérèse of St. Augustine came to see the new applicant and said over and over again, as so many people had, what a pretty little girl this was, only this time it was a Carmelite nun who had said the happy words and there was no Louis around to make forbidding signals. "I had not intended to enter Carmel to have praises bestowed upon me," Thérèse muses about the event, "and when the parlor was over, I told the Lord many, many times that it was for him alone that I wanted to become a Carmelite." There were depths, undoubtedly, to Thérèse's ambition. It was, she knew as soon as she began to meditate on Pauline's explication of the Carmelite life, the most certain of vocations. But it also had, it clearly had, the additional charm of continuing the community life of Les Buissonnets just a few hundred yards away—as the magpie flies.

It was a very hard year for Thérèse. She was intensely aware of her position as the youngest of the Martins. Céline had had her first Communion and though she had tried to share her happiness with her sister, there was now an unbridgeable gulf between them which only Thérèse's coming of age could narrow. For the present the little girl was haunted by the need, in every sense of the word, to communicate. When she saw the Bishop in the street, she ran up to him to ask him, please, to allow her to receive her first Communion a year ahead of time; how hard it is, she explained, to have to wait a whole year, until January 2, to be born.

First Communion was a signifying occasion, as Thérèse saw it, not only for the uniting of her spirit with Céline's, but for what it augured of the life to come with Pauline in Carmel. Thérèse and Céline were dedicated to making Pauline's last days in the Martin community unforgettable. They brought her cake and candy and sweetmeats of every kind, and brought them to her without fail every day, because soon she would be giving all those things up for good. They pestered her with their presence, not giving her a second to herself if they could help it. It was a way, too, of filling the time with Pauline so that they could somehow, in anticipatory celebration of her departure, forget that she was departing.

Finally, the day came, October 2, a "day," as Thérèse narrates it, in full diapason, "of tears and blessings, in which Jesus gathered to himself the first of his flowers. . . ." As she looks back on the wonderful day, on the sorrowful day, she remembers the precise spot where Pauline gave her her last kiss—though she doesn't name it—and the movement of the Martins to Mass, *en famille*, if "family" was still the correct word for the Paulineless Martins, the tearful Martins, who moved, crying, all of them, into church, shepherded by their aunt. "If everything had crumbled about me, I shouldn't have paid any attention. I looked up at the blue sky and marveled that the sun could shine so brightly when my own heart was flooded with sorrow."

Do you think I exaggerate? Thérèse says to Mother Agnès, Pauline who was. Do you think perhaps I exaggerate the pain I felt? She knows, she tells her adoptive mother, now, at the time of writing, her mother in God, she knows her grief should have been more measured; she did hope, after all, to join Pauline in Carmel.

78

But, she explains, using her special kind of typographical notation to intensify the power of her adjectives, "my soul was *FAR* from being *ripe.* . . ." She still had to be tested many times before achieving her great end; she knew that.

One trial came quickly enough. That same Monday, October 2, 1882, was the first day of school, and she had to go in spite of her misery. Was the misery softened or concentrated by the visit that same afternoon, after school, to her "darling Pauline," now to be seen only behind a grille? "Oh," moans Thérèse, "how I have suffered in this *parlor* at Carmel!" She must tell all, she insists, in writing the history of her soul. The sufferings were grim before Pauline entered; they were grimmer after she was in. Every Thursday the Martins trouped to the Carmel parlor, which, one might have thought, would have been an improvement on those embarrassing games to which Thérèse was earlier condemned. Not so, not so. Thérèse, who had had Pauline for the closest of confidantes, was able to get only two or three minutes with her at the end of the afternoon, and that only at great pain. And then what did she do when she had her beloved sister to herself? She cried. And then went away in agony. She could not make sense out of Pauline's treatment of her, spending all her time with her cousins, Jeanne and Marie Guérin. "I've lost Pauline" was all that Thérèse could conclude. It was some years before she could understand the delicacy of feeling that had prompted Pauline to speak at such length and with such concentration to her cousins. Thérèse's ironic commentary on this series of setbacks is, "How surprising it was to see how my mind developed in the depths of my suffering; it developed to such a point that I didn't waste any time before falling sick."

How much, too, has been made of this illness of Thérèse's! What cloudbursts of rhetoric, what sunbursts of perception! The illness is not easy to explain. It is fascinating to speculate upon, and nobody who has thought long about Thérèse, has come to like or dislike her, to adore or to abhor her or just to be pleasantly puzzled by her, has long resisted this line of inquiry. Around her behavior during the several bouts of this illness, most of the serious psychoanalysis of Thérèse has taken shape. Upon this upsetting experience of hers hangs one's understanding of her spiritual strengths and weaknesses and really her physical frailties and endurance as well. And in this illness, if you follow my conception

79

of Thérèse as a prodigy among saints, emerges a spirit remarkably precocious even among that rare species.

If one follows Thérèse's own diagnosis of her illness, it was beyond any doubt the work of the devil. Why? He was furious at the attenuation of his power which the Martins were, in effect, plotting, as their vocations developed, one by one, until each of the girls was safely secured in the religious life, four at Carmel, one at the Visitation. If one follows Father Étienne Robo's skeptical explication, it is all to be understood in the light of the fact that Thérèse "was a neuropath as well as a saint. . . ." Understand this and one sees that "many otherwise inexplicable episodes of her life can be linked together and make a coherent whole." This diagnosis "explains her constant unconscious preoccupation with herself. Neuropaths have an intense interior life, and because their sensations, their perceptions, are unusually keen, they have artistic gifts. They are dreamers. . . . given to self-analysis, they attach an enormous importance to themselves, to what they feel, to what they do."

No diagnosis was made, even when Thérèse was attacked by continual and violent headaches, toward the end of the year. She was capable of getting to school. It did not seem important to do anything about her. But in Easter of the next year, 1883, near the end of March, the illness came to an open crisis. Louis had taken Léonie and Marie with him to Paris; Thérèse and Céline were left with their uncle and aunt, the Guérins. One night, her uncle took Thérèse out and began to talk to her about Zélie and what he remembered of her life, talking, Thérèse says, "with a kindliness that touched me profoundly and made me weep." Uncle Isidore's perhaps kind, perhaps unkind response was to reprove Thérèse for her tender heart—one suspects he meant her touchiness. What you need, my girl, he said, is distraction, all you can get, and he and his wife decided promptly that she must have all sorts of fun during her Easter holidays. They were, in fact, ready to go out with her that night to some sort of Catholic social group, but Thérèse, her aunt thought, was too tired to go. She was more than tired. She began to tremble when she was undressing and continued to shake and shiver under piles of covers and with several hot-water bottles, too, and so it went throughout the night. When next day Dr. Notta, a learned man in his profession, according to Marie, was called in, his diagnosis was chorea, or St. Vitus's Dance.

The name of the disease is romantic. It means, if one inflects its Latin root, a dance in a ring; if its Greek root, a choral dance. St. Vitus comes into it because his was a name regularly invoked in cases of epilepsy; the fact that he was mistreated by his parents has nothing to do with it, nor does his martyrdom under Diocletian. In any case, for all its engaging verbal associations, chorea is an ugly disease, involving irregular and quite involuntary muscle spasms that contort the patient, usually a child just entering upon puberty, and make over his movements into a grotesque human parody of a marionette on a string. Thérèse certainly had some of the symptoms. Her body jerked in the classical manner of the victim of chorea. She had often shown herself a delicate child, of the sort that often falls prey to the terrible Dance. Louis and his older children were frightened, especially since Dr. Notta's treatments did not seem to be doing any good. Thérèse's condition grew worse. In addition to her convulsive movements, she was beset with angry apparitions that made her cry out in fear—nails on the wall grew up into great charred fingers; Louis's hat was transformed into a big black animal. She threw herself into great turns and twists in bed, and once vaulted right over the high railing around her bed onto the stone floor of the Guérins' house.

Remarkably enough, she remained conscious through most of her fits, and even when she seemed comatose, far away from everything and everybody, she knew what was going on, she followed the conversation. Father Robo should be pleased—neuropaths are, we must remember, "unusually keen . . . [and] attach an enormous importance to themselves. . . ." This particular "neuropath" was also unusually lucky. When she sailed over the bed rail onto the stone floor she did not even scratch herself, according to Léonie, who found her there, stretched out. And according to Marie's testimony at the trial for canonization, no matter how athletic Thérèse's movements became, no matter how she twisted and turned and tumbled about, her nightgown never opened or rose in any way that could be called "immodest." This remarkable fact—if fact it is—is one of three listed by Father Rohrbach in his book on Thérèse to support this as perhaps "another case of diabolic obsession." The others are Thérèse's continuing consciousness during her attacks—"her complete possession of her interior faculties"—and the fact that she remained unharmed, despite being dashed against the railing and thrown onto the stone floor.

Whether the first mover in Thérèse's illness was or was not the devil is not likely to be decisively settled on earth. The Church did not make any official pronouncement about diabolic visitation, as it never does, and Pius XI's apparent acceptance, in the decree of beatification, of the opinion held by Thérèse and her family that she had been victimized because the devil anticipated the injury she would do him, is not to be interpreted as any definitive certification of that interpretation. Neither, for that matter, does the Church support the precise terms of Thérèse's miraculous cure. It is clear that her illness was mysterious and its cure mysterious and all we can do now, it seems equally clear, is to speculate as intelligently and intelligibly as possible upon the several mysteries involved in the illness.

I myself am convinced that Thérèse was suffering neither from St. Vitus's Dance nor from a mental breakdown. I say this with full awareness that I have something less than the competency of a pediatrician or a psychiatrist in these matters. But I have the impressive witness of Father Thomas Verner Moore, both a pediatrician and a psychiatrist, with all the necessary academic degrees, who at various times was head of the Department of Psychology and Psychiatry and Director of the Child Guidance Center at Catholic University in Washington. In his book *Heroic Sanctity and Insanity* Father Moore disposes of the attestations of mental breakdown as the cause of Thérèse's illness as well as the general analysis of Thérèse as a saint who suffered all her life from neuropathy and sanctified herself by dealing with it. He shows beyond argument, it seems to me, the awkwardness of Robo's terminology and the inappositeness of his conclusions. He sums up: "St. Thérèse was not a neuropath if by that you mean what was once termed a constitutional psychopath by psychiatrists. But she did have various emotional difficulties. But who goes through life free from emotional difficulties?" Fair question and fair conclusion, I think. But far more interesting, to me at least, is Father Moore's diagnosis of Thérèse's physical symptoms.

Father Robo rests his analysis of Thérèse's illness upon her response to her mother's death: "The shock had been too much for her, and it left a permanent scar on her nervous system. It would have been better had she been able to give an unrestrained expression to her grief. . . . she had been happy, lively and demonstrative, now she became timid, retiring and so sensitive 'that a look,' she says, 'was enough to make me burst into tears.' Was Mrs. Martin's death the cause of this nervousness that never left her altogether, even after she had become a Carmelite, or was it only the occasion that released a weakness already part of her constitution?" Father Moore dismisses these speculations as so much "pseudo-psychology," which "supposes that Thérèse's illness was purely mental and that she was not suffering from a dangerous physical disorder." But five symptoms indicate, as he sees Thérèse's disorder, a diagnosis of physical rather than mental breakdown:

1. The unremitting headache "demands a differential diagnosis" and the examination of physical elements along with the mental.

2. The sudden aggravation of the headache, with accompanying chills and fever, "points to the acute onset of an infectious disorder."

3. The fact that she collapsed again the day after she got out of bed to attend Pauline's Clothing ceremony "again points to an infection of some kind."

4. "Severe physical prostration with a period of delirium is not found in purely mental conditions and points to a toxic delirium due to an infection."

5. The fact that this *physical* prostration continued, with great corollary pain, is "further evidence of a serious physical disorder."

One particular infectious disorder seems to Father Moore—to Doctor Moore—to fit these symptoms: *pyelonephritis*. Pyelonephritis is a disease of the kidney which may start with pyelitis, inflammation of the pelvis of the kidney. An acute form of the infection usually comes all at once, with accompanying chills, and then fever, with all sorts of related miseries, from head to stomach, touching every spot where Thérèse was disturbed and with all the same manifestations—violent headaches, convulsions, coma. Today, medicine has the equipment with which to deal with pyelonephritis in a child of ten. In 1883, a child suffering from that or any related condition almost always died; there was no accurate diagnosis generally available—an early and correct one, according to the history of the treatment of the disease given by Father Moore, was lost—and hence no useful treatment. "Only a true miracle," says Doctor Moore—says Father Moore— "could possibly have brought about her sudden cure. Our Lady manifested herself to the child, clothed in her immaculate beauty. The expression on her face was ineffably tender and sweet. She smiled upon an innocent child whom she loved and who had a mission on earth that was to be continued in heaven. And as Our Lady smiled all the child's pain vanished. Two big tears of unmixed heavenly joy started from her eyes and flowed silently down her cheeks. Thérèse was cured."

The sequence of events is clear enough. Thérèse recovered enough at the house of her uncle and aunt to be taken in a carriage to the Carmel on April 6 for Pauline's Clothing, and not only to go to it but at the convent to jump onto Pauline's lap and to "cover her with kisses. I could contemplate her beauty in her white wedding-dress." Afterwards she was taken back to Les Buissonnets and, reasonably enough, put to bed again. By the next day she was as sick as she had ever been, beyond the possibility of human cure, Thérèse says. It was Marie's turn now to bear the brunt of her illness, though the Guérins were still in constant attendance, Aunt Céline coming in every day, to Louis's great relief. Little Céline spent all the time she could with her sister and Léonie did her best to amuse Thérèse. Others, friends of the family, came to visit, but Thérèse begged Marie to put them off; Thérèse explained she couldn't stand "seeing people sitting around her bed like a string of onions and looking at me as if I were a strange beast of some kind."

Marie played mother for Thérèse in great earnest and with great skill during her illness. It took great patience, too. For though Thérèse called her *Maman* often enough, there were times also when she did not recognize her and would not respond to her most tender and affectionate words and there was one terrible moment when Thérèse, in delirium, responded to Marie's attempt to give her a drink of water with a screaming rejection: "You want to poison me!" Though there were times when Thérèse was very pleased to have Marie with her and showed it, her most enthusiastic response was saved for the letter that Pauline sent her from Carmel, which she read over and over and came to know by heart, and for the hourglass that Pauline also sent her and the little doll dressed up as a Carmelite, which made her uncle frown; he thought she should forget all about the convent; it had too many painful associations for the little girl. But for Thérèse, it was the hope of one day becoming a Carmelite, she says, that sustained her, and the association, however painful, was one she kept very firmly before her mind as she cut various decorative objects out of *papier bristol* (cardboard) for Pauline and made a crown of *paquerettes* (Easter daisies) and *myosotis* (forget-me-nots) for the beloved statue of the Virgin that stood in the sickroom, the miraculous statue that had given Zélie such encouragement when she needed it, Louis's statue from the Pavilion.

Thérèse prayed to be cured. She longed to leap up from bed and cheer her poor despondent father with a triumphant announcement of her recovery. Louis, as always, had put his trust in his devotion to Our Lady of Victories, whose church in Paris was a place of pilgrimage for him, whose novenas had proved so powerful for the family. He did not let up now in his bombardment of the blessed damosel. "A *miracle* was necessary," Thérèse sums up, "and it was *Notre-Dame des Victoires* who would work it." Thérèse had her miracle. Louis had his. Marie, kneeling beside Thérèse's bed with Léonie and Céline, after one of Thérèse's terrible rejections, had hers.

Thérèse herself had been aware of what she was doing in this last of her spurnings of Marie. She had been yelling at the top of her lungs for "Mama! Mama! Mama!" But when Marie came hurrying to her she could not quite make out who it was—or was not. There was nothing to do but to go to supernatural sources, Thérèse felt. She turned her face where her sisters were looking, at the statue of the Virgin, and in that kind of wordless prayer in which her illness had tutored her, she lifted her heart in hope of the Lady's intercession. Then *"Tout à coup la Sainte Vierge me parut* belle, *si* belle *que jamais je n'avais vue rien si beau, son visage respirait une bonté et une tendresse ineffable. . . ."* "Suddenly the Blessed Virgin glowed with beauty for me, a beauty beyond any I had ever experienced before; her face radiated an indescribable kindness and love. . . ." It was the smile above all that caught Thérèse, lifted her in a seizure unlike all the others of recent months, a seizure of immediate and entrancing joy. Father Moore's description, quoted above, follows Thérèse's own

85

words—"Two big tears started up from my eyes and ran silently down my cheeks . . . tears of unmixed joy." She was cured.

Everybody in the room felt the change, saw the change. Marie looked at Thérèse with special understanding. She had guessed, Thérèse thought, what had happened. Both sisters had been granted their wishes, and both knew it. When Marie was able to talk with Thérèse alone, in private, she pressed her little sister for details. Thérèse could not resist her sister's loving eagerness. She told her what had happened; she told her about the *"enrapturing smile of the Blessed Virgin"*—both underlined and in quotation marks in Thérèse's manuscript. She told her, but with some reluctance. She felt there was something wrong about doing so, and for four years she was plagued by the effects of that disclosure. It was, like the experience itself, *tout à coup*, all at once, a great revelation, to everybody. Marie begged Thérèse to allow her to tell them at Carmel about the apparition and Thérèse once again could not say no. When Thérèse herself was recovered enough to go to see Pauline at the convent, she wasn't long with her sister, didn't have long to admire her sister in "the habit of the Virgin," which filled Thérèse's heart with joy, or to bask in the kindness of the Prioress, before the other nuns began to ply her with questions about her "grace." Did the Blessed Mother have little Jesus in her arms? Was she surrounded with a lot of light? Etc., etc., etc.—all the questions one might expect of holy women eager to share in the transcendent experience, but to share as women, with all the little details. Thérèse does not record more than a couple of questions, but we can be sure she was asked to describe the Virgin's dress inch by inch. She was able to respond to these worrying questions with one answer only: "The Blessed Virgin looked very beautiful, and I saw her smile at me." After all, Thérèse reflects, it was only the Virgin's face that had "struck her" and held her attention and there she was, surrounded by all those Carmelites, determined almost, it seemed, to get things wrong. Had she been telling lies? Thérèse developed out of this one of the Church's great cases of scruples, that terrible infestation of self-doubt that makes one's every act, and especially acts of a spiritual kind, an occasion for a crisis of conscience.

If, Thérèse reasoned, she had kept the whole affair to herself, she could have remained happy and at ease in her extraordinary experience. But perhaps the Virgin had allowed this torment for the good of Thérèse's soul, perhaps because she was in danger of giving way to pride in an accomplishment that was, after all, not hers to begin with. Instead, she would now be able to accept the fact that humiliation was her role and would be able to look upon herself with the requisite abnegation. "But how I suffered!" Thérèse laments; "I cannot describe it, not this side of heaven."

Rather than describe her sufferings, Thérèse lapses in her story for several pages into a long discourse about some of her childhood delights in pictures, in reading, and especially in the exploits of the remarkable people who led hidden lives. French-women who loved their country deeply and heroically, with a sense of divine mission, such as Joan of Arc, impressed her as a child, she remembers, and she remembers with this impression her own urge to greatness. It was not glory in human eyes to which she aspired, but, as always with her, a hidden achievement, something for him who would alone be truly pleased with her efforts, and who, drawing her to him and covering her with his limitless merits, might make her a saint. What, she, Thérèse? She, with all her faults, faults which linger on even after eight years in religion? Yes she, even she. The ambition, she tells her sister, Mother Agnès, the ambition has never left her, an ambition which, she seems to be suggesting with a brief addendum on suffering, was quickly enough confirmed by the trials that fol-lowed.

If we see these events entirely through the eyes of the mature Thérèse, the nun, the Carmelite, who has for long years now been meditating upon them, we miss, I think, their real impact and their real significance. They did not occur to a woman of twenty-two; they happened to a girl of nine and ten. They were not merely rough or remarkable events softened by the rule and regi-men of a life of prayer in the convent; they were the most star-tling events, the most terrifying events, made more harsh by surrounding circumstances that must have seemed to the little girl, if only in her subconscious, to be the product of a conspiracy against her. Louis was in Paris with Marie and Léonie when the first violent attack came. Pauline was beyond reach, in the Carmel. Only Céline, of the family community, was with her, and while she was a more than ordinarily resourceful thirteen-year-old, and very close indeed to Thérèse, she could not make up for all the missing Martins, nor could the Guérins, uncle, aunt, or cousins. Without any help from the devil, Thérèse was *tout à coup* subject to the demons of normal human society, which were suddenly unleashed upon her. She was alone, as almost never before. She was not at home, surrounded by protecting, comforting, endlessly attentive elder sisters. Her daily walks with her father were suspended, if only temporarily. A trip into the jungle would not have been much more frightening.

By present-day standards, Thérèse's fright—if she was as frightened as I think she was—must seem at the very least disproportionate, and at worst a pathological response to inconsequential stimuli, a response that justifies Father Robo's diagnosis. There was too much "preoccupation with herself"; she was too much "given to self-analysis," too much of a "dreamer." Perhaps so, but such a soul as Thérèse's is by everything in its nature self-preoccupied. She had, at two and three and four, not simply at nine and ten, the gift of discursive meditation, and perhaps even more, perhaps the first stages of a contemplative skill that went quickly and easily beyond words. The conditions of her family life, protective to an abnormal degree, affectionate to an abnormal degree, immersed in love, were the necessary conditions for the development of such a soul. But each abnormality in such an environment deepens and intensifies the other—the protection augments the affection; the affection demands the gestures and postures of protections; the constant soliciting of love and the equally constant response of love make love as much a daily requirement in the lives of such a family, especially the young lives, as food and drink and sleep—and more, really. The least withdrawal of any of these would be painful. When the withdrawal is not accompanied by substitutes of a like quality, some significant derangement must follow, some weakening, which makes an experience like Thérèse's almost inevitable.

There was no substitute in Thérèse's case for the love that had left her home. Marie was a sensitive and deeply concerned godmother who tried earnestly to replace Pauline, but Pauline, from her first election to the role of confidante by Zélie, was not to be replaced; she listened and she talked, she explained and she understood with an arch-especial authority that no one else could match. When one adds to this the less than salubrious circumstances of the abbey school, one sees the intensity of Thérèse's misery. Her illness occurred, one can say, on schedule. It was bound to come when it did and as it did.

Thérèse did not suffer a mental breakdown. That seems to me to be beyond argument. She was weakened, however, by everything that happened around her, psychologically weakened, physically weakened. That also seems to me to be beyond argument. Her illness, when it came, was surely of the kind we now call psychosomatic. The physical symptoms, as Thérèse describes them, as Marie describes them, suggest exactly that disorder diagnosed by Father Moore: pyelonephritis. And we know from his description, and the standard descriptions to be found in the medical texts of today, what a cruelly painful infection that is. But do we also know how valuable that infection was for Thérèse? Do we accept, with her, the providential nature of the disease, its accompanying miseries and—I think the word is appropriate —values?

Until now, Thérèse's faith had been largely theoretical. I do not mean that she did not practice it with conviction. But necessarily, she lived at some distance from it. She had reflected at some length, and with remarkable depth for a four-year-old, upon the death of her mother. She had spent hours, days, in visits to church, which had involved long periods of silence, and though she had had no training in systematic meditation—and who would have expected a five- or six- or seven-year-old girl to have such training?—she had begun to fashion for herself the rudiments of spiritual exercises. She had been deeply disturbed by her experience of Céline's first Communion, in which she was both nearer to her sister and further from her than she had ever been before. She had been nearly shattered by Pauline's departure for Carmel and had found peace only at the last moment in the sudden welling up within her of a religious vocation, now not a child's vocation but a young woman's, a vocation almost certainly confirmed by the response first of Pauline and then of Mother Gonzague. Still, for all the intensity of these experiences, she had only been playing at religion until the Easter uprising came to throw her body around the room and to storm her soul. Religion until then was a toy altar in a recess in the garden wall at Les Buissonnets. Religion was the life of an anchoress in the cozy Lisieux desert. Religion was descending in state on a Sunday morning to be royally greeted by King Louis. Religion was sweet, was touching, was a joyous entertainment. It was not the cross.

Thérèse at ten was ready to emerge from a religion of childish delights to one of adult experiences. She was ready, this child in ringlets. This little girl who was protected on all sides—overprotected, some would say—this sensitive flower—oversensitive, Father Robo and others would say—was ready to be stripped. If she had not been, what would have happened to her? Could she have developed a spirituality of any great depth on an unending diet of sweetmeats? Would religion ever have been more than a joyous entertainment for her? These are not rhetorical questions, nor are they superficial, I believe. They go to the heart of Thérèse's spirituality and the life out of which it grew.

In the Easter experience, Thérèse leaped over superficiality and sentimentality. If ever these were threats to her spirit, they were now dissipated, not wiped out, perhaps, but reduced to minor verbal decorations, speech mannerisms, unimportant atmospheric pressures to which she never really yielded, however much they may seem to show on the surface of her prose, like condensation on a humid day. In the Easter storms, Thérèse found herself and found herself as she had eventually to find herself, as we all do, alone. The very conditions of her misery were the conditions of her freedom. With so many of her family away from her and forced, as she was for a while, to languish in a strange bed, she was able to make that stern confrontation with suffering, with the cross, without which any ambitions to sanctity or any sort of significant Christianity are meaningless.

Christianity is a religion of the cross. It requires somewhere in the annealing process which brings a soul to maturity a clear facing of this fact. Suffering is in its essence, suffering and solitude, and not merely suffering and solitude, which may come uninvited, which must at some time come to everyone, but suffering and solitude willingly accepted, if not greeted with joy. If any man would follow me, Jesus said, then let him leave—which is what he meant when he said "hate"—let him leave his father and his mother, his brother and his sister. Thérèse's imitation of Christ required that at this point in her short term of days she leave her father and her sisters, in the spirit, in the flesh. And so she did. For her failure to recognize Marie, her long periods of coma, her convulsions, coupled with the brief absence of Louis and Léonie and Marie and the continuing effects of her mother's death and the permanent departure of Pauline and the sojourn at the Guérins'—all these were for her the most unmistakable separation in the flesh. The separation in the spirit came almost as soon as Pauline left for Carmel; it reached its highest point of intensity when she met the apparition of the Virgin on her own and then could not really share the experience with anyone else, when, in fact, she discovered that sharing it meant only anguish, an anguish of uncertainty about the accuracy of her words and the intelligence of her listeners and finally uncertainty about the experience itself. It was not just a trivial case of scruples, it was a set of well-founded doubts, which came and went for four years, with an irregular periodicity but with an ever wider and deeper amplitude.

It is possible to dismiss Thérèse's scruples, indeed all scruples, as foolish—"Senseless," is Father Robo's word for them—even though one realizes how much suffering they involve, as even those who scorn them generally admit—"Senseless as scruples are," Father Robo says, "they are very real and very painful to the sufferer." If one has contempt for scruples and something less than respect for the scrupulous, one is bound to lose all contact with Thérèse's kind of experience and with that to lose as well any depth of understanding of what suffering means to the saint. Thérèse "does not say," Father Robo writes, "what was the particular subject of her scruples, but it was certainly some absurd trifle, for if scruples had a reasonable cause they would no longer be scruples." Thérèse does not say? She has been saying over and over again at this point in her story, which is about a year after the Easter crisis, explaining why she has scruples at this stage in her life by explaining the texture of her life at this stage. It is not remarkably different from what it has been ever since the first headaches began, ever since the first of her separations from her family, ever since the beginning of her spiritual maturing process. But to understand it one cannot dismiss either her scruples or anybody else's as foolish or senseless, however little objective basis there may be for them. One must instead contemplate the cross, think long about the multiple ways of the cross in human experience, and recognize, finally, I think, that for some deeply religious people scrupulosity is inevitable and quite useful.

St. Alphonsus Liguori, whose compassion for those who suffer from scruples is legendary, or at least should be legendary, sums up his lengthy advice to them this way: "Let scrupulous souls, then, suffer this cross of theirs with resignation, and not perplex themselves no matter how great the distresses God may send or permit. It is for their profit, that they may be humbler, may guard better against occasions of sin which are beyond doubt and seriously dangerous, and that they may commend themselves more often to the Lord and learn to put greater trust in divine goodness." That is Alphonsus's general summary. His practical advice is a reasonable conclusion from that summary: get yourself a spiritual director and do what he says, follow his advice to the letter —scrupulously, he might have added. Unfortunately, even less today than in Alphonsus's time are spiritual directors widely available and not all of those who do exist have a saint's sympathy for those possessed with scruples. The scrupulous soul who wanders from confessional to confessional, from parlor to parlor, in fruitless search for the understanding director who will free him from the shackles of his disease, may very well end up with a worse case than he started with. He would do better, often enough, to ponder Alphonsus's words of general summary, as deeply as he knows how, and perhaps other diagnoses of the same kind, and to let it go at that. If he reads Thérèse on her scruples he will discover the same thing, less generalized, dramatized in terms of her own experience, but still substantially the same thing, the same advice, the same understanding.

Scruples are a disease of conscience. When a conscience becomes tender enough, it is fair prey for scruples. By this sign you shall know it—you are the proud father of a tender conscience; congratulations! For Thérèse, the conscience itself, a conscience not merely tender but raw with sensitivity, was a sign. It was the assurance to her that she had come through, that she had passed her postulancy of suffering, one which for her at least could not be an experience shared with anyone else. She had had an enormous clarification of her faith; she knew now, with something more than a theoretical knowledge, what the cross was about. She knew that the cross, when it comes, is splendidly adjusted to the conditions of your own being. It does not mean hanging, literally, from a cross. It does not necessarily mean desertion as Christ was deserted, your disciples—that is, those closest to you—turning from you in fear or aversion. But there is a good chance that those closest to you, those whom you love the most and who most love you, will be physically absent in your time of trial. For chance is very much in it: by chance your mother may die when your mother is very young and you are still dependent on her; by chance your father and two of your sisters may be away from home; by chance you may find yourself the youngest in your class and the smartest and the least befriended; by chance you may find that a general debility which has begun with the joyous departure of your favorite sister, your adoptive mother, for a life she has long wanted with all her heart, has left you open to an infection that cripples and convulses your body and darkens your mind and brings you close to death. But then, if you are Thérèse, you may find that all that chance has done, providence may undo, that in the dark, in the solitude, in the suffering, there may be an encounter of such grace that it transforms all the misery into joy, even if only for a moment, and leaves you, with scruples, yes, but also with a conscience now so exquisitely tender, so open to the human and to the divine, that it is worth all the debility before and the doubts afterward and everything that has come between. And this, if you are Thérèse, you will never deny was an agony and is an agony, but an agony that has brought with it delights.

SIX

THE rapprochement between theory and practice which her illness had effected in her life fascinated Thérèse. It absorbed her attention, if not wholly, at least enough of the time so that the discontent she felt when she returned to school in October did not trouble her too much and even the temptations she had felt when she had visited Alençon with Louis at the end of the summer could be transformed into lingering meditations on the transitory nature of worldly pleasure.

The temptations in Alençon were real enough. The people were attractive. They had moving associations with Zélie to bring up. They admired Thérèse, they petted her, they fêted her. It was, she decided, her first *entrée* into the world, and she was, she says, dazzled, "as at ten one is so easily dazzled." At ten? Shouldn't we say at twenty? at thirty—forty—fifty? Wouldn't her contemporaries, or at least her father's contemporaries, have said that? The point is that Thérèse was in some ways twenty or thirty when she was ten. In that very slight experience that Alençon afforded her of frivolous pleasures, of fondling, of coddling, of easy admiration, the world really was too much with her. She was glad to be able to visit her mother's grave and to muse there awhile about death, as the memory of the trip twelve years later makes her think again about death and the faint consciousness of death that her Alençon admirers had, and then presses her to ask herself what has happened to the things that were at the center of their consciousness, when death was only peripheral to it. The châteaux and the parks, where are they, what are they now to that generation, so many of whom have died? She echoes words of the Book of Wisdom, of Ecclesiastes, and delivers herself of a brief reflection on commodity that recalls the Bastard's great speech on the same subject in Shakespeare's *King John*—not, one can be sure, by direct influence.

Never again after Easter 1883 could Thérèse disengage herself from reality, from the large reality to which she had now been made free. If earlier she had had no certain contact with that reality, now it was rare that she had none. She was to prepare for her first Communion in March of 1884 and the preparation filled all the interstices of her days. Pauline, with the awareness of a sensitive sister and a wise friend, drew her close to her own life with a book she prepared at Carmel. It was a notebook of pious practices—acts of love for each day, sacrifices, brief prayers, translated into Thérèse's favorite rhetorical figures, each act signified by a flower or its identifying fragrance. The associations were traditional enough, violet for humility, rose for sacrifice—two months and nine days of acts, sacrifices, and prayers, of which Thérèse kept precise count. When the book was returned to Pauline, Thérèse had totted up 2773 acts and 818 sacrifices! Ida Goerres sees here possibly "one root of that habit of excessive self-observation which burdened Thérèse all her life," as she also finds in the flower symbolism the possible source of "that 'style' which was later so to characterize and distinguish her saintliness: to conceal from others and from herself elements of pain and harshness under sweet pet names." What neither Mrs. Goerres nor anybody else seems to have noted is the antiquity of the practice. Such a spiritual horticulture goes back to the Old Testament, through the herbals and garlands of medieval literature. Walafrid Strabo's *Hortulus* moralizes a ninth-century monastery garden. In the thirteenth, fourteenth, and fifteenth centuries, the Virgin's bower absorbed the attention of all poets as a matter of convention—sweet convention. The rosary, that universally popular devotion, is based on flower symbolism. Pauline invented nothing. Thérèse yielded to no remarkable saccharinity of her own. Both accepted as a matter of course the confluence of nature and supernature, as Christians and Jews had been doing for several millennia.

The systematization of acts of virtue and of sacrifices is no newer, really, than the floral rhetoric with which Pauline chose to wreathe it. It is standard practice among religious and has been far, far back into antiquity, as far back as we have any record of monasticism. The rosary as a device for metering prayers is ancient among the Buddhists. Jews, Moslems, Hindus—all have, one way or another, at some point or another in their religious lives, kept track of acts of the kind Pauline recommended to Thérèse, of prayers, and all the other accoutrements of the religious life. If, of course, the bookkeeping becomes all, then one has turned every sacrifice, every prayer of love, every attempt to do good, into a parody of its intention. It is unlikely, I think, that Thérèse ever was guilty of an accountancy spirituality, even in her first enthusiasm for Pauline's notebook. She had been shifting beads on her chaplet of the virtues off and on since the age of four. Now she had a fuller, richer way of recording her life in God, as her ardent letter of gratitude to Pauline makes obvious.

There was much to thank her for, and others too. Sister Thérèse of St. Augustine, who had complimented her prettiness on her visit to Mother Gonzague, had embroidered a cover for the book. Mother Gonzague deserved a kiss, just on general grounds. But most of the warmth was for Pauline, who had produced the "lovely," the "entrancing," the "beautiful" book. Every day, Thérèse says, she does her best to do as many practices as possible. She finds the prayers "sweet-scented like roses." The picture in front, showing a small dove making a present of its heart to Jesus inspires Thérèse to proffer her own: "I'll adorn it with all the lovely flowers I find, so as to offer it to the Child Jesus on the day of my first Communion; and truly, as it says in the little prayer at the beginning of the book, I want the Child Jesus to be so happy in my heart that He won't think of going back to heaven. . . ."

Sticky? Intolerably gooey? In the same way that the greeting cards of the eighties and nineties are sticky, and many of the place cards that were used at formal banquets, and the advertising cards, and the book illustrations, and the embroidery of the period, and the lacework, and the petit-point, and the ornamentation of chairs and sofas and beds and desks and dining-room tables and walls and ceilings and everything else. Thérèse and her sister were products of their own time as well as of the ancient traditions of all the religions. Their time does have charm, we are now perhaps beginning to see, even in its most rococo furbelows and fustian. But we can take it more easily, see it more easily, in the visual arts than in the verbal. Certainly there never was more bad poetry, rarely worse fiction. Some of the ornamental writing is unstomachable, no matter how one approaches it. But not, I think, Thérèse's, if we see it for what it was, understand it as she understood it, make some effort to penetrate her feelings.

This was reality for Thérèse. She was now ready to share not only Céline's religious life, after her first Communion, but Pauline's. She was taking instruction from every possible source, eating it up with her food, drinking it, sleeping it, living it. Marie assiduously prepared her with little lessons ingeniously constructed to emphasize little things, to win the child's affection for them and to make her see with what an extraordinary fullness everyone was endowed if only one remained conscious of the marvels around one. She seems, without realizing it perhaps, to have paraphrased the magnificent rhetoric of Gregory the Great in his *Magna Moralia* on the Book of Job, the great passage that ends, "Full of wonder then are all the things which men never think to wonder at, because . . . they are by habit become dull to the consideration of them." She gave Thérèse a little booklet "On Renunciation," by her own beloved director, the Jesuit, Father Pichon. Thérèse found matter in it for a lifetime of meditation, matter that a full-fledged religious would still find quite acceptable, quite mature enough for her reflection.

Thérèse herself was as full of reflection as she was of the acts she was noting every day in Pauline's notebooks. She thought much about Marie's doctrine of the marvels of the world that so many people passed by and she reasoned that if she were so touched by this spirituality then the greatest sinners must be too. Why shouldn't they gather up from the world what was really lasting and prepare themselves, by their reflective gatherings, for heaven? One day, she notes, one of her teachers at the abbey school asked her what she did with herself on those holidays when she was left alone to herself. Thérèse told her that she used to get behind her bed, where there was an open space large enough for her, and enclosing herself in the curtains, would just sit and think. "But think what?" the teacher asked. "I think about God," Thérèse answered, "and about life, and about eternity . . . . I just *think!*" The nun sat back and roared, and afterwards enjoyed twitting Thérèse about her *thinking* days. "Do you still *think?*" she used to ask the girl, undoubtedly with a broad smile. When she thought again about her thinking days, when she was at work on her autobiography, Thérèse decided that what she was doing was practicing mental prayer. She was demonstrating, as I think many children could if they were given any encouragement, the naturalness of this sort of lifting of the heart, of moving the soul beyond words and perhaps beyond images as well, to where it simply fastens on states of being, familiar ones such as joy and sorrow, gratitude and praise, mournfulness and melancholy, and unfamiliar ones that may be nothing more than degrees of the joy, sorrow, etc., or may not be anything that has a name for any of us. Just thinking, "I just think," was Thérèse's reply to the nun. "Just feeling" would perhaps have been more precise, but feeling in all its wide round range of meaning: examining, perceiving, touching, tasting, groping, reconnoitering, sympathizing, becoming one with spirits and essences. She had probably passed into what St. Thomas calls the third degree of abstraction, beyond material objects and extrasensory objects, such as lines and planes, to the world of pure concept, but you couldn't have proved it by her. She didn't have the vocabulary to describe it, but then neither did she have the vocabulary to block her attempts just to think or to feel.

I say "the third degree of abstraction" and I think that accurately describes Thérèse's experiences at eleven, shortly before her first Communion. But none of her thinking or feeling could ever have been altogether *abstract* if by that word we understand something cut off from persons. Thérèse invariably brought her meditations back to the person, and the higher they rose in degree of abstraction, in Thomas Aquinas's use of the term, the more centered they became upon persons, human persons, divine persons, until they concentrated directly upon the figure of Jesus. When she went into a week's retreat at the Benedictine abbey school, along with a few other girls, as final preparation for her first Communion, it was like a girl getting ready at enormous length, hours, days before the time, and with unbelievable care, for her first date or first series of parties or her debut. She was going to meet a person, not a thing, not a mere object, not an abstraction. She was going forward, going into an intimate experience for which she had yearned, ardently and for oh, so long. She trembled and glowed and mused and marveled with all the intensity of an aroused puberty graced with a supernatural love.

There was no discontent at school for Thérèse in the week of retreat. There would have been no discontent if it had been conducted in a piggery or a glue factory. But it was good to have the week in the midst of a quiet religious community, a little more subdued than usual because of the death of its prioress. It was good to have daily visits from Marie and Léonie and Louis, aware now, as they must have been, of the perils of departing too far from Thérèse. And it was a sign of special joy to have such attention from the headmistress, who each night kissed Thérèse good night, and was rewarded by a revelation of her precious book of sacrifices and prayers on the part of the little girl. The attentions extended as far as daily combings of the hair by the nun in charge of the children's dressing; Thérèse still did not know how to do it herself and probably never would if Marie did not leave Les Buissonnets soon or somehow bring herself to end the morning ritual with her youngest sister's beautiful long hair.

Thérèse was allowed once in the week to see her playmate sister, Céline, when, one morning, she began to cough a great deal and had to be sent to the infirmary. Céline brought a picture with her for Thérèse, "The Little Flower of the Divine Prisoner"—it was of Thérèse standing before the tabernacle of the Blessed Sacrament. Thérèse was touched by it and by such news as Céline had been able to snatch for her of her retreatmate sister, Pauline, who was preparing for her day of profession as a nun, the same day as Thérèse's first Communion. Father Pichon, to whom Thérèse had written, asking for prayers and appointing him her director for the days ahead at Carmel, sent word that he was going to say Mass for Thérèse and Pauline on the great day, and Thérèse moved through everything serenely. She moved soberly, delightedly through general confession on the eve of first Communion. She looked unbelievingly, delightedly, at her Communion dress, white, like all the others spread out for the girls, "snowflakes," in which each girl was dressed in turn, like the slowly revolving members of a stately corps de ballet, stiffly, formally clad in white tulle. Everything delighted her, even the hymn.

Communion itself was— The only possible words are Thérèse's, but not Thérèse's really, either, but the words of the Song of Songs, that song above all other songs, which is what the Hebrew means, that song which Thérèse was from now on to sing over and over again, because now she knew of what she was singing at first hand.

It was a kiss of love. I felt myself loved and I said, in my turn, "I love you and I give myself to you forever." There had been no demands, no struggles, no sacrifices; we had exchanged looks a long time ago, Jesus and poor little Thérèse, and we had understood each other. And now, on this day, it wasn't a look any more, but a perfect joining together; there were no longer two of us, Thérèse was gone, like a drop of water lost in the ocean. Jesus alone remained, the master, the king. Hadn't Thérèse begged him to take away her freedom, because she was afraid of what she might do with it; she was so frail, so helpless, she longed only to be united now and forever with the divine strength. Her joy was too profound, too overwhelming for her to contain it. Soon sweet tears were pouring down her cheeks to the great astonishment of her companions. "Why is she crying? Is there something troubling her? No, it must be because her mother isn't here or the sister she loves so much, the Carmelite." They didn't understand that when all the joy of heaven comes into a pouring heart, that heart, long banished, cannot take it all without bursting into tears. No, no, it wasn't Mama's absence that hurt that day of first Communion. Didn't I have all heaven in my heart and hadn't Mama taken her place there long ago? In taking Jesus into me, then, I was taking my darling mother, too, and her blessings and rejoicings in my happiness. I didn't weep over Pauline's absence either. Oh, I would have been happy to have her at my side, but this was a sacrifice I was used to. On that day, joy alone filled my heart. I was giving myself completely, as she was too, to him who came in all love to me.

Thérèse recited the act of consecration to the Virgin for all who were receiving Communion for the first time, quite properly, she thought, she who had lost her earthly mother, talking in everybody's name to her heavenly mother. Once more she goes to the Song of Songs: the Virgin seemed to smile at her, in her imagination now, not as an apparition, and Thérèse remembered the smile she had actually seen with her eyes, the smile that had cured her, and now, she thought, "she has placed in the calyx of her little flower, Jesus, the rose of Sharon, the lily of the valley." It is a felicitous use of the floral rhetoric of the Song. Just as in that incomparable poem, the rich names and richer descriptions are handed back and forth between the bride and the bridegroom, so Thérèse now makes a present of these epithets of the rose and the lily, which are the bride's in the original, to her bridegroom. It was still another way of saying, "There were no longer two of us. . . . Thérèse was gone, like a drop of water lost in the ocean." He alone remained.

The rest of the day was Papa's and then the sisters', Pauline's most of all, as they moved the party to the Carmel to rejoice with another girl dressed in white, another bride, veiled, like Thérèse, in white, and with a crown of roses. Greeting cards, place cards, advertising cards, embroidery, lacework, petit-point, furbelows and fustian. . . . But nothing extrinsic to the interior experience had any significance for Thérèse that day. The family party, the dresses, the happy exchange of greetings and presents—all were engaging enough, but briefly only, for a moment, and then, blessedly, they were over, so that the little girl, the big girl, the girl of treasured intimacies now could think a little more to herself, feel a little more of those intimacies, of the interior peace. Marie took her into her bed, to sleep with her in the darkness that had to come, "for even the happiest times here below must end in darkness. . . ."

Two weeks after her first Communion, Thérèse asked permission of her confessor to go again to Communion and, to her surprise, he consented. It was a rare request; it was a rare enough occurrence in those years before Pius X, but sentiment was moving in the direction of frequent Communion and the priest must have heard the little girl with some pleasure. Her response, the next morning, on Ascension Day, was much as the first time. Tears again and every sensible assurance of her lover's presence, around her, near her, in her. Over and over she said to herself St. Paul's words that all who have loved as she loved have taken as their own, "And I live, now not I, but Christ in me." And if Christ lived in her, then the cross too must be hers, and hers with no revulsion or fear. And so it was.

Thérèse had thought much about suffering, with particular concentration ever since Marie had talked to her about it at some length. Marie liked to turn the vigils of great feast days into spiritual conferences. On this one, she told Thérèse she probably would not have much suffering in her life, that she would always be carried along by God, like a little child. But when she thought about these words at Communion, she felt something quite different. She wanted to suffer. She wanted suffering because now she loved suffering. She had suffered before, but without love. Now living for her love alone, living fully in her love, taking pleasure in her love alone, finding pleasure in her love alone, she was able to say those moving words from the *Imitation of Christ*, those terrible words: "O Jesus, unspeakable sweetness, turn all earthly consolations into bitterness for me." It was a prayer that now came to her lips without constraint of any kind. "I felt," she says, "that I said it not through any act of will of my own, but like a little child who automatically repeats the words of a person she loves." Suffering became, in time, her only consolation. For the present, it was in her, very much a part of her, but to some extent, perhaps, swallowed up in its own rhetoric. When she made her retreat in preparation for the sacrament of Confirmation, three weeks after her second Communion, she had two days to meditate on suffering instead of the usual one, because the Bishop had had to change the date, and we can be sure she used it to think some more about suffering. Her thinking days were not over. On the day of Confirmation, she found herself warmed by the thought that her development as a Christian had reached one kind of perfection: a fullness of the sacraments. And she carried on her concentrated reflections on suffering; the most interesting of the ceremonies for her was that in which the Bishop traced "the mysterious sign of the cross" on her forehead, a mark to stay with her, she knew, forever.

Once again she was conscious in her senses of a supernatural presence. When the Holy Spirit descended, she says, "I did not feel a strong wind, but rather that light breeze which the prophet Elias heard on Mount Horeb." She was referring to that moment —the exact reference is 3 Kings 19:13—when the Lord speaks to Elias on the mountain and asks him what he is doing there and Elias answers several times, "With zeal have I been zealous for the Lord God of hosts," in those words and in others which specify the nature of his devotion. And the Lord answers Elias and gives him tasks to do and, one assumes, the strength to do them. Thérèse felt she also had been appointed her task and equipped with the necessary strength to do it: "On that day I was granted the strength to suffer, for soon my martyrdom was to begin." Léonie stood up for Thérèse as her sponsor and offered, along with her sponsorship, her tears.

There is nothing harder to understand and accept in Thérèse than her joy in suffering. If one grants her the need to take some solace in it when it becomes all her life, at the end of her life, when she is dying of tuberculosis, one finds it difficult to accept this same attitude at eleven and twelve and thirteen. If one grants her the need to prepare herself for the possibility of another attack like the Easter crisis, one finds it difficult to understand this new attitude, not of preparation or acceptance, but of eagerness and longing. Suffering she saw, and was happy to see, would be her only consolation. This was the meaning of her Communions, of her Confirmation.

Difficult as it is to understand, Thérèse's is a classical attitude in Christianity. She knew the *Imitation of Christ*, and knowing it meant knowing suffering, and, if one sympathized at all with its spirituality, meant loving to suffer. All its admonitions point to a life of solitude in which one empties out everything that is not God, experiences, memories, friends, until the only truly permanent friendship remains, friendship with the Lord. But the admonitions go beyond this internalizing of one's life and experiences to a following of the way of the cross. The true lover of God must moderate the stirrings of his heart, be meek as Jesus was meek, make all desires the desire of oneness with Jesus in his pain, in his loneliness, in his sorrow, in his desolation. The *Imitation* promises no consolations as the world understands comfort, but only that tranquility and peace of conscience that follow upon total self-abnegation. "Set your axe to the root of the tree," the author of the *Imitation* says. "Fully cut away and destroy in yourself all inordinate inclination that you have to yourself or to any private and material thing." There is no vice greater than inordinate love of self in the *Imitation's* arraignment of human failures. Mortify this and you will be ready to accept the supreme sacrament, the sacrament of the Eucharist. The book ends with a eulogy of the Eucharist and frequent reception of it, eloquent by the standards of any century, astonishing for the fourteenth century. Undoubtedly Thérèse found in it a chart for her own behavior, she who enjoyed so much keeping records of acts and prayers. In the last chapter of the book, she also found a formula for the offering of oneself that she never forgot. Its language is the language of Mary's Magnificat; it is also the language of Thérèse, as this sample will show: "I desire to reserve nothing to myself, but I offer myself and all mine in sacrifice to you freely and liberally. And also my Lord God, my Creator and my Redeemer, I desire to receive you this day with such affection, reverence, praise and honor, with such thanks, dignity and love, and with such faith, hope, and purity as your most holy and glorious mother, the Virgin Mary, desired and received you with, when she meekly and devoutly answered the angel that showed her the mystery of the Incarnation, and said: Behold the handmaid of the Lord; be it unto me according to your word."

Thérèse at eleven had caught the sense of the *Imitation*, had caught its spirit, and was determined to live it. She didn't go about it in any slavish literal-mindedness. She was no masochist. She did not walk morosely about the abbey school, when she returned in the fall of 1884. She tried once again to play the other girls' games, but she enjoyed much more making up stories, which her fellow students found engrossing enough, but which the nun in charge of recreation soon stopped. Thérèse says this with a nice play on words: "*voulant nous voir jouer et courir et non pas discourir*"—the nun wanted them to exercise the strength of their bodies, not of their minds, to run, not to run on in words. She made a valiant attempt at friendship with two girls, to which they responded with a nominal show of affection, but no more. When one of them, who had given Thérèse a friendship ring, returned to school after a short absence, her response to Thérèse's joy at her return was nothing but indifference. Thérèse could not return coldness for coldness, she says; hers was not a fickle nature. "When my heart loves with a pure intention, it does not stop loving, and so I still pray for my old friend and I love her still."

Thérèse several times and in several ways expresses her distrust of earthly affections, but she is not saying that one must not love those around one. It is impossible, she thinks, to give oneself over entirely to love of creatures without being poisoned—that is her exact language. She speaks, she says, not from experience— she has never felt such an exclusive ardor for any creature—but from close observation. She has seen too many burned by that love. She thanks the Lord for having preserved her from such temptations—not, she hastily adds, from any merit of her own. And then she goes on in her fever of gratitude to thank God for remitting her sins in advance, for keeping her pure, and even greater mercy than he showed the Magdalen. "Oh," she exclaims at this point, "how I wish I could explain what I mean!" It is a fair exclamation, and a necessary one. Without it, she sounds impossibly complacent and smug. Without it and the parable that follows, Hans Urs von Balthasar seems to be justified in his criticism of her when he says that she was without a sense of sin, as a result of her confessor's ill-advised declaration to her at the time of her entry into Carmel, that she had really "never been guilty of a single grievous sin." Balthasar concludes that "at a vital moment she had been withdrawn from the community of sinners, divided off from them and banished into a life-long exile of sanctity. She is to make superhuman efforts to escape from this cage but never completely succeeds, because she is fenced in by obedience." Thérèse seems to anticipate this criticism in her parable of the doctor's son. It is a crucial tale for the understanding of Thérèse. It explains much about her own childhood and what she made out of it when she began to construct her spirituality.

She tells her story two ways. In the first, the son of a gifted doctor trips over a stone in the road, falls, and in the fall breaks a limb. His father runs to him, picks him up gently and tenderly, tends to his wounds and using all his considerable skill soon brings him back to full health. Now certainly, says Thérèse, "that child has good reason to love his father!" Good enough. Now she tells her story another way. Suppose the father sees the stone in the road before his son does and runs ahead and removes it, without anyone seeing what he is doing. Certainly the boy, not knowing what his father has done for him, will not express any gratitude for his father's foresight. He will, in effect, love his father less than he would have if he had been cured by his skill. But if later he does discover the danger he has escaped because of his father's intervention, will he not love him all the more? Well, then, Thérèse sums up, that is my case. I am the child of an all-loving father, whose foresight has left me in such great debt to him. He did not spare her just a little, she says, but everything, *TOUT*, in capital letters and italicized. He didn't wait for her to love him, like the Magdalen, but wanted her to know how much he loved her, with what providential fullness, so that she might love him madly.

To Thérèse, loving God *à la folie*, to the point of madness, does not merely make up for everything; it transcends everything. She fully anticipates Balthasar's criticism, I think. He says: "The combination of . . . two factors, her privileged position as a *miraculée*, and her sinlessness, was sufficient to block the development of something that had played an important part in her childhood —a profound understanding of confession. All the faults which

Thérèse speaks about date from her younger days. Later she does not commit any. She could not, in her condition. Therefore certain of the central mysteries remain unacknowledged in her theology: the mystery of bearing sins, and of solidarity in sin, the mystery of how love may be coupled with an awareness of sin, above all the mystery of confession." She says: "I have heard it said that a pure soul cannot love with the ardor of a repentant soul. How I should like to give those words the lie!" She makes no elaborate defense of herself. Prevenient grace, as it seems to have worked for her, or for anybody else, should need no defense. Does one have to speak up for goodness? Yes, of course one does, especially when it seems to smirk and to hide smugly behind its glossy surfaces. But then it isn't goodness, is it? Pride of this sort, naked spiritual pride, is not goodness and is not defensible. Is Balthasar accusing her of pride, without perhaps being fully aware of making the accusation? Aren't most of those who can't stand Thérèse, and almost cheerfully admit to it, accusing her either of pride or of lying? Either she committed some sins she does not admit, or she is an impossibly smug young woman, that is to say, a proud one, in the worst sense of the word. Worse still, she talks of joy in suffering, of finding her only consolation in suffering, this silly girl, this pompous girl, this vain and strutting little girl!

Balthasar springs to her defense. "But we owe a debt of justice to Thérèse—it is hard for a person to live in the knowledge that she is holy." Thérèse was burdened with the certainty of salvation, and certainty, says Balthasar, "in the highest degree. . . . She knows how welcome she will be in heaven, and is already making arrangements here below for what she is going to do in the next world." It is true that she made such plans at the very end of her life, in her last days, really, if her sisters' record of her dying conversation is altogether accurate, in her last days and not before then. It is true that she had off and on, maybe most of the time, that certainty of salvation of which Balthasar speaks. But she was also assailed by terrible nagging doubts, which became through much of her career in Carmel a constant temptation against faith; the certainty of salvation is surely meaningless against such a temptation. What salvation? By whom? For whom?

Yes, it is hard for a person to live with the knowledge that she is holy and hard to live with the knowledge that she is not holy. It is, as Jewish mothers have been telling their children for centuries, it is hard to be alive, just plain hard to be alive. This, Thérèse knew too. Unless all her miseries are invented ones and all her reflections mere copybook maxims which she had committed to memory with the kind of extra effort she had to make to learn her Catechism, she was well acquainted with suffering, heroically acquainted with it, and she knew in detail how to put that suffering to good use.

Thérèse was aware, in her precociousness, of the significance of her Easter trials, I think. Her translation of the effects of that storm of physical and psychological and spiritual pain into a battering of her heart by God was not something she understood only ten or twelve years later. I am convinced that with her spiritual genius she made great and lasting sense of the experience almost while it was happening to her. It was, in fact, the making of her genius. It prepared her for the expanding reality to which she was being brought, step by step, experience by experience. Thus she could face the bad taste left in her soul when Marie extracted the details of the miraculous cure from her and the nauseating badgering of the good women of Carmel pressing her for more details of the experience. Thus she could face the almost impossibly intense encounter with love in her first Communion, a ravishing of her soul which she felt at least as keenly as any woman does her first encounter with physical love, and felt, what is more, in much the same way. And thus, all over again, she could know joy, know pain, know God, as the Bible uses the word "know," and stand up to such a totality of knowledge—in her second Communion, in her Confirmation, in her experiences at school, in her attacks of scruples—with a stalwartness, with a resilience, that few adults have ever matched. And let us remember, too, that however precocious she was, she was only ten at the time of the Easter attacks, eleven at the time of her first and second Communion, twelve when the attacks of scruples became most fierce and unrelenting. And for all her extraordinary openness to the experience of God, her incomparable receptivity to her lover, she still could not fix her own hair, she was still in many ways a little girl.

It would have been intolerable to Thérèse's family if she had lost all the characteristics of young girlhood as she became more and more learned in the ways of suffering and the ways of love. It would be foolish for us today to think of her as looking any different from the way she did look, any less ingenuous, any less simple, any less charming. Still, however innocent her charms may have been, however naïve her airs, however girlish her appearance, inside her there was a depth of experience that cannot be described with the same adjectives. It is not enough to say of somebody who has been so transformed by suffering, that she is innocent or naïve. It is ridiculous to describe a girl who has the ecstasy of love that Thérèse experienced in the sacraments as simple or ingenuous, whatever her appearance. She knew passions which the girls with whom she went on retreat could not guess at, which her schoolmates would have goggled at, if there had been a language in which her feelings could have been communicated to them. Does the average woman, full grown, fully fleshed, know as much of passion, feel as much of passion? Does the extraordinary woman, extraordinary in the intensity and depth and range of her feelings, ever taste a love as rapturous as this little girl's, as transforming, as transfiguring?

This was Thérèse's way of reaching out to sinners and of understanding them, in her life and after her life. As love had transformed her, she offered them, she offers us, a transforming love. It was a love strong enough to transform an eleven-year-old into a passionate lover. It is a love strong enough to transform anybody, who at any point, for whatever reason, can respond as Thérèse responded to the same love and to the same lover. It is a love that is always compassionate to suffering, because it rests upon suffering, because its essential language is suffering, because it draws all its feeling from suffering and extends all its feeling toward suffering. It offers no comfort, it finds no consolation in anything except suffering. Isn't this the best possible way to reach out to, and to understand, sin and sinners?

Suffering is a stripping of the person, whether it is physical or psychological or spiritual or any combination of the three. Something goes out of one with suffering, a degree of consciousness, a degree of ease, a degree of balance. We become ungainly with suffering. We do not need to be tossed around in our beds or thrown onto the floor; we do not need convulsions to show us our awkwardness, our imbalance. Something, somewhere, hurts inordinately. It is enough. If we are twisted within, no matter how untouched we may actually be on the surface, we feel as if we were twisted on the outside, and if we feel as if we were twisted on the outside, then there is a good chance that we will show it and others see it and know it. Suffering, then, has visible signs; it is often a visible stripping. It is to these signs that most people's compassion or pity responds. They see the marks of pain, either the bandages or the crutches or the casts, the marks of external damage, or the twistings or grimaces that are the marks of internal damage, and they are moved and they let us know that they are moved. But some people respond even before the damage, external or internal, even before the marks become visible. They anticipate the suffering and compassionate it in advance. They live with such a constant awareness of it that they feel it in everybody to whom suffering comes—which is to say, they feel it in everybody—feel it before it comes and when it comes and after it comes. This is Thérèse's kind of compassion, this is her kind of love and understanding.

Sinners suffer, not only as the sinless suffer, but with all the special misery of those who give themselves knowingly and willingly to what they are convinced is wrong. One need no more suffer that particular misery at that particular time to feel for it and even to feel with it than one need be torn apart to feel for and with the soldier whose body is ripped by bullets, or need fall apart to feel for and with the civilian whose body is rotted by cancer. One cannot become one in any significant physical sense with an animal that has been chased and killed and disemboweled by a particularly savage hunter, but one can be touched to tears and to prayer and the deepest compassion by the sight. Even the crushing of an insect bothers some people that much and evokes that much compassion. Death in any form evokes in someone, somewhere, a response of sympathy or concern or love. All animate creatures that are visible to the naked eye elicit the response at some time or another, even, I suspect, the deadliest of them—scorpions, cobras, tsetse flies—if their anguish in any way parallels the human. The death of a leaf, of a flower, the frustration of life in an unopened bud—these too can hurt. And if a bud, a leaf, a deadly fly, then a sinner too can at any time touch our pity, rouse our compassion, spur our love. Thérèse, who spent so much time burying dead birds, was not one to turn away from live sinners, however little she may have been attracted by sin. She always responded to suffering.

Franz Kafka, who was a near contemporary of Thérèse's, born

just ten years after her and dead the year after her beatification, responded as insistently as Thérèse to suffering. Though he was as uncertain of personal salvation as she was sure of it, he was as caught up as she in the ubiquitous drama of suffering. At his most exposed, in the collection of aphorisms and *pensées* that he called "Reflections on Sin, Suffering, Hope and the True Way," he insists upon the universality of deception, of sin, and of suffering. We overrate evil; we run away from good—that is the price of deception. We cannot miss sin, because it "always comes openly and can at once be grasped by means of the senses. It walks on its roots and does not have to be torn out." The omnipresence of suffering is just as unmistakable; it creates the essential brotherhood of man:

> We too must suffer all the suffering around us. We all have not *one* body, but we have *one* way of growing, and this leads us through all anguish, whether in this or that form. Just as the child develops through all the stages of life right into old age and to death (and fundamentally to the earlier stage the later one seems out of reach, in relation both to desire and to fear), so also do we develop (no less deeply bound up with mankind than with ourselves) through all the sufferings of this world. There is no room for justice in this context, but neither is there any room either for fear of suffering or for the interpretation of suffering as a merit.

Thérèse would have argued that there was an ultimate justice involved in suffering, which would be clear in eternity. But she would not, I think, either as an eleven-year-old or as a twenty-four-year-old, have disputed the assertion that justice in suffering was not discernible here. She would have insisted, too, that there was an unmistakable merit in suffering, the merit of becoming one with others who suffer, the merit of uniting oneself, as best one could, with the suffering Christ. But all the rest would fit comfortably into her doctrine; all the rest reads like her doctrine, for it insists upon the inevitability and universality of suffering and the need, therefore, to hold oneself open to it, without taking pride in it or setting up elaborate defenses against it.

Thérèse never held herself back from suffering, perhaps because suffering never held itself back from her. One way or another, she was faced with it steadily, either because her temperament insisted, erroneously, upon making serious sufferings out of minor hurts, small disappointments, the thousand little shocks which each day everybody must face, or because she saw with absolute clarity the large unhappiness which the little shocks contained and rated accurately, with a justice that was as divinely inspired as it was humanly centered, the unkindnesses that we regularly visit upon each other. The profundity of her response to suffering goes beyond this sort of perception, however, wise as it may appear to be. She finds her depth in her unwillingness to rail against suffering. Nowhere does she indict suffering as the incarnation of evil. She does not indulge herself in any invective directed against pain and suffering. To her that would have been wasted emotion. Nor, on the other hand, does she underestimate the force of suffering, and pretend that with the right attitude its pains will somehow disappear. She is, like her mother before her, utterly honest with herself and a realist. Suffering is everybody's lot. We must accept it as we accept life. We can grow with it. We can even go out to meet it with a welcoming warmth. We can find solace in it, we can discover in it the surest adumbrations of eternity.

No matter how much she may appear to be, Thérèse is never complacent about suffering, her own or others, nor is she woodenly submissive to it. If she finds joy in suffering, as I think one is bound on close analysis to see that she does, it is because her own analytical mind is always so hard at work upon this above all other experiences, this constant experience, this experience which teaches so much. Suffering the harassment of scruples, she forces herself to a greater candor with Marie and discovers in her oldest sister a confidante and a spiritual director, endlessly patient in the face of Thérèse's tears and torments. Céline reaches the age at which she must leave the abbey school and Thérèse is separated from the only attraction school still holds out to her. She "wasted no time in falling sick," she says wryly of herself, and her father wasted very little time, when he recognized the intensity of her misery, in removing her from the school. She suffers but she meditates upon her suffering and develops the kind of detachment which permits her to make wry remarks about herself. She judges herself and others' judgments of her with balance and when, occasionally, that balance is upset, she can redress it; she has the necessary interior resources.

After leaving the Benedictine school, Thérèse was sent for private tuition to a Mme. Papinau, a bright woman, she thought, with some of the charm of an older world about her. There, in a room full of furniture at least as ancient as Madame, or her still more faded mother, Thérèse learned what she could between bouts of wresting her books from under the cat and twisting and turning attention to herself in and out of the constant talk that went on between the junior Madame and the senior Madame and all their many visitors. Thérèse soon discovered she preferred not to have anybody's attention. At first she enjoyed listening to the compliments that were paid to her, by visitors who didn't think she could hear them, compliments about her hair, about her face, about her general attractiveness. Then she decided she did not want to hear any more compliments, because she was fattening on them, enjoying them much too much. "Oh!" she exclaims, thinking about the flattery and her susceptibility to it, "what compassion I feel for people who lose their souls!" And once again she thanks the Lord for his prevenient grace, for directing her to something higher than worldly praise. That's not enough for her, she reflects, but not with scorn for those who find it enough, and not with a superior pity either. She speaks with a heart that yearns for only the most lasting love, and in terms of the allegory, which she never forgets in her autobiography, she associates with her all others who have such longings, not only all those who know they have such longings, but all the rest as well, all who, without knowing it, in seeking their pleasure in the world have tricked themselves into accepting caricatures of reality for the real thing. Her own pleasures were as deliberately unworldly as she could make them at puberty. In reflection and rumination, in solitude, she found her joy and contentment.

At thirteen, Thérèse became the *solitaire* she had played at being with her cousin Marie Guérin, the hermit she had so long yearned to become—and without benefit of clergy. She led the life of a solitary, both alone, by herself, and with people. She went back to school two afternoons a week, so that she, like her sisters, could become an *Enfant de Marie*, a Child of Mary, if the nuns thought her worthy of the sodality, but she might as well have been alone. She had never been on close terms with any of the nuns and so there were no whispered conversations, no giggling, no confidences of great seriousness to be exchanged with any of the teachers. The girls were not interested in talking with her, even over sewing. Her only real ease was in front of the Blessed

Sacrament in the chapel, where she waited for Louis to call for her at the end of each day.

It was just as well that nobody wanted to talk to her. She had little use for conversation with people. Even pious conversation bored her, she says. It was always better, she felt, "to talk *to* God than to talk *about* God." With people, she felt in exile. With God, she felt at home. It was as simple as that. She was being cut off from her family, bit by bit, to reinforce the conviction that Jesus was her *unique ami,* her only friend. The summer before her brief return to the abbey, she had a double experience of this kind of separation. Louis went off in late August on a trip to Constantinople, by way of Munich and Vienna, not to return until he had visited Athens, Naples, Rome, and Milan, in late September and October. Papa's name day, August 25, the feast of St. Louis, a major event in the Martin calendar, had to be celebrated with the main personage absent. Thérèse sent him a warm letter, with a flower sewn on to the notepaper and verses enclosed that Pauline had written for her to recite to her father on the great day, "Wishes of a Little Queen for the Feast of the King, her Father." Louis responded with more than the requisite tenderness, telling all his children how he imagined he could see them gathered around him in the Belvedere, "and my little Queen with her sweet, pleasing voice reciting her little speech." He was so touched, he said, that he wanted to be back in Lisieux and to hug and kiss them all. But he was not in Lisieux, he was in Vienna, and while he never forgot the "Queen of my heart," nor his "Pearl," nor his "good Léonie," nor his "brave one," Céline, nor his "poor big girl," Marie, to whom he addressed his letters, he was out of the family circle.

Thérèse had a good month with the Guérins at Trouville, while her father was gone, playing with Céline and her cousin Marie. But even with company she enjoyed so much, she had the problems of a solitary. She was able to take shrimping and riding on a donkey in stride, but she feared she enjoyed too much a blue hair-ribbon her aunt had given her and so she dutifully—scrupulously —confessed her excessive pleasure as a sin. She was suffering all the while from headaches, too, but saying nothing about it until she noticed the attention that Marie's constant debility and tearfulness drew to her. Then she decided to try some of the same techniques, to sit in a corner and cry, and, when pressed, to admit

113

to her headaches. She found her corner. She cried. And she was pressed. And she admitted to her headaches. But nobody quite believed her—the headaches were not due cause for her tears; there must be something else, her aunt thought, something that was troubling her conscience. It was all too much like LaFontaine's fable of the ass and the dog. Thérèse was the ass who, hoping to be petted like the dog, put his great awkward hoof on the table, and instead of the kisses he had looked for received a beating. "If I wasn't beaten like the poor ass," Thérèse says, "I was paid back just the same. The experience cured me for life of the desire to attract attention."

Back to solitary. Thérèse found her only real pleasure at Les Buissonnets. When in the summer of 1886 she was taken to Deauville by her aunt, she quickly fell ill, and had to be sent home. She had fallen heir to Pauline's old attic studio and there could while away many hours amid sketches Pauline had left behind, a solemn portrait of Pauline at the age of ten, and her own collection of pious objects and natural curiosities. She had flowers, she had a cageful of birds, she had holy statues, and in front of the statue of the Virgin a row of candles. There was doll furniture, a watchcase, an inkwell, an hourglass. There were notebooks, ribbons, boxes, shells collected at the beach, almost every genus and species of collection that a lively young mind could envisage, with rather more of both nature and supernature than most girls her age would want. But the whole collection faded from sight and interest when Thérèse heard that Marie was the next to go to Carmel. The ritual was clear; she must spend as much time as possible with her godmother, her second adoptive mother, her third mother. Every time she passed Marie's room, she knocked until her sister opened the door, then she grabbed her and covered her with kisses, enough to last, says Thérèse, through all the years in which she would be deprived of them. A month before Marie was due to enter the convent, Louis took the family to Alençon for a visit, a bitter visit for Thérèse. She was without consolation at her mother's grave, sobbing over the catastrophe of the cornflowers she had picked so carefully and had then forgotten to bring with her. She was able, she says in her wry way, to make a great affliction of anything in those days. She longed, in the words of the *Imitation,* to have full rule over herself, to be the mistress, not the slave, of her impulses. But she was still a child, and at Alençon, at least, she gave the impression of being not only young but weak-willed.

What other impression could she give? She was more solitary than she had ever wanted to be. Marie was about to leave, and while the family was in Alençon, Léonie had entered the Poor Clares. She had gone to visit the cloistered Franciscan nuns with Louis and while there had so clamored to be admitted to the community that she had been taken in. Poor Léonie; she *was* taken in—by her own enthusiasm, by emotions over which she had even less control that Thérèse had over her tears at her mother's grave. Léonie liked the habit and did it credit. She fell in happily with the customs of the Poor Clares. Look your last at my eyes, she told her family when they came to say goodbye, for the *clarisses* keep custody of their eyes and always lower them in public. But "God was content with two months of sacrifice; Léonie returned and we saw her blue eyes again, often wet with tears." When they left Alençon, however, there were only three girls with Louis, and one was due to leave Les Buissonnets for the family convent on October 15, in a week, no less.

Thérèse expected to be desolate on her return to Lisieux, but instead found an unlooked-for peace, a sudden answer to her prayers. When Marie entered Carmel, Thérèse was still plagued with scruples. She decided to pray to the family's Holy Innocents, the four Martins who had been the first to go "up there"—the two Josephs, Hélène, and Mélanie-Thérèse. They, "who had never known troubles and fears must take pity on their sister. . . ." Their answer was immediate, says Thérèse: an ocean of peace. "If there were people on earth who loved me, there were others in heaven who loved me too." She set about showing her new balance, sharing her new peace with everyone, Céline most of all. She began to do more fixing up in their bedroom; for the first time in her life she made the bed! But she was still touchy, still needed to be confirmed, if not in grace, then at least in human respect. If Céline did not notice what she had done, Thérèse burst into tears: "I wept like the Magdalen and then as soon as I began to feel a little better, I started to cry about having cried."

She really was over her scruples, even if there were still some tears and touchiness left in her. Léonie was back. It was time to celebrate Christmas. Early on the morning of December 25, 1886, just after midnight Mass, the family, with one girl more than was originally expected, was ready to gather around the fireplace where Thérèse had left her Christmas slippers. It was a delight to which Thérèse still looked forward, the slippers, like the stocking in English-speaking countries, filled with little surprises. She ran upstairs to put away her hat. As she did so, she heard her father say about the slippers, with fatigue and, one suspects, with an unmistakable sigh, "Well, happily this is the last year of that. . . ." Thérèse started to cry. Céline, seeing her tears, told her not to come down yet; she would only be miserable if she looked inside her slippers just then. But something had happened, a larger change than the first waves of peace that her prayers to her dead brothers and sisters had brought. Thérèse smiled, ran down as quickly and happily as she could. Holding back not only tears but a wildly beating heart, she took hold of her slippers and each of the presents in them, and examined and exclaimed over them with the serene air of a queen. Louis responded with smiles, laughter. "Céline thought she was dreaming!" No, Thérèse says, not at all. She had recovered *la force d'âme*, the strength of mind and soul she had lost at four and a half and "recovered it for ever."

SEVEN

*O*N Christmas night of 1886, Thérèse began, she says, the third period of her life, "the most beautiful of all, the richest in heavenly graces." She calls it *cette nuit de lumière,* that night of illumination, and it was all of that. It brought to an end her period of purgation in a great burst of enlightenment. While she did not follow mechanically, like a soul on a conveyor belt, the classical stages of the mystical life, she did move in a clear progression from purgation to illumination to union. Her progress was more like a spinning spiritual top that keeps going back and forth across its own path than anything that goes straightforwardly ahead. She was given tastes of union during her time of purification. There were moments that were composed almost equally of illumination and union. And all through the second half of her life, from Christmas of 1886 until her death on September 30, 1897, she was being purged, steadily purged, to the point, some of the time, where illumination seemed farther away than the missions of China and union was only a dim distant memory, something that had occurred to a little girl and a very young nun, and would not come now to a wasted ancient of twenty-three and twenty-four.

All the stages of the mystical life had to be mixed up and thrown together in Thérèse's life. All the stages of life had to be compressed. She was fated to live seventy years in twenty-four and not to scant any of them because they were compressed or mixed up with other stages. They might be in miniature, but the reduction in size was no real reduction in spiritual stature. Great things were accommodated to a little girl, to an obscure nun, to a short life, to unimportant events, but they remained great things, grew greater, actually, for being adjusted to such littleness, such obscurity, such a short term of years. A series of

117

headaches and an attack of pyelonephritis lead to an apparition with a mysterious smile that ends an incurable illness with split-second precision. A first and a second Communion bring a little girl's soul and its creator together with all the shattering beauty and intensity of the Song of Songs. A mild rebuff from a tired father, accidentally overheard, leads the same little girl all of a sudden, as quickly as she had earlier been cured of her terrible illness, to spiritual maturity. Little moments in a little life, astonishing moments, emboldening moments, they gave Thérèse courage to ask for anything and to experience everything.

Free of her scruples, free of her tears, Thérèse could now look far outside herself for her experiences. Somebody had once said to her, "If you cry so much during your childhood, later on you'll have no tears left," and it was true; the tears had dried up at their source. After "the Christmas conversion," as she called it, she was dry-eyed most of the time; she did her weeping within. She contemplated a picture of the cross, on a Sunday morning, and saw and felt the blood that flowed from one of Jesus's hands; she felt herself wounded by the indifference of the world to its redeemer. She would gather up the blood that was being wasted. She would give it to those who needed it. She heard her Lord's cry, "I thirst," as if it were addressed to her, and she determined to respond to it by giving him the souls for which he thirsted, sinners now, sinners above all at this point in her life, she so longed to save them.

Thérèse had heard much in the summer of 1887 about a murderer named Pranzini. In the course of a robbery that spring, he had murdered two women and a child. His trial, in July, was brief; he was quickly condemned to die at the end of August. Nothing about him suggested there was a chance of repentance of any kind, but Thérèse saw him as one of the souls she could save, or rather that she could plead for with such persuasiveness that he would be saved. She asked Céline to have a Mass said for him and was encouraged when Céline didn't mock her either for her wild hope of retrieving the lost soul or for the shyness that made it impossible for her to speak to a priest herself. Thérèse was certain she would be successful this time, that God would be merciful to Pranzini, but she asked in her prayers for a sign of some kind so that she might know that praying for sinners made sense. She was given her sign, not only given her sign, but given the opportunity to read about it. It was rare to come upon a newspaper at Les Buissonnets. Only the Catholic daily, *La Croix*, was allowed in the house, and even that was not for the younger girls to read. But Thérèse found a copy at home on the day after Pranzini's execution, and in it she read that, though he had not gone to Confession, at the last moment, just before his head was about to be fitted to the guillotine, the criminal had snatched at the crucifix that the priest offered to him and had kissed "the sacred wounds three times!" There was her sign. "It was a true exchange of love," Thérèse says. "To souls, I offered the blood of Jesus; to Jesus, I offered the same souls, brought to life again by the dew of his precious blood. . . . And the more I did so, the more he increased in me the thirst for souls. . . ."

If she had been bored by commonplace subjects, discussed in a commonplace tone by commonplace people, before this, Thérèse was now altogether unfitted for such conversation. Fortunately, in the last of her confidantes, Céline, she had someone quite up to the only topic that really interested her, and as passionately interested in discussing it as she. They talked together of the divine lover in the room appointed for such discussions, the Belvedere, at the time appointed for such talk, after the stars had come out, a girl of fourteen and a girl of eighteen. Their conversation was interlarded with quotations from the *Imitation*, from Scripture, and from a book the Carmelites had lent to Louis, *The End of the Present World and the Mysteries of the Life to Come*, by the Abbé Arminjon. Since Christmas, Céline had felt entirely at ease with her younger sister; she knew her for her contemporary in everything that mattered now. By May, Thérèse was in constant ecstasy. Her confessor had urged her to receive Communion at an almost unheard of frequency, four times a week. At the end of the month, he raised it to five Communions in all the weeks that contained a major feast day. The only tears that Thérèse shed nowadays were of happiness. There seemed something providential too in the brevity of her sessions in the confessional. No talk about her interior life. No questions about her reformation and conversion. Nothing about the prayers to her brothers and sisters. Nothing about the sudden maturing. It seemed as if she needed no other direction than the lordly guidance of her lover. She saw confessors as "faithful mirrors" that accurately reflected the way of the Lord in men's souls. God did not seem to need much of an intermediary in dealing with her.

Thérèse was not finished with intermediaries, but they were now to be a very different kind from what she had been used to, a much higher kind, as the world rates such functionaries. She needed no one to intercede between her and God. Anybody who did could only get in the way, as embarrassing and as obnoxious an intruder as a spectator at the marriage bed. Her interior formation was not complete. Whose ever is? But she was far beyond mere ambitions now; she was leading a life in God, and yet it was not enough of a life. She wanted to give all of herself to God, and to give herself all the time. One can withhold some of oneself from a human lover; indeed one really must withdraw some of the time in order to preserve one's sanity, to hold on to one's individuality. It is very different with a divine lover. A man and a woman may become one flesh in marriage, but their souls remain independent. I am not underestimating the psychological element in the joining of people in the flesh, but it is not quite the same element as the supernatural, it does not act with the same intensity as the divine force does in those who are called to the mystical marriage. In the union of the soul and God, human marriage is merely allegorical, as Edith Stein pointed out. Because Thérèse felt called to that highest of unions, for which all other unions are analogical, toward which all other unions lead, she needed, actually needed, to go to the convent, to become a Carmelite, and as soon as possible. To hasten that going, to make it smooth, Thérèse needed human intermediaries, highly placed intermediaries, her kingly father, the spiritual director of the Carmel, her bishop, perhaps even the Pope himself.

There was little enough encouragement for her vocation from the sources that should have been most encouraging, the sisters already at the Carmel. Marie flatly refused her support; Thérèse was still a child, it was ridiculous really to see her trying to enter the convent at fourteen. One understands this: Marie was twenty-six when she entered; she was twenty-seven now. With every kind of love and respect for her gifted sister, she could not understand the hurry. She had herself come slowly, carefully, with every deliberation, to the tremendous decision that is involved in forsaking the world, not only for the religious life, but for one of the most severely cloistered communities in the Church. Pauline was only a year younger, but she had entered at twenty; she could be counted on to be more encouraging. Yet in fact she was not. Thérèse says, charitably, that Pauline, when she seemed to reject her advances to the Carmel, was merely testing her vocation.

Rebuffed by her sisters at the convent, Thérèse tried for a while to withhold her secret from Céline, but less for fear of more discouragement than that she might hurt Céline, who was, after all, four years older than she and had her own ambitions to the religious life. But Céline was larger than life, heroic really, in her generosity. The size of that generosity is not to be underestimated. She found out, she understood, she accepted the fact that if Thérèse were to be received in Carmel, all would fall on her, all. Léonie would be off soon to try her flickering spirits again, this time at the Visitation. Louis had had the first touch of the cerebral congestion that was ultimately to disable and to kill him, and though on the first of May 1887, when it occurred, it did not seem likely ever to become so serious, he was close to his sixty-fourth birthday at a time when sixty-four was considered to be old age. Céline would be left with an elderly father, perhaps a sickly one, without the company of any of her sisters, all of whom would be leading the life she wanted so much for her own. Her vocation would be suspended, her life would be dangling in midair. But Céline saw Thérèse's vocation as her own too and gave her the buoyant support which it was her special grace to do. And then, to Thérèse's everlasting joy, in that sweet Pentecost of 1887, Louis also gave his consent, and more. Tears came to his eyes, matching Thérèse's own tears; he cried out that the Lord was doing him a great honor in taking each of his children, and then he performed his symbolic action, his regal action, plucking and presenting her with her blazon, with her allegorical model— her little white flower.

Louis was easy; Louis was tender. His consent seemed to come from another world. With extraordinary gentleness, he pulled the little flower out of the soil by the roots, without damaging any of it. And so, in the same way, in spite of some tears and a momentary nervous walking back and forth, he yielded up Thérèse, his youngest, his little queen, a child of fourteen. But it was not so easy with Uncle Isidore. As guardian of all the Martins until they reached their majority, he had to give his consent too. Too young, too young, was his response. "It would be a real *public scandal*," Thérèse sums up his answer in a letter to Pauline, "to see a *child* entering Carmel. I should be the only one in the whole of France, etc. Still if God wants it, He will find a way to show it. . . ." Uncle Isidore thought he understood God's time-table fairly well. Thérèse must not even consider entering until she was seventeen or eighteen. Pauline was not as certain as M. Guérin about these things. When Thérèse came to see her two weeks later, doleful as she had not often been since Christmas, Pauline was moved to write her uncle and to select from Thérèse's eloquent and moving pleas just the right ones. "Our poor little Benjamin of a Thérèse was so pale, sad, and wretched this morning . . . a whole week of agony. . . . In her eyes—so loving but so tearful—I thought I detected something more than a child's trouble." The nun asked her sister if she were sick. "No," Thérèse replied, "but I have never suffered like this; if it goes on, I shall die of anguish. I can see that Uncle is waiting for a miracle, but of course God won't work a miracle for me. They say it's extraordinary to enter Carmel at fifteen. It's most unfortunate that it should be extraordinary; but it seems to me that the good God never asks the impossible, and He is asking this of *me*. . . ."

The very same day that Thérèse visited Pauline and that Pauline wrote her uncle, he announced his change of mind. When Thérèse came to see him, on a Saturday visit, before she could say anything, he took her into his study and told her he was no longer opposed to her entering Carmel that year, at Christmas, if she could, as her father had agreed to let her do. She was, he said, a little flower that God wanted to pick. . . . Enough! Thérèse wrote the next day to Father Pichon, whom she had told of her hopes and ambitions three years earlier, just before her first Communion, and who had solemnly agreed to say his Mass on that day, which was also Pauline's day of Profession, for both sisters. "I think the moment has come," Thérèse wrote the Jesuit. ". . . Father, I ask you please to pray for your youngest child. I am just back from the Convent; my sisters there told me that I could write and tell you quite simply all that was going on in my heart. You see, Father, I have done so, hoping that you will not refuse to take me as your little daughter."

Father Pichon never gave Thérèse anything but encouragement, even too much encouragement, if one accepts Balthasar's interpretation of his action as a confessor in declaring her always without sin. Father Delatroëtte, pastor of St. Jacques and chaplain of the Carmel, was exactly the opposite. He would give no encouragement at all. He had declared himself firmly on the subject of early vocations: no one under twenty-one was to be admitted to the Carmel. He was moved neither by Mother Gonzague nor by Mother Geneviève de Sainte Thérèse, one of the foundresses of the community, whose words there normally had the unction of the tablets of the Law. As ecclesiastical superior of the Carmel, he said, he was unalterably opposed to Thérèse's entering before she was twenty-one. Well, not exactly *unalterably* opposed. There was always the Bishop. He told Louis, who had come with Thérèse and Céline to see him, that the Bishop could overrule him.

Thérèse and Louis made a trip to Bayeux to see Monsignor Hugonin, the Bishop, with eager hopes that counted upon everything going right, including the weather, and so they dressed for sunshine. When they arrived at the Cathedral town, it was pouring rain. They took a bus and managed to stay dry. At the Cathedral, they found the Bishop involved in a big funeral; but there was no place they could go, it was too wet. What did Papa do? With "his patriarchal simplicity," he marched Thérèse right down to the front of the great church, with everybody dressed in black staring at her light clothes and white hat. She was nothing but a distraction, she was sure, to all the "good folk of Bayeux," whom she devoutly wished she had never seen. She felt almost the same way about the Bishop after she met him. His vicar-general was kind; he was kind. When she cried outside the Bishop's study, the Vicar-General said, "Ah, I see diamonds. Let's not show them to the Bishop!" When she cried inside the study, the Bishop put his arm around her neck, lifted her head onto his shoulder, and patted her with an affection, she was told, he had never shown anyone else. But his affection knew a limit. How long had she had this hope of becoming a Carmelite? A long, long time. Not for fifteen years, the Vicar-General interjected; you're not going to say that. As long as I have been able to use my reason, Thérèse insisted. Wouldn't you be of more use to your father at home, more comfort? the Bishop asked. Louis, to Thérèse's surprise, then pleaded for her. But the Bishop said he would have to talk with the Father Superior of the convent. In the meantime, it was good that she was going on pilgrimage to Rome, in celebration of

Leo XIII's golden jubilee as a priest; the Bishop would see to it that his decision reached her in Italy.

Before letting them leave, the Bishop took Thérèse and Louis through his quarters as far as his garden. Louis delighted him when he told him that Thérèse had put her hair up for the meeting with him, to make herself look older. The Bishop never forgot it; he never spoke of his *petite fille*, Thérèse says, without telling the story of the hair. Louis asked the Bishop several questions about the pilgrimage, about how one dressed for a papal audience—would the clothes he had on do? And he told the Bishop that if he did not give his permission to Thérèse, she would "ask that grace of the Supreme Pontiff." And so they left, well mannered, but terribly let down. Thérèse was in tears again, pouring like the heavens outside! Louis, who had hoped to send a jubilant telegram back to Lisieux, was not in much better control as they walked back into the wet day.

Thérèse was being treated like a child, and yet not like the child she really was, the special child anyone would be if she were looked upon with enough respect and brought up with enough love. This was the Thérèsian revolution, to lead small children to spiritual maturity and to lead adults to childlike simplicity, to bring all people back to first principles, loving principles, the principles of her lover who was Love. This was a revolution her parents had initiated and which she had supported early, as far as she was able. When a relative of the Martins' nursemaid was dying, with three children left untended, Louis took in the two younger ones, both under six, and gave them to Thérèse to take care of during the day. She found the *candeur*—the ingenuousness and simplicity—with which the children took to her revolution in child-raising a deep pleasure. She talked of God to them. She did not threaten them with loss of toys and candy or promise them more of either when she found them squabbling with each other and tried to get them to reconcile their differences. She talked instead of the rewards in heaven that the Child Jesus would give to good children, and apparently talked in terms the children could understand and accept. The older looked at Thérèse "with eyes shining with joy" and asked a "thousand" questions about little Jesus and his heaven and promised, with "enthusiasm," to let her sister always have her way. Thérèse understood now, she says, what Jesus meant about "scandalizing one of these little ones"—that is, that "it were better for him that a millstone should be hanged about his neck and that he should be drowned in the depth of the sea."

Like flowers which are entrusted to skillful gardeners, souls are given to parents and teachers, Thérèse mused. What if an idiot gardener tried to graft a rose onto a peach tree? He would kill a perfectly good tree altogether capable of producing its own fruit. With souls, we must first try to discover what God's intention seems to be for each one, and then, without rushing too fast or waiting too long, we must try to encourage that intention in the child. Holiness in children comes, as it does in birds, from the example of their elders. Thérèse remembered in particular detail the linnet she had trained from the beginning, before it could even fly. It had no parents from which to learn to sing. It could only follow the example of the canary with which it was caged. How could it imitate the quivering sound of the canary with its soft voice? It was delightful and moving to see how it finally did just that, achieving some of the vibrant texture of its master's voice without losing any of its own sweetness. That is Thérèse's method; that is the method of the Martins. It had been used effectively enough with her. She was her father's child, her mother's child; she was Pauline's child, she was Marie's child. She had learned from all of them, imitated all of them, and whether M. Delatroëtte and Monsignor Hugonin recognized it or not, she was ready for Carmel; readier than many older girls, she and her sisters and her father and her uncle would have said; readier than any older girl, I think we should have to say, on the basis of what we know about her extraordinary preparation and her great gifts. She was a linnet that had learned to sing from a whole houseful of canaries and could outsing any of them. What was there among religious exercises that she really could not do?

Most of the friends of the Martins thought that Louis was taking Thérèse with him and Céline on the pilgrimage to Rome to show her the marvels of the world, to make her reconsider her decision about Carmel. Not so at all, not for Thérèse, not for Louis. He and she were both well aware of the real aim of their journey—to see the Pope and get him to endorse Thérèse's early entrance into Carmel. Louis loved traveling, but he always kept before him the cautionary lines from the *Imitation* that remind the travel-hungry that all the world and all the heavens are right before their eyes, wherever they are, that nothing under the sun can last, that everything here below is only an empty representation of reality. Thérèse was as eager as anyone else in the train, which carried 187 pilgrims, to greet the Pope on his jubilee and thus to give token of the support of Catholics all over the world to the "prisoner of the Vatican," as Leo XIII described himself. She looked forward with some interest to the stops coming and going, to the historic sights, to the famous places, but it was hard for her to take her mind off her one real concern, the center of all her interests, especially in the 3 A.M. darkness, leaving Lisieux. When the Martins arrived in Paris three days before the pilgrimage was officially to begin, Thérèse found only a crush of people and carriages. "Céline will tell you, if she likes, of the marvels of Paris," she writes her sisters at the convent; "but, for me, all I have to tell you is that I *keep* thinking of you; the beauties of Paris do not win my heart in the least. . . . O my darling Sisters, all these beautiful things I see do not bring me happiness; I shall only have that when I am where you are now."

There was one moment of happiness in Paris, at Notre Dame des Victoires, so long the special object of veneration in her family, as a devotion and as a church. Kneeling before the statue of the Lady of the Victories, she felt once again the Virgin's smile, felt confirmed in the earlier experience, felt so close to the great lady that she could no longer call her "Mother"; only the tender name of "*Maman*" would do. Through her and through St. Joseph, to whom she prayed with an equal intensity, she looked for protection from the harsh intrusions of the world, tensions that might upset her so hard-won balance, tarnishings of mind and senses, anything that might bring evil into her life. She had not yet learned "from experience," she says, that, as St. Paul writes, "'all things are clean to the clean,' and that simple souls and good hearts see evil in nothing, for evil exists only in an impure heart and not in senseless objects."

The Martins found their Norman companions on the pilgrimage pleasant enough to be with, though they came, most of them, from higher worlds. There were priests, and from their behavior and the way others responded to it, Thérèse learned why Carmelites make priests the special object of their prayers. It wasn't any particular wrongdoing that caught her eye; it was the constant attention that the priests were given; it was the strength of their good example, when they gave it, the absence of that strength when they did not give it—"if the salt loses its savor, wherewith shall it be salted?"

Thérèse kept her eyes fully open to the beauties of Switzerland, as the train passed the mountains and the lakes. She dutifully climbed up to the roof of the great cathedral in Milan and all the way up to the top of the bell tower in Venice, while Louis went round San Marco, across the way. In Venice she resisted the importunings of Céline long enough to write a sweet rambling letter to her cousin Marie Guérin, full of a pleasure she was not always sure she felt in all that was "really marvelous," in all the "lovely things," in the Italian language, of which she retains just one word, *Signorella*, as "the hotel people call me . . . 'little lady.'" The letter comes most to life when she tells Marie how often she thinks of her, "in the beautiful churches" especially, where undoubtedly Thérèse came to life. But also, she says, "I have thought of you also in the presence of the wonders of nature, amid those Swiss mountains that we crossed; one prays so well then; one feels that God is there!" This was her old comrade in the solitary life, after all, her fellow anchoress; she could not forget her in the high places.

Thérèse had been frightened by the crush of people and traffic in Paris. In Bologna, separated for a moment from her father as they were leaving the train, she was suddenly the object of attention of a mob of students who had come out to welcome the French pilgrimage. One of the young men seized on her as the youngest in the party and lifted her high in the air and started to carry her around like a triumphant athlete or a trophy of victory. Seeing her clear distaste for the whole thing, he quickly put her down. She was glad to leave Bologna for Loreto and the Holy House, where she and Céline insisted upon receiving Communion inside, in Jesus's "own house," in spite of the fact that the basilica had been so constructed that altar, tabernacle, and Sacrament were all outside the house, which sits in the church, says Thérèse, "like a precious diamond in a white marble casket." Louis received according to the rule and custom of the place, while Thérèse and Céline ran down one of the priests in their group who had the special privilege of saying Mass in the house and got him to put two hosts in the paten for them. And thus they achieved that special joy which Communion in this special house meant for them.

There was no question in Thérèse's mind about the House of Loreto. Of course it was in fact the Virgin's house in Nazareth. Of course angels had lifted it from its original site, in the thirteenth century, and carried it here. Of course this was where Mary had walked back and forth with the child Jesus and Joseph had worked till the sweat dropped from him. Thérèse put her rosary in a bowl which she was certain was one from which Jesus had taken food. She stopped in the room of the Annunciation. To her, these were all patent realities and she thrilled to them as she did not to Paris or Venice or Bologna.

Thérèse was an unabashed collector of religious experiences: the holy building in the Loreto basilica, the tongue of St. Anthony preserved in Padua, the body of St. Catherine in Bologna "which still holds the mark of the kiss of the Child Jesus." In Milan she revelled in the Campo Santo sculpture, a cemetery full of mottled marbled grief. She stored up the snow-topped mountains of Switzerland to meditate upon later. When she was confined to the convent—*prisonnière au Carmel* is her forceful way of putting it—she would remember what she had seen and she would be able to forget her "poor little interests in contemplating the power and the glory of God" which she had felt in the mountains. It was all, for her, a foretaste of "what God has prepared for those who love him." She quotes the end of the famous passage in the first letter to the Corinthians in which Paul's heart leaps with the thought of the marvels to come—"eye has not seen, nor ear heard, neither has it entered into the heart of man, what God has prepared for those that love him." Her heart had, now, an unmistakable presentiment of those marvels.

Rome should have held everything for Thérèse. Her visit began dramatically enough with an awakening in the middle of the night, the porters yelling "*Roma! Roma!*" and Thérèse coming alive to the fact that they really had come to the end of their journey. The countryside was beautiful, she saw the next day, when they began their sight-seeing, and all around her there were the marvelous marks of antiquity, still bold and clear in the bright sun of modern Rome. She and Céline had a glorious time at the Colosseum, breaking away once again from the main party in order to get down into the holy dust where the martyrs had shed their blood. Louis just gaped at his two adventurers, but they ran sure-footedly over the barrier, across the disheveled rows of seats, down onto that piece of pavement which Céline had heard the guide describe as the particular place of martyrdom. There they knelt in the dust and then once more Thérèse offered herself to her lover, this time asking for the grace that would make her an adequate witness to her love, a martyr. Again at the Catacombs, the girls crept off by themselves to pray at the bottom of the tomb where St. Cecilia was buried—or so it was generally believed. Thérèse discovered there and in the church which had been made of Cecilia's house a devotion to the saint that she had never felt before. Everything about Cecilia delighted her, but especially "her abandon, her unlimited confidence which made it possible for her to virginize worldly souls. . . ." She was, Thérèse decided, the patron saint of music, not because of a beautiful voice or any particular talent, but "in memory of the pure chant that she sang in the depths of her heart to her heavenly bridegroom. . . ." She, the saint whose existence many now doubt, became Thérèse's true friend and her new confidante.

Rome should have held everything for Thérèse; if it did not, at least it was fairly liberal to her in the relics it let her take away. She and Céline, like all the scavenging tourists of history, took away some small stones from the Colosseum and scooped up some dirt from Cecilia's part of the Catacombs. At the Church of St. Agnès, Thérèse tried in vain to buy a relic to take back to Pauline, Sister Agnès of Jesus; then suddenly she came upon a little red stone "which had detached itself from a rich mosaic" which dated back to the time of St. Agnès, which the saint herself must have looked at, or so Thérèse thought: "Wasn't it charming of that saint to give us exactly what we were looking for and were forbidden to take? I've always seen it as a mark of sweet concern on her part and a proof of the love with which this dear saint looks down on my darling Mother and protects her."

Rome should have held everything for Thérèse, but it did not. "You see, little Sister," she wrote the co-foundress of the *Solitaires de Lisieux*, her cousin Marie, "there is nothing for me in Rome! Everything is for the artistic! If only I could have a word from the Pope, I should ask no more of Rome." She did have her word—well, if not *her* word, *a* word, anyway. After six days of seeing the wonders of Rome, she writes, on the seventh she saw "the greatest of them, Leo XIII."

She was deeply impressed by the solemnity of the occasion. There were two Masses in the Pope's own chapel. The Pope said the first, then there was a Mass of thanksgiving, and finally, in an atmosphere of monarchical splendor, with a plethora of prelates—cardinals, archbishops, bishops—around him, Leo gave his audience. Much kneeling, much kissing—a foot, a hand, for each pilgrim—followed by the papal blessing and a gentle push from a member of the Swiss guard to get the pilgrim off his knees and on his way. When Thérèse came up, she found M. Reverony, her bishop's vicar-general, standing at the Pope's side, and a minute later heard the word he had ordered to be passed around among the pilgrims: the audience was already overlong; not a word was to be spoken to His Holiness. Thérèse turned to Céline for advice. "Speak!" said her sister. Thérèse spoke. "Most Holy Father," she said, "I have a great favor to ask of you." Leo leaned forward and his dark black eyes seemed to penetrate right to the bottom of her soul. "Most Holy Father," she continued tremblingly, "in honor of your jubilee, please let me enter Carmel at the age of fifteen." The Pope indicated to M. Reverony that he had not quite understood Thérèse's words. The Vicar-General explained her request and added that the superiors of the Carmel were considering the matter right at that moment. "Good enough, my child," the Pope told Thérèse; "do what your superiors tell you to do." Thérèse dared one more time to make her plea. Putting her hands on the Pope's knees, she implored him: "Most Holy Father, if only you would say yes, everybody would agree." The Pope sent her on her way with his last word: "If God wills it, you will enter." Thérèse found the vigor and directness of the seventy-seven-year-old Pontiff very moving and his apparent concern for her encouraging. She wanted to continue the conversation, but two of the guards lifted her up by her arms, and seeing that her hands were still on the Pope's knees, with the help of M. Reverony they yanked her away with force, but not before the Pope could lift his own hand to Thérèse's lips. Then as she was being led away, he raised it in blessing, following her for some time with his eyes. When Céline, who was next in line, came up, all she could think of was to ask the Pope to give Carmel his blessing. M. Reverony said with some crossness that it had already been done. Yes, the Pope agreed—but in tender tones—it has been done. When Louis came along, with the men of the pilgrimage, M. Reverony was much pleasanter. He introduced him as the father of two Carmelites and the Pope pleased the two future Carmelites by the gracious way he put his hand on Louis's head.

Thérèse wrote a letter full of pain to Pauline. The substance of it was that she had "nothing but God, alone, alone. Goodbye, dearest Pauline, I cannot go on telling you, I'm afraid Papa may come and ask to read my letter, and that is impossible." She did not want Louis to know how severe her pain was. In the same letter she speaks of herself as the *jouet* of Jesus, his toy. This was her constant meditation for the rest of the trip. She was a ball to be kicked around by the Holy Child, not an expensive one, either, just any old ball that a child might take apart to see what's inside, and then throw away. She was resigned to it, to being the most prosaic of playthings for her lordly lover, but like Zélie she was honest with herself; she couldn't deny the great pain she felt.

Before they left Rome, Louis and Thérèse went to see Brother Simeon, principal of St. Joseph's College, run by the Brothers of the Christian Schools, and a figure of importance in the French colony in Rome. They found M. Reverony there too, but that didn't deter Louis from telling the old religious the whole story. "You don't see that sort of thing in Italy!" Brother Simeon exclaimed about Thérèse's determination to enter Carmel and M. Reverony now at last seemed altogether convinced about Thérèse's vocation. All through the rest of the trip, the Vicar-General went out of his way to be gracious to Thérèse, as if to make up for his roughness at the papal audience and to give continuing witness of his support. When she lost her belt at Assisi and had to spend a long time looking for it and then to scramble for a seat on the only remaining carriage, M. Reverony's, filled with the notables of the pilgrimage, he did not treat her as a child, but rather like a lady of considerable importance, and he refused to allow her to tip the driver; it was his pleasure. When she sat next to him on a bus, he chatted to her about Carmel and promised to do all he could to get her into the convent.

She was not at her liveliest on the return trip, but she did manage to *ooh* and *ah* a little at Vesuvius's smoke—What power God has!—and to be startled at what the volcano had done to Pompeii.

She didn't miss a single holy object either. She was a great toucher. She touched one of the nails that were venerated as having fastened Jesus to the cross; it was in a reliquary without glass and Thérèse managed to get her little finger into it—she thought of herself as a child who feels absolutely free to do what she pleases with her father's treasures. Why, she wondered, was it so easy for a woman to be excommunicated in Italy. At every moment, some one was saying, "Don't go in there! No, not there! You'll be excommunicated!" Poor women; no respect for them anywhere. And yet there are more of them who love God than men, she mused, and it was the women who showed courage at the time of the crucifixion, braving the soldiers' insults and daring to wipe the face of Jesus. Well, Thérèse dared, dared anything if the end in view was large enough. In Rome, at a Carmelite monastery, while everybody else stayed in the outer galleries, she made her way into the cloisters. Suddenly she saw in the distance an old monk signaling to her to get out. She signaled in return that she was enjoying the beautiful pictures around the cloister and he, perhaps thinking she was younger than she was, because, Thérèse says, she had her hair down that day, let her stay and moved off himself. She wanted to tell him that she was a future Carmelite, but "the builders of the tower of Babel made that impossible." Once more, in Florence, at the Carmelite church, she dared to go beyond the rules and the rails, but this time with encouragement from everybody. The Carmelites themselves opened their large grille so that the pilgrims could see the body of St. Mary Magdalen de' Pazzi, but only Thérèse had small enough hands to get through the remaining grille to touch the tomb of the saint, and so everybody passed her their rosaries and she fulfilled with distinction her high office of toucher-in-chief.

On the way back to France, the train moved along the Italian Riviera and Thérèse stored up more scenes for meditation in the convent. Now it was seaport lights and then the matching lights above in the heavens. She had a full treasure of earth's beauties. Now she wanted to be imprisoned in Carmel. There was nothing more to hold her outside. When Louis suggested that they follow the pilgrimage to Rome with another which he had always been eager to make, to Jerusalem, she could produce no enthusiasm at all. It was Carmel she wanted and it was to Carmel she ran when they returned home to Lisieux, to share her miseries, to share her hopes.

On December 16 she wrote the Bishop, simply, openly, imploringly. Louis fixed up the letter according to the stiffer forms he had been used to in business and in Catholic organizations, making the letter less felicitous, but not entirely un-Thérèsian. Fortunately, the original is preserved. In it, Thérèse pleaded, "O Monseigneur, it is said that trials are a sign of vocation; so indeed they are; you know that the good God has not spared me trials, but I felt that I was suffering for Jesus, and not for a single instant did I cease to hope. The Child Jesus has made me feel so strongly that He wants me at Christmas, that I cannot resist the grace He is giving me. . . . It is true that I am very young, but, Monseigneur, since God calls me and Papa is in favor . . ." Just to make sure her plea was well represented, Thérèse wrote M. Reverony the same day, reminding him of his promises. "All the distractions of the journey to Rome could not drive from my mind for one instant the ardent desire I have to be united with Jesus," she wrote the Vicar-General. "Ah! why should He call me so powerfully, if I am to be made to languish far from Him?"

She awaited Christmas with the utmost longing of her life, but nothing happened, except the warm and imaginative displays of affection of her sisters. Céline fashioned a ship out of a kitchen bowl; on its side she wrote *Abandon!*, Renunciation; in the bowl she placed a baby Jesus and next to it a little ball; on the sail she put words in the mouth of Jesus's plaything, the little ball: "I sleep, but my heart is awake." This tableau greeted Thérèse when she returned from midnight Mass. At the Carmel, on Christmas Day, Thérèse was greeted even more theatrically, though the terms were the same. When the grille was opened there was another infant Jesus at the center of the stage, holding in his hand a ball with Thérèse's name written on it. Pauline had composed a song for the occasion and the nuns sang it for Thérèse: "every word brought sweet consolation with it. . . ."

On New Year's Day, the answer finally came, an answer which had been known at the Carmel for three days, since December 28, but which was delayed because Thérèse's entrance was to be delayed until Lent. The Bishop had left it up to the Prioress to make the final decision and she decided on a three-month postponement. A new cross! That was Thérèse's disconsolate response, though she knew well enough that miracles take a little time, at least a little. Should she practice more rigorous mortifications? Should she give up her self-made, self-imposed rule, since everything was now settled? No, her life would be still more *sérieuse*, earnest, grave, and mortified. When she says "mortified," she explains quickly, she does not mean that she took up a severe penitential life. "Alas," she sighs, "I've never done that." She has heard all about those saintly people who practiced the most rigorous mortifications from childhood. Céline could always find a thousand little ways of making herself suffer. Not for Thérèse— there was never any attraction to such hand-crafted physical mortification in her. She had allowed herself to be swathed in cotton and to be handled like a pet bird. Her mortifications were, she sums up, to crush her own will, which was always eager to break through; to suppress cutting replies to people, harsh words of any kind; to do small kindnesses without inflating their value; to sit straight in her chair, rather than all bent over, as any self-respecting adolescent prefers to do. These "nothings," as she calls them, were her way of preparing for her nuptials. The three months would pass quickly and easily; her little way almost assured her of that. But if they did not, if they brought pain and difficulty, *tant mieux*, so much the better; her little way was prepared for that too.

EIGHT

*I*N her last letter to Pauline, written two weeks before entering the convent, Thérèse wrote, "O Pauline, I want always to be a *little* grain of sand. . . . I should like to say many more things about the little grain of sand, but I haven't time. . . . *I want to be a saint.*" That was her transfixing ambition as she moved toward Carmel. As Teresa of Avila said "I want to see God," and meant it, and made everything in her life take shape under its inspiration, so Thérèse declared her hope and toward its realization constructed and reconstructed every minute of her life. She had read somewhere, she wrote in the same letter to Pauline, she didn't remember where or what saint was speaking, the words, "I am not perfect, but I want to become so."

It was to be her own perfection, not someone else's. She would not achieve the heights of sacrifice through scourging. No eviscerating mortifications for her. She had no image of herself as a large figure, as an awesome object of veneration, nor did she desire any transformation along those lines. Her devotion to littleness was as intense as her ambition to sanctity. Indeed for her the things were identical: little flower, little bird, little vessel, little grain of sand, little saint. It was fitting, then, that she left for Carmel from the little dining room at Les Buissonnets, a really small room, filled by its heavy round oak table and high-backed chairs, its serving tables and sidepieces, and stretched to the point of bursting by the Martins, even without Marie and Pauline, and the Guérins, even without the Maudelondes.

The remaining sisters hugged and kissed Thérèse with all sorts of ardor. Léonie was back from her first try at the Visitation, had been back since January, when it was clear her health was being affected by her postulancy. She saw her little sister, her littlest sister, ten years younger than she, go off to the convent, and go

135

off with ease, with joy, with certainty, while she faltered, for the time being anyway, slapped down once again, apparently unequal to her majestic vocation. Céline too was deeply involved. She was as certain of a vocation as Léonie, and as determined to attain Carmel as Thérèse. That night, their last night together in their own room, Céline and Thérèse filled their long whisperings with anticipations of life in Carmel. But before Carmel and before whisperings about it there were the night's earlier ceremonies: a full drama of tears, smiles, and last long affectionate glances. *Tante* Céline did most of the crying. *Oncle* Isidore and Papa did most of the glancing. Everybody smiled and looked affectionate. Jeanne Guérin was generous with her *délicatesses*. Marie Guérin took Thérèse aside, her fellow *solitaire*, and asked her pardon for all the pain she had caused her, pain of which Thérèse had no memory.

The ceremony was repeated the next morning at Mass and Communion, which everybody received, as a family. Everybody cried too, as a family, and then, after a solemn blessing from her father, Thérèse was received behind the doors of the Ark. She felt, really, that she was being received into the tabernacle itself, that is surely the meaning of the rhetorical figure of the Ark. She was in now, finally, living with her lover, having given herself fully, not for a moment's surrender, now and then, but forever, in a constant surrendering. The only possible analogy to her feeling is marital. Her surrender was total submission, but not into a limp passivity. She gave with high and constant consciousness. She had entered Carmel to make a career of that giving, no matter how much anguish was involved. And anguish would be involved. For as in the most joyful and satisfying of marriages, if one tries to keep going, to keep giving, beyond one's resources, a certain physical and psychological pain accompanies the joy and the satisfaction, so in the great spiritual encounters, when one insists upon pushing on beyond one's endurance, suffering comes to join the joy, to join to almost every pain an equal and opposite pleasure. Indeed, every pleasure involves a pain, but equally, every pain involves a pleasure. "Yes," says Thérèse of her introduction to Carmel, "suffering held out her arms to me and I threw myself into them with love."

The life of a religious was just as expected, "more thorns than roses." This brambly summation of Thérèse's is frequently under-

stood as a description of her first five years under the steward-
ship of Mother Marie de Gonzague, for indeed she says, just a
few lines below, that for five years the way of suffering was hers
and those five years do coincide with the two terms of Mother
Gonzague as Prioress before Pauline was elected to replace her
for a term. It is not enough, however, to think of Thérèse's sufferings as a Carmelite as a five-year term, soon enough to be relieved
with the succession of Pauline to the seat of authority. She had
no illusions about Carmel, she says, and no surprises awaited her.
She was delighted with her austere cell, more than content to
throw herself into her daily tasks, noble or ignoble, doing laundry,
sweeping stairs and cleaning under dormitory beds or praying in
choir, just thinking by herself, alone, as for so many years she had
been doing, or joining with as much outward pleasure as she
could muster in the recreation activities of the other postulants.
This was life in the Ark, this was how one joined one's lover if
one's lover lived in a tabernacle. There were, besides, the lovely
apparitions of a day at the Lisieux Carmel. There was Sister
Agnès of Jesus, her own sister, Pauline. There was Sister Marie of
the Sacred Heart, her own sister, Marie. There was Sister Augustine of St. Thérèse, warmly receptive to Thérèse always, who had
had compliments for her from their very first encounter in the
parlor. There was her novice mistress, Sister Marie of the Angels
and the Sacred Heart, who had authority and understanding to
back up the authority and love to support both. And there was
the great venerable figure of the Lisieux convent, Reverend
Mother Geneviève of St. Teresa.

When Thérèse was first taken to the choir, the first presence of
which she was conscious, after the presence in the tabernacle,
was of Mother Geneviève; she was suddenly aware of the eyes of
"our holy Mother Geneviève fixed on me." For the nuns at Lisieux, Mother was holy, as holy as she was ancient. She was one
of the founding mothers, second Prioress of the convent, and a
fixture at the Carmel since its first days in March 1838. In 1888,
she was eighty-five years old. She had survived the physical torture of inadequate buildings, leaky roofs, poor diet, poverty in all
its religious guises. She was always available to the nuns, even in
old age, for serious conversation, and, to the extent that the rule
and the hours of recreation permitted, for trivial conversation.
Austerity and severity reached their outermost boundary at her

skirts. She kept the rule, which she herself had helped to make commendable, with exemplary precision, but with none of that surface sternness, that grim setting of the lips and emptying of the eyes, which makes some religious superiors so forbidding and makes one doubt that they are in fact superior. For the three years she was still alive after Thérèse's entrance, she was for her an embodiment of authority both loving and regal; like Louis, worthy of fealty and the utmost affection. Suffering had extended its arms to Thérèse at the Carmel, but so had love, and not merely love, but love in the familiar gestures and postures of the family, a family that stretched back fifty years and that still had with it its grandmotherly Mère Geneviève. It was not unlike living in the Convent of the Incarnation or at St. Joseph's in Avila, at the time of St. Teresa.

Family contacts at the Lisieux Carmel were of every kind for Thérèse. There was the official family, into which she had first been introduced when she discovered her vocation at the age of nine and with which she had continued to have a significant relationship in her parlor visits during the intervening years between Pauline's entrance and her own. There was her own family, not only the two Carmelite Sisters who were Martins, but all the other Martins with whom she continued her relationship, even after taking the veil. Louis, always a generous patron of the convent, noticeably increased his benefactions with Thérèse's entrance. "How good you are to your *little Queen!*" Thérèse writes her father after just three weeks in the convent. "Hardly a day passes but she receives some gift from her King!" She thanks him and once again assures him of her love: "If you knew how the little *Orphan of the Berezina* loves you! but no, you will discover that only in Heaven." She reminds him of their pilgrimage to Rome, which she contrasts to heaven where "indeed we shall see lovely *statues* on lovely *cornices;* then we shall really be able to go into an ecstasy. And then, what a *guide* will be there, to show us the wonders of Heaven!" The family jokes remain too: in her reference to the Napoleonic Wars; in the wild coinage of their Italian guides—*estatues* for statues, *cornichons* (which actually means a ninny or a greenhorn) for cornices, and *estasaison* (a strange Italo-French hybrid which means nothing) for ecstasy.

Thérèse was, if not a tireless correspondent, a faithful one. She kept the ties with home fixed and firm. She continues to thank

Louis, for candles, for fish, for a spade, for pears, onions, plums, apples—"so many things that I must simply make one thank-you cover everything, but all the same each separate thing gives its own pleasure." She asks Céline to do some stitching for her on the Martin sewing machine and some weeks afterward asks for some material and some ribbons, just before felicitating Céline on Louis's approval of her Carmelite ambitions: "Now you must belong wholly to Jesus, more than ever He is wholly yours. He has already placed on your finger the mysterious ring of the espousals. He wills to be the one only Master of your soul." Louis's ready acceptance of what he saw as God's desire to grace all of his family leads Thérèse to two heartfelt salutations: "Dearest sister, we are SISTERS indeed in all the force of the word," and "Goodbye, my heart reads yours from far off." She sends consolation to both Guérins Senior on the fatal illness of one of Mme. Guérin's cousins and congratulations to M. Guérin on having brought the dying man to reconcile himself with the Church. She jokes with Marie Guérin, who also has to be thanked for gifts, but for none quite so warmly as for her letters—"if Mme. de Sévigné had written to me, she would certainly not have given me so much pleasure."

Thérèse also kept up a vigorous intramural correspondence. She dashed off notes to Pauline and Marie on whatever piece of paper she could find, some simply sweet with sisterly love (in both senses of the word "sisterly"), some crackling with her own intense religious experiences. The language is rich and strong; the images and figures remain consistent, for long before she was called upon by Mother Agnès to write her story, she had begun to give shape to her little way and to find a rhetoric appropriate to it. When her sister Marie goes off on retreat in May of 1888, to prepare for her final Profession, Thérèse writes her, "You, who are an EAGLE called to fly in the upper air and gaze upon the sun, pray for the little weak reed in the depths of the valley, the least puff of wind bends it over. . . . Pray that your little girl may remain always a small grain of sand, very obscure, hidden from all eyes, that Jesus alone may be able to see it. Let it become smaller and smaller, let it be reduced to a *nothing*. . . ." She begs Marie's pardon for hurting her feelings, for not having welcomed more eagerly her assistance in preparing to recite the Divine Office. Thérèse does not say so, but it is clear she thought she could keep the Carmelite silence from the very beginning and make her way through the complexities of convent life with a minimum of help.

It was at the time of Marie's Profession that Father Pichon heard Thérèse's general confession, made with a thoroughness she had never achieved before this, and it was then he blessed her thoroughness with the assurance that she had never committed a mortal sin. The Jesuit's declaration brought her joy and gratitude. She was not in the least offended at being told that her sinlessness was not because of any merit on her part, that left to her own resources she would be not a little angel, but a little demon. The point was that she had not been left to her own resources.

Father Pichon would have been Thérèse's spiritual director as, after a fashion, he had been Marie's, but he was soon off to Canada, where he was to spend much of the rest of his life in missionary work, and therefore could only turn up from time to time in Thérèse's life, the way he did in the lives of others, as "God's traveling salesman," which he liked to call himself. His language was often bluff, journalistic, deliberately banal. But his spirituality was not without its depths and was always accommodating, psychologically as well as spiritually, to the vagaries of religious temperament. When Thérèse says that he was a director of the sort Teresa of Avila required, she was, I think, entirely right. He knew Teresa's work well and turned to it often. He was especially learned in its attitudes and textures of joy. To nuns he says forthrightly: "Our recreations must be veritable re-creating exercises. If we are not naturally light of heart, we must learn how to rejoice. There are gifted temperaments who have the talent of inspiring a certain warmth, a heartiness in recreation. I congratulate them. I beg of them never to permit their talent to become rusted from disuse." He recalled with joy St. Teresa's inculcation of a joyous spirit in her convents. When she called for an extra period of recreation on one Easter and a religious begged off, preferring "to meditate rather than make merry," the saint, "the dear saint," as Father Pichon calls her, permitted the sober Sister to remain in her cell; "but permit your Sisters," she said wryly, "to rejoice, to expand their hearts in the Lord." For Father Pichon that clinched the case. Don't act like a stranger, he tells his religious; no gloom, no long faces. "Learn how to jest, how to joke during recreation. Humor is a necessary element in life. It lubricates emotions, eases tension, drives away sadness and discouragement, and even aids good health."

In a delightful and wise conference on "Our Spiritual Temperature," Father Pichon seems to anticipate the criticism his reading of Thérèse's soul will later arouse in Balthasar and others. He deals with the cases of those who "never commit mortal sin, yet who are ungrateful," and in doing so outlines that pattern of gratitude without which sinlessness is worth little more than sinfulness. What shall we do with the sinless who "complain to their spiritual directors . . . behold their lives in a somber light, enveloped in a dark cloud. They are bored in the service of God." But what should they be? "My dear friends, you should thrill with joy, should fall upon your knees to send forth your alleluias of gratitude to the God who has accorded you the greatest of all graces—the grace to live in His love. . . . Leave tears to those who have had the misfortune to offend God." This leads him, then, to an excoriation of tepidity. With the aid of a fine line from St. Bernard of Clairvaux—"It is easier to find sinners who will be converted from crime to virtue than religious who will leave tepidity to re-embrace fervor in the service of God"—he indicts the tepid with all the strength of conviction and not a little of the scorn Dante brings to the same exercise in his *Inferno*, when he places the *ignavi*, the trimmers, the tepid, outside the gates of hell. The "little good" that the tepid do "is tainted with self-interest, self-love, spoiled by vanity, impatience, and a hundred other defects." The tepid "do not dare to confront themselves, to feel their spiritual pulse. They resemble the unhappy man who avoids returning to his family for fear of meeting with reproaches."

Thérèse delighted in Almire Pichon and he delighted in her. But her direction was left, at least as far as the world could see, in the hands of Mother Gonzague. "I could not meet her without having to kiss the ground"—the standard posture of humility for a penitent Carmelite. On those occasions, in that posture, Thérèse received direction from Mother Gonzague. Fortunately, the occasions were not so frequent. The Prioress was often ill and too busy, in any case, to bother with Thérèse. There was little chance under this superior that Thérèse would be spoiled, as she so dreaded being, and almost as little opportunity for human direction. She says she liked Mother Gonzague a great deal, but with that sort of pure affection which left her free to move toward her spouse, her divine lover. And it was in him and from him that she received her spiritual direction. "My child," Father Pichon had said to her, "let Our Lord be your superior always, and your novice master." And that, says Thérèse, is exactly what happened —or almost so. In fact, she had an excellent novice mistress in Sister Marie of the Angels, with whom even the long days that Thérèse had to spend being instructed in the ways of Carmel in general and her own work in particular, did not prove tiresome. She was a saint of the old school, as Thérèse sums her up, of the kind produced by the first Carmelites. But for all her virtues, Sister Marie did not draw Thérèse's confidences. At fifteen, Thérèse was not used to speaking her mind to anyone except her closest confidantes—and as for speaking her soul, she had had no practice in the art; she didn't know where to begin. One of the older nuns pleased her with the accuracy of her observation when she said she didn't think Thérèse had much to tell her superiors. "Your soul is extremely simple," the nun explained her observation; "the more perfect you are, the more simple you are. The closer one gets to God, the more simple one becomes."

Nothing about Thérèse's time at Carmel was ordinary, nothing followed a line of easy or familiar development, for all the consolation that the presence of her older sisters brought and the continuing warm support that her father's presents and the letters from Céline and Marie Guérin offered her. She never suffered from tepidity. She pulled no long faces, brought no gloom with her into the laundry or the recreation room, the dormitory or the choir. But neither did she fall with graceful relaxation into spiritual converse with her novice mistress or the Prioress. Poor Thérèse—there always seemed to be something—someone—missing. For years she had been eager for Carmel. And now that she was there, she was just as eager to have Céline with her. The same soul animates us both, she wrote to Céline: "There is between our souls something so evident and so alike. Always we have been together; our joys, our griefs have all been shared." She is certain they will not be separated for long. Only the "yellow lily"—symbol of marriage—"could have made some slight separation." But Céline's future is signified by the white lily of purity, and more, the lily-immortelle, for Céline's purity will never be mottled, will never fade. Therefore it makes little difference that Thérèse preceded Céline into Carmel; Céline's goodness and endurance are such that she can come at any time; she can follow Thérèse's frailty with her own strength, just as long as both sisters give all, for Jesus demands all of them.

"Life is often a burden," Thérèse laments to Céline, "but such sweetness! Yes, life *costs*, it is *hard* beginning a day's work, the frail bud has known it and so has the beautiful lily. . . . If only one felt Jesus close at hand! Oh! One would do all for Him . . . but no, He seems a thousand leagues away, we are alone with ourselves; oh! how wearisome is company when Jesus is not there!" She is painfully aware of her loneliness, perhaps because she is still a child, in spite of all her gifts, her precociousness, her prodigious understanding, her remarkable religious experiences. She is impatient for Jesus to say to her—"Your turn now." She wants immediate evidence of her election. "What can that loving Friend be doing? Doesn't He see our anguish, the weight that is crushing us? Where is He, why does He not come to console us, since we have no Friend but Him?" Maybe that is not exactly what she meant to say. Maybe she cannot really say at all what she meant to say. "What a poor muddler Thérèse is," she mourns —"such a letter, such a fuss! Oh, if I had been able to say all I think, how long it would have taken Céline to read. . . ."

Céline would not have had time to read a very long letter. She was too much taken up with the work of looking after her father. She knew how much of a burden life could be. Her election was clear enough; it was to the pain and anxiety of taking care of a dear old man in whom mortality was shaking its sands like an angry hourglass. His arteries were hardening. His mind was not always accessible to him. He suffered from a congestion of thoughts, experiences, fears, hopes, speculations, meditations—a turmoil of fragmentary impressions which he could not sort into any orderly form. Mixed with his ancient hope of a monastic life was his present fear of outbreaks against the Church of the severity of those in the Revolution of 1789. What would happen to Christians? to his daughters? to himself? He made plans for escape, the hazy plans of a hazy mind. Suddenly, on June 23, 1888, he left home. For three days nothing was heard of him. No one— not the well-placed and resourceful Isidore Guérin, not the helpless and harried Céline, not the police, not any friends—no one knew where to look or even really how to look for Louis. Léonie was terribly frightened by her father's absence; just down the lane fire consumed a house and she could feel the heat creeping toward Les Buissonnets: a nightmare! At the convent, the Martins knew Louis was missing and with as much calm as they could muster prepared themselves for terrible news. On June 26, Mother Geneviève told the girls not to worry; she had had some sense, in her prayers for Louis's safety, of a consoling dénouement. On June 27, a telegram from Le Havre announced that Louis had turned up. Céline and her uncle went off to the seaport to bring him home.

No, there was little peace for Céline. Louis had two more strokes in 1888, one in August, one in November, at Le Havre again, where he had gone with Céline to see Father Pichon off for Canada. There too he began to fulfill in detail Thérèse's strange prophetic vision of his illness. Without any clear sequence of cause and effect or any verbal excuse for doing so, he found a covering for his head, like the veil which Thérèse had seen, and was rarely without a cloth of some kind around his head.

There were periods of lucidity, given unction for the family by Louis's intense religious activity. He made large bequests to the Lisieux churches. He spent hours in prayer. He frequented the churches as often as he could, as thoughtfully as he could. He never altogether lost the semblance, at least, of recollection. It would not be an exaggeration to say that he was never altogether lost.

It was in the course of Thérèse's first six months at the Carmel that the Martins discovered their devotion to the Holy Face, more or less *en famille*. For Thérèse in particular the mixture that Jesus's face presented of anguish and love, both hidden away from the world, was irresistible. It did not matter how it was revealed, whether in an image one could see with one's eyes or in some daguerreotype of the mind. "If only my face could be really hidden away," Thérèse prayed, paraphrasing Isaiah (53:3), "so that no one on earth would recognize it. . . ." When Louis disappeared, the sisters prayed with special fervor to the Holy Face and soon afterward had an ex-voto tablet placed between candelabras in front of an image of the Face, with due praise to the Lord, and signed with the family's initials, *F.M.—Famille Martin.* There was something to celebrate; Louis was back, for the moment at least, and he was managing to survive his strokes and would perhaps even be able to attend Thérèse's Clothing Day ceremonies—if the conventual chapter could ever make up its mind and would actually choose a day.

Thérèse should have been clothed at six months, to the day, after her reception. Postulancy was not supposed to last any longer than that. But the convent's religious superior, M. Delatroëtte, cast a large shadow over chapter meetings. He had declared himself firmly enough about under-age Carmelites in general and Thérèse Martin in particular. They would have to wait at least until her sixteenth birthday. And so finally, January 10 was fixed upon and Thérèse could look forward not only to the day itself but also to having her father with her, for he seemed to be well enough recovered by the end of the year to come to the ceremony. "My dearest King," Thérèse wrote Louis on December 30, 1888, "What a happiness to be able this year to send you my new year wishes from the *Kingdom* of Carmel. Never has your *little Queen* been able to offer her affection with more joy. . . ." What a great happiness this double happiness was for her! She summed it up in typical Thérèsian style, keeping her rhetoric regal: "The Kings of the earth are most happy when they succeed in contracting noble alliances for their daughters, and what gratitude these children feel for their parents! . . . For your little Queen it is a very different matter; you, *as father* and truly *as King*, chose to entrust her to no other than to the King of Heaven, Jesus Himself; from *Orphan of the Berezina* I have passed to the most noble title of Carmelite." Her compliments to Louis are more than merely rhetorical and he surely must have felt their very large force, not in the least diminished by his daughter's tender wit: "If our Roman guide were here, he might say: '*Messieurs les Abbés*, I am going to show you such a Father as you have never seen, there is that in him which will make you fall down in wonder.'" She managed once again an example of their guide's original word coinage—*emerveillaison* for *merveille*, wonder. "Isn't it true, darling Father," she continued, "that you could not do more for your *little Queen!* If she isn't a saint, it will certainly be her own fault, for with a Father like you, she has the means!"

One more thing Louis could do for Thérèse—he could turn up at the Clothing, and this he did, to share his daughter's visible rapture. Her letters to Pauline during the retreat before the Clothing are full of her suffering, of her lack of consolation, of the pinpricks with which she is riddled—"the poor *little ball* can take

145

no more; all over it are tiny holes which cause it more suffering than if it had but one great gash!"—but they also admit to her happiness, even if it is happiness in suffering. Her Clothing brings her so much closer to the outside world, to everybody in it, here on earth, and elsewhere. She wants to love with an incomparable love. She wants to do her lover's will with an inflexible determination. She wants him to end his suffering, "to dry the tears that sinners cause Him to shed. . . . Oh! I want Jesus to have NO pain the day of my espousals, I wish I could convert *all* the sinners on earth and bring all the souls in purgatory to heaven!"

Writing is forbidden during retreat, Thérèse tells her father in a short note to him, but she has been given special permission to write him—and Pauline—and Marie—and she doesn't fail on Clothing Day itself to scribble a note to her fellow novice, Sister Marthe of Jesus, a lay Sister who had entered the Carmel when Thérèse herself had hoped to do so, at Christmas 1887, but was not to be clothed until May. "To my dearest little Sister in memory of my beloved Clothing," she begins. Soon, she tells Sister Marthe, you will be the bride of Jesus too. Ask him, she beseeches Marthe, "that I may become a great saint. I shall ask the same grace for my darling companion." And she signs herself for the first time "Sister Thérèse of the Child Jesus of the Holy Face."

The Clothing of a Carmelite in Lisieux at the end of the last century was a ceremony comparable to the richest of weddings, with outer magnificences striving to match inner glories. The dress of the bride was invariably ornate, but not with an empty finery; it proclaimed, wherever it could, the bride's vocation, her hopes, her faith. Thérèse wore a white velvet dress, with a veil of *Point d'Alençon*—Zélie was properly represented—and a crown of lilies over all. She burst upon Louis and Céline and Léonie and the Guérins at the door of the enclosure like a field of lilies suddenly coming alive. It was a gray day, drizzly, inauspicious, one might have said, but the ceremony held its own brightness and Louis's firm attention was so pronounced, and he seemed so much his old self, that, says Thérèse, everyone could not help admiring him, this great giver of gifts to God, who now that he had accepted Céline's announcement had no more children to give. The procession of Carmelite nuns, each holding a lighted candle, escorting the new bride back into the enclosure, was for Louis a family procession: there was Pauline; there was Marie; soon, Thé-

146

rèse would take her place as Céline received her brown and white habit, and Léonie would as soon as possible return to the Visitation. What a sense of fulfillment the old man must have had! He had given food, money, statues, contributed liberally toward the high altar at the Cathedral, but most of all he had given of himself, and nothing with more joy than his daughters, insofar as they were his to give. With what fervor he must have heard from behind the grille the Bishop begin a *Te Deum* after the Clothing! It was wrong, according to the rubrics: the *Te Deum* belonged to the ceremony of Profession, not to the Clothing. But once begun, it had to be finished, and after all the majestic words of praise were not inappropriate. They gave to Louis's last participation in his family's feasts a fitting sonority and fullness.

But the fullness was not yet, not for Thérèse. When she returned to the cloister, after kissing Louis for the last time, the first thing she saw was her favorite statue of the Child Jesus, smiling at her, she says, from among the flowers, and then, all of a sudden, snowflakes. What a gift from her lover, she thought, something no mortal lover could provide. It was a miraculous event on such a mild day, totally unexpected, as the world makes its expectations, but not as startling as all that to Thérèse, who was always alert for a sign from her beloved, and not the least on this day. Perhaps it was a strange taste of hers, she muses, to be so fond of snow, but so much the better that it was strange—it showed to what lengths that bridegroom would go, that lover of the pure, that lover of virgins, that admirer of snow-white lilies.

To be fond of snow was not really Thérèse's strange taste. It was her fondness for suffering that more properly qualifies for the adjective, and in this too she was thoroughly indulged. For a week or two after her Clothing, things went well—or rather they went poorly, if suffering is to be our index of well-being. Thérèse was happily ensconced in refectory duty, serving in the dining room with Pauline. Louis continued to show improvement. He was well enough to undertake one of his periodic trips to Alençon. But shortly after the beginning of February it was clear to Céline and Léonie that their father had reached the point in his mental wanderings where they could no longer cope. His memory was unreliable. He was still worrying a great deal about the fate of Christians in anticlerical France. His daughters could not trust him to stay at home. They arranged for him to go to the huge establishment of the Good Saviour at Caen, a little more than halfway between Lisieux and Bayeux. The institution of the Bon Sauveur was a town within a town, a small fortress of good works, with schools for boarders and the students who lived in town, schools for the deaf and for the mute, with full hospital facilities and a special home for the mentally ill. On February 12, Céline and Léonie took their father to the Bon Sauveur, after allowing him to make one last benefaction in person at the Carmel, a gift once again of fish, but without any visit with any of his girls at the convent, for fear he would not be able to survive the meeting.

Thérèse spoke of February 12 as the Martins' day of "great riches" and in her list of the special graces given by Jesus "to his unworthy bride"—fifteen special graces, from her birth to her Act of Oblation two years before her death—she lists this one too, right after her taking of the Carmelite habit. "One day, in heaven," she tells her sister Pauline in her autobiography, "we will enjoy talking among ourselves about our glorious trials, and even now aren't we happy to have suffered them? Yes, the three years of Papa's martyrdom seem to me to have been the most moving and the most fruitful of our life—I would not give them up for all the ecstasies and revelations of the saints. . . ." It was a full measure of suffering, all she had desired and much more; it was a fulfillment of her prophetic vision; she was being consoled, as she had asked to be consoled, by suffering alone; her love was being returned as she had demanded that it should be; pain for pain, ache for ache, she was being drawn into the union of victims which for her was the only possible union, the inevitable end and confirmation of love. To all the sufferings of a protracted postulancy and novitiate, to all the many small scourgings of the cloistered life of Carmel, there was added Louis's humiliating illness and the trials of Céline and Léonie. And then to these sufferings of the family, which Thérèse shared stroke by stroke and trial by trial, there was added dryness in prayer, which became her "daily bread." Deprived of "all consolation," she says, "I was nevertheless the happiest of creatures, because all my longings were satisfied."

Neither Céline nor Léonie records quite so much satisfaction with their lot, though neither complains about the multiple hardships that fell to them. They took up quarters with the Sisters of St. Vincent de Paul in Caen. Louis had planned to buy Les Buissonnets, but now there was no point in it. The two girls planned to stay as close to their father as they could, and, whenever they should be free, to take up their delayed vocations. They did not regret the termination of the lease on their home in Lisieux. They were free to attend Louis—as much as Bon Sauveur rules would permit. At first they were able to see their father fairly often, but as he fell into the general routine of the home, so did they, and the general routine permitted only one visit a week. They called at the hospital every day to get news of Papa and most of the time, though the news did not promise any recovery, they gathered that he was a great favorite at the Sauveur. He shared everything that was sent him. He went, when he was well enough, to daily Communion. The religious superior of the house, Mother Costard, who looked after him herself as much as she could, persuaded Céline and Léonie to go back to Lisieux. They could still come to see Louis every week. If there were any significant change in his condition they would be notified. So back they went, to live with their aunt and uncle, who had just retired to spend his time between Lisieux and a country place at La Musse, living handsomely with the aid of a large inheritance from the cousin whom he had brought back to the Church on his deathbed. Louis was particularly delighted to hear that Céline and Léonie were in the country at La Musse. The ancient angler and meditative country hiker could settle them perfectly in his mind among well-remembered birds and flowers and trees, houses and hills and roads.

It was during this time of "great riches" that Thérèse settled on her full name in religion, Sister Thérèse of the Child Jesus and the Holy Face, and received permission to add the second possessive to the first. Her devotion was shared by Céline, and more than shared. The whole family ached with sorrow over Louis and shared the ache and yet gloried in it. Céline insists upon "rejoicing" in the family's trials—all of them, Louis's, her own, everybody's—after first hoping that at least their father's condition might be ameliorated. She sees Louis's purgatory more than fulfilled here below. Léonie throws herself and the whole family upon the heart of Jesus: "But do not let us complain. We are not merely the friends of Jesus, we are His brides. . . . In Heaven we shall see our darling father, brought so low here on earth, crowned with glory. . . . Let us be his crown . . . worthy of such a father." Pauline prays that they will all become saints. Marie invokes the example of Job and sees Satan asking that Louis be tested, as Job was tested, and sees the Lord consenting to the test. Thérèse writes a litany of suffering in her letters to Céline, her own words interlaced with Scripture and the wisdom of Father Pichon and quotations from almost every book on the Carmel shelves that she had been able to read, from Father Arminjon to Teresa of Avila. At no point does she say what she has to say more skillfully than in her letter of May 1889 to Marie: "Before my entry into Carmel, our *incomparable* Father said, as he gave me to God: 'I wish I had something better to offer the good God.' Jesus heard his prayer. . . . The something better was *himself!*"

Thérèse keeps the long view. She sees her father's sufferings as she sees her own, in terms of ultimate purposes. She and her father are caught in God's nets—to use the metaphor with which she explained to her cousin Marie Guérin the firmness of God's hold upon her. Eternity is constantly in her thoughts. She longs to see God face to face, and forever. She longs for that moment when, as Arminjon put it, "God will cry out, 'My turn now!'" He is crying out for his turn with Louis; he is detaching him, as she marvels to see her lover do, from all created things. He is making Louis's martyrdom a true witness to love—Louis's for God and God's for Louis. That is a spectacular performance and one to be applauded as such. But there are little performances too, hundreds, thousands, millions. The little events, the tiny happenings, which are over so quickly, are also part of the divine plan. It is only in the preparation they give us that most of us can be sure of our encounter with God. We may not be called to heroic martyrdom; our witness may be minuscule, written in very small letters, but that is enough. A little is enough, as long as it is all our littleness, given gram by gram, but given willingly and without regret. On New Year's Eve, at the end of 1889, as she keeps the Carmelite vigil of the last hour of the year, she writes Céline, "Ah! let us profit, profit by the shortest instant, act like misers, be jealous of the smallest things for the sake of the Beloved!"

More and more Thérèse is obsessed with images of smallness. She really thinks of herself as a grain of sand. When she asks Pauline, off on her annual retreat in May 1890, to pray to Jesus to penetrate the grain of sand with his eyes, she speaks of something obviously tangible to her. The eyes of her lover are "night lilies" and they have rays that can pierce the sand. It is a wild fantasy, surrealist in its imagery, but real enough to Thérèse, for whom the "Flower of flowers" can, merely by opening its petals, send forth "melodious sound" and "set its mysterious teachings vibrating" in her heart. She inhabits the world of the emblem books of the seventeenth century, with all their astonishing extravagances of verbal and pictorial metaphor; she really lives in that world. For her flowers do talk and do send forth penetrating light rays. And why not? Supernature could do anything it willed with nature. If supernature had to do mayhem to our idea of nature in order to explain itself to us, why so much the better, especially if it did so in terms of little things, fitted to the proportions in which Thérèse best understood herself. She says, not long before the end of manuscript A, that she attaches little importance to her dreams, which were full of commonplace objects—woods, flowers, brooks, the sea, little children, butterflies—and, after daylong concentration on God, quite free of his presence. The only strange elements in her dreams were birds unlike any she had ever seen. There was no significant symbolic apparatus in them. However poetic they may be, she tells Pauline, they are far from being mystical. But are they not mystical? Or rather, do they not feed her daytime contemplation of God with its necessary images, not really the images of a poet, which live at a metaphorical remove from experience, but rather the images of a plastic spirituality in which one actually becomes for all practical purposes a little flower or a grain of sand? *Actually* becomes? Yes, actually becomes these things to the extent that they so color one's understanding of oneself that one can no longer altogether detach oneself from this way of speaking and thinking and feeling about oneself. To the same extent that one's name stands for one, the very small flower and the particle of sand become one's surrogates, one's doubles. A metaphor, in this way of using words, is such a heightening of language that it can never be altogether separated from the language. When Thérèse says, "Surely our family is a virginal family," the statement is incomplete until she has added her appositive, "a family of lilies." She is not incapable of direct speech, but it never fully accomplishes her end. "Céline,"—she addresses her sister, who is on pilgrimage in Tours, in the spring of 1890—"pure hearts are often ringed with thorns, often in darkness; then the lilies think they have lost their whiteness, think that the thorns which ring them round have actually torn their petals!" Then, in case Céline doesn't understand, she explains herself, with a quick moralization torn from the Epistle of St. James: "Do you understand, Céline? The lilies in the midst of thorns are those whom Jesus loves, it is in their midst that he takes His pleasure! 'Blessed is the man who has been found worthy to endure temptation.'" And so with that image firmly planted in Céline's garden, Thérèse sends word to Marie Guérin, whom she had meant to write: "I keep praying," she says, "that the Blessed Virgin may make her a *little lily* which thinks of Jesus a great deal, and *forgets itself*, and all its miseries as well in the hands of obedience." Her cousin Marie had been suffering from scruples—thorns ringing *her* petals. But they had not actually torn the petals and they need not. Marie, under obedience to a director of souls, could become that lowly object, a little lily, which is to say one of the largest figures in the Thérèsian pantheon.

To what extent is Thérèse aware of the metaphorical structure of her words? Is she saying more than one thing when she writes, for example, to her sister Pauline, "If it were possible for a *grain of sand* to console Jesus, to dry His tears, there is one that would so love to do it"? Does she mean, in addition to speaking her own longing to console Jesus, that if in the course of nature a grain of sand can offer consolation in any way, can in fact dry tears, then, as sand absorbs moisture, she will soak up the tears of Jesus? Does she have a clear image before her when she writes, "Let Jesus take the poor *grain of sand* and hide it in His adorable Face . . . there the poor atom will have nothing more to fear, it will be *sure to sin no more!*"? I think she does see or feel the sand absorbing wet tears. I am convinced that she does have a sharp impression of some infinitesimally small particle of sand being caught up in the scarred face of the Jesus of the Passion, and there hidden from all, from everybody but him himself. She ends the letter to Pauline in which she says these things with an amusing demurrer, amusing because in the course of denying meaning to her words, she uses the same devices which she is apparently shrugging off: "Dearest *Lamb*, understand the *grain of sand*, it does not know what it has said tonight, but quite certainly it had no intention of writing one word of all that it has scribbled." And all of this too may have still another meaning. Thérèse may be saying that she simply writes what she is commanded to write; the spirit speaks and her pen moves.

In every way, Thérèse was trying to make her will conform to the Lord's will. In her meditations she had become more and more convinced that she was afflicted with an inordinate degree of self-love. She saw the postponement of her profession as a nun, at the end of her first full year as a Carmelite, as more than just the intransigence of M. Delatroëtte. This was a long engagement which gave her time to prepare an adequate trousseau, and especially to bejewel her wedding gown with trials of a sufficient unpleasantness which she suffered with a sufficient pleasantness. She began to delight in ugly things and in deprivations. She stumbled almost happily to her cell when someone, by mistake one assumes, took away her lamp, the lamp with which she was used to lighting her way in the dark corridors. It was during the period of the convent's Great Silence, so she could make no inquiries or representations about it. She could have complained, however, when someone removed the pitcher from her cell, a handsome little jug, and replaced it with a large one that was chipped all over. She could have explained what had really happened, too, when the novice mistress, seeing a broken vase on the floor near Thérèse, automatically assumed that she had dropped it. She had had nothing to do with it, but she simply kissed the ground, in the consecrated tradition of penitent Carmelites, and promised to take better care in future. It wasn't easy to do any of this, she confesses. It cost her dear, is the way she puts it. It would all come straight on Judgment Day. Till then, it was apparent that when you do your duty, no one notices, but mistakes show up at once, for all to see.

Thérèse had asked for a hidden life. She did and she didn't have one. She went round the convent doing what she could of little jobs that nobody noticed, tidying up, folding mantles that Sisters had carelessly tossed away over chairs, doing whatever she could to bring ease to others and mortification to herself. When she sat in a chair, she tried now, as for so long she had before Carmel, to sit straight, according to the Carmelite rule, without leaning for support against the back of the chair—to symbolize the fact that the Carmelite leans on nothing but God. She was promptly told that she was developing a stoop: Lean back! Finally came word that her profession had been set for September

8 and at the end of August she was off on retreat in preparation for the great event and right from the very beginning she was subject to dryness. "The most absolute aridity," is the way she puts it. She felt almost forsaken. "As always, Jesus was asleep in my little boat." Let him sleep; he has enough to do for others; she won't bother him. He won't come altogether awake for her, she guesses, until the great retreat, the retreat of eternity. It shows, really, how far she is from being a saint, she concludes. Not enough fervor. Her faith too weak. And what excuse has she, she asks herself as she meditates on the retreat some years later, what excuse after seven years in the convent for sleeping through her prayers and religious offices? But still she is not greatly distressed. She thinks of herself as a little child lying peacefully asleep under the watchful eyes of its parents. She will be fed, she will be graced, whenever she needs to be. As she writes to Céline the month before her retreat, God sees us with the distance of eternity, already sees us in glory. Here, we live as in a mirage, in a dream, in which the reality is the leprous image Christ gives us of himself—she is moved to quote at length from the prophet Isaiah's eloquent characterization of the suffering servant, of the hidden and despised just man, which the Church has from the very beginning interpreted as a prophecy of the Passion of Jesus.

There are excruciating aridities on retreat, but no loss of perspective for Thérèse. She dreams, perhaps, but she dreams in the bright colors of the Song of Songs. Céline's weak heart makes her wonder if her sister may die soon; she asks for her as for herself nothing but a fullness of love. She had promised Céline, she writes Pauline, "to make profession for us both, but I shall not have the courage to ask Jesus to leave her on earth if it is not His will. It seems to me that love can substitute for long life." And if love can do all, if love *is* all, why worry about sensible impressions of love? "I do not desire love that I feel, but only love that Jesus feels." All, all is to be his, nothing hers, except that which comes from giving herself completely to him: "Tell Him to take me on the day of my profession if I am ever to offend Him again. . . ." She means it, I think we can be sure of that; she wants to arrive in heaven purified, without stain. One way to assure herself of that is to die now. Another way, this realistic girl, this honest girl, this daughter of Zélie, realizes, is a form of prevenient grace: "Jesus could very well give one the grace never to offend Him again, or rather to commit only faults which do not OFFEND Him, but merely have the effect of humbling oneself and making love stronger."

The notes tumble down from her exalted aridity to her sisters, in profusion. To Pauline: "My Spouse says nothing to me, nor do I say anything to Him either, save that *I love Him* more than *myself*. . . ." To Marie, who had asked the "little bride" if she understood "the celestial harmonies which already hymn our divine union": "I assure you that she is not hearing celestial harmonies! . . . Certainly her Spouse leads her by fertile and magnificent countrysides, but the *night* prevents her from admiring anything. . . ." The notes go back and forth. Thérèse exults in a papal blessing, which she had secured for herself through the good offices of Brother Simeon in Rome. She rejoices in a paternal blessing, secured through the good offices of Céline. Leo XIII's blessing was for herself and Louis, a response in grace for his gift to her of the trip to Rome. Louis's blessing was over the wreath she was to wear on her day of profession, a double blessing, as she arranged it, not only in words and feelings on Louis's part, but through Céline's placing of the wreath on her father's head, a symbolic action to show Louis's share in the offering of Thérèse to God, and at the same time to show Thérèse's part in the offering of Louis, to make the ceremony in effect a double oblation. At least this way Papa could be present at the ceremony.

At the last moment, like any nervous bride, Thérèse was not sure she herself should be present. She felt enveloped in darkness. Only one thing was clear—she didn't have a true vocation! She stammered out her terror to Sister Marie of the Angels, her novice-mistress, and that was enough. As she said them, her doubts vanished. Unquestionably, Sister Marie's gentleness helped. When Thérèse, to make her act of humility "complete," told Mother Gonzague about her "strange temptation," that worthy just laughed. When on the day of profession, she told Mother Geneviève, that splendid ancient did not laugh; she told Thérèse that she had had exactly the same doubts just before taking her own vows.

A great sense of peace swept everything aside on September 8. It was a day of many births, the day celebrated as the birthday of the Virgin in the calendar of the Church. Thérèse felt herself reborn. She was truly a queen now, with the privileges of a

155

queen: prisoners could be freed, the king could be persuaded to bestow favors even on his most ungrateful subjects. She yearned to empty purgatory, to convert sinners everywhere. She prayed and prayed, for everyone, but especially for Louis. She made, once again, a total offering of herself. In her *billet de profession,* composed by herself and worn over her heart, as Carmelite custom required, she voiced again her desire to die at once rather than commit a fault; she implored Jesus to take all of her: "let creatures be nothing to me and me nothing to them, so that you, Jesus, may be *all!*" She offered herself for a martyr's death, "in soul or in body, or rather, both." She wanted, she said, never to be a burden to the Carmel community; she wanted no one to be bothered with her, except as a grain of sand to be stepped on and forgotten. She asked that this day be one on which no soul should be damned and all the souls in purgatory should be saved. Finally, she asked Jesus's pardon if she had said anything she should not have said: "I want only to bring you comfort and joy."

Two weeks later, on the day before taking the veil, Thérèse had to face the fact that Louis would not be at the ceremony. His lucidity and composure in this period had made the Martins plan to bring him to the Carmel for the great occasion. But in the end M. Guérin thought the confrontation with his daughters in the convent would be too much for him and so Thérèse was left, as she wrote Céline, "all torn. . . ." Everything was ready for her "espousal," but something was "lacking to the feast. . . ." Consolation, as always, was in recognizing that everything will someday be added; for the moment, "our Spouse is a Spouse of tears not smiles; let us give Him our tears to console Him, and one day these tears will be changed into smiles of inexpressible sweetness!" They have no shelter, the Martins, not here on earth, she laments. They have thorns, as Father Pichon had written Thérèse from Canada. She copies out, for Céline to read, a passage from his eloquent letter: "Oh! my *Alleluia* is drenched with tears. Neither of your fathers will be there to give you to Jesus. Need you be much pitied here below when the angels in Heaven are congratulating you and the saints envying you? It is your crown of thorns that makes them envious. Love these thorn-pricks as so many pledges of love from the Divine Spouse!"

It was a good day, the day of Thérèse's veiling, thorns and all. It was another feast day of the Virgin's, of *Notre-Dame de la*

Merci, Our Lady of Ransom, celebrating the founding of the Mercedarian Order in the thirteenth century by St. Peter Nolasco and St. Raymond Pennafort. Under the patronage of the Virgin, the Mercedarians vowed to give themselves as hostages for Christians imprisoned by the Saracens. It was a vow Thérèse could well understand, with all her unquenchable ardor for souls, even to the point of martyrdom. She felt, that good day, a little like a hostage herself. Neither of the fathers was there; she was prepared for that. The Bishop had planned to come, and then to go to dinner at her uncle's house, but at the last minute he too fell ill. She was not prepared for that and she burst into tears, a rare enough occurrence by then with Thérèse to cause some remarks at the Carmel. But deep inside her there was peace, and a real sense of accomplishment. She had come through. Her espousals were complete, at least as far as the ceremonies were concerned.

A week later, Thérèse's cousin Jeanne was married to Dr. Francis La Néele, in Lisieux. When Jeanne came, soon afterward, to visit at the Carmel, Thérèse was full of questions about the way she treated her husband. She did not want to do any less for her Jesus than Jeanne did for her Francis. She delighted in the comparison of the two marriages and "amused" herself, she says, by working out a wedding invitation based upon Jeanne's; with parallel wording and typography:

Letter of Invitation to the Wedding of Sister Thérèse
of the Child Jesus of the Holy Face

Almighty God, Creator of Heaven and earth, Sovereign Ruler of the world, and the Glorious Virgin Mary, Queen of heavenly court, invite you to take part in the wedding of their august Son Jesus, King of Kings and Lord of Lords, and Mademoiselle Thérèse Martin, now Lady and Princess of the Kingdoms of the Childhood of Jesus and of His Passion, given to her as dowry by her divine Spouse, her titles of nobility being Of the Child Jesus and Of the Holy Face.

Monsieur Louis Martin, Lord and Master of the Noble Manors of Suffering and Humiliation, and Madame Martin, Princess and Lady of Honor of the heavenly court, invite you to take part in the wedding of their daughter Thérèse to Jesus, the Word of God, Second Person of the Blessed Trinity, now by the operation of the Holy Spirit made Man, and Son of Mary, Queen of Heaven.

As it was not possible to invite you on the occasion of the nuptial blessing, given on the Mount of Carmel on the eighth of September 1890—to which only the Court of Heaven was admitted—you are asked to come to the renewal of the nuptials, which will take place tomorrow, the day of eternal reckoning, when Jesus, the Son of God, will come on the clouds of Heaven, in the full state of His Majesty, to judge the living and the dead.

The hour being still uncertain, you are invited to hold yourselves in readiness and to be on the watch.

Sticky? Corny? Coy? Impossibly naïve? The performance may be all of these things and worse—"a document of blatant teen-age tastelessness," according to Ida Goerres—if you do not accept Thérèse's world of the imagination on its own terms and if you have no appreciation of a feminine flight of fancy. Call it credulousness, gullibility, whatever you like. Thérèse was only too ready to believe, but in what? In the precise terms of her wedding invitation? No more than Dante believed in his trip to the next world or any part of it, did Thérèse accept the literalness of "the sentimental, romantic betrothal allegories dear to the convents of her time," as Mrs. Goerres describes them. Her belief was in the affiancing of her soul and Jesus; that was quite precise, literal even. Her faith was in the absolute reality of her joining to her beloved, bride to bridegroom, soul to soul, person to person. In that sense, she took with dead seriousness her wedding garments and her wedding ring and the whole elaborate ceremony, first of the Clothing and then of the profession and finally of the veiling, as nuns have for so long and will undoubtedly continue to do. In the same context, she took with playful wit the language of the wedding invitation, neither so playfully that it had no meaning at all nor so seriously that she can be accused of adolescent foolishness. If these are signs (as Mrs. Goerres suggests) of Thérèse's "human limitations," if these are among those "respects" in which she shows herself what she "remained all her life, a provincial child, a middle-class girl who had attended school for barely five years," then they betray similar limitations in all the other passionate women who use the same kind of language, Catherine of Siena, Jeanne de Chantal, Teresa of Avila, Gertrude the Great, Mechtild of Magdeburg, etc., etc., etc. Thérèse had the misfortune, for the sensibility of her detractors, to write in late nineteenth-century French rather than sixteenth-century Spanish or fourteenth-century Italian or medieval Latin.

What the squeamish readers of Thérèse are objecting to is not her verbal style, really. They are objecting to the passion of the bride for the bridegroom in spiritual espousals. It is not only Thérèse who is guilty of "blatant teen-age tastelessness" but the Shulamite in the Song of Songs, who first presented lovers of God with such fervent language in which to express their love. Is there a better language?

NINE

*I*N the same year that Thérèse was born, 1873, Arthur Rimbaud wrote *Une Saison en Enfer, A Season in Hell,* the most considerable literary investigation of the lower world since Dante struck bottom. Amid madness and delusion, Rimbaud has visions of peace, of a "celestial and ethereal calm." He envies the saints their gift of prayer. In the farce without end, which is the life we are all condemned to lead, the prayer of the saints is strength.

In the years exactly contemporary with Thérèse's career in religion, the late eighties and nineties, the French Symbolist poets were agonizingly seeking the same vision. They were concocting myths and legends to help them penetrate the mysteries, or once pierced, to find some way of expressing their experience of the mysteries. They were mixing arts, finding correspondences and analogies in words, sounds, colors, events, persons, looking for some ultimate revelation which, they were well aware, if they ever discovered it, they would not be able to articulate. Some, like Mallarmé, were as determined to evoke purity as a chastity-obsessed missionary heaping clothing on a naked Polynesian. But Mallarmé, and many who came to learn from his poetry and from his talk about poetry at his Tuesday *salons,* courted purity by stripping away outer layers, not by adding to them. It is what you do not see that you see, what you do not hear that you hear. Silence must somehow be given a vocabulary. That elusive calm, celestial and ethereal, must be isolated in this earthly hell whose seasons we all know so well, too well, this noisy place, this murky place, this place crowded beyond endurance with images and impressions.

Mallarmé chased the phantoms of purity beautifully, ceaselessly, and without any real hope of catching them. He tried to trap them with a prismatic glass—at least a wandering ray, a trembling particle of the elusive light. He found an image, a sound, a form which may suggest to us what he felt—or tried to feel. In lines full of whiteness, of colorlessness, of suspended animation, he communicates something we should understand if our understanding has been counseled by Thérèse:

> *Le vierge, le vivace et le bel aujourd'hui*
> *Va-t-il nous déchirer avec un coup d'aile ivre*
> *Ce lac dur oublié que hante sous le givre*
> *Le transparent glacier des vols qui n'ont pas fui*

> This virgin, bright, and beautiful day—
> Will it tear open with a stroke of its drunken wing
> The hard, forgotten lake which haunts below the frost
> The transparent glacier of flights that have not been flown!

Chance stands in the way of Mallarmé. There are many great shudderings of wings, but the flights remain unflown. In the sonnet of which these are the first four lines, "sterile winter" inflicts its *ennui*, its terrible boredom, upon his days, upon the bird of his imagination, a swan. The swan's plumage is caught in earth. If we respond to the poem with any great feeling, we may be caught too, caught in an icy despair. But it will be, like Mallarmé's, a creative despair.

Thérèse never achieved such poetic crystallizations of her feeling—not in verse, anyway. But she came close enough in content, in texture of thought, in tonality of feeling, to be worth inspecting in this same context. When she sings her "Song of Today"—"*Mon Chant d'aujourd'hui*"—her perceptions are tuned to the same transparent glacial strings; her flights are also unflown:

> *Ma vie est un instant, une heure passagère,*
> *Ma vie est un moment qui m'échappe et qui fuit.*
> *Tu le sais, ô mon Dieu, pour t'aimer sur la terre,*
> *Je n'ai rien qu'aujourd'hui!*

> My life is an instant, a passing hour,
> My life is a moment that escapes and eludes me.
> You know, O my God, to love you here on earth,
> I have nothing but today.

The day is Thérèse's prism. In it she captures the wandering rays and trembling particles of her lover's light. The day has its purity: the day has its silences. Those are what she seeks, the silences. In the instant which is life, elusive as it is, silence can be caught and held. That is her prerogative as a Carmelite, that is her vocation as a virgin, that is her special majesty.

Virginity for Thérèse is not a negative state, though it does shut out all the noises of the world. But to feel what she felt, to know what she knew, we must think not of the absence of noise, but of the presence of silence, that deepest of silences, from which all cares are exiled, by which all cares are banished, and "not only useless cares," she writes Céline, "but *all cares.*" What is it to be a virgin? It is to be without any thought except of "the Spouse who will have nothing near Him that is not virginal. . . ." She rhapsodizes about virginity—Jesus's native land, the identifying texture of his life and of the lives of those in whom and with whom he lived his life on earth, Mary, Joseph, John the Baptist, John the Evangelist. All the rhetoric of Thérèse's musings on virginity is, like Mallarmé's on the virginal day, a rhetoric of whiteness—a "dazzling whiteness." Virginity is best configured by flowers, white flowers, by lilies and by the flowers of Normandy which she always gave to Céline on her sister's name day, little white asters. She didn't know the proper name of the flowers, so she called them "Céline-flowers."

On Céline's name day, October 20, in 1890, Thérèse sent her two of her flowers joined together on a single stalk: "one same sun caused them to grow together, the same ray brought them to blossoming, and surely the same day will see them die!" The rhetoric is transparent. The Céline-flowers are also Thérèse-flowers—but this she doesn't have to say; her sister will understand her, as she had understood her earlier when she signed a letter to her with the initials "C.T."—both names together, like two flowers on a single stalk. People do not stop to meditate on a little Céline-flower, Thérèse tells her sister; "yet its white cup is full of mystery," she says, speaking of its rather flat calyx. It contains quantities of other flowers in its double soul, and then, in addition, "its white calyx is red within, as though it were stained with its blood!" But most remarkable of all, she points out, is its sturdiness: "Céline, the sun and the rain can fall upon this little insignificant flower and do not wither it. No one thinks to pick it, so it stays virgin." It is a dedicated strength, like the gift of prayer Rimbaud envies the saints. Created by Jesus for himself alone, "it is more fortunate than the glowing rose which is not for Jesus alone." Once again she apologizes for her "stumbling words," though she is confident Céline will understand them, and once again, as she does almost always, she adds to her name in religion the identifying description "r.c.ind."—usually it is "rel. carm. ind.", meaning unworthy Carmelite religious.

The letters of this "unworthy" to Céline kept her older sister in close touch with the convent which she so longed to enter, but which, apart from this contact, seemed more and more remote to her. Céline could move about and among holy places. She went often on short pilgrimages in France; the letter in which Thérèse rhapsodizes about virginity was sent to Céline at Paray-le-Monial, site of the Visitation convent where their aunt had been a nun, where Léonie had made her second attempt at a conventual life and where she was eventually to settle down, a place consecrated for its associations with Margaret Mary Alacoque, who had also been a nun at the Visitation. Yes, Céline did get about, moving from Lisieux to La Musse and back again with the Guérins, and making pilgrimages, but Louis's condition generally determined her condition and Léonie's, and effectively limited the range of her movements. In Thérèse she had a direct contact with the life in Carmel that she was so eager to lead—and more, she began to live it through Thérèse, entered into its prayers with her sister, examined its spirituality, meditated on the requirements and implications of Carmelite life. Thérèse frequently uses the first person plural in talking to Céline, for they share their riches and their poverty, their famines and their feasts, their aridities and their graces; Céline's sufferings in the world, as Louis's doyenne, are Thérèse's too; Thérèse's sufferings in the convent, oblations to bring souls to salvation, are Céline's as well. They are in exile together, Thérèse tells her sister when she felicitates her on her twenty-second birthday, or rather on their dual birthday, which is a much more advanced one than twenty-two: "Do you know that we two together are forty, already? It is not surprising that we have already experienced so much, do you think?"

Thérèse cannot wish Céline what she would not wish herself— "not health, happiness, fortune, glory, and the like. . . ." With a garland of scriptural flowers, she toasts her stalk-mate, her soul-mate, for her good fortune, which is her bad fortune; she salutes all the sufferings she has had in common with Thérèse. "Together we have grown up," she exults; "together Jesus has instructed us in His secrets, sublime secrets which *He hides from the powerful and reveals to the little ones* [Matt. 11:25, Luke 10:21], together too we suffered *in Rome;* our hearts then were closely united, and life upon earth would have been ideally happy even if Jesus had not come to make the bonds that bind us closer still. Yes, in separating us, He united us in a fashion till then unknown to my soul, for from that moment I have been able to desire nothing for myself alone, but only for us both."

This was Thérèse's genius for taking advantage of everything, good or bad, everything, whether it seemed the result of mere chance or seemed to be directed by Providence. Separation was a grace for *C.T.*—Céline Thérèse—for the two sisters, yearning to be together, were actually drawn much closer to each other. In her eagerness for Céline's welfare, Thérèse found another way to conquer the excessive demands of self-love. Every affliction brought its signal compensation. The early deaths of their brothers and sisters gave the Martin children quick representation in the next world. Zélie's death, which was an affliction for the family, and Louis's sufferings, an even greater affliction, forced the girls to recognize that here below they were only in exile: "this foreign land has for us nothing but wild plants and thorns—but is not that the portion it gave to our Divine Spouse?"

Thérèse did her utmost to share her own tough-mindedness with her sister. This is the way it must be in the world, she says in dozens of different ways to Céline: those to whom we are most devoted sicken and die, like our mother, or suffer excruciating pains in a lengthy separation from this life, like our father. Mother Geneviève, to whom Thérèse expected Céline to be as devoted as she was herself, was in great pain throughout 1891, but we— you—I—the pronoun doesn't matter—must not be too sad; this is the identifying mark of the living. Besides, there was reason to be pleased. Mother Geneviève was in good enough condition at the end of July to participate in the celebration of the diamond jubilee of her profession as a Carmelite, a rich feast sweetened by the gifts sent by the Martin girls on the outside and the Guérins— fish, the provender that Louis was so delighted to offer, fruit, cakes, and a graceful letter from Céline to the venerable old foundress.

Thérèse brought Céline into her special works, her special prayers, her special concerns. Carmelites make it their particular work to pray for priests, something Thérèse had been doing with intense devotion ever since the trip to Rome. But now, in the last years of her life, she was particularly taken up with the case of an apostate priest, Hyacinthe Loyson, a Carmelite who had left his order, his celibate life, his Church. But had he really left? He and his wife frequented churches, making sweeping dramatic gestures of devotion, carrying with them a huge crucifix. He lectured all over France, gave great scandal to many, but also evoked the compassion of many. A great sinner, yes, Thérèse agreed, but all the more to be recommended to Jesus, who must wish to do something for Loyson, she was sure, or else why "would He have put into the heart of his brides a desire He could not fulfill?" At the end of her life, Thérèse offered her last Communion for the good of this ex-priest, and when he died in 1912, the large numbers who by then knew of Thérèse's concern were moved to hear from the Jesuit who occupied the position of "grand exorcist of France," Father Flamérion, that in his opinion Loyson was surely saved, and he gave credit for this to Thérèse's intercession. At the end, Father Hyacinthe, surrounded by clerics —from the Armenian and Greek churches, from Protestant churches—made some sort of peace for himself, saying over and over again, "O my sweet Jesus." No, there must be no end to our praying, Thérèse insisted, no weariness: "Confidence works miracles. . . ."

Thérèse's confidence was not entirely in prayer. She also used spiritual books as a resource in time of suffering, for herself and for others. While she was not a constant reader—she still spent hours "just thinking," in mental prayer that was less and less verbal, one would guess—she did have her favorites, those volumes she had learned at home and in Carmel to trust. Scripture is foremost—the Gospels most of all, then the Psalms and the Song of Songs, Isaiah, the Book of Wisdom, Ecclesiastes, Proverbs. At the convent she read Teresa of Avila and John of the Cross and it is especially John whom she cites in her letters and in her autobiographical manuscripts. And from home she brought with her a spirituality formed in the language and convictions of *The Imitation of Christ* and a very high regard for the Abbé Arminjon's *End of the Present World and the Mysteries of the Life to Come*, which had come to Louis Martin from the Carmel to begin with. It is a book she recommended warmly to her clients, those who came to see her at the Carmelite parlor to ask for help, for even the eighteen-year-old Thérèse, as some family friends of the Martins saw clearly, had wise counsel to offer. When a distressed woman insisted no book was worth anything to her, Thérèse asked Céline to give her Arminjon, for in his book "she will certainly find the answer to many doubts!" It was fitting that Céline should be entrusted with this mission, for she and Thérèse had read the book together in the Belvedere at Les Buissonnets, the year before Thérèse left for the Carmel. Céline would have the guile, too, to sneak the book into the young woman's possession without her husband or Mme. Guérin or anybody else knowing about it.

It is extraordinary how few people who have written about Thérèse know Arminjon's book. They depend, as Ida Goerres does, on a listing of the table of contents supplied by Abbé Combes, or on a few quotations that Thérèse had copied out from the seventh of the book's eight conferences. It is true that *Fin du monde présent* has been out of print for almost a lifetime, but not, as Mrs. Goerres believed when she wrote her biography, that it "can no longer be located." It has never ceased to be available at the Bibliothèque Nationale in Paris, from which I was able to obtain a microfilm copy of Arminjon as easily as I have other microfilms. And now, in any case, it has been reprinted, and the somewhat agitated speculation about its contents can be stilled, as of course it could have been years ago, if in the simple, conventional way of trained scholars, all those so deeply concerned had repaired to the extensive catalogues of the Bibliothèque Nationale, which all the great libraries of the world possess or to which they have access, and had checked the call number of the book and arranged for microfilming.

Arminjon's book is neither impossibly dull nor scandalously sticky as uncharitable and unreading detractors have assumed. It is, within the limitations of late nineteenth-century French spiritual writing, a passionate book. It is the book of a preacher, a retreat-master, formed by the Jesuits, himself for some years in charge of the seminarians at the major seminary of Chambéry, but always, before all, a giver of conferences. Eight of those conferences form the substance of this moderately heated eschatology, completed a few years before the end of its author's life. There seem to be in it more than a theologian's presentiments about the next world. It is no Dantean excursion. The writing is vigorous at times, elevated at times, and filled with the rhetorical inflations of a century that insisted upon its preachers writing out their sermons and conferences. Still, with all the limitations of its time and its genre, *Fin du monde présent* has an agreeable presence of its own, the effect of the Abbé's irresistible conviction about the life to come and the firm eye he keeps on eternity, so firm one sometimes believes he knows its geography like a guidebook. He offers his readers a fair share of tremblings before the terrors of damnation. He also invites their confidence, *une vive et inébranlable confiance,* a lively and unshakable confidence. For while we are only voyagers here below, with shipwreck always possible, we know exactly where we should be going to claim our great inheritance in our true home.

Thérèse liked that sort of language; she enjoyed reading it; she enjoyed using it. She couldn't be bothered about the clichés with which its pictures were made. She saw the reality where others saw—or see—only the dim images of reality, made dimmer by each uninspired repetition of a figure of speech which was less than strong to begin with. But since, for Thérèse, a just metaphor was much more than a mere figure of speech, the voyager-ship-wreck-inheritance-homeland imagery was entirely acceptable. It rested for its insights upon Scripture, and Father Arminjon assiduously canvassed Scripture for support of his eschatological doctrine. His first resource, always, was the Bible. After that foundation, he built a few arguments on lines from Augustine, Gregory of Nyssa, Bonaventure, Thomas Aquinas, Suárez, Ignatius Loyola, Bellarmine, Cornelius à Lapide, and one or two other glossers and commentators. His doctrine was sound. Through him, Thérèse was being introduced to the central traditions of Christian thought, researched with less than major force, perhaps, but more than superficially culled. She was wise enough, in giving advice through Céline to the worried woman to whom she recommended Arminjon, to suggest skipping the first two conferences of the book, "On the End of the World and the Signs That Will Precede It," and on the "Persecution by the Anti-Christ and the Conversion of the Jews." There, the Abbé is too literal-minded a reader of his august sources: his insistence, for example, on the Anti-Christ being Jewish and the product of what he calls an illegitimate union—those details and a chapter full of related certainties do not warrant continuing confidence in Father Arminjon or his book. But as he moves on—to deal with the resurrection of the body and universal judgment, with heaven, hell, and purgatory, with the final beatitude, the vision of God face to face, and with the machinery of redemption to be found in Christian sacrifice— he gathers strength, wisdom, and sureness of touch. When he comes in his ninth and last conference to the mystery of suffering and its direct bearing upon the future life, he delivers us into Thérèsian spirituality as earlier he had delivered Thérèse into the words and thought of a remarkable set of witnesses, from Job and the apostolic Fathers to a tale out of Joseph de Maistre about a young girl in St. Petersburg whose dignity and repose while being "devoured" by cancer inevitably suggest Thérèse's own behavvior at the end of her life. Arminjon's sensitivity to classical culture, as revealed in this conference, is touching. He uses Plato and Horace effectively, appositely. He moves with ease across a wide range of materials, and with more than ease, with sophistication. But he is naïve, too, and simple, as Thérèse was naïve and simple, full of apologies for the weakness of his book, as he ends it, but even fuller of conviction about "our apostolate." It is the apostolate of hope, the energizing force which directs the earthly pilgrimage. Remember how quickly the last hour approaches, he reminds his reader, his friend, *ami lecteur,* "when the heavenly Spouse who has loved and served us will say to us: *Move on, come to me, enter into beatitude and eternal rest!*"

There are elements of scholasticism in Arminjon. He was a systematic thinker. He discusses conflicting theory with a medieval monk's concern to see all sides—where there are many sides—and to give adequate examination to each. On whether or not purgatory exists in a specific place, for example, he finds impressive witness for an exact location in a letter of St. Augustine's (94, *ad Evod.*) in which Augustine describes Jesus's descent into hell, not only to rescue Old Testament figures from limbo, but also, on a supplementary journey, to deliver captive souls from purgatory. Against this, he cites opposing testimony from St. Victor and St. Gregory the Great. He examines the possibility of a material fire with which souls may be purged with the same attention to divergent views and leaves the answer where it must be left, in the realm of mystery.

Thérèse could find in *Fin du monde présent* a delicate balance of the scholastic and the simple believer. The Abbé was a trusting soul who was not put off by the possibility of apparitions and other miraculous events. He was also a trained analyst, acute enough to follow fairly complicated theological discussions to ends that were not ends at all, but necessary and proper impasses. Best of all, from Thérèse's point of view, everything was given coherence for him in the Christian doctrines of sacrifice and suffering. For him, we are all neighbors of death and brothers in pain. In the torments of their suffering, human beings confirm their sacredness, their relationship to Jesus, their imitation of him. He is positively eloquent in his glossing of the text of St. Paul in which he vows to "fill up those things which are wanting of the sufferings of Christ, in my flesh, for his body, which is the Church" (Col. 1:24). For, as he tries to show in some detail, the Passion was not ended on Golgotha. This is Thérèse's deepest point of contact with Arminjon. It was her constant prayer to relieve Jesus of some of his suffering, or at the very least to assuage it in part by suffering it in part. This was where life in general—and her own life in particular—became coherent. Her expanding consciousness was a growth in suffering. When she wrote Céline on her name day in 1891, the same year in which she entrusted her with the delicate mission of bringing Arminjon to a suffering friend, she described her growth and Céline's in these terms, the terms of suffering. The Céline-flower has been chosen for instruction purposes, she tells her sister; unlike all other flowers, it blossomed "a month before its proper time. . . . The frosts, the rigor of winter, instead of retarding it made it grow and flower. No one paid any attention, the flower is so small, so very ordinary. Only the bees know the treasures enclosed in its mysterious calyx, composed of a multitude of small calices all equally rich. Thérèse, like the bees, has grasped the mystery. The winter is suffering, suffering not understood, hated, regarded as useless by the eyes of the profane. . . ." She identifies the honey contained in the calices as souls, children, all of them, of the virgin flower.

Thérèse was making her symbolism of the soul well enough known to those close to her. She used her letters, her poems, her words set to music for the entertainment of the nuns at the Carmel. She drew doctrine into everything she did. As a gift for her aunt's feast day, she plaited some of her own hair, cut from her head on the day of her Clothing, into the form of a spray of lilies over a cross. She added to the framed picture a nicely turned compliment, reminding her aunt of the pleasure Louis used to take in her hair and would take in such a gift as this one, and telling her how pleased she was to give it to Mme. Guérin, "who, after my dearest father, is dearest to me in this life." The letter also contains tender memories of Zélie and Thérèse's deep affection for "a maternal heart," for "a mother's tenderness," and hence for her aunt: "Darling Aunt, since she has been upon Mount Carmel, your little Thérèse feels still more deeply, if possible, the affection she bears you. The more she learns to love Jesus the greater grows her love for her dearest relations."

Did Thérèse tell each of "her dearest relations" that she loved them each more than anyone else in this life? It sometimes seems so. Certainly her compliments to Pauline, Marie, and Céline vie with each other for intensity of superlatives. And certainly she lavished a thick lot of sentiments upon her aunt, with this general tone, placing her right after Louis in her affections. What could she have had in mind? Nothing, I would answer; she had nothing in mind. There was no guile in any of this. For Thérèse, writing to anyone at any particular time, was at that moment enamored of that person almost beyond all other persons. She gave herself in each of her letters completely. It was not the same sort of surrender with which she gave herself to her lover, but it participated in it—she surrendered precision of value judgment, she gave up all the distinctions that would have stood in the way of the unbroken warmth she felt as she addressed now her sisters in the Martin family, now her Sisters in Carmel, and now her aunt or uncle or cousins. Like a little child who calls each of a dozen colors her "favorite color," or, asked to name her favorite friend, lists one favorite after another, Thérèse had a whole corps of favorites, each one of whom was "dearest to her." Her salutation at the end of her aunt's feast-day letter is in perfect keeping with this practice: "Your little girl again sends you all her good wishes and begs you, darling Aunt, to believe in all the tenderness of her child's heart."

At the end of 1891, nearing the close of her nineteenth year, Thérèse was an astonishing mixture of a very little child and a fully grown woman, one well into middle age in her constant exposure to suffering, her own and others', and in her willingness to accept it, her own and others'. The sweetness and simplicity of her childlike self protected her from turning bitter and resentful under the assaults of suffering. The depth of her experience of pain and the maturity of her response to it kept the sweetness from turning into a cloying sentimentality and the simplicity from turning into simple-mindedness. She loved people very much, in spite of all her detachment from this world and her frequent derisive cries of "Creatures! Creatures! How they fail one!" Exile on earth was general. One shared one's banishment with others equally distant from home, from peace, from purity of vision. Difficulties there were, torments, even, but they were universal; affliction visited everyone. If, in this view of life, Thérèse sometimes seemed to emphasize the dismal and the despairing elements out of all proportion, she could just as easily be reminded of the sweetness and the simplicity which were also part of the human lot by some of those to whom these elements had been made attractive and convincing by her own example. So it was that Mother Geneviève, on one of Thérèse's regular Sunday visits, when the sick old nun seemed occupied with two other visitors, called to her to wait; she had just a word to say to her: "Everytime you come, you ask me to give you a spiritual bouquet. Well, today I have one for you: Serve God with peace and with joy. Remember that our God is the God of peace." Thérèse was deeply moved by this echo of St. Paul—"For God is not the God of dissension, but of peace" (1 Cor. 14:33). She felt that Mother Geneviève had spoken out of a supernatural insight into the state of her soul, but when she asked Mother, a week later, what special revelation she had been given, Mother said she had had none at all. That only convinced Thérèse all the more that Mother Geneviève was always moved in her words as in her actions by an acute awareness of the presence of Jesus, who seemed literally to live in her and to direct her.

When Mother Geneviève died, Thérèse had a sense of release; she was filled with joy. It was her first experience at a deathbed and it was *"ravissant"*—enrapturing. It was, she thought, as if Mother were sharing her happiness with her, and it reminded her that when she had said with fervor to the old lady that surely she would not have to go to purgatory, Mother had replied sweetly, "That's what I hope." The convent could look forward to a blessed intercessor in Mother Geneviève and Thérèse to another exalted confidante. When she saw, in the last moments of the nun, that one shining tear remained wet and bright on her eyelid, she longed to collect it for herself. She saw that it was still there when Mother lay in state in the choir and so she took a small piece of fine linen and gathered the tear as a relic to be carried always in the little sachet in which her vows were also locked away. Fortunately no one saw her do it; nor did anyone at the convent have precisely her experience dreaming about Mother Geneviève a few nights after her death. She dreamt that Mother was making her last will and testament, bequeathing something of her own to each of the nuns. When it was Thérèse's turn, it looked as if there were nothing left for her. But Mother raised herself up and said to Thérèse, not once but three times, and in a "penetrating" voice, "To you, I leave my heart."

It was not only Mother Geneviève who gave Thérèse heart in the fall and winter of 1891. On retreat in October, she was full of her customary dryness and was beginning to feel the temptations against faith which were to plague her off and on for the rest of her life. She even asked herself whether heaven really existed, she who had such great certainty of her own salvation! But she asked only herself. She did not ask the retreat master; at first she couldn't see how to put her doubts into words. Suddenly in the confessional, it all came right. As soon as she began to talk, the words came; she felt the priest, Alexis Prou, a Franciscan Recollect Father, understood her better than she understood herself. She felt her heart and her soul expand under the priest's direction. He told her that her faults gave no pain to God. Speaking as a priest and God's representative, he said he was sure that God was really pleased with her.

It was another assurance like Father Pichon's at her general confession when she entered Carmel. She had not fully grasped before this that it was possible to have faults that brought no suffering to God. That assurance overwhelmed her with joy; it was possible now "to support the exile of this world patiently." She expatiates on her joy; it obviously stayed with her a long time. God seen in this light has the qualities of a tender mother—but, of course, he is infinitely more tender than any mother. Nothing makes his mercy more clear to her than the caresses of her mothers. To Pauline, she says, "That's my nature: fear makes me curl up; with love, I don't simply move ahead, I fly." That's why she treasures Mother Agnès's readiness to forgive. She says she withered at a reproach, but that isn't altogether true. At least as far as one can see, she was quite up to the stern reprimands of Mother Gonzague and others in the community. When Sister Vincent de Paul, not long after the retreat, scolded her for her poor arrangement of the flowers which the Carmel received all the time from its friends, she turned a contrite and humble face to the nun, but showed no sign of inner curling. On the other hand, when Bishop Hugonin came to the convent on November 24 to celebrate the three-hundredth anniversary of John of the Cross's death, she beamed at the signal honor shown her when the Bishop took her head in his hands and gave her "a thousand caresses" of all sorts and kinds. It was another suggestion of the joys to come, a foretaste of the caresses of heaven. She was resigned to exile in this world, but she purred every time some of the loving kindness of the next world was evinced to her.

Caresses, verbal or physical, brought great balm to Thérèse's soul. She did not fight them off. Her spirituality required no such bleakness of response to human warmth. She thrived, like a hardy Céline-flower, in the winter frosts, but not because she rejected the sun. And the sun would search her out, would give her inner warmth, calm and confidence even in the most desolate circumstances; that was an aspect of her life which she herself was not always as clear or candid about as she might have been, though she certainly was not hesitant to admit it when she saw it clearly, as she did in the winter of 1891–92, when a terrible influenza epidemic struck the community and she was one of only three Sisters to remain on their feet. On her birthday in January, a nun died, Sister St. Joseph of Jesus, the first of three to go. Then two days later, the sub-Prioress, Sister Fébronie, died. And three days later, when Thérèse was getting up into the dark morning, she had a "presentiment" that Sister Madeleine of the Holy Sacrament was dead. And so she was. When she entered Sister Madeleine's cell, there she was, stretched out on her bed, the door open, no one paying any attention to her. Thérèse felt no fear, not the least. She simply went and got a candle for Sister Madeleine and a wreath of roses.

Thérèse was thankful for the strength that remained with her all through the epidemic and that made it possible for her to attend to the stricken community. She did it with such distinction that M. Delatroëtte, the canon who was the very least of her admirers and the last to grant her even grudging support, was forced to take notice, to approve, even to speculate about what graces the baby of the community had brought to it. This new approval, this too brought pleasure. But Thérèse's special enjoyment was to be able to receive Communion daily. Special enjoyment? She calls it an "ineffable consolation." She felt spoiled by her lover. What a privilege he had worked for her through the papal decree of 1890 that permitted confessors to decide for themselves how frequently religious communities could receive! It was a privilege Thérèse continued to enjoy even after the epidemic and she reveled in it, as she did in her duties in the sacristy. She was still a great toucher and she took particular pleasure in touching the "sacred vessels and in preparing the altar linen" for the Mass, that is for the coming of Jesus. She remembered as particularly apposite the lines from Isaiah (52:11) which are addressed to deacons at their ordination: "Touch no unclean thing . . . be clean, you that carry the vessels of the Lord."

This was the heart of Thérèse's life: she was doing every day what she had so longed to do and every day she was being confirmed in her vocation. The signs were abundant and Thérèse, without superstition, but with every respect for the signifying figures of the life of the spirit, even those which required very close scrutiny to make them out, never failed to find her signs. As in October 1890 she had found a pair of asters on a single stalk with which to salute Céline on her name day, so in April 1892 she found two daisies in the Carmel meadow with their stalks so tightly joined together that they became one. With this double daisy, she greeted Céline on her twenty-third birthday. It was a good sign, the two daisies on one stem; it was another opportunity to tell Céline that their double vocation, their mutual life in Carmel, was safe. They were still being watched over, still being protected.

Thérèse needed some signs to assure her that Céline was still directing her steps—and being directed—toward Carmel. The week before her birthday, Céline had been invited to a dance to celebrate the marriage of Henry Maudelonde, Mme. Guérin's nephew. It was a festive occasion for the Guérins and all their relatives. Thérèse worried about the extent of the festivity; it might distract Céline from her Carmelite ambitions; it might—well, who knew what it might do? Thérèse asked for some supernatural help. Keep Céline from dancing! That was her prayer.

Céline was actually a fine dancer; perhaps that was Thérèse's worry. But on the night of April 20, 1892, Céline did not celebrate Henry Maudelonde's marriage on the dance floor. The boy she was with begged her to dance; she would not—or could not. In some confusion and embarrassment, he was forced to escort her to her place—and then he disappeared. Another good sign—at least for a girl making her way into the religious life in 1892. Céline knew nothing of Thérèse's prayer, but she could not and would not dance, perhaps for the first time in her life. Thérèse's confidence in signs was increased, for as her forehead had been stamped by her lover with his identifying mark, so now had Céline's.

Another signifying event, the great one of the spring, was the return to Lisieux of Louis. His legs were now completely paralyzed. With the threat of vagabondage gone, Léonie and Céline felt quite capable of taking care of him. And so their uncle brought him to stay in a house just a street away from the garden entrance to his own house in Lisieux, with a cheerful man to look after their father, who was himself a most cheerful old man to look after. He wasn't always aware of his surroundings; his alertness came in waves. But just two days after the return, he was spry enough in all his senses to visit his daughters at the Carmel. What a meeting it was, the first trip of Louis since illness to the convent parlor—and the last. The girls talked; Louis responded with signs. His responses were all the more moving for being reduced to stiff gestures. He was an emaciated old man at this point, very thin, very weak, palsied. But in his great infirmity, he still preserved some of his dignity. He understood his daughters' words. He was still capable of some useful meditations of his own. When he left the parlor, he pointed up in the air with his finger and managed two clear syllables, "*Au ciel!*"—To Heaven!

It was possible to live something of a life with Louis at the house in the Rue Labbey which Isidore Guérin had rented for the old man and his two daughters. Desiré, the manservant, was tall and strong and quite capable of lifting Louis in his arms, so the old man was not condemned either to his invalid's carriage or to his armchair. There were days, too, when Louis could sustain the rudiments, at least, of a reasonable conversation. He took great pleasure in the music of Marie Guérin, who was a passing good pianist, and would respond to a performance he found particularly moving as he did to words that caught fire with him, as if entranced. But for all his moments of joy there were almost as many of unhappiness and anxiety, and of an equal intensity. He would cry out, "Pray, pray for me, children," and the tears would spill down his cheeks. Death was on his mind, when anything was on his mind, and he asked some of the time for specific prayers for a happy death. He looked and acted years older than he actually was, not almost seventy, but nearer ninety, a patriarchal ninety, however; he was a sad, sick, but still handsome old man, with unmistakable distinction in his ravaged face, and it stayed there till the very end, as the pictures of the next year and on his deathbed show clearly.

There was no separating of life in Carmel from life lived as a Martin. Thérèse was now, however indirectly, in constant touch with the affairs of her family. Louis's condition was reported to her in some detail in visits by Céline or Léonie or her aunt or her cousin Marie. She was always aware of Céline's suspended vocation and of Marie's steps approaching the Carmel. She was always aware of family needs, family illnesses, family problems of any kind. She knew that Jeanne La Néele had been praying to St. Anne because she wanted a baby very, very much, and she knew too that Jeanne had been sick in the fall of 1892, as her mother, Mme. Guérin, had been too, and she kept up a merry chatter in her letters to the Guérins, especially to Marie, to show both her concern for their well-being and her conviction that all will be well. She did not preach to the family any more than she preached to her Carmelite contemporaries, but she did constantly invoke prayer and extol it. Prayer was to her an unmistakably higher apostolate than preaching—she said as much to Céline in her summer letter, written to La Musse in August 1892—and she was always anxious to draw souls to it, and beyond all others the members of her family, for they were most easily accessible to her, and could be led up the mountain without too much trouble. It was her way of extending to those closest to her the graces of her state.

The outer forms of Carmelite prayer contained the inner strength for the kind of mountain-climbing Thérèse was so determined to make commendable to others, and especially her family. Hence, she frequently used the language of St. John of the Cross, usually in paraphrase or some other kind of adaptation,

176

occasionally in direct quotation. When she wrote Céline in the summer of 1892, she quoted from the "Songs between the Soul and the Bridegroom" of St. John, the opening of the fourteenth stanza,

> *Mi Amado, las montañas,*
> *Los valles solitarios nemorosos.* . . .
>
> My Beloved [is] the mountains,
> The lonely wooded valleys. . . .

At key moments in the autobiography, written three years later, she turned to St. John again, to the same set of verses, to find appropriate ways of explaining her intoxication with love—

> *En la interior bodega*
> *De mi amado bebí.* . . .
>
> In the inner cellar
> Of my beloved, I drank. . . .

How else to explain herself—except with more of the same? Drunken shepherdess, drunken lover, she would abandon everything, anything, everybody, anybody, for her beloved. She was stunned, woozy, crocked with love, and she didn't care who knew it—or rather, she did care; she wanted everybody to know it, starting with Céline and Pauline and Marie and going on through all the members of the family, perhaps a little more restrained as she came to the outer circles, but not so reticent ever that there would be any question about her condition. Perhaps others would emulate her example as she had followed her sister Pauline, first because she had herself so much wanted to do so and then because, once again, the signs seemed to point to her doing so when she was encouraged by her superiors to paint, just as her sister did, starting in the late spring of 1892.

It was Pauline's example that first inspired Thérèse to write poetry and to attempt to compose her own prayers. It was Pauline's example now that she held before her as she began to paint. Was there anything special about her painting? Did she show any marked skill for the art? Other nuns thought so, but the family continued to think that Céline's was the larger talent for painting and drawing, and if that was a fair judgment then we must assume that Thérèse's experiments in the visual arts were of no great importance, for the best one can say of Céline is that she

was an engaging primitive some of the time, a retoucher with
little taste or skill some of the time, and all of the time too little
tutored to be able to do much with whatever small grasp of the
art she had. The best thing that Thérèse gathered from her three
or four years of painting in the convent was another figure of
speech for her rhetoric, one which she used with enormous skill
to make a delicate point in the third section of her autobiography,
the one written for and addressed to Mother Gonzague.

All artists, Thérèse explains to Mother, need more than one
brush, at least one large one for the more significant strokes, the
central structure of their canvases, and at least one small one to
work in the details. Neither brush can, of course, take any credit
for the finished performance; that is all the artist's. Thérèse, the
little brush—could she be any other?—was first used on December 8, 1892, by Jesus to supplement the efforts of his major instrument in the community, Mother Gonzague. Thérèse never
forgot the date, perhaps because it was a major feast day, the
Immaculate Conception, perhaps because the work she did that
day involved so many masterly little strokes.

Thérèse had been very close to Sister Marthe of Jesus, who had
come to the Lisieux Carmel just a few months earlier. Sister
Marthe was eight years older than Thérèse, but like so many
older women, she felt at ease with the girl at once and made her
the recipient of all sorts of little confidences, of minor gossip, and
of major rhapsodizings about the older nuns, especially the Prioress, Mother Gonzague. The Prioress had quickly seen how well
the two novices got along and had decided that they should be
allowed to spend a fair amount of time together, using that time
for talk of spiritual things. But the talk stayed on a plane more
worldly than spiritual, and Thérèse thought she knew why.
Marthe was an innocent creature but a passionate one too. She
had bestowed her affections, with a great burst of emotion, upon
the Prioress. It was now Thérèse's responsibility to tell Sister
Marthe what she was doing and what was wrong with it. Amid
blushes, tears, and in Thérèse's enveloping arms, Marthe faced
herself and found herself capable of facing herself. See, Thérèse
said to her, see whom you really love. It isn't Mother Gonzague,
it's you yourself you love. Look, Thérèse went on, I had the same
sort of problem to face when I entered. I had to keep from developing an attachment to Mother Gonzague of this kind, an alto-

gether *material* attachment, like a dog's to his master. In order to arrest this feeling, Thérèse explained, she had had to make many sacrifices, but that was fine for love; love subsists on sacrifices and the more a person refuses natural satisfactions, the stronger his love becomes and the more selfless. Thérèse's little brushstrokes were amply supported by the large ones of the Prioress, she says, and both were directed, of course, by a lordly artist who was merely making use of them.

This is no conventional discussion of a commonplace conventual problem. It is an adroitly managed examination of emotional tensions that nuns have never noticeably been eager to discuss or even, I think, to admit to themselves. That today such problems should emerge in an occasional book or article or conference about the religious life is not really remarkable. Such realism is long overdue. But how impressive it is, really, that Thérèse should have had the quick wit and easy conscience that she showed in her conversation with Sister Marthe and in her discussion of that conversation in the pages of her autobiography. Her constant dreaming about her lover—her fantasy-life, as some have called it—had not unfitted her to face life as it was lived by those around her nor to deal with that life when she had to. One can believe, I think, that she felt an attraction to Mother Gonzague of the kind Sister Marthe felt and one can also believe that she knew how to deal with it. She didn't have to take cold showers— the only baths that were possible at the Carmel were cold, as her cell was, as the cloister was, as everything was. But in any case, Thérèse didn't have to suppress her burgeoning sexuality with such ancient and not too successful panaceas for rising passions. She had elsewhere to direct those passions and to the extent that her feeling for the Prioress continued to bother her, she had the resource of a strong will that had been made stronger with each of the delays in her entrance, each of the trials that stood between her and Carmel. Oh, she had her tense moments, all right, she confesses. How often as a postulant, she says, she made excuses to find the Prioress, to talk to her in her *dépôt*—her office —or anywhere else she might be, to spend time with her on any excuse. But she recognized the excuses for what they were and dealt with them severely. It meant rushing by the *dépôt* at a great speed or holding on to the banisters for dear life. She did it; she practiced her asceticism of the hallways and the staircases and she was amply rewarded for it, with the reward that is generally given, she says, to those who fight bravely against their temptations. Namely? The temptations cease to be a great problem. She doesn't have to suppress all her natural feelings; she admits them and transforms them into stronger and better feelings. Whatever her heart yearns for, it is a much smaller desire than her central longing, her longing for him whom she loves above all else. In loving him, she has discovered, her heart has expanded enormously. It has grown and grown, so that now she can give more affection—"incomparably more"—to those whom she holds dear than if she had yielded to a selfish and fruitless kind of love.

Thérèse apparently understood precisely what sort of attraction she and Sister Marthe had felt for the Prioress. She probably would not have called it homosexual; such words were no part of her vocabulary. "Material attachment" was one way of describing it; a "merely natural affection" was another for her. It was nothing much more, perhaps, than the strong affection young girls often feel for older ones as their sexuality begins to make itself clear. It was certainly no indication of sexual deviation of any kind. There was strength of feeling in Thérèse; there had to be. She brought to her supernatural love every natural gift for love, and among those, necessarily, would have been a thoroughgoing physical response to physical stimuli. When Thérèse opened her heart and soul to a person, she opened her arms as well. All her life she had been opening her arms to girls, to women—to her mother, to her sisters, to her cousins, to her aunt, to girls at school, to the nuns she visited at the Carmel, and now to the nuns with whom she lived at the convent. The men in her life were as few as could be imagined—her father, her uncle, Father Pichon, the Bishop and his vicar-general, three or four other priests, the retreat masters at the convent. Those she knew really well, with whom she lived closely, were exactly two, Louis Martin and Isidore Guérin. To them she gave exactly the same affection she gave to everybody else close to her: within the limits of a family relationship, an affection that could be called wild, reckless, abandoned, for she loved those near to her with that sort of passion. In it there were grave and formal handshakings, bows and curtsies, liftings by the arm. But there were also great enveloping embraces, suffocating hugs, nuzzlings under chins, squeezes, kisses—all the physical manifestations of love that children can show for each other and for their elders and their elders for them, but not, apparently, those claspings and graspings that push the relationships out of control.

It is unlikely that Thérèse often found herself under unbearable sexual tension. The extraordinary warmth of her family's affection, so eagerly and easily displayed, was one way of absorbing her own abundant tenderness. And then quickly enough she developed in her religious life the sexual passion which infused all her thinking and feeling about Jesus and gave to her relationship with him, whether in fantasy or in actuality, its great majesty. But she did have moments of attraction to girls or women—perfectly reasonable and understandable moments, without which she would not have achieved the stature she did as a theologian and psychologist of love. She responded so warmly and so spontaneously to other people's suffering because she knew it so well herself—all of it, or at least some part of every kind of suffering. She had had close relationships with other girls —two, to be exact—at the Benedictine abbey school, had given herself with enthusiasm to those friendships, and had been rebuffed, turned from in that clumsy parody of adult sexual rejection which children practice so entertainingly and so cruelly. She found herself drawn to Mother Gonzague, at her entrance in Carmel, with the fervor of a fifteen-year-old girl that has so much in it of an aroused sexuality. For all her precociousness, in this she was simply following the glandular chronology of the calendar. Her body-mind responses in this, as in some few other things, were exactly right; they were on schedule. As a postulant she felt what she called just a few years later "such violent temptations" —"I had," she sums up, "such violent temptations to get in to see you, just for my own pleasure. . . ." This was as close as she ever came, as far as any of the records indicate, to that sort of temptation. And even this was quickly dissipated, for everything was happily set against it, Thérèse's own conscious drive toward greater self-control, her overweening passion for her divine lover, and Mother Gonzague's own solid common sense.

The Prioress must herself have recognized the signs of inordinate affection in Thérèse as in other postulants and novices, and in older nuns as well. Devotion to her person was a commonplace at the Carmel in Lisieux; it accounted for her regular election to the post of religious superior, with the exception of that one odd upset in February 1893, when Pauline was chosen to be Prioress. There is no indication that Mother Gonzague ever encouraged any of these merely natural affections (so foolishly called "unnatural affections" in the euphemisms of family fiction), in spite of a certain tendency to pamper herself and her beloved cat and her insistence on maintaining something like a full family life, even in the convent, a life that had about it the marks of the kind of relaxed and decadent socializing that so appalled Teresa of Avila when she began her reform of the Carmel three hundred years earlier. Yes, Mother Gonzague regularly entertained in the parlor—saw friends who came to her with local gossip, had lengthy chats with her relatives day after day, put up her sister and her sister's children in the convent grounds and put the nuns at their disposal for all but the most menial tasks, for repair work of all kinds, sewing, painting, refurbishing family belongings. Yes, in all of this she was weak and self-indulgent. But Mother Gonzague was also iron-willed, cold-lipped, stern-faced in her personal relations with her nuns wherever or whenever any sexual tension arose—to a fault, perhaps. She kept her arms closed; if they embraced anyone, it was herself. It is hard not to believe that she knew exactly what she was doing. I cannot say, as Ida Goerres does, that "from the first day the Prioress treated Thérèse with incomprehensible sternness," or that her conduct toward Thérèse was a "cold repudiation of her loving heart." Rather, I think, we must accept Thérèse's own warm estimate of Mother Gonzague and simply assume that she lacked the sound instincts of a Thérèse in dealing with the embarrassing supererogation of affection that came her way. For her the best way to deal with it was not to deal with it at all or to turn flatly from it, to offer for every warm show of affection an equal and answering coolness. Besides, she always had her cat.

Thérèse's instincts *were* sound, psychologically sound, spiritually sound. They had been well rehearsed in conversation and discussion at home and with the Guérins and on both sides of the grille at the Carmel. They had been nurtured by brief but effective direction given to her and her sisters by Father Pichon. Her retreat masters at the convent had been unusually good, with unlooked-for discernment of spirits—her own individual spirit as well as those of the community at large. And her reading had been helpful. The books of the Carmelite masters had served her well, John of the Cross in particular. In her third and fourth years at the convent, at the ages of seventeen and eighteen, John had been, she says, her "only spiritual food." But afterwards, she found little satisfaction in such reading. More and more she was left dry even by such masters. She would open a book and find immediately that her heart was set against it; the words barely made sense to her as she read, or if her brain understood the words, her spirit did not, and she found she could not meditate, which for her was a nerve-racking experience. In this "impotence," as she calls it, her only resource was Scripture and the *Imitation of Christ*. In them she found the necessary purity of vision, the solidity, which were still capable of attracting her by means of words. But beyond everything were the Gospels, which spoke to her with the directness of persons. In them there was no end of meditative matter. In them was all the instruction she needed at this point. In them was generous confirmation of her own experience of God, by example and aphorism, by the word of Jesus and his disciples and apostles. God was within her; she felt it, she knew it. It was that feeling, that knowledge, that the Gospels fed. She started with her instincts, when she began her great pilgrimage to Carmel, as a little girl. She ended, in her last years at Carmel, with those same instincts. They were broadened now and deepened, by people and books, but whatever their breadth and depth and whoever their instructors, she was back again "just thinking," having gone through wise books and wise people to get to Wisdom itself.

Thérèse specifically rejects books and people at this point in her life, all but the *Imitation* and the Gospels, and even they have only a limited use to her. "Jesus has no need at all of books or of teachers to instruct souls," she thinks. "He, the teacher of teachers, he teaches without the noise of words." She says, in an important admission for one's understanding of her life with God, that she has never heard him speak, but that she knows he is with her, in her, moving her soul, stilling her soul, inspiring her when she needs to be inspired. When is that? When she least expects it. Light comes, oh, so many different ways, new light, odd light, good light, valuable light, but not often during prayer. As so many of his intimate friends say, so says Thérèse: Jesus comes most frequently *"au milieu des occupations de ma journée,"* in the middle of the work of the day. Like Margaret Mary Alacoque before her, like Sister Josefa Menéndez after her, she is surprised (one gathers) on her knees, in the course of a quick trip down a dormitory corridor, perhaps even in choir. The Lord is no respecter of person or protocol, even when the person is bent on doing his, the Lord's, business and the protocol follows rubrics that spring right out of sacred texts. Thérèse's interruptions are never as brusque or rude as Margaret Mary's or Sister Josefa's or any of the others who report long colloquies with Jesus that keep them from finishing their work, from sweeping up or making the bed or even listening attentively to their superiors. Thérèse reports no colloquies. The talk is all one way—from her to him. What he gives her is a leaping insight, a startling new perception, something that comes from inside her, where he dwells, the guardian truth within that St. Augustine spends so much time waiting for, whose counsel seems always to be available for the greatly attentive among the saints, such as Augustine and Thérèse, and for everybody else as well, according to these same experts, if everybody could just make the necessary sacrifice of time and attention.

The Lord is endlessly gracious, Thérèse is quick to add. He doesn't demand that everybody conform to the same pattern. His mercy is such that he offers himself in different ways to different souls and in so doing also reveals different aspects of himself, to be appreciated, a perfection at a time, by each of the different kinds of person. For Thérèse the center of any contemplation of God must be his infinite mercy; through it she sifts and examines, feels and is moved by all the other divine perfections. All, all seem to her to be infused with love. Even justice seems to be clothed in love. Even justice? Perhaps justice more than everything else. She cannot fear God's justice. He, who pardoned the prodigal son, won't he be just as just in his treatment of Thérèse, who, like the elder son in the parable, is always at his side?

If she prayed such prayers in the winter of 1892–93, Thérèse must have been delighted with her responses. It was a season of continual rejoicing. She broke into prayer and into poetry, an *Hommage* to the Trinity, composed for Sister Marthe, and her first formal poem, "*La Rosée divine*," The Divine Dewdrop. She was confident of her lover's favor, confident to the point of ecstasy—but ecstasy was not her way. Her way was littler. Her way was a bubbling letter at the end of the year to her aunt and uncle, full of love for everybody, with an entertaining salutation from

"Your ELDERLY Niece"—she was within three days of her twentieth birthday. Her way was a long letter of congratulations to Pauline who, on February 20, 1893, was elected Prioress of the Carmel. Thérèse bursts with pleasure: "If today is so beautiful even here upon earth, what must it be like in Heaven?" What joy for Zélie to see "the one she loved, the one who drew her most . . . become a Mother in her turn, the Mother of many virgins, among them her sisters!" What joy for Thérèse "to be able to give you that name!" It is, for the moment, her most satisfying pleasure, though she cannot say it as often as she would like to Pauline herself, but "One day, when the shadows have passed, I shall lie at rest upon your heart and say over and over the sweet name: *my Mother.*"

There were not too many shadows at first. In the first months of Pauline's regime, Mother Gonzague seemed willing to accept the change, and Pauline with some shrewdness appointed Mother Gonzague novice mistress. With a greater shrewdness still, she named Thérèse sub-Prioress, putting her in direct charge of her two good friends, Sister Marthe of Jesus, her old companion in the lists, and Sister Marie Madeleine of the Blessed Sacrament, a fairly recent arrival at the convent. Both were lay Sisters. Neither was likely to receive much useful guidance from Mother Gonzague. From Thérèse, both could expect loving supervision, guidance, and counsel. For them, the formal exercises of Thérèsian spirituality would now begin to be worked out, for two little lay Sisters. Were there any more appropriate subjects for the little way of Thérèse?

TEN

THÉRÈSE'S special skill as a mistress of novices was her ability to live at several levels of consciousness at once. Her acts
could be intentional or spontaneous, as situations required. She
could live with Sister Marthe through her crisis of love for the Prioress. She could translate her own experiences of rejection into the
rejections, real or imagined, with which every beginner in the religious life is afflicted, and with the deft use of a fragment of her
own life she could give rationality and dignity to the lives of her
poor affronted novices. She was, it is clear, an endlessly resourceful improviser, open to every divagation of mood and attitude
on the part of her charges as she was sensitive to her own vagaries
of tone and temperament. She had to be. It was an article of faith
to her. For in these changes of human texture, in others as in herself, she found the marks of divine direction. No matter how slight
the variation might be, to remain insensitive to it or unmoved by
it was to run the risk of not heeding supernatural guidance or
counsel.

Her method seems paradoxical, if we look at her own summary of her work as a director of novices. She saw immediately,
she says, that she was unequal to the task. Inevitably, then, she
gave the job over to more certain hands: "I threw myself into the
arms of the Lord, like a little child," and there, cradled against
him, she explained that providing such nourishment for souls was
beyond her. He would have to give her what the girls needed and
she would pass it on to them, implacably, she says, refusing to be
troubled if they were troubled. She would try to persuade them
that the direction came from God and she would not—could not
—look for any other. At the same time, she states what must seem,
at least superficially, like the critical answer to this procedure.
From a distance, it all must seem very simple—"doing good for

186

souls, making them love God more"; it's just a matter of modeling them after your own ideas. But close up, it's not like that at all. One must give up one's own ideas; everything personal must disappear. It is the way of the Lord that must be followed, not one's own way. But if she insisted that this way of the Lord, once she had perceived it, must be followed to the letter, was she not doing exactly what she wanted no part of—forcing her novices to adhere to her own views, to her own tastes? She may have insisted all she wanted on the high sanction for her commands, to her novices they were bound to seem her commands and only hers.

Thérèse was painfully aware of the difficulty anyone faces in giving commands and getting obedience, but that a superior in the religious life must find particularly troublesome. One gives orders as surrogate for God—Prioress, sub-Prioress, novice mistress, sub-novice mistress—anybody, everybody, who stands even the smallest step over anybody else in the community hierarchy. A mistake made in the name of the Lord is a particularly ugly mistake. In order to avoid such errors, or even the appearance of committing them, many religious superiors become either martinets or laggards, imposing a military discipline against which there is no appeal, or imposing no discipline at all. The result, then, is either a religious community which is distinguished only for its remarkable resemblance to the army or one which achieves a model chaos. In neither case do relationships often reach beyond the human. Either because there are no exercises or because there are too many exercises, the spiritual life of the community is slight or nonexistent. The encounter between the soul and the Creator for which the religious life was designed becomes the rarest of events. This, Thérèse could not conceivably accept. She would willingly do anything to encourage and facilitate the encounter to which she had dedicated her life. Paradox or the appearance of paradox—it wouldn't matter which—anything that brought her charges closer to Jesus, and herself with them, was acceptable.

Did Thérèse then have to find some golden mean between the ruthlessness of the martinet and the too great ruth of the laggard? No, I think not, for there is no such neat mathematical line to follow in human relations, and especially not in those relations between humans which are designed to end in union with God.

Thérèse would have to give the appearance of a drill sergeant some of the time, scrupulously observing and marking down every little infraction, the slightest fault or imperfection, while detesting this duty of hers, detesting it all the time. She was suspicious of those people to whom it comes naturally to tell others their faults. She would rather "a thousand times" be told her own faults than scold others. Those who enjoy fault-finding and scolding fully deserve the reproaches of novices who blame everything on the terrible temper of the novice mistress and nothing upon themselves. But still she must be on watch, like a vigilant sentinel. She must find the minute lapses, the tiny imperfections, and attack them like deadly enemies, even if in doing so she must seem so strict that her little Sisters think she is a true devotee of strictness, who runs after them and scolds them for the sheer pleasure of running after them and scolding, l'art pour l'art.

How, then, could Thérèse wrest any dignity for herself in this pursuit? How could she protect herself and her charges from that reduction of the most subtle and tender of vocations to a military performance the cruelty of which is exceeded only by its silliness? It is in this stage, after all, that the sweetness of the religious life is established or a sourness takes over that ultimately chases a soul out of community life or makes its continuing presence there poisonous to almost everyone else. Thérèse's simple answer is to let the Sisters say what they will—they must know how much she loves them, that she would give her life for them, yet, paradoxically, her love for them is such—"so pure," she calls it—that she would rather they didn't even know about it. "Never," she says, "have I tried to draw their hearts to me. . . ." Her job is to lead them to God and to realize that the visible form Jesus takes in their lives is that of the Prioress.

This is the point at which Thérèse could have become a stiff-necked and pompous little flunkey, in the worst possible way old before her time. But she didn't, if the testimony of her novices at the beatification proceedings can be trusted. We have, furthermore, her own emphasis upon the differences among souls—"They differ more than faces do," she quotes Father Pichon. There is no one way to treat them all. With some, she must make herself very small, humiliating herself, if necessary, by showing them her own failures, her own imperfections, her own struggles. Nothing brings a more fruitful rapprochement between Thérèse and her

188

novices than this fraternity of failure. Her charges are delighted to know that Thérèse speaks with personal experience of their faults, not out of a frigid application of a spiritual manual.

Sometimes Thérèse was cautioned by a novice not to use force. Gently, gently, she was told by a protesting young Sister. But nobody is a good judge of her own cause, Thérèse avers. She must be like the doctor who with some patients must prescribe a bitter medicine and insist on it all the more when his patients protest that the remedy is worse than the illness. Let them scream. Some souls are like that. You cannot change your mind or soften your ruling. That would be weakness, not humility. You know how right you have been, sometimes, anyway, when a day later one of these violent protesters, with whom you have been very strict, comes to you and tells you how she feels about the whole thing. Yesterday she was all ready to go to Reverend Mother and explain to her that she was finished with Sister Thérèse of the Child Jesus; she would go to her no more. But then, suddenly, she thought maybe it was the devil who was inspiring her and wasn't Thérèse really praying for her?, and listen, I have some ideas of my own on the subject—shall we discuss them? Fine, says Thérèse, who much prefers sweet conversation to bitter words, let's talk.

Here, too, Thérèse insists on being very cautious. Not too fast. Let's not upset the whole handsome structure, built with so many tears. One wrong phrase that even seems to attenuate the force of what she had said yesterday and all of Thérèse's careful planning will be destroyed. The recalcitrant novice will jump on that phrase and off they will go again, and again, and again. So Thérèse says a prayer—but only interiorly, deep within herself, not audibly—and "always," she says, "always, truth triumphs."

Truth did triumph, truth does triumph, but the action is never entirely supernatural. It is only in a confluence of the natural and the supernatural that such discernment of spirits as Thérèse practiced could have reached so far into the lives of people and could continue to do so now. Concentration on her lover—on divine aims and divine motivations—gave Thérèse a lively consciousness of persons, for as with any passion that is directed to a person, hers made her more and more aware of other persons, that is of those qualities in them that defined them as individuals, qualities that made each one in many fundamental ways utterly unlike all other individuals. But she was aware of these distinctions not simply as the passionate lover of a person, nor even as the ardent wooer of the second person of the Trinity, but as one who found in her great love personhood itself. What's more, she found it by a constant searching beneath surfaces. No religious exercise could reveal enough in itself. It needed a brooding kind of meditation, one that scraped the bottoms of words and went as far beyond words as this sort of intense probing could lead— into trance, one would say of somebody else; into some sort of abstraction more subconscious than conscious, one might say of somebody other than Thérèse. But Thérèse neither sought nor found extraordinary manifestations of her own fervor or of God's answering enthusiasm for it. No blotting out of awareness for her. Her affective states seem always to have been accompanied by some clear reasoning process in which she pondered events even as she experienced them. The pondering need not have been verbal. A reflective gaze of Thérèse's could have involved any organ of her body and I suspect that at one time or another her musings touched every organ of her body. For she functioned as a totality —body-mind-soul—and responded as a totality—body-mind-soul. And so to a ruly or an unruly novice, her response would have been the triumph of her own truth as well as of an intervening supernatural grace.

She speaks of God always being close to her, when she seems to be reading someone's soul. The novices taunt her—but admiringly—with having an answer for everything. They try to trip her up, with no success. God is there. But not God alone. Thérèse is there too. Her power of concentration, her summonings up of consciousness, gave her much of her penetration into states of soul. When she surprised a novice, who thought she had altogether hidden her anxieties from her, by asking her what bothered her, she was not exhibiting precognitive gifts or even perhaps any great talent for reading faces. She herself denies any such special skills and we must, I think, accept her denial. The wisdom of Thérèse is rather in the fullness of her consciousness, in her own sense of the fullness of human reality and the curious contrapuntal ways in which that fullness shows itself. Her own behavior always follows at the very least the interweaving motions of a two-part invention, such a simple canon, say, as "Row, row, row your boat, gently down the stream. . . ." Now her exterior line is clear, now her interior. And then, by a felicitous inversion, the interior becomes the exterior and the exterior turns inward. Thus it is that an unruffled surface is accompanied by an inner sense of humiliation, somewhere deep down inside Thérèse, but not so far down that it is buried in her subconscious. She knows about it, she thinks about it, no matter what sort of external self she shows to the world. And equally, when she appears devastated by some turn of events, by a run-in with the Prioress, or a protracted tension between herself and one of her novices, she may well feel inside her a continuing calm, a sweet peacefulness. She longs to make corrections in herself as well as in her novices. She wonders why the community doesn't recognize the defects inside, her foolishness, her poor judgment? If she were really seen for what she is, she is sure she would be scorned. But, she explains, she has been veiled by God, who has covered all her imperfections and faults, exterior and interior, with a disguise, and it is this disguise that attracts the novices and wins their compliments, not the real Thérèse.

Fortunately, there are times when her desire—her need, really —to be excoriated for her faults was recognized, if not by a nun or a novice, then by a beneficent deity who inspired one of them to curse her out, to provide some of the vinegar that her spiritual appetite demanded. She was as disgusted with a constant diet of sugary phrases as the most dyspeptic of her detractors. Enough of all that! Enough of sweet praise. "You know," she tells Mother Gonzague, "that I prefer vinegar to sugar. . . ." Vinegar and spices, please, she says. And then, happily, her request is granted. The veil is lifted and her "dear little Sisters" suddenly see her as she is and let her have all the acid and fire she wants.

Did they really see her? Maybe for a moment, or perhaps they saw some small part of her, either by seeing far into her or by recognizing, just as it came to the surface, some element of her interior life which in her counterpoint of emotions, thoughts, prayers, contentments, humiliations, faults and virtues, had just been made exterior. Did she really see herself? She distrusted anyone's acting as judge of his own case. She was, for all the fine edge of her consciousness and its fullness of lines, less than the best judge of her own case. She knew herself well enough, I think, at the far extremes of her life, whether those extremes complimented her or detracted from her. She was capable of an astonishing breadth of consciousness. But I wonder whether at any point she was altogether capable of experiencing such a polyphony of feelings—perhaps as much as a double-fugue's worth—and of judging them at the same time, or at any time.

It is enough that in her marvelous candor about her inner states and outer appearances, she goes so far beyond conventional expressions of spiritual malaise or self-deprecation and permits us, just as if we were her specially graced novices, to dig into her life and to recognize in it a full measure of human experience, the unflattering as well as the gratifying, the spiritually dry and empty as well as the grace-filled. And by the terms of her writing, just as by the terms of her relationship with her novices, to us "*tout est permis,*" everything is allowed us. We are free to say what we think, "without any limitations," to say the good and the bad, the favorable and the unfavorable. It is easy for her novices to treat her that way, she explains, because they don't have to give her the respect they owe a real novice mistress. And it is easy for us. She has made it wonderfully easy to take her up or put her down, like the most familiar and battered old possession, a family possession. She's ours, all ours, to do with as we like.

We tend to see in Thérèse all our own faults as well, perhaps, as some, if not all, of our virtues. She has laid herself open to such treatment, and deliberately, I believe. She knew that the only way to feed her lambs, as she was enjoined to do by her two prioresses, using the consecrated rhetoric of the last chapter of the last Gospel, was to offer herself to them. She did so with a moving openness of manner and honesty of phrase that, if it stopped short of the candor of the autobiography, went much further in self-analysis than novice mistresses or sub-novice mistresses or anybody else in religious life was going in those days. Like Sigmund Freud, whose first significant publications parallel her years in the convent, she was intent upon freeing as many as possible of those around her of their inner agonies, especially of those they didn't know they had, so that they might be left open to all the impulses of love which, in their agonies, they were truncating or even destroying altogether. Unlike Freud, she thought only in terms of a small community of nuns—at least to begin with —and unlike him, too, she could depend only upon one case history, her own. But that one she felt she could share, with varying degrees of completeness, with everyone with whom she had anything to do. She could confess her faults. She could admit with ease, almost with pleasure, her periods of dryness in prayer and her inability or unwillingness to search out "belles *prières"—beautiful* prayers—in books of *beautiful* prayers. It gave her a headache, she said, this looking for artful phrases with which to address the Lord. Her approach to prayer was precisely the same as her approach to her lover, simple and direct. Like a child who has not yet learned to read, she just said what was on her mind or in her heart. For her, prayer was an *"élan du coeur,"* a leaping of the heart, a simple lifting of the eyes toward heaven, a cry of joy or despair; but it had its own great energies and didn't need any borrowed ornamentation to give it the strength of conviction. All this, and more, Thérèse was happy to admit. Neither in dealing with her charges nor with her superiors could she pretend to be someone other than she was. She was one of God's great lovers, but she loved as herself, not as somebody else, and because she was so thoroughly honest about being herself she frees us too to be honest *about* ourselves and *to* ourselves in our spiritual life.

This is an honesty we underestimate at our peril. For if we cannot see the central importance to our sanity of recognizing what we are really like in those close bouts of self-examination which to a large extent prayer must be, then we are unlikely ever to discover who we are. Worse, with every protraction of our unwillingness to face ourselves as we actually are when we pray —or when we yield to whatever urgings of the heart may pass for prayer in our lives—our identity slips further and further from us. For the fact is that it is not enough to fall into the conventional language of prayer. There must be some real confrontation with ourselves before there can be any significant lifting of the heart to God. Children do it easily—most children, anyway—until they are taught to overlay and interrupt their colloquies with elegant phrases, with decorative indirection, with all the multiplicity of evasion with which prayer life has become cluttered over the centuries. Even the most consecrated practices can at times be nothing more than an evasion. Even the most hallowed of approaches to God, hallowed by millions of performances over thousands of days and nights, even they can become a way of deceiving ourselves about ourselves. Thérèse had no compunction about admitting the simple facts: "saying the rosary is harder on me than scourging myself with an instrument of penitence." She tried very hard, but it made no difference. She could not fix her attention on the mysteries of the rosary. She could recite it in common. The fervor of her Sisters' piety supported and bulwarked her own. But alone—nothing!

A small thing, this? Perhaps as people living in the modern world think and act, it is of no great consequence, but for a nineteenth-century Carmelite nun, it was like confessing a terrible secret vice to admit to this failure to get anything out of the meditations of the rosary. And even today, in a lay Catholic environment and in the religious life, if there were any large-scale defection from the rosary, with open admissions like Thérèse's, there would be great scandal. How many would dare to be as bold as Thérèse in writing her pages for Mother Gonzague—to say that the rosary is a scourge for her, a whipping of her soul more fearful than a lash of a chain across her body? And how many, that terrible truth acknowledged, could be serene about their relationship with God or the Mother of God?

Thérèse found her serenity only at the edge of desolation. She had to confront herself steadily, closely, in the raw center of her spirit, before she could face the emptiness she felt saying the rosary alone. She had to reflect on her love for the Virgin and be certain that it was exactly the kind of love she thought it was. That it was, two things seem to prove—one, that her invocation of Mary was constantly and quickly responded to; and two, that she was able finally to achieve the necessary serenity in the face of her utter lack of devotion to the rosary and absence of feeling for its way of commanding and organizing prayer. It certainly wasn't the prayers themselves. The Our Father and the Hail Mary remained central to her life. In the grip of aridity, it was enough for her to recite these fundamental prayers of the Church, to recite them *very slowly*—she italicizes the adverbs—and she was once more close to God, her soul nourished much more than if she had rushed through them a hundred times. She was a client of the Virgin herself, not of her beads. She made direct appeals for aid, with the simple confidence of a child that the appeal would be heard and answered and with the disrespect of a child for anything that is superfluous or gets in the way.

Nothing superfluous was allowed into Thérèse's conduct of the novitiate either. As much as possible, she treated the souls under her the way she treated herself. She scheduled no formal conferences at all in the years she acted as mistress of novices, until the replacement of Pauline by Mother Gonzague as Prioress, in 1896, and even then her instruction hardly deserved the name of "formal," although she used the standard Carmelite sources —the Rule and Constitutions of the Order, its great Testaments of Carmelite spirituality, and the somewhat less sacrosanct Custom Book. Her examination of doctrine and tradition was dialectical; she talked things over with her novices, with some heed to Scripture but even more concern for common sense and common experience in her exploration of theological and psychological points. She was full of hypotheses, Céline tells us, especially in her weighing of one novice's complaints against another. Now let's see, she would speculate, what if what you say is true? What happens then? By such conjecture, entertained in a very deliberate manner, she would lead her novices to mitigate or altogether to dismiss their own complaint, perhaps even to take the blame for the other Sister's fault. As Céline records so well in her memoir of Thérèse, *Conseils et Souvenirs*, a cloistered nun is often capable of bearing up with heroic strength under physical torture, but may find the *"menus incidents,"* the petty incidents, of convent life more than she can take. "My chalice," Céline quotes an old religious as saying, "is community life."

Thérèse worked hard with her novices to prepare them for a life of petty incidents, to which they would have to bring a heroism as great as torture might require and far more readily accessible to them. Torture is, after all, a rare occurrence in Carmel. It has been centuries since the Mitigated Carmelites of Toledo threw John of the Cross into one of their dungeons and left him for nine months to subsist on a daily ration of one piece of dry bread and a single sardine. Thérèse knew the dry bread and sardine diet of the spirit; she lived on it much of her time in Carmel. It usually took the form of other people's orders, which so easily shatter our happiness and peace. Everything has been fine until suddenly we find that we cannot have our way; our opinion is pushed aside, contradicted, overruled—then what do we do? If we follow Thérèse, as she tried to persuade her novices to do, we welcome the opportunity to follow that ancient piece of advice from the *Imitation of Christ* to be submissive to everyone, which means, Thérèse told Céline, actually to rejoice when we are blamed for something. She recognized the difficulty of this. Our face may betray some of our tension, as we take criticism, even if our words do not. Others may see that we are still far from perfect. So much the better; we can be happy that others think us imperfect and even say it out loud. So the very difficulty adds to the quality of the humiliation and we make more and more progress in this essential channel of spiritual development.

Humility above all things, that is Thérèse's leitmotif in her spiritual direction. "It seems to me," she tells Céline, "that humility is truth." It is a truth she finds everywhere, whether or not she herself achieves an unmistakable humbleness of spirit. It is a truth she proposes that her novices revel in: "It is so sweet to feel weak and little!" When Céline records this dialogue, she is quick to add a footnote exonerating Thérèse from the possible charge that she accepts sin or faults passively. Shades of Mme. Guyon and the Quietists! Please, no heresy here! Nor is there any, for all of Thérèse's emphasis upon trust in divine mercy, even to the point of a daring abandonment, and with it an accompanying acknowledgment of our human frailty. No, we may not merit forgiveness all by ourselves, but we can move some distance toward a just pardon with our openness to our own defects, our sweet openness, our humble openness. This is where good will enters Thérèse's speculations and becomes the mechanism of her therapy.

Céline, once she became a Carmelite novice herself and was entrusted to Thérèse's direction, was led through the course of self-abandonment, rejoicing in her defects, looking for the happiness of humiliations—everything that Thérèse had discovered just before entering the convent and had reinforced in practice in her half-dozen years in Carmel. Céline complained to Thérèse that for all her ardent desires to become "sweet, patient, humble, charitable," she was getting nowhere. The more she craved virtue, the further from it she fell. She found some solace in a passage in the life of St. Gertrude in which that exemplary religious was counseled strongly by Jesus to cultivate good will above all things, for everything that was in the virtues was established upon a foundation of good will. Céline brought the passage to the attention of Thérèse, who had another example for her, from the *Life of Father Joseph Surin*, the seventeenth-century Jesuit who found himself so grievously involved in the affairs of the nuns at

Loudun who were thought to be diabolically possessed. After an exorcism that he had performed, according to the *Life* of Father Surin written in the 1870s by Marcel Bouix, some of the little demons told him that in spite of their wide conquests they were helpless against "this little watch-dog of *good will.*" So, said Thérèse, "there you are. If you have no other virtue, at least you have a little watch-dog that will save you from every danger. Be consoled; it will lead you to Paradise." And in the same conversation, Thérèse reminded her sister that everyone wants to possess the virtues. Who among us doesn't? But how rare it is to find someone who will willingly accept the stumbling, bumbling life our weakness imposes upon us, and happily will see himself fallen, prostrate, and just as happily allow others to see him there in that abject position.

She insisted upon good will in such a way that those who followed her, through anecdotes from the saints and the devils, and maxims out of the *Imitation,* and incidents from her own life, could understand that what she really meant was a kind of sweet detachment about oneself first of all and then about others. One would have to view oneself from a distance, just far enough away to see oneself with accuracy and honesty. Stop blaming the weather or weariness in your bones, she tells her sister. See your discouragement as a mode of humiliation. Enlist yourself where you belong, among the *petites âmes,* the little souls, since you can practice virtue only so feebly. Never mind, she says, never mind about heroic virtue. Accept these humiliations as valuable reminders of your imperfection. This way, she explains, Céline will not become smug about herself, but with every reminder of her defects will find herself prodded to think of her true stature and not to seek a specious glory.

Thérèse was neither practicing nor recommending a sense of failure in the life of the spirit or a groveling before men as a sign of abasement before God. Humility above all, yes, but not what we should today call masochism. Let others think what they may of us; if they judge us critically, they don't really hurt us; if we judge them favorably at the same time, we all gain from the exchange. We must not stab ourselves with our wretchedness, but we must keep the right spiritual distance. She tells Céline with evident relish the story of a man with a great reputation for holiness whom a bishop came to see, surrounded with the pomps and the people his station permitted. Seeing the episcopal procession coming toward him from the distance, the holy man was for a moment tempted to think of himself with pride. He quickly chastened himself for the moment of vanity and seeing some children nearby playing on a seesaw, he took one step down and took his place among them. When the bishop found the man seesawing away with the children, far from thinking him a saint, he took him for a madman. So it is, says Thérèse to Céline, with some of us who are not strong enough to take praise. We must sacrifice even "an apparent good" to achieve our sanctification. Rejoice, then, when you fall, and if necessary contrive to stumble clumsily as a means of humbling yourself. But even this must not turn into an extravagance of self-abnegation. As she tells her sister in her annual birthday letter in 1893, no extra-fine thoughts, please, no complexities conceived to please "our beloved." No, she says, "it is not intellect or talents that Jesus has come upon earth to seek. He became the Flower of the fields solely to show us how He loves simplicity." Because it is so difficult to remain pure, one must not be too conscious of oneself. It is Jesus's delight to contemplate souls beloved to him, souls only He notices; "and they, not realizing their value, think themselves below other creatures."

Thérèse's letters to Céline in 1893 are an addendum to her autobiography of delicate beauty. With that gift she had for preparing those around her for the depths of the riches to come, she was leading Céline into the cloister, and not simply into the cloister but right up to the *mysterium tremendum* at its heart. Yours is the most select of missions, she tells Céline, and "all the more beautiful because, while you remain the visible angel of our dearest father, you are at the same time the bride of Jesus." She anticipates Céline's rejoinder: "'That is true,' perhaps my Céline thinks, 'but after all I do less than the others for God, I have many more joys and therefore fewer merits.'" And she answers her out of the great forty-fifth chapter of Isaiah: "'My thoughts are not your thoughts,' says the Lord. Merit does not consist in doing or giving much, but in receiving, in loving much." Her specific for all spiritual problems is summed up concisely in the middle of this letter, sent to Céline at La Musse in July: "O Céline! how easy it is to give pleasure to Jesus, to enrapture His heart! All one has to do is love Him, not considering oneself, not examining one's faults too closely. . . ."

She had been writing at a tremendous rate, until her ink ran out and she had to spit into the inkwell to make some more—"that makes you laugh, doesn't it?" She might have made one of her homely parables out of the event. Certainly it reflected her little way perfectly, and in her next letter to Céline she found an analogous situation upon which to moralize. We must feed the fire of love—she echoes Teresa of Avila. When in our darkness—our aridities—we can find no wood, what can we do? We are "obliged at least to throw little bits of *straw* on the fire." Of course Jesus needs no help in keeping the fire going, but this "delicate attention" delights him and then he responds by heaping the fire with wood. Thérèse knows what she is talking about. She has done just that: "when I *feel nothing*, when I am INCAPABLE of praying or practicing virtue, then is the moment to look for small occasions, *nothings* that give Jesus more pleasure than the empire of the world, more even than martyrdom generously suffered. For example, a smile, a friendly word, when I would much prefer to say nothing at all or look bored, etc. . . ." Rejoice when you fall, that is what she is saying again. If necessary contrive to stumble clumsily as a means of humbling yourself.

There was peace for a moment in the Martin family; it had been possible to bring Louis to La Musse this year, into the great park of the château, onto the knoll over the Iton River where the big house sat in its splendor. There Céline could meditate in both comfort and solitude. Léonie left on the twenty-third of June for the Visitation convent at Caen; her mind was now firmly set on the religious life after a visit to Paray-le-Monial; "now at last," Thérèse wrote her in August, "our saintly Aunt's prediction is fulfilled. The child of Blessed Margaret Mary is in the Visitation, and for ever she will be the bride of Our Lord." Thérèse took great joy in Léonie's vocation, but "obviously" her joy must be "wholly spiritual, since from now on I am never again to see my dear Léonie here below, or hear her voice, or pour out my heart in hers." But they can look forward to the same end, in heaven, and to reunion there with the whole family, "our dearest Father . . . ringed about with glory and honor for his perfect fidelity, and above all for the humiliation of which he has drunk so deep; we shall see our kind mother, who will be full of joy at the trials which were our lot during the exile of our life, we shall enjoy her happiness as she gazes upon her five daughters in religion, and we shall join with the four little angels awaiting us there. . . ."

Céline did not, however, have uninterrupted peace in which to probe and settle her state of soul. When the Guérins returned with her and Louis from La Musse to Lisieux in August, she found herself with servants who were not entirely trustworthy, especially the woman of the pair, who had at first seemed to offer such warm and competent assistance in taking care of Louis. "Your poor servant," Thérèse called her—"to have such an ugly fault—dishonesty is specially ugly—but perhaps you might convert her like her husband." A novena to St. Joseph that Céline had made had brought the man back to Christian practice; why not the woman? But even if a conversion is not quick to come, this is simply another of the inevitable miseries of exile. Thérèse compared Céline to a peach despoiled of its surface beauty but absolutely safe and whole within, in the kernel of its being, and in her next letter applied a passage from the Song of Songs to her sister's scarred life: "What do you see in the bride, but choirs of music in the camp of an army?" Céline's life, she comments, "is indeed a battlefield." But she can still sing the songs of the Lord; "her life must be a *melody,* 'a choir of music.'" She heaps comfort upon her forlorn sister. For after a blissful summer with her father, who had come marvelously alive listening to the song of the nightingale in the La Musse forest and had looked with joy all around him from the high château at the great country feast spread before his hungry old eyes, Céline had come home to a wearying fall. There was the servant trouble; Louis was not so easily aroused by the back-street gardens of Lisieux as by the La Musse countryside. Céline was fixed all the more, at least in the kernel of her being, upon Carmel. Thérèse's effulgent rhetoric was well placed. Céline needed every consoling word, needed urgently to believe, as Thérèse wrote, that it was indeed doubtful whether God had "often made two souls that understand each other so well: never a discordant note. Jesus's hand, touching one lyre, instantly sets the other vibrating. . . ." With such loving consolation, with such buoyant support, Céline's vocation never faltered. She remained faithful to her Lord, to her convent, to her sister; she must have believed she was already with her sister, in Carmel, a bride of Christ, even if not clothed and veiled and professed. If she believed anything Thérèse wrote her, she must have

200

believed this; she was assured of it often enough and winningly enough. Certainly she was as far removed from the world, though living in it, as any nun at the convent.

In part, at least, because Thérèse was looking forward with such expectation to Céline's physical entrance into Carmel, she was not particularly disturbed at having to remain in the novitiate even when her official time was up in September 1893. Three years after profession one was supposed to leave the novitiate; that was an almost inflexible rule. But there was another rule, or "interpretation" of a rule, as Céline calls it, which prohibited more than two members of the same family taking part in the chapter of the community. Since Pauline and Marie had already been admitted, Thérèse was automatically precluded, but not at all to her unhappiness. She remained the *doyenne* of the novices, their dean, until her death, and by doing so was in a position to guide Céline through her first years in the convent and to give her life there the remarkable foundation her own considerable distinctions deserved.

Thérèse never missed an opportunity to link herself with the other members of her family. For even when most deeply absorbed in her speculations about the nature of worldly exile, and fully aware of the multiple separations which tear families apart, brother from brother, sister from sister, child from parent, and especially severely those who are in the religious life, Thérèse held firmly to her family ties. Her vision of heaven was filled with families, more tightly united than ever before. Her life on earth, insofar as she was able to control it, was always a family life. She had discovered herself, found her identity, plighted her troth, declared her love and followed its urgings as a member of a family. Where else, how else could she have been so early and so deeply involved in Carmelite life? With what other father and mother would she have been so warmly encouraged to seek a supernatural relationship as a little child? What other family could have provided such a succession of substitute mothers? In what other kind of environment could the sedulous courting of the most passionate possible encounter with God have been so warmly encouraged, and more than encouraged, positively solicited? Even the Guérins, with all their devotion to the Church and an intense religious life, when faced with the desire of Marie to follow her cousins into Carmel, showed themselves lacking in the Martins' kind of unquenchable passion, a thing in itself not altogether surprising; such furious love is not merely uncommon, it almost never attacks a whole family, much less two families, even when they are as tightly intertwined as the Guérins and the Martins. Thérèse did not propose to lose any of the ardor with which her family had been so remarkably endowed, so much more than any other she knew or even knew about. Unless forced to do so by the command of her superiors, she would not diminish any of her sweet and intensely satisfying relationships with her family, neither in the parlor nor inside the cloister nor on letter paper. She would not—she did not—neglect her duties. She didn't seek long sisterly conferences and indeed when Pauline was elected Prioress she kept herself at a discreet distance so that Mother Agnès should never be accused of showing favoritism to her family or her family judged wanting in respect for conventual decorum. She did write notes to everybody, at all times, under almost every set of circumstances, meticulously getting permission when permission was required, using scraps of paper, torn halves of used stationery, anything to conserve the convent's niggardly supplies. And she never wrote frivolously, just to fill in her time or to entertain those with whom she corresponded. She wrote as a theologian and director of souls, really, though she would never have applied such high-sounding titles to herself. She wrote, as she directed her few novices, to explicate her own relationship to Jesus and to lead others, especially those in her own family, to the same exalted intimacies—those who shared one form of kinship with her should by all means share the other.

At home, Léonie had never been very close to Thérèse, or at least not as close as Pauline, Marie, and Céline had been. But when Léonie entered the Visitation, she was automatically lifted to a special rank of tenderness and concern. She soon became her "darling Léonie," her "darling sister." The faint marks of formality which one may spy in the first letters from the Carmel to the Visitation quickly disappear. Léonie must be saluted now on her name day. Like Céline, she is worthy of a running commentary on the religious life, on its bleaknesses and blessednesses, and most especially on the way in which one may seek and find Jesus in the world of the cloister, under what guises, in what conditions. She never forgets, either, that Léonie has twice failed to sustain her vocation, and subtly or openly she extends her support in this too: she tells Léonie that her letters show her to be really happy now—"I do not doubt that God is giving you the grace to remain forever in the ark of holiness." In case Léonie forgets for a moment the stature of her community, or thinks that others—especially all the other members of her family gathered together at the Carmel—may forget it, she tells her that they have been listening in the refectory to the life of St. Jeanne Françoise de Chantal, the foundress of the Visitation, and that it is "a real joy . . . to hear it, it brings me even closer to the dear Visitation, which I love so, and again I see the intimate union which has always existed between it and Carmel, which makes me bless the good God for having chosen these two Orders for our family." When Léonie received the Visitation habit on April 6, 1894, and took the name of Sister Thérèse-Dosithée, Thérèse was overjoyed. The family ties could not have been more overt in the names, her own patron saint united with the name in religion of their aunt who had been a Visitation nun, Sister Marie-Dosithée.

To Léonie, Thérèse confided her doctrine of littleness and humility but with rather less insistence than she did to Céline. Léonie deserved more congratulation on having come through the wintry exile in the world that led her to this final solace, and so she sent her a letter bursting with the radiant words of the second and the fifth chapters of the Song of Songs—"Winter is now past, the rain is over and gone. . . . Arise my love, my beautiful one, and come. . . . Open to me, my sister, my love. . . ." She sees Léonie touched by the same love that animates her own days, eager to receive it, open to the full expression of that love: "He desires to give you His *kiss* before *the whole world,* so that none may fail to know that He has placed His sign upon your forehead and that never shall you receive any other Lover than Himself."

It was not necessary to stress the hardships of this world to Léonie; she had known them well enough, firsthand. She had lived all her life at some remove from the family. Her years at the Benedictine abbey school were as a boarder, not, like Céline and Thérèse, commuting from home. She was never a significant part of the budding Carmelite cloister within the family. She was not one of Thérèse's adoptive mothers. She was worried over by Zélie and clumsily befriended by a family servant, whose attentions, at first endearments, turned to perverse commands before

Zélie intervened to break up the relationship. She stumbled into the religious life and stumbled right out again, as a Poor Clare and a Visitation postulant, before finally finding her ease in the community at Caen, and even there she had to undergo trials again, the shock of her father's death, the departure of Céline for the Carmel, the final isolation from her family, forever. No, there was no need to emphasize the miseries of this world to Léonie. The troubles she had seen had made her an expert. For her the key notes were of union, with Jesus and with her family in the life to come. After Louis's death, Thérèse asked Léonie, "Darling Sister, are we not still more united, now that we can look toward Heaven and there find a Father and a Mother who offered us to Jesus?" Hold on to this vision of the future—that was Thérèse's continuing advice to Léonie, that and her own great confidence in Léonie's ability to sustain any trial now, to be asked for any sacrifice, to take any suffering.

If Thérèse ever said to herself in 1894, "All my confidence is in my confidence," the brilliant, terse prayer of Claude de la Colombière, she would have said exactly what she should have said to describe her state of mind and the behavior that followed from it in that remarkable year. She was at the very beginning of the year herself beginning to suffer the pains in her throat that anyone else would have taken in fear and trembling to a doctor, pains that presaged something quite as serious as the tuberculosis that followed soon enough. But in her judgment, this was nothing important, or if important, was only more of the kind of suffering she had asked for and now must welcome in good spirit. Besides, what was the point of complaining? As a postulant, she had been ordered by the novice mistress, Sister Marie of the Angels, to tell her whenever she felt stomach pains. She had felt them every day and loyally reported them every day. With what result? Sister Marie, forgetting what she had required Thérèse to do, came to a simple conclusion, "Why this child does nothing but complain!" So now Thérèse made up her mind by herself: no more complaints; full confidence in the Lord.

With the same certainty of judgment she went ahead with her painting and her poetry, with the composition of prayers that spoke directly to the conditions of her novices and with the preparation of quite elaborate *Recréations pieuses*. What with her extensive correspondence, her direction of souls in and out of the family, her work as assistant novice mistress, her menial jobs in the convent and her life of prayer, alone and in concert with the other nuns, Thérèse was a very busy Sister. She had a particularly active January. For her sister Pauline's first feast day as Prioress, January 21, 1894, she painted a picture of "The Dream of the Child Jesus," which is no merely sentimental outpouring, for while the infant is seen clutching flowers in his hand, behind him, equally visible, is the Holy Face, a chalice and host, and the instruments of the Passion. The Child dreams of "the happiness of His beloved bride," Thérèse wrote in an accompanying commentary on her picture. But in the distance he "catches glimpses . . . of strange objects bearing no resemblance to spring flowers." The flowers—Thérèse explained in a note which further explicated her commentary—represent Mother Agnès's virtues. These flowers—these excellences—given to Jesus by Pauline to comfort him on earth, will be returned to her in glory in the world to come. Thérèse ended her second note with a tender plea to Pauline to lead her "still towards the Beloved. . . ." She wanted that skill in the virtues that her sister and superior could teach her so that in heaven she might occupy a place not too far from Pauline and so that Pauline might still "recognize me as your child and your little sister."

To fill out the community's ceremonial observance of Mother Agnès's feast day, Thérèse wrote the first of eight religious entertainments (*Recréations pieuses*), celebrations in prose and verse of signal feasts—three were for Mother Agnès, given on successive January 21s, in 1894, 1895, and 1896; two were for Christmas, in 1895 and the next year; and the others were written on the occasions of a feast of the lay Sisters, a golden jubilee of a nun, and Mother Gonzague's feast day, once she had become Prioress again. From the first, these were fairly ambitious little entertainments, lacking any very precise dramatic structure (though at least two were divided into acts or scenes), but tidily set to familiar tunes and allowing the community's actresses a considerable histrionic range, from Joan of Arc, and a substantial number of the royalty and nobility of France and of heaven, to the Holy Family. If they followed any religious or literary tradition, it was that of the medieval Lauds or sacred representations; those attestations of piety often enough allowed room for a vigorous spirituality and a vivid poetic talent, as is shown by the performances of such very different writers as Jacopone da Todi, the thirteenth-century Franciscan who is sometimes credited with creating the first Christmas carol, and Lorenzo de' Medici, who is often credited with being the most gifted of literary politicians.

All the late winter and early spring of 1894, Thérèse was occupied with composing handsome compliments in prose and verse, in letter and prayer, for her family, for her friends, for her novices—for her favorite people. To Céline Maudelonde, cousin of a cousin and an old school friend, she sent felicitations on her approaching marriage, not conventional congratulations at all, but memorable words of hope and encouragement, of delight in the "great peace" she sensed in Céline and of pleasure at what she could offer her old friend, even from Carmel: "The grilles . . . are not made to separate souls which love each other only in Jesus; they serve rather to strengthen the bonds that unite them." To Sister Marie Aloysia Vallée, the teacher of Pauline and Marie at the Visitation, she sent first a copy of her painting "The Dream of Jesus" and then warm acknowledgment of the nun's enthusiastic response to it, full of her own enthusiasm for the Visitation, whose mothers must really be hers too, she says, "seeing that they formed the heart of the *two angels* on earth who acted as my mothers in fact." For Céline on her twenty-fifth birthday, she painted another little picture, prepared a letterful of meditations on Céline's vocation, and a poem, "The Melody of Saint Cecilia," saint of abandonment, as she identified her in the letter. The poem is not a masterpiece, however one looks at it. It moves easily along its alexandrines and clicks its alternating rhymes neatly into place. It says its say, of love and renunciation,

> The love that does not fear, that falls asleep and loses itself
> In the Heart of its Lord, like a little child. . . .

It says its say, and after one hundred and twelve lines collapses of genteel exhaustion. There is more vitality in the succeeding poem, written about ten days later, a *Cantique* "to obtain the Canonization of the Venerable Joan of Arc." In it, a soldier speaks his mind in support of Joan and the Church as a compliment to "the valorous *chevalier* Céline Martin," to whom the poem is dedicated.

There were other poems of the same sort that spring. One, "The Portrait of a Soul that I Love," was written for her sister Marie's feast day (now that she was Sister Marie of the Sacred Heart), June 1, the feast of the Sacred Heart. Another was dedicated to her old companion in the novitiate, Sister Marthe, a "Song of Gratitude to Our Lady of Mount Carmel." The real accomplishment in verse was none of these, however, but one written at the request of Marie, "My Song of Today," surely the best of Thérèse's early verses, the one that begins

> My life is an instant, a passing hour,
> My life is a moment that escapes and eludes me

and returns regularly and reasonably and sweetly to its insistent refrain,

> *Rien que pour aujourd'hui!*
> Just for today!

The meaning? She can take the suffering, she can bear any trial, for one brief and passing day; and what a reward for just this day's tedium, the reward of "eternal today."

A few weeks after producing her poems for Sister Marie of the Sacred Heart, another Sister Marie entered the Lisieux Carmel, Sister Marie of the Trinity, and for her Thérèse quickly indited four little prayers, terse, bright with hope, and mounting in loving intensity to a crescendo of passionate ejaculations. This newest of the novices was soon enough to become Thérèse's favorite among them. She had, like Thérèse, made an early entry into Carmel, at the age of seventeen, in Paris, but she had fallen sick and had had to retire for several years before entering Carmel again in Lisieux. Into her quite willing and entirely worthy hands were thrust these prayers. There were two to the Eternal Father, asking him to open heaven's gates "to an uncountable host of little ones," and also asking him, in return for the offering of the Face of his Son, that blessed inheritance of Thérèse and all others who would claim it, "to pardon all poor sinners." The third, to the Holy Child, asked for all the necessary graces and virtues to make the supplicant recognizable in heaven as the "little spouse" of the little Jesus. The last leaps into burning rhetoric— "adorable Face of Jesus, the only beauty that ravishes my heart. . . ."—and willingly forswears the sweet glances and ineffable kisses of Jesus here on earth, as long as she may carry his likeness in her heart, so that he may not look at her without seeing himself; she begs him, too, so to inflame her with his love that she may be quickly consumed and rise to see his face in heaven.

Thérèse's thoughts were very much upon heaven, even more than usual. The Guérins had been able to take Louis with them once again to La Musse in May, but he was very weak, it soon became apparent, and on May 27 he was anointed; he seemed about to die. He recovered briefly, but it was not likely to be a long recovery. The news from Léonie in June was not good either. Her recovery of her vocation was a tremulous one. And then came word from Céline that she might be going elsewhere than to the Carmel after Louis's death. There was always the possibility that the ecclesiastical superior of the convent, M. Delatroëtte, would prevent her entering as once before the fourth member of a family had been refused entrance. There was, in addition, a request that Céline could not make clear, which she could only talk about in disguised terms. Father Pichon, seeing the likelihood of her being refused permission to enter the Lisieux Carmel, had suggested another work for Céline, a projected religious foundation in Canada, where he was stationed. To this last set of possibilities, Thérèse responded with a great outburst of words, a long letter in the middle of July, full of love and sympathy and more than a hint of the suffering that even the possibility of lifelong separation from Céline brought to Thérèse. "Never, never will Jesus separate us," she cried. "If I die before you, don't be afraid that I shall be far from your *soul*, we shall never have been more united! That perhaps is what *Jesus wants* to make you realize in thus talking to you of separation. But above all do not be alarmed, I am not ill. . . ." She suggests they forget all this talk of the future, but she cannot quite stop herself. There must be a little more about the storms she has passed through that Céline must now experience before she can relax into genial conversation about Marie of the Trinity and send a bouquet of remembrances to "all the dear travellers" at La Musse. There is much, then, that indirectly seeks to keep Céline's gaze fixed on Carmel, and at the same time to offer consolation if she should be forced to go elsewhere. She doesn't neglect to send her most recent poems, set to religious music, and to ask her to show them and "My Song of Today," which her sister Marie had sent to Mme. Guérin, to her cousin Marie. There was to be no lack of communication in the family, no matter what trials or separations it had to face. It would storm heaven as a unit.

Louis's earthly storm was finally at an end. On July 28, two months, almost to the day, after his anointing, he was once again *in extremis*, and this time to stay. But his death had the requisite majesty for such an old courtier of the Lord. His breathing remained fairly strong and quite even until nearly the very last second. He kept his eyes shut, until early in the morning of the twenty-ninth, when in response to three invocations of the Holy Family by Céline—"Jesus, Mary, Joseph, I give you my heart, my soul, and my life . . . assist me in my last agony . . . may I breathe forth my soul in peace with you"—he opened his eyes, looked directly at Céline with tenderness clearly written on his face and, says Céline, with "inexpressible gratitude," his eyes "filled with life and understanding," before he closed them for the last time. Céline was devastated by the death agony, but not for long; there was good purpose in Louis's death, after such an anguishing terminal illness, and there seemed even to be supernatural signs accompanying his departure. In any case, Céline took great comfort in a luminous globe that she saw shining in the sky on the night of Louis's death, when she woke suddenly from a fitful sleep. She looked, she saw its brightness, and then watched it slowly disappear in "the immensity of heaven."

M. Guérin's allegorical figure for the patriarchal old man was an old tree, with beautiful pieces of fruit on it. As each one ripened, the Holy Child passed and made a sign over it, and each time, without complaint, the old tree bent down and let one of its pieces of fruit fall into the hands of little Jesus. "What a great soul!" Isidore Guérin exclaimed in his letter to Marie Martin: "Beside that man, we are pigmies!" The funeral Mass was held at the Lisieux cathedral, with a separate service at the Carmelite chapel. On the family's mortuary card, the symbol chosen by Louis's daughters as most fitting for him was a picture of the Holy Face, framed by texts associating Christ's suffering and Louis's, at least by implication, ending with a prayer that the girls certainly offered with fervor: "Lord, hide him in the secret of your Face!"

The Holy Face was a good sign for the family. Under its aegis, Thérèse had offered Céline to her lover's service. Under its protection, her own vocation had prospered. Under that name,

Céline would soon enough enter Carmel, under that name two others, as Sister Geneviève of the Holy Face and of St. Thérèse, a commemoration of all the great benefactors of Thérèse Martin, not the least of them the co-foundress of the Lisieux Carmel. Céline was herself very clear about her destination. If the Carmel would have her, that was where she wanted to be. Father Pichon would have to get along without her. "In the end," Thérèse says, it was Louis, her "darling King, who never could stand slowpokes, who hastened to straighten out Céline's entangled affairs. . . ." One day, when everything seemed impossibly mixed up, Thérèse spoke very directly to her Lord and lover: "You know how much I want to be certain that Papa has gone right to heaven. I don't ask for a word, but do give me a sign." If there were no further opposition from an old Sister who was then the only obstacle to Céline's entrance, then she would know that Louis had gone straight up. The first person Thérèse met after making this prayer, was the old Sister in question, who asked Thérèse to go with her to Mother Agnès's room, where, with tears in her eyes, she spoke warmly to Thérèse about Céline. The signs were clear, about Louis, about Céline, and, of course, about Thérèse, who had, after all, invoked them.

ELEVEN

*A*ND now," says Thérèse, a few pages before the end of the autobiographical manuscript she wrote for Pauline, "there is nothing else I want except to love Jesus madly." The only childish desire she still has is to arrange flowers on the altar of the Holy Child, and even that has lost much of its savor since she has been given the flower she wanted most, Céline, the most exquisite anyone could offer. She wants neither death nor suffering, though she is attracted by both—love alone really appeals to her. She used to think that with suffering she would be gliding along the shores of heaven, and that her death would be an early one—"that the little flower would be plucked in its springtime." But now abandonment is all; resignation to God's will provides her with her only compass.

Thérèse no longer reads John of the Cross; she prays his prayers, instead; she lives his life. She enters with him into the wine cellar of her lover's heart, and soaks up the love she finds there. She flames with her love, as she was gathered into it. Yes, she says, "you may fall, you may commit infidelities, but love, knowing how to profit from everything, quickly burns up anything that may be displeasing to Jesus, leaving only a humble and resounding peace in the depths of your heart." Oh, she says, with a heart bursting with love, if everyone had graces such as these, no one would fear the Lord. He would be loved madly all the time and by everybody. And out of love—not in fear and trembling—everyone would take care not to bring him pain, displeasure, sorrow.

Her meditation at the end of this, the longest by far of her three autobiographical statements, is a burning one, in which the rhetoric sears the pages. She tells Mother Agnès about her own experience of love, the experience that led to her great Act of

211

Oblation, offering herself to God's "merciful love," rather than to the divine justice which claims so many eager victims. Her eagerness is to make this love better understood, to draw others to it as she has been drawn, to be consumed in it as she has been consumed. "O my God," she cries, "is your despised love doomed to remain imprisoned in your heart?" If the demands of God's justice, she reflects, extend to the ends of the earth, how much more strength and love must there be in God's mercy, which reaches right up to heaven!

As mistress of her own small community of novices, Thérèse did not neglect the Rule. She inculcated its every codicil, by the letter and by the spirit, as best she could, in fairly formal lessons and in allegorical explications in poetry and prayer, which she wrote at a great rate in 1894 and 1895. But the Rule was significant only for what it offered the soul of love. And "significant" is the word: the Rule signified love, it was a whole series of emblems proclaiming the marvels of the encounters of love—if you would only search them out assiduously enough, scratching away at the surfaces of the words until you had found the profound meaning at the center, locked away inside the words. Thus, for example, you followed the injunctions of poverty, as Thérèse did, even to the point of the most narrow-minded literalness, or so it must have seemed to those lacking the spirit to follow the letter so closely until it revealed the spirit. Thérèse scraped the gilt off the ends of the pages of the books she was given for herself; she rubbed the shining gold from holy pictures whenever she found it a distraction from the poverty of holiness or the simplicity of love. She had been pleased to lose each of the attractive implements of her cell—her pitcher, inkwell, and holy water font, one by one. When somebody did not take one from her, she gave it away. She gave Céline several of her things in September 1894, on her entrance into the Carmel, not the nicest things—they were already gone, and besides they would not have inspired Céline with devotion to poverty—but serviceable ones, in fairly good repair, and she found replacements, as close to useless as they could be and still be kept, in the Carmel's attic junkheap. When her workbasket was about to fall apart, one of the other nuns took pity on her and pulled the bedraggled old thing together with an ancient velvet ribbon which could be used for nothing else. But while acknowledging its usefulness, Thérèse wanted—again—

nothing in which she could take pride of possession, nothing with which she might find herself distracted; she turned the velvet over on its drab side and gave the basket its requisite impoverished appearance.

Thérèse's acts of mortification were all of this sort. She simply took the day as it came, with its multiple opportunities for self-abandonment. Each sacrifice was enough in itself. She was content to do what each moment presented to her. When a novice rubbed linseed oil into her humble cell desk, she insisted upon the same girl's scrubbing it all away; she wanted the original drab finish, or something as close to it as possible; she was mildly disturbed that a certain sheen remained from polishings by previous occupants of the cell. When she was forced to borrow something —Céline instances a penknife—if she could not return it at once, she left it outside the door of her cell, to indicate that it was not an object she was allowed to have in her cell. For her poems, she used any piece of scrap or waste paper she could find, the back of an old used envelope, half a piece of notepaper, anything. For her autobiography, she used two school notebooks of the cheapest kind, that she had asked Léonie to buy for her—one at a time. She was surprised to find she needed a second—she was never willing to waste a sou by inexact anticipation of her needs. She ate as little as possible, within the requirements of the rule to keep one's health as best one could; she had little taste for the social experience that mealtime brought and no taste at all—at least no expressed taste—for one kind of food over another. She found it difficult to eat at all while anything closely related to the life of Christ was being read, especially the details of the Passion during Lent. When she found that certain foods pleased her a great deal, she mixed bitter-tasting herbs, such as wormwood, with them, and practiced a parallel mortification when a bitter-tasting medicine was prescribed for her by drinking it very slowly. "Greater penances are forbidden me," she explained to Céline, who tried to stop her doing some of these things, "so won't you let me profit by these small opportunities?"

Self-denial never reached the point with Thérèse of insisting that others follow the same asceticism: what she denied, she denied herself, not others. She did counsel a constant awareness of the other. At recreation, she told her novices, go to entertain others, not to enjoy yourselves. This sort of self-denial she did encourage, but only in such a way that if it were practiced no one would be aware of it except the one perfoming its delicate little exercises. For example, when you are interrupted in telling a story, she told Céline, even by someone who bores you with her interruption, don't try to go back to what you were saying, "and in this way, you will leave recreation filled with great interior peace. Because there was no self-seeking on your part, you will find yourself endowed with fresh strength for the practice of virtue."

Special strength came from that special exercise of abandonment which is best summed up as leading the life of hiddenness. In the parlor, and frequently at other times as well, Thérèse would speak only after someone had spoken to her, even if it left some friends or relatives with the impression that she was not quite right in the head. She delighted in the presence of her family; she wrote notes to her sisters and stayed, within reason, as close to them as she could, but that did not mean breaking the Rule or coming anywhere close to the point of breaking it. In fact, she was so anxious to keep her sisters from turning their relationship in Carmel into a mere extension of life at Les Buissonnets, that she asked them please to hold their confidences with each other to a minimum, to ask for no special parlor permissions except when they had something useful to offer a visitor, and to be particularly alert about these things after her death. But that did not mean she would not spend as much time with a visitor as was necessary, if it were really valuable for the visitor, and especially if she could offer her time and counsel unostentatiously. Nor was she ever without great warmth for those close to her, however little the surface evidences of that warmth. She was not one of those holy people who thought they had to sever all family ties. There are many mansions in our Father's home—whenever she dwelt on that text, Thérèse made clear which was hers: "Mine will be not with the great saints but with those little ones who always retained a great love for their family."

Her way of showing her love for her family was not exactly hidden, but it was not obtrusive either. She wrote poems and prayers for Céline, but she also wrote them for other novices. She composed *recréations pieuses* for Pauline, after she became Prioress, with clear relish, but she did handsome service in the same genre of religious entertainment for other nuns as well. And even when she wrote directly for one of her family, her sentiments were never so specialized or her love so personalized that what she had written could be understood only by the person for whom it had been done. They all demanded, really, to be shared, and they were.

The fifty-three stanzas of *"La Cantique de Céline,"* like her long Act of Consecration to the Holy Face, were written to solemnize the happy events of the late winter and early spring of 1895, when Céline took the Carmelite habit and later when she celebrated her birthday for the first time inside the convent. The long Canticle opens with Céline's childhood, but it is any childhood of grace, destined to be completed in a womanhood of grace:

> Oh! how I love the memory
> Of the blessed days of my childhood!
> To keep the flower of my innocence,
> The Lord surrounded me always
> With love.

She remembers for Céline, in verse after verse, her affection, "in the springtime of her life," for Jesus and Joseph and Mary and every reflection of heaven on earth. In the poem Céline loves, each in its turn, wheatfields, distant hills, gathering bunches of grass and flowers, Sunday promenades, her mother's smile, her father's sweet kisses, the flight of swallows, the plaintive chant of turtledoves, the noisy wings of insects. The list is long and the pleasures longer, but none so lasting or so profound as those she feels now that she belongs entirely to love and the making of love and to its especial Maker:

> Now I am a prisoner;
> I have fled the groves of the world,
> I have seen that in it all is fleeting,
> I have seen all my joys pass by
> And die.

But this death kills nothing, for

> In you, Jesus, I have all things;
> I have the wheat, the half-open flowers,
> Forget-me-nots, buttercups, exquisite roses;
> I have the bloom of the lily of the valley,
> I have its fragrance.

In her love, she has the harmonious solitude and the gracious melodies of rivers and rocks and tumbling waterfalls and the gentle murmur of brooks and birds. She possesses the rainbow, the dawn, the line of the horizon, the greenness of grass. In her lover, she has found permanent peace.

As in the poem, all was for love, so was it in the Act of Consecration. "Dear Spouse," she cries out in its opening words, "Dear Bridegroom of our souls, if we could love with the love of all hearts, that love would be yours. Give us, O Lord, this love. Then come to your brides and satisfy your thirst." But it wasn't only his thirst she longed to satisfy, it was the thirst of the brides as well: "And give us souls, dear Lord. We thirst for souls—above all for the souls of apostles and martyrs, that through them we may inflame all poor sinners with love for you." The Holy Face, greeted with such passion in this act of deep dedication and devotion, is both a means and an end. From this blessed face come what dedicated souls now know of love and what they may in future learn of it. From it come all the favors they seek, as they try so earnestly to make their way out of exile into their true home, to that exalted moment when they can look and look, to their hearts' content.

Thérèse was on fire with these words and others like them. She slipped verses into Céline's slipper on her first Christmas night in Carmel, in 1894, as a little offering to her from the Virgin, promising her sister a crown woven by Jesus and a day of eternal light to follow the darkness of this life, if only she would keep his love steadfast in her. Earlier on the great feast day, Céline had listened to the sound of "The Angels at the Crib," Thérèse's dulcet caroling of the newborn infant in prose and verse, arranged to fit nine different tunes. Around the Holy Child, five angels are joined in happy harmony: the Angel of the Infant Jesus, the Angel of the Holy Face, the Angel of the Resurrection, the Angel of the Eucharist, and the Angel of the Last Judgment. The verse is fullsounding, easy upon the ear, undemanding on the mind. We contemplate the Word in heaven and, made flesh, on earth. We ask, who really understands such a love, and then fall into sentimental musings about the Christ child. This is Thérèse at her most unabashedly sentimental. The words flow on, soft, simple, sweet. But all that is sweet is not sticky:

Douce mélodie,
Suave harmonie,
Silence des fleurs,
D'un Dieu vous chantez les grandeurs.

Sweet melody,
Smooth harmony,
Silence of flowers,
You are singing the grandeurs of a God.

That was Thérèse's constant point—she sang not of the wrath of Achilles nor of arms and the man, but of the Supreme Being, a Supreme Being who was supremely accessible. She never could get over the fact of his accessibility, over the possibility that, having granted so much to us, he might grant even more.

Every pious entertainment, every poem, every prayer was another opportunity to reassure those around her of their certain salvation. How little they had to do! All they needed was confidence, trust, acceptance, however uneasy, of the trials of this world. As she wrote Sister Marthe when that most uneasy of her novices was on private retreat at the end of 1894, "It is a great trial to see everything *black,* but this is a matter not wholly within your control. . . ." What to do, then? What you can. What is that? Detach yourself from the nagging troubles of this world, even from creatures, and then stop worrying. Not a chance of your falling into the swamps of misery and sin you fear so much, she tells Sister Marthe; Jesus would never allow it. Instead of thinking about all this blackness of earth, think of the whiteness of heaven. And then Thérèse adds, in a kind of undertone, "above all, *let us be small, so small that everybody may trample us underfoot,* without our having the least air of noticing or minding." The words in italics are from the *Imitation of Christ,* but she is pushing its doctrine further surely than the fourteenth-century writer had intended. Thérèse thought, felt, lived, preached, and consoled as a woman. No Brother, she. She led women in a woman's way, with a fearless display of emotion and something close to a single furious direction of feeling. On the outside she could be—she would be—as little as the least form of vegetation, as humble as a creature could be. But inside, she would be swelling with a gigantic love that threatened to burst through her flesh.

In those first months of 1895, her heart beating with the joy of Céline's presence, Thérèse turned over and over the words of love, turned many of them onto paper and into eloquent passages of prose or verse. She was beginning to write her autobiographical memoirs; her sister Pauline, both as adoptive mother and as mother in religion, had asked her to get them onto paper, so that none of the remarkable events of her life, which from time to time turned up in stray conversation during recreation, should be forgotten. And as so often proves true, a spate of writing of one kind led to a flood of writing of another. In the same month in which she began to set forth her *Springlike Story of a Little White Flower*, she produced her most ambitious religious entertainment, "Joan of Arc Accomplishing Her Mission," and her most considerable prayers apart from her Act of Oblation, the Act of Consecration to the Holy Face and a prayer inspired by a statue of Joan of Arc.

Joan of Arc was a great heroine for Thérèse, one of those to whom she looked for exemplary guidance as a child, when she first began to conceive the possibility of stretching her own stature to heroic dimensions. Her *recréation pieuse* built around Joan occupies fifty pages of a notebook. It moves in its two parts and five scenes from the victories of the French armies under Joan, through heaven and back to earth again with Joan's capture and martyrdom. It has fourteen characters, among them Saints Michael, Catherine, Margaret, and Gabriel, and whether or not she wrote the part for herself, it possesses a title role that Thérèse herself played, to the great delight and warm acclaim of the convent. The pictures we have of her dressed as Joan show a composed young actress with some of that special kind of self-assurance we normally associate with a true professional. Certainly, there are unmistakable changes in her face as she moves, in the photographs, from Joan's triumphs as a soldier, to Joan enjoying a foretaste of the glory of heaven, to Joan despondent in prison. Only in a photograph with Céline, who played St. Margaret, does she show the unmistakable signs of a somewhat self-conscious amateur, rather rounder in the eye with piety than a practiced actress would be.

Just what Joan inspired in Thérèse is shown in the prayer that a statue of the then Venerable Joan elicited. Her invocation is to the Lord God of Hosts. "I burn to do battle for your glory," she says. With the Lord's aid, she will be able to cry out "with holy

David," in the words of Psalm 143, "You alone are my shield; you, who teach my hands to fight." Thérèse's fighting is, of course, not literally the same as Joan's: "it is not on the open field I shall fight. I am a prisoner held captive by your love; of my own free will I have riveted the chains which bind me to you, and cut me off forever from the world. My sword is love! With it, like Joan of Arc, I will drive the strangers from the land, and I will have you proclaimed king over the kingdom of souls." She acknowledges her weakness for the task, but the battle is joined; she must fight "until the evening of my life." She ends the prayer in full rapture: "To be with you, to be in you, that is my one desire, and your assurance of its fulfillment helps me to bear my exile as I await the joyous eternal day when I shall see you face to face."

If the words she was putting on paper are the indication I think they are of Thérèse's inner state in the first months of 1895, she was close to constant ecstasy. Céline was with her; what a great pleasure it was to realize that! Her taking of the habit on February 5 intensified the pleasure. It was a clear pleasure, too, unbroken by any sorrow of any kind, or even by the faintest of upsets to mitigate and minimize the high joy of the occasion. Thérèse had always noticed, she says in pages of her autobiography written about this time, that on the day of their betrothal to him Jesus does not seem to want his children to undergo trials. This great day must always be cloudless, a real foretaste of paradise. Five times in her own family's experience, the day of Clothing had been such a day, starting with Pauline's Clothing—which is the immediate occasion of these remarks of Thérèse's—and ending with Céline's. The atmosphere remained serene for some time for Thérèse, in spite of a few small disappointments. Léonie seemed to be fighting another losing battle with her vocation at the Visitation. And there was a disappointing change for Céline. She had entered the Carmel with the very satisfying name of Sister Marie of the Holy Face, Thérèse's own long-standing choice for her, but now the family's old nemesis, Canon Delatroëtte, suggested that the name of the recently dead foundress of the Lisieux Carmel would be better for Céline. At a recreation one evening in January, the new name was announced publicly —Sister Geneviève of Saint Thérèse. That was a sad fact to have to record, but Thérèse did so with good cheer, slipping a piece of paper into Céline's pocket that same evening, on which she had written,

Sister Geneviève of Saint Thérèse
Little Thérèse was the first to write it!

Nothing could dismay her—not in those months. Before the month of February was out she produced her most enduring piece of poetry to attest to the intensity of love she was feeling and living. In fifteen stately stanzas, she offered a philosophy of love, a theology of love, a multiplicity of experiences of love. "Vivre d'amour," she called it—"To Live for Love," or, as Ronald Knox translates it, "All My Life Love." Each of the stanzas except the first and the last two begins with the title words; the opening is "Au soir d'amour," in the evening of love; the closing strophes start, "Mourir d'amour," to die of love, so that they can end, they and the poem itself, with a triumphant last echo of the poem's refrain, "to live for love," as Thérèse finds her destiny, her heaven, and her final embrace.

It is not a poem that translates easily, in spite of the simplicity and directness of the opening lines:

> Au soir d'amour, parlant sans parabole,
> Jesus disait: "Si quelqu'un veut m'aimer,
> Fidèlement qu'il garde ma parole,
> Mon Père et moi viendrons le visiter;
> Et, de son coeur, faisant notre demeure,
> Notre palais, notre vivant séjour,
> Rempli de paix, nous voulons qu'il demeure
> En notre amour."

> In the evening of love, no longer speaking in parables,
> Jesus said, "If anyone loves me,
> As faithfully as he keeps my word,
> My Father and I will come to him;
> And in his heart make our abode,
> Our palace, our everlasting home;
> Filled with peace, we will that he shall live
> In our love."

It is a poem instinct with love in which, for no reason at all except her love, Thérèse was determined to make love speak, to make love heard, to make love all the life of others as it was all hers. And so, forswearing parables and every oblique device, she must somehow penetrate to the very essence of love, to reveal the inner life of life itself, and to do so, in effect, in words of one syllable. She obviously felt she could do what she had set out to do. The poem arose spontaneously, without feast or devotion to explain it, with no immediate need on anyone's part, not even a faltering novice, with no excuse at all except that of love. Out of love, then, came love, in a series of robust rhetorical outbursts. "The spirit of love inflames me with its fire," Thérèse says in the second stanza; that is what moves her. Her love is a constant exchange, a constant interchange. In loving Jesus, she explains, she draws the Father to herself, and she doesn't stop there:

> O Trinity! you are the prisoner
> Of my love.

And so *she lives in love*—a multiple play on words beyond any altogether rational sort of explication. She is in love. Love is her end. Love is her beginning. Having fallen in love with love, with Love Itself, she lives right inside It. On one level, she plays at it, she revels in the totality of life that love must be at some stage for all lovers, when nobody else, nothing else, matters at all:

> Lovers must have solitude,
> Heart to heart, day after day, night after night;
> My bliss, just one glance from you,
> I live in love!

She longs all through the poem for all the treasured pleasures of love, but not an unbroken sweetness. To live with *her* love, to live in him, is to live in and with and of and on the Cross. No mountain peaks for her, not even the consecrated heights of Mount Tabor, one of the Lord's special homes in the Israel of the Old Testament. For her, the road to Calvary is the bower of bliss; all love is centered there; there, all love ends and all love begins. But none of this is by calculation, unless there is some sort of numbering involved in giving without measure, giving all she has to give of her riches, "my only wealth," she says—"To live in love." That is what she has and what she gives away and—happy paradox—has all the more the more she gives away.

The more she gives of love, in this life that is all love, the more she loses fear, the dimmer her memory of her faults, her imperfections, her limitations. Sin is burned away to nothingness in the fire of love. Even if she were to fall, to fall regularly, to fall every hour, her lover would pick her up, would hold her in his arms and surround her with his grace. How, then, with such a pilot can she fail to distribute peace and joy as she sails through the world? And even if her blessed lover sleeps, she has enough faith to pierce the veil that separates them, enough hope to sustain her through the long day of life, and enough love to provide the motion necessary to push her through her course.

Now for three strophes—the tenth, eleventh, and twelfth—Thérèse feels the buoyant motions of love. She begs her lover to kindle his fires in priestly hearths, until each priest of his is purer than a seraph; let us join together, she prays, in the fiery work of the Church. She begs for the pardon of sinners; for them, she wipes the tears and sweat and blood from the Holy Face. That is what it means to live in love, to bring everyone back to him, her lover, to make them all bless his name forever and ever. Blasphemies dig deep down into her heart, where she repeats each one to efface each one. She wants, in all these movements of love, to emulate the Magdalen, to bathe his feet with her tears, with precious oils, to feel the rapture that the Magdalen felt when she kissed his feet with her great long hair, as she dried them with that same long hair. But what has she to offer of fragrance for that face? Only her love.

To live in love—what madness, the world thinks. Enough, the worldly cry; stop wasting all your sweetness, all your life; find a more useful way to expend it. But Thérèse's answer is as blunt as the world's accusation:

> To love you, Jesus, what a fulfilling loss!
> All my sweetness is yours, I shall save none.
> I want to sing on and on as I leave the world, to sing:
> *I die of love!*

The poem's ending is a crescendo of feeling. To die of love—what a sweet martyrdom! That's what she wants and implores the cherubim to tune their lyres to this song of her heart. She feels it, she knows it—her exile is almost over. She cries out,

> Burning arrow, burn me away until nothing is left,
> Take my heart, here in this sad sojourn, here below.
> Jesus, my Lord, let me live my dream,
> Let me die of love!

This is all her hope in life, to die of love, to lose the chains that tie her to this world. God will be recompense enough; she needs no other reward. And so she sinks into the blessed fantasy, pierced with love, burned with it, on fire with it forever. The French has a good sound, a romantic one, even a little of the sound of a popular song, but that's fair enough, since, as with most of her poems, Thérèse wrote to the model of a song, whose tune she borrowed for her own use. Here are the concluding lines of the poem:

> De son amour je suis passionnée;
> Qu'il vienne enfin m'embraser sans retour!
> Voilà mon ciel, voilà ma destinée:
> VIVRE D'AMOUR!

> I am impassioned with his love;
> Oh, that he would come at last to inflame me forever!
> There lies my heaven, there rests my destiny:
> TO LIVE IN LOVE!

According to Céline, all of "Vivre d'amour" was conceived and composed "d'un jet"—in one spurt—in the course of the hour assigned Thérèse on February 26, 1895, in the convent's Forty Hours Devotion before the exposed Holy Sacrament. As a result, Céline claims for the poem "supernatural promptings." But do we need any special witness to such inspiration in Thérèse? "I do not believe," she once told Céline, when asked how frequently she lost all sense of the presence of God, "I have ever been more than three minutes at a time without thinking of him." However hidden her life with God may have been, it was not a fragmentary one, lived in an alternation of sudden outbursts and long dry periods. Even in the dry periods, even amidst the worst of her temptations against faith, she was aware of God, thinking of Jesus, caring, hoping, longing, feeling something tangible, unmistakably real to her, almost all the time. When she cries out in the last verses of her poem—

> Qu'il vienne enfin m'embraser sans retour!

> Oh, that he would come to inflame me forever!

—she was crying out of an ecstasy of burning love. She had been inflamed, fiercely embraced, hugged in the fire of love. That lovely French verb s'embraser—to blaze, to shine with a glowing fire, to be inflamed, to fall in love—has an unmistakable echo of embrasser—to embrace, to kiss—in it.

Oh, yes, she knew desolation, too. She did not have to be pleaded with to add to the fourteen stanzas, which came pouring out of her on her knees there, before the exposed Sacrament, a fifteenth in which she acknowledged the force of Calvary, of the cross, in her life of love. Céline had only to mention it and Thérèse wrote a set of lines to go after the third verse, the set in which she says with such strength of conviction that Tabor's heights are not for her, but rather the hill of Calvary, where all love must eventually end, from which all love ultimately comes. She had felt the wounds of love as wounds. She knew their hurt. She had no inflated or distorted idea of the peace that comes with a life of total dedication to love. Before she died she was to have a year and a half of the most anguishing doubts about her faith, believing and yet not believing, because she could never know in her moments of anguish what she really believed and what she did not. She had already had most of the small disappointments and derelictions to which we are all heir, and in much greater abundance than most people have them. She had felt again and again the withdrawal of God, almost sensibly, I believe, and with how much pain, for to her there was nothing, no completeness, no life, really, when Jesus departed from her, when she lost, even for a few seconds, the awareness of his presence, the strong feeling of him inside her.

Her sense of desertion was so great at times that, like an amputee reaching for a lost limb, she groped for her lover, grasped at shadowy presences, dipped wildly into the air for some touch, some taste, some quickening of the senses that would assure her he was there with her, had not deserted her. That is why her poems are full of gropings and graspings and nearly frenzied entreaties to be swallowed up in love, to be hugged and kissed and lost forever in the living flames of love, to die of love. And that is why she cannot beg for any more suffering; she had had enough, was having enough, would continue to have enough, without asking for anything more. Consolation was in suffering alone. Comfort was only in the cross, but she had, she knew, limited endurance, and she was realistic enough to confess it. "I did not ask for suffering," she said at the end of her life, "for if I had prayed for it, then it would have been my own suffering and I should have been afraid that I wouldn't have the strength to endure it." It wasn't mere suffering she wanted—that was clear—but complete abandonment to love and everything love demanded of her, "joys, labors, trials," Céline says, whatever Providence was "pleased to send her. . . ."

Sometime after her sister's canonization, Pauline was able to change some words in the Office of Saint Thérèse to make Thérèse's attitude toward suffering clear forever, at least to those who said or read the liturgical Office and meditated on it. At the end of the ninth lesson of Matins, there originally appeared these words: "*inflamed with the desire of suffering,* she offered herself, two years before her death, as a victim to the merciful love of God." No, not at all, that was not Thérèse's fire for a moment and Pauline was determined to set the world straight about it. She finally won her point with the Sacred Congregation of Rites and in May 1932 the italicized words were changed to read: "*on fire with divine love.* . . ."

This is no mere quibble, nor does it represent any change in Thérèse's attitude toward suffering. She came to welcome suffering as a child. Her whole life was a series of steps in suffering, a progression in pain. But never, not before her great Easter illness or after her Christmas conversion, not at any point on her turbulent journey to Carmel or after entering the convent, did she go out of her way to solicit suffering for its own sake. She detested the physical scourgings to which so many religious submitted themselves. She found herself unequal to most of the traditional mortifications of the religious life, in and out of the convent. For her the consolations of suffering were those that came to remind her of her oneness with Christ on the cross. Suffering's comfort lay in that not quite credible exchange of feelings that followed the exchange of beings, when Jesus entered into her and she entered into him and she could not say who was who. Suffering's joy was redemptive, not masochistic. When she gave her pleasure, such as only she could give, to God, she shared that pleasure with everyone. The pleasure was somehow salvific, supporting all souls, freeing all souls, bringing love in some mysterious manner to replace hate and terror and misery, even if only for an instant, in one spurt of supernatural feeling. Her attitude was very simple: Whatever Jesus wants, Jesus gets. She was, as her Office now quite properly reads, "on fire with divine love."

There is an important secret buried away here. It is a central secret of the spiritual life; it is a central secret of psychological health: One must love one's own way, no matter how awkward, and in one's own words, no matter how inadequate. Thérèse was burning with love—but her own love, not somebody else's. Let those who would be bloody. Let those who could be brilliant, or self-scourging, or whatever their gifts permitted them to be. She could offer her lover only what she had to offer. She never tried to offer him anything different from that or anything more. She was in love with him *à la folie*—to the point of madness. That was enough to make her yield all of herself. And *that* was enough. "Me," she told Céline one day, when she found her sister uneasy about being asked to do more than others, to give up what other Sisters permitted themselves, "Me, I am always happy with what God asks. I don't worry about what he asks of others and I don't think I have more merit because he asks more of me than others. What pleases me, what I will always choose—if I have the possibility of a choice—is whatever God wants of me. My lot is always a beautiful one, I find. Even if others merited more in giving less, I should want less merit for myself in giving more, just because in that way I would be doing what God wants me to do."

Thérèse was not fazed by her limitations nor by the accomplishments of others. Everybody's accomplishments are useful. If somebody else does something well, she explained to Céline, take joy in it; it obviously gives joy to God. And if you take the kind of pleasure you should in the accomplishments of others, you grow rich in that pleasure, and more and more joyous in life. She quoted the fourteenth-century Dominican mystic Johannes Tauler to Céline to drive her point home. "If I love the good that is in my neighbor," Tauler said in one of his sermons, "more than he loves it himself, then this good becomes mine more than it is his. If I love in Saint Paul all the favors God has accorded him, all these then by the same title belong to me." In this "communion," Tauler said, everything that is good in the universe, even in the saints and the angels, enriches me. And in this way, Thérèse added, if you really want to do good, any good, whatever it is, and struggle over your small talents, your precious virtues, your own little endowments, whatever they may be, the very struggle to use what you have will accomplish the ends of goodness, and you will do as much good as anyone else, no matter how richly endowed. This is another presentiment of heaven, as Thérèse comments upon it to Céline, a foretaste that the least gifted may have, that, it may be, the least gifted may have more richly than the more liberally endowed. For "the Doctors of the Church tell us," she says, "that the love that unites all the elect in heaven is so great that the happiness and merit of each one makes for the happiness and merit of all." So here below, if one takes enough pleasure in the achievements of others, one comes to share in the happiness that comes with achievement and even, it may be, comes to merit that happiness, just as if one were directly responsible for the achievement oneself.

Thérèse had dozens of rhetorical devices to explain the ardors of her love to others and to bring them, somehow, to participate in it themselves, so that whatever their intrinsic worth as lovers, they would find love at the highest level, if only by the absorption they found in the love of others such as herself. No small bargains for her, she says in one of her driest and most terse figurative explications of love. "There are some souls who make their spiritual living in niggling little affairs, who always look for exact returns, a little for a little. But as for me, *I speculate in the Bank of Love,* and I play for high stakes. If I lose, I'll know about it soon enough." But, she says, she is not worried about sudden reverses; Jesus will take care of all that for her: "I don't know whether I'm rich or poor—later on, I'll find out." The important thing is to stay at the center, love's center, our center. To illustrate this, she uses the figure of the kaleidoscope, a toy which had fascinated her as a child, as it does all imaginative children. She had taken a kaleidoscope apart and had teased out of that wonderful invention of Sir David Brewster its secret, the three mirrors that reflect the pieces of glass or paper or wool, or whatever colorful scraps are used to make the patterns, in an infinity of circular mirrorings. For her the peephole through which one looks into the kaleidoscope is a rhetorical figure for God himself, looking through himself, and thus finding even our most clumsy and insignificant efforts handsome to his eye. But if we withdraw from the center— that is, if we run away from love—all that will be left for God to see will be some scraps of wool and some bits of paper, the poor leavings of our love.

The surest way to remain at the center of things was to offer everything in her life for that center, to make a total consecration of herself to love. This would satisfy all her urgings, all her passionate desires, at once. The grievous misapprehensions about love under which most people lead their lives could be corrected by such an offering. Love could begin its reign on an equal footing with Justice if souls could be brought to understand how, simply by throwing themselves, with all the love that was in them, into the arms and heart of love, they would find all their love answered with love and all their shortcomings and miseries comforted with love and all the nagging smallnesses of their lives wiped out, burned away, altogether erased by love.

On June 9, on the feast day of the Trinity, Thérèse made her great offering of love, her *Acte d'Offrande à l'Amour Miséricordieux*. It was offered in a great rush of words to her head, to her heart, and to her hands; to give it its full title, it was an *Act of Oblation as Victim of Holocaust to God's Merciful Love* which she hastened to get down on paper. But it was far more than a set of words on paper; it was a sequence of experiences. In every line there is gathered some moment of her life, some instant of her love or of her suffering, of her most blessed moments and her most desolate and deprived. In every line there is a great mixture of longing and of satisfaction, alchemical in its magical joining of quantities that are frequently and confoundingly opposed.

There is some disagreement between the accounts of Céline and Pauline as to just when Thérèse invited Céline to participate in the offering of victimhood, but there is no question about Thérèse's first action after she had made up her mind to make the offering. She quickly asked the Prioress—Pauline, that is—for permission to do so. According to Céline, she stammered over her request in a way unusual for her; Céline does not remember whether or not she actually used the word "victim." But the substance of her request was clear enough and the intensity of her feeling was written all over her. Two days after Thérèse composed the Act, she and Céline knelt together in the room next to Thérèse's cell, where the nuns usually did their art work, and before the Virgin of the Smile, Thérèse spoke the words of oblation and the two Sisters offered themselves together as victims.

On a hasty reading, the Act of Oblation seems little more than a dedication to victimhood, rather more intense in its rhetoric than most ascetic documents, but essentially a statement of devotion in a familiar tradition. It has that legalistic tone reminiscent of so much writing in seventeenth-century French spirituality—

Francis de Sales in particular, but also Pierre de Bérulle and all those whose doctrine in any significant way associates them with Bérullian thought, Condren, Olier, Lallemant, Surin, etc. The doctrine set forth in the Act of Oblation is very much like Bérulle's spirituality of self-abnegation. Everything is directed toward an inward annihilation, in which, with the deepest conviction, the soul confesses itself to be nothing before God, who is all. But confession is not enough. There must be some unmistakable outward sign, and so the soul almost literally contracts to demonstrate its nothingness, and not simply its nothingness, but its profound awareness of it. Thus, and almost is these words, the soul, as the party of the second part, agrees to offer itself—in capital letters—AS A BURNT OFFERING to the party of the first part, God, represented here as—and again in capital letters—MERCIFUL LOVE.

All of this is true enough. The Act is a contract of victimhood. But it is much more than that. It is a translation into the logic of spiritual action of Thérèse's doctrine of merit, with a daring and a depth that she had never before attempted. For now, as a basis for her actions, she was claiming not only the merits of the saints and the angels, but the merits of Jesus himself, and claiming them with the utmost directness and certainty. Those who see in Thérèse's Act of Oblation only the formulas of victimhood or find freshness of thinking only in the second part of the document, where she gives herself up to her longings for eternal possession by Jesus, miss the great strength of this work, I think. They fail to see Thérèse's brazenness before God, her holy arrogance, which inflates her smallness to the size of infinity and makes her worthy of God's company. What is even more important, her breathtaking doctrine of merit associates with her anybody else who wants to share her august company. For all anyone has to do is to claim with her the merits of those who have so lavishly offered themselves and their love to others—saints, angels, the Virgin Mary, Jesus, the Trinity—and the merits will be his. Even if one's desires are *infinite*—the Holy Office softened this word to *immeasurable*, thereby showing at once humorlessness and tone-deafness—even if one wants all, God will listen, God will respond. "Whatsoever you shall ask my Father in my name, he will give it to you!" —that is the fulcrum of Thérèse's leap into high heaven. With that certainty, she can plead for the eternal embrace of her lover and the marks of that embrace, the five wounds, the stigmata, to be hers in heaven forever. With that assurance, she can ask for permanent possession of Jesus; she can ask that he be housed in her as in the tabernacle. And what is more, she can ask for these things in such a way that she seems to be assured of receiving what she asks for.

Were these only religious formulas? Or even, at a somewhat higher level, were they only the impassioned words of a zealot, so deeply committed to the religious life that she had become a little unbalanced as a result? Is there any significant connection to the lives of the rest of the world, the less deeply committed, the less zealous or the altogether passionless? What can a balanced person, who leads his life in the world with calm and satisfaction, find in such a document? Is it worth disturbing one's equanimity about? What, really, is all the shouting about?

If I answer all these questions by saying that Thérèse's Act of Oblation is a great document of love I will not be saying enough, I will not satisfy the perplexity which an open and honest scrutiny of the Act must surely arouse. But if I say that it is a set of responses to every nagging ache of love anyone has ever known, no matter how slight or how great, no matter how defective or excessive or perverted, then, perhaps, I may suggest the majesty of Thérèse's accomplishment and its relevance to everyone, everywhere, who has reached the point in life where it is possible to think seriously about love and not simply to allow its anxieties to wash over one in a seething sea of anguish. Thérèse is calling an end to those dreadful desires for self-gratification which convulse the goodness which is in all love, however much or however little that goodness may be, and often destroy it altogether. But she is not offering instead a total mortification of gratification for oneself. She has found a balance of pleasures—for herself and for her lover—and with it a pattern of performance that could, for anyone caught in any tangle of love, cut the knot, break it forever. If one can bring oneself to accept the terms of this Act of Oblation, one can look forward to something like Thérèse's depth of satisfaction. If, that is, one can associate one's love for a thing or an idea or a person with the love of God, then one can be assured of something like Thérèse's love for Jesus and his love for her, and without any loss of whatever really is loving in one's desires for anything or anybody. When we make offerings like Thérèse's we ourselves do not diminish, nor do our affections for others become smaller or less important, nor does their love for us.

The exact terms of Thérèse's Act of Oblation are worth examining in some detail. The opening paragraphs are a *mélange* of many things, all of them important. She addresses herself to God, to the Trinity, and states her purpose. Her underlinings and punctuation are not quite as idiosyncratic as usual, but there are the inevitable oddnesses, which are worth preserving, no matter how strange they may look in English. They say something about the feeling underlying every statement of Thérèse's.

> O my God! Blessed Trinity, I desire to *Love* you and to make you *Loved*, to work for the glorification of Holy Church by saving souls on earth and delivering those souls that are suffering in purgatory. I desire to accomplish your will perfectly and to attain the degree of glory that you have prepared for me in your kingdom; in a word, I want to be a Saint, but I feel my powerlessness and I ask you, O my God, yourself to be my *Sanctity*.

Then comes the first appropriation of merits:

> Since you have loved me enough to give me your only Son as my Saviour and my Spouse, the infinite treasures of his merits are mine; I offer them to you with great happiness, begging you to look at me only through the Face of Jesus and in his Heart burning with *Love*.

Then follow more appropriations of merit and the rich certainties that such appropriations assure her:

> I offer you in addition all the merits of the Saints (those in Heaven and those on earth), their acts of *Love* and those of the Holy Angels. Finally I offer you, *O Blessed Trinity,* the *Love* and the merits of the *Holy Virgin, my darling Mother;* it is to her I relinquish my offering, begging her to present it to you. Her Divine Son, my *Beloved* Spouse, said to us in the days of his life on earth: *"Whatsoever you shall ask my Father in my name he will give it to you."* I am certain, then, that you will grant my desires; I know it, O my God! *for the more you want to give, the more you make us want to give.*

She feels a great confidence, now, and asks God to take all of her and to do so immediately, finding in her the same fullness and ease of habitation he does in the church tabernacle:

In my heart I feel immeasurable desires and with confidence I ask you to come and take possession of my soul. Ah! I cannot receive Holy Communion as often as I want, but, Lord, are you not *All-Powerful?* . . . Remain in me, as in the tabernacle, never leave your little victim. . . .

The Holy Office was uneasy with the next codicil in Thérèse's contract of oblation. She asked the Lord to take away her freedom to displease him, an old prayer of hers, reaching back at least to the time of her first Communion. With that request she coupled a plea that if, through any failure on her part, she were to fall, God should purge her on that instant, burning away all her imperfections. She was begging, in her strong emotional way, to be lifted up to the highest state in the moral life, following the classical procedure outlined by St. Augustine, from the lowest level (*posse peccare*), where it is possible to sin, through the level one attains with the support of the sacraments, from baptism through the Eucharist (*posse non peccare*), where it is possible not to sin, to the peak of salvation, where, in answer to lives and prayers like Thérèse's, it is no longer possible to sin (*non posse peccare*). There is no real loss of freedom here, but simply the free election of a sinless state, confirmed in God's grace. God's freely given gifts support the soul's desires. Without them, the desires remain only desires. With them, the soul is transformed. But the transformation is effected only by the freest of exchanges, individual soul to Creator, bride to bridegroom, lover to beloved. She says: I freely give up all desire to sin or to be able to sin. He says: I freely accept your offering and promise to support you if at any point you stumble or even appear to stumble. When Thérèse asks for suffering and the marks of the Crucifixion on her body, to last through all eternity, it is as confirmation of this exchange. The stigmata will be visible signs of her acceptance in heaven, birthmarks of her rebirth. Thus the impassioned rhetoric of the next paragraphs in the Act of Oblation.

> I want to console you for the ingratitude of the wicked and to beg you to take away my freedom to displease you; if at times I fall through weakness, I beg that your *Divine Glance* may purify my soul instantly, consuming all my imperfections, as fire transforms everything into itself. . . .
> I thank you, O my God! for all the graces you have granted me, in particular for having made me pass through the crucible of suffering. It is with joy that I shall contemplate you on the last day,

bearing the scepter of the Cross; since you have deigned to give me this most precious Cross as my portion, I hope to be like you in heaven and to see the sacred stigmata of your Passion shining in my glorified body. . . .

Now Thérèse turns to making her motivation clear. She is not accumulating merit badges like an eagle scout. She is not ambitious for a high place in heaven, though she does not abandon for a moment her hope of being caught up there forever, in Jesus. But it is not through being singled out for a high rank, because of high achievement on earth, that she will be enfolded in the arms of her lover; it will be the intensity of her love alone that will yield her an eternity of love. She could not care less for those orders of achievement which some theologians and spiritual writers see as intrinsic to the structure of heaven, those ranks in which exaltation is granted all, but in a clear sequence of class and priority, as Dante, for example, indicates in his arrangement of the blessed in Paradise, following the order of the planets. There is only one order for Thérèse, the one in which love is everything and in a constant ecstasy one can sink into its joys, not for a day, not for a passing moment, but forever.

> After earth's exile, I hope that I shall enjoy you in the Homeland, but my wish is not to amass merits for Heaven; I want to work for your *Love alone,* with the single aim of giving you pleasure, of consoling your Sacred Heart, and of saving souls who will love you forever.
>
> In the evening of this life, I shall come before you with empty hands, for I do not ask you, Lord, to count my works. Before your eyes all our justices have stains. I want, then, to clothe myself in your own *Justice,* and to receive from your *Love* eternal possession of *Yourself.* I want no other *Throne,* no other *Crown* than *You,* O my *Beloved!* . . .
>
> In your eyes, time is nothing; a single day is like a thousand years, so that in an instant you can prepare me to appear before you. . . .

The conclusion of the Act is a summary one in every sense of the word. It is brief. It sums things up. It brings things to a conclusion. But while it does all of this in summary fashion, it does not do so coolly. The heat of Thérèse's love does not at any point simmer down. How could it, when she was faced more and more clearly, with each word, with a vision of complete absorption in her love, in perfect love, in Love Itself.

So that I may live in an act of perfect Love, I OFFER MYSELF
AS A BURNT OFFERING TO YOUR MERCIFUL LOVE, im-
ploring you to consume me unceasingly, while you let the floods
of *infinite tenderness* pent up in you flow into my soul, so that I
may become a *Martyr* to your *Love*, O my God! . . .

After this *Martyrdom* has prepared me to appear before you,
may it make me die, and may my soul, without a moment's delay,
leap into the eternal embrace of *Your Merciful Love*. . . .

O my *Beloved!* at every beat of my heart I want to renew this
offering an infinite number of times, till the shadows have disappeared and I can tell you my *Love* again and again, looking at
you *Face to Face forever!* . . .

> Marie, Françoise, Thérèse of the Child Jesus
> and of the Holy Face, rel. carm. ind.

Feast of the Most Holy Trinity
The ninth of June of the year of grace 1895.

This text of the Act of Oblation is a slightly corrected one—not
corrected by the Holy Office but by Thérèse herself. The corrections are chiefly underlinings and punctuations and paragraph-
ings. There are no significant changes in the wording of the first
version, which is reproduced in facsimile in the holograph edition of the autobiographical manuscripts. That early version fills
all of one side of an eight- by five-inch page, from top to bottom
and side to side, and about a third of the reverse of the page. The
firmness of the writing is impressive, with only a very few addi-
tions in the cramped spaces between the lines, only one or two
changes by erasure and rewriting, and only one long crossing-out,
and that of an addition in the first paragraph that Thérèse re-
considered. The motion of the writing of the Act of Oblation is
like the motion of Thérèse's soul in making her offering, straight
ahead, firmly forward, with a military precision. She knew the
state of her soul perfectly on this day.

Once again, Thérèse was experiencing all the stages of the mystical life at once. As so often was true of her experience of God,
when she offered herself in purgation, she demanded—and received—an almost simultaneous illumination with the purification.
She knew human imperfections; she knew her own imperfections.
She didn't use language as strong as some ascetical or mystical
writers; she never characterized the soul of sinful man as beast-
like, as Walter Hilton did, nor did she consign "all creatures who
are of the Devil's sort in this life" to endless damnation, as Lady

Julian of Norwich did. She didn't linger long over the temptations of the flesh or of the spirit, though she knew them well enough from her terrible Easter struggles of 1883, when she thought she had been given the strong personal attention of the Devil, and though she was probably never altogether without some concern over the strength of her own faith in her last years. But imperfection—fault—sin—however deliberate or indeliberate, was accompanied more and more for her with sudden inward illuminations, signs of the Lord's presence, which burned away all memory of failure, all inclination to fall, all preoccupation with her weakness. If she felt her weakness strongly, she could rest upon the strength of Jesus; that was a constant resource in time of failure. Her own nature unfolded to her in an expanding awareness of herself, in which with ever more intense feeling she saw God mirrored in herself. Her ritual of purgation was—to use that figure so beloved of the mystics—to wipe away all trace of herself from her inner looking-glass, so that only God might be reflected in it. Or, to use Richard of Saint Victor's version of the same rhetoric in his *Benjamin Minor*, she cleansed her mirror of all its downward images and then held it straight up, so that, in the words of the fourth Psalm, the light of the Lord's countenance could be sealed upon her and gladness could settle in her heart.

Purgation and illumination were not enough. Union must come. This is the ultimate object of the Act of Oblation, the necessary sum of all her days. She will not be guilty of that spiritual avarice against which John of the Cross so sternly warns the beginner in the spiritual life; she was no beginner and furthermore she had never been attracted to any of the devices or devotions or mortifications which John is so anxious about; she would not be lost in a feast of penances or a banquet of fasts. She would go where the Lord led in her quest for union; she would ascend Mount Carmel at any pace, along any route that her lover designated, and if he required her to turn back at any point, or to wait here or there for a time, she was docile enough to do so. But her docility never strayed into apathy. She burned with love. Every heartbeat was a palpitation of love, as she reminded her lordly bridegroom in the Act of Oblation. She was not impatient, exactly, but she was, oh, so eager.

Thérèse's eagerness was rewarded quickly, piercingly, violently, almost, just five days after she made her burning offering of herself. She was in the choir and beginning to say the Stations of the Cross, when *tout à coup*, she told Pauline, suddenly she "felt wounded by a dart of fire so ardent" that she thought surely she was about to die. She said she had not words to describe it, but she found some familiar figures at hand with which to make something of her experience accessible to others: "it was as if an invisible hand had plunged all of me, completely, into fire. Oh! and what fire and what sweetness at the same time! I was burning up with love and I felt that not for a minute, not even for another second, could I stand such violent feelings. . . ." She must surely die. But she did not die; she was experiencing, as she realized soon enough, the raptures which many saints had described.

Tom Clarkson, in his fine little book about Thérèse, *Love Is My Vocation*, calls the experience "a kind of spiritual orgasm" and compares it to Teresa of Avila's piercing with a golden arrow or spear, which, Teresa says, she had herself actually seen an angel thrust into her heart several times. If one doesn't know Teresa's experience from reading her own account of it, one may know Bernini's translation of it into sculpture. Thérèse herself may have seen the sculpture at Santa Maria della Vittoria in Rome and marveled, as so many of us have, over the mixing of physical and spiritual states which the seventeenth-century sculptor achieved in that altar group—angel, arrows, and saint. Teresa is clearly spent after her great moment of ecstasy, as drained as after the most intense sexual experience, her mouth slack, her eyes drooping, her naked foot hanging limp. Somehow Bernini manages to add a spiritual dimension to his portrayal of Teresa's mystical experience, but not by compromising the intense sexuality of the experience. It is in the attitude of Teresa's body, perhaps, or in the benevolent expression on the little angel's face, as he gazes on his passionate victim. It may be that our sharp impression of a merging of flesh and the spirit, of a complete and total union of two worlds, is simply the result of placing such urgent fleshliness in the surroundings of a baroque church, where the spirit is everywhere manifest in unmistakably human terms and yet remains the spirit. Whatever it is, it is a palpable reality and we not only know it, we feel it.

The pitch of Thérèse's feelings was unspeakably high and intense—and instantaneously over. Right afterwards, she says, she relapsed into her habitual state of aridity. It was a steepness she reached only once, according to her own testimony. She had known *assauts d'amour*—assaults of love—from the age of fourteen, she told Pauline, and, oh, she said, how she loved God in those moments! But they were not at all like the experience of June 14, that true consummation of her mystical marriage, when she felt herself burned by a flame the reality of which she could not question, when she knew as surely as if she had received the stigmata that her burnt offering had been accepted.

TWELVE

*I*N the summer of 1895, Léonie left the Visitation for the second
time. She was not alone. Her generation of novices at Caen
was afflicted with a literal-minded superior, who was incapable of
adjusting the Visitation rule in any way to fit the temperaments
of her young charges, a fact noted with sadness by the Mother
Superior at the time of Léonie's death in 1941, when she was a
venerable religious of forty-two years' standing. For Léonie did
return, in January 1899, and to stay. In her own way, she was as
persistent in her courting of religious life as Thérèse. Her obstacles were temperamental, but they were not always in her own
temperament, however capricious or unyielding it may at first
have seemed to her superiors. The fact that in her departure she
was accompanied by other novices is indication enough that the
failure was not hers alone, and one can only smile at the reason
the convent gave for the novices leaving—their "delicate health."
Later the failure of the "older Mothers" to "use the mitigations
now seen to be indispensable in the formation of subjects" was
also admitted to be a cause of the mass exodus.

Delicate health was not Léonie's failing, any more than caprice
or obstinacy. She was an "original." She did not conform easily to
accepted patterns of behavior, and hence she was not always acceptable to those around her, from her mother at home to her
mothers in religion. She was undoubtedly slow in her movements,
slow in her thoughts, and especially slow to take commands, except in her strange relationship with Louise Marais, the servant
Zélie had left express orders to fire after her death. In a family of
quick-witted girls, Léonie's taciturnity was bound to seem odd
and more than once to be a cause of irritation. Her laconic style
was not often seen as a real style, even, perhaps, a witty one. No
one seemed to recognize that this style could be a function of

metabolism, to give it a physiological explanation, or of a fine detachment, to give it a spiritual explanation. She was clearly a problem—everybody saw that, Zélie most of all. Nothing bothered Zélie so much at her death as her fear that Léonie would not be able to get along without her. But Léonie did, surviving the mild mockery of her solitary ways to which she was exposed in the family, the laughter at her warm but clumsy efforts to end her mother's mortal illness with sacrifice, even her own death, if she could somehow contrive it. The point is, she was not only solitary, she was stubborn, and her stubbornness was engaged as never before in her efforts to find a life for herself in religion.

We know less about Léonie than we do about the other sisters of Thérèse. The textures of her personality assured her of a certain mystery, the mystery of shyness and containment and retreat, the mystery of few words and no vain posturings, the mystery of stillness. Does this make her, in Ida Goerres's (or her translator's) ungrammatical comparison, "spiritually the most unique and original of the sisters—not excepting our saint herself"? It is enough, surely, to say that she was herself, that it was a good self to be, and that she was really like no one else, not even Thérèse. But it is questionable to conclude, as Mrs. Goerres does, that "Léonie lived what Thérèse lived and taught, the Little Way of perfect humility and simplicity," and what's more, "did so wholly unconsciously and without ever suspecting that she was acting in any extraordinary manner." Consciousness is an essential part of the Little Way. No matter how remarkable one's spiritual gifts, if one follows this way of responding to harshness with gentleness, to insult with compliment, to every slight with extra-special consideration, one must know what one is doing, why one is doing it, and one must do it with every kind of conscious care. If, as Mrs. Goerres concludes her long note on Léonie in the back of *The Hidden Face,* Léonie "in her actions . . . followed the Little Way with a force fully the equal of her sister's," then, I would insist, she must either have thought a great deal about what she was doing, just like Thérèse, or have been utterly unlike her sister in doing spontaneously, and altogether without effort, what it cost Thérèse, as she keeps telling us, a very great deal to do.

Everything Thérèse did, she did with consciousness. I think that is true, even allowing all one must for the life led below the level of full consciousness, but insisting that she had been remarkably skillful in her efforts to dredge up from the darkness within all that could move her closer and closer to love and, just as firmly and clearly, all that could separate her from love or make her in any way falter in her attempts to love and to make love understood, to introduce others to the joys of love as she understood it. Such comfort as she is able to bring Léonie comes from a firm facing of herself. Look, she tells Léonie, just before her sister is about to leave the Visitation, look at me, faced with a predicament not unlike yours. You are unhappy at having your profession postponed. The same thing happened to me.

She had been a novice for a year, Thérèse goes on, when she found that no one was paying any attention to her, thinking that was the best way to follow M. Delatroëtte's thinking—she was, after all, just too young. "I felt great pain, I assure you," she wrote Léonie in April 1895, recalling that tense moment in her life, "but one day God showed me there was a good deal of self-seeking, so I said to myself: 'For my Clothing I was dressed in a lovely white robe adorned with lace and flowers; but who has thought to give me a robe for my espousals? That robe I must prepare myself, *by myself;* Jesus wants no one but Himself to aid me. . . . Creatures will not see my efforts, for they will be hidden in my heart. Trying to be *forgotten,* I shall wish to be seen by none save Jesus. . . . What matter if I appear poor and totally lacking in intelligence and talent."

Léonie learned to live with a reputation for a total lack of intelligence and talent, learned so well that before she died she found herself appreciated as both intelligent and talented. Inevitably, sooner or later, she had to learn something of Thérèse's spirituality, of her Little Way, as a conscious doctrine. She was regaled regularly, in her several abortive trips to the Visitation and in her years outside the convent, with instructions from Thérèse. She may not have had the full course, as Céline did, and as in somewhat different ways Pauline and Marie did, but she was given all the allegories, all the rich rhetoric of the Little Way, to meditate on. Thérèse reminded her frequently, as she did everyone, of her small size, of her littleness in the gaze of God. Remember, she told her in April, how I compared myself to a little toy, Jesus's little toy. And think, she tells Léonie, how many toys Jesus has, how many souls, and reflect, if you will follow *my* reflection, that the others are his fine toys and that you are, if you think as I do, "a small toy of no value." The psychological strength of this fancy of Thérèse's is in its concluding excursus. Little children, Thérèse remembers in her turn, often enjoy most of all those toys they can do anything at all with, toys which are easy to *"pick up* or *lay down, break* or *kiss."* The very valuable ones are hardly touched; they do not dare. So, then, how good it is to be poor and with what joy Thérèse prays each day to become more poor, "that every day Jesus might find more pleasure in *playing* with me."

Thérèse was very busy in the summer of 1895 with the affairs of Léonie and of her cousin Marie Guérin, who was about to make her entrance into Carmel. Thérèse worked on her uncle and aunt; softening them up, a cynical reader of her letters might say, preparing them to accept the sacrifice of their daughter, with flattering reflections on their own holiness. She told Aunt Céline she was saintly, however much she might herself deny it. And more, she was the sainted wife of a sainted husband. Sainted aunt, sainted uncle! Uncle Isidore seemed positively "transfigured," she told her aunt; "his speech," when he came to see her in the parlor with Marie, "was not the speech of the faith that hopes, but of the love that possesses." She remembered to quote that wry remark of Teresa of Avila's, "when she said to our Lord, who was laying crosses upon her at a time when she was undertaking mighty works for Him: 'Ah! Lord, I am not surprised that you have so few friends, you treat them so badly!'"

Of Marie, Thérèse's words were, if not more guarded, at least more precisely adapted to the present situation. She had "enough *energy* to become a saint. . . ." Energy, she explained, is the indispensable virtue in the making of saints. And she asked her aunt, in effect, to bring Marie closer to Léonie with that energy. One day in July, Léonie had come with Marie to see Thérèse and Léonie had been so full of emotion that she literally could not speak. She wept and wept until, at last, she was able to muster the strength and self-control to look up at her sisters. Léonie was obviously ashamed of her record as a religious, frustrated as she was in every attempt to become a nun, unequal to the demands of the religious life as perhaps she thought she was, and in comparison to her four sisters in Carmel a great failure, as anybody could see she was. In response to this display of Léonie's, Cousin Marie was "truly a 'valiant woman,'" Thérèse told her aunt. The compliment gave Marie no pleasure; she preferred to be called

"Little Angel," the title Thérèse hastily substituted for "valiant woman" when she saw her cousin's displeasure. "She is merry enough to make stones laugh, and this is a distraction for the poor girl with her," Thérèse explained.

To Marie, just before she entered the Carmel on September 15, Thérèse wrote a bubbly little note, full of warm love for Marie and for her parents and with just a hint of the possibilities of expansion through diminution to which she introduced all those close to her. She hoped above all, she told her cousin, that "dear Marie may keep her promises, staying as quiet as a small child in its Mother's arms." To Marie's sister Jeanne, Mme. La Néele, the only member of the Guérin family to be seriously disquieted at the entrance of Marie into Carmel, Thérèse wrote to assure her of the community's delight at the presence of the new postulant, Sister Marie of the Eucharist: "Her lovely voice makes us happy and is the delight of our recreation; but what especially rejoices my heart much more than all the talents and exterior qualities of our dear angel is her disposition to virtue." As for Jeanne's sacrifice—and how tactful it is of Thérèse to call it Jeanne's sacrifice and not Monsieur or Madame Guérin's or even Marie's—as for that, hasn't the Lord promised to all who leave fathers or mothers or sisters "for His sake a reward a hundredfold in this life"? Jeanne surely knew the scriptural reference; the line turns up in the Gospels of both Mark and Matthew. Thérèse promised her every return; she speaks with a becoming boldness about her lover's generosity. And then, before she finishes, she changes the subject entertainingly. She wants to thank Jeanne for her generous gifts of food, but, she explains, Jeanne's father keeps the Carmel more than well supplied with food; no one in the community is dying of hunger. What Thérèse wants is not fish but flowers. Could Jeanne send along a branch of eglantine, or maybe a periwinkle, or a buttercup, or any other quite ordinary flower? She wants to copy the flowers for her paintings. Later, if fish is needed, she could always sell her paintings and with the money buy the food, which she herself does not really like very much or want to think about very much. If this request is not quite right or proper, then Jeanne should forget it and send on the fish; Thérèse promises to be thoroughly grateful for it—especially grateful if Mme. La Néele is "kind enough" to include the beads of which she had spoken to Thérèse. See, she boasts, see what a convert I am, not at all silent about my needs or desires or the convent's but, if anything, too bold in my requests—"it is so difficult to keep the golden mean! . . . Luckily a Sister forgives everything, even the importunities of a little Benjamin."

She did not pester the Guérins with her letters, but she kept in touch with them. She knew how much the family was bound to be concerned about its girl in the community, and she knew just how to reassure everybody, uncle and aunt and cousin and cousin-in-law, about Marie. She sent her own few letters to the family and then tactfully, tastefully, briefly, added a line or two from time to time to the letters Marie sent home. She was saying, in almost so many words, that Marie was still with her family in the convent.

There must have been added consolation for the Guérins in knowing that Marie was almost immediately to be entrusted to Thérèse, who was *de facto* novice mistress. And certainly, Thérèse was quite prepared for the joyous occasion. Three days before Marie's entrance she wrote a tuneful religious poem, "My Heaven Here Below," to celebrate the twenty-first birthday of her great favorite among the novices, Sister Marie of the Trinity; now she quickly ran up a pious greeting in rhyme to give the day of entrance a properly festive air—"Song of a Soul Having Found the Place of Its Repose," suitable in theme, in tone, and with the best of melodic and rhythmic inspirations for such a performance: Thérèse based it on Ambroise Thomas's major achievement in his opera *Mignon*, the highly hummable *"Connaîs-tu le pays?"*

Thérèse was especially busy in 1895. It was as if her great burst of love, her Act of Oblation and dart of fire, had opened her to unceasing activity. She was surrounded with souls with whom to busy herself, and the more she desired to lead a hidden life with Jesus, the more claims were made on her attention—by her novices, by her correspondence, by her tasks as a writer. She was poet and dramatist and autobiographical memoirist, and she gave all the necessary time to these exercises, which to her had a tonality as unmistakably spiritual as her conferences with her charges or her prayers in choir or in her cell. But she had even more she could give and Mother Agnès knew it and took advantage of it. She was given a priest to help. The special devotion of the Carmelites to the needs and difficulties and the support and sanctification of priests was to be crowned in Thérèse's case by a brother, a younger brother, as she described the priest now entrusted to her help and hope and love.

For oh, how long, she had been gripped by a desire that was patently unrealizable, she says, as she introduces her younger brother into her memoirs. What if those two little boys of the family had not been sent off to heaven? What if she had been able to watch them ascending the steps to the altar? Well, that was quite impossible, but suddenly on her feast day, the day of Saint Teresa of Avila, she was startled to discover she had such a brother. Mother Agnès pulled her out of the laundry to read her a letter she had just received from a young seminarian attached to the Bishop of Bayeux. His name was Maurice-Barthélemy Bellière and he hoped to be a missionary, he wrote on October 15, 1895, from the Major Seminary of Sommervieu. Would Mother Agnès please ask a member of her community "in the name and on the feast of the great St. Teresa" to offer prayers and sacrifices in his support and in support of his missionary efforts? It was for this that Pauline came to Thérèse, then busy with the dirty linen. She read Thérèse the letter, in which M. Bellière promised always to remember his sister in religion in his Masses—when he was able to offer the sacrifice of the Mass. Thérèse, said the Prioress, was the choice; she would be the sister of this future missionary.

The joy this announcement let loose in her, Thérèse explains to Mother Gonzague in the third part of her autobiography, can only be called *enfantine*, childlike. To match it, she had to go back to the kind of pleasure she associated with her childhood, to joy of such acute intensity that the soul seems too small to contain it. Not in years had she tasted such happiness. She felt as if her soul were being constructed all over again: "it was as if one had stirred for the first time chords of music which until then had rested untouched and forgotten." She meditated on what this choice meant and realized that it carried large responsibilities with it for which she would have to prepare assiduously. So to all the other obligations of that heavy year—family, novices, community writing, autobiography—she added this new one. She prayed with redoubled fervor, she says, and looked forward to a still larger family and a spiritual life that would contain the marvelous dimension of a priest's sacrifices directly tied to hers, a priest's prayers offered up in unison with her own.

The immediate response to all of this was an undramatic thud.

The young seminarian—he was just a few months beyond his twenty-first birthday—wrote "a charming letter," says Thérèse, "full of warmth and noble sentiments," to thank Mother Agnès. A month later he sent a card bluntly announcing that he was on his way into military service. After that, there was "no sign of life" from him until the following July.

The immediate effect, then, was anticlimactic. All that drama of expectation followed by the poorest of responses, like a flat and feeble third act after a violent second-act curtain. But there was far more to the experience for Thérèse than immediate effects. It was another manifestation, precise and intense, that her communication with the next world was not merely fanciful. It was no hallucination, this dream of hers of sharing the life of a priest, ridiculous as it so often seemed upon what the world calls sober reflection, that is to say, unimaginative reflection. It was part of her life, a life in which reality and fantasy were never altogether separated, because her fantasies participated, all of them, in the only significant reality as she understood reality, the reality of eternity. For her, thought and action could not be long split apart without permanent damage to both. If thought did not lead to action, then there was some falsification or misapprehension involved. If her beliefs and motivations, her central convictions, made sense they did so because constantly there was clear evidence for them. Events like this one, bringing her the priest-brother she had long hoped for, occurred just often enough to confirm her in her ways. And what is more, they occurred in patterns as complex as this one, confirming her in those ways far more than they seemed to, at first, anyway. For it wasn't just the sudden appearance in her life of the young seminarian, but also the way it came, on the feast day of Teresa of Avila, her patron saint and Carmel's. And it wasn't simply the fact that her sister was Prioress and knew better than Mother Gonzague would have known how good a choice Thérèse would be for the blessed intercessor M. Bellière requested. It was also, in the remarkable chain of events, the fact that after the first flamboyant fireworks of the letter, the seminarian shut up, closed off all communications, for almost a year, except for the toneless announcement of his call to the army. That was the final touch, the appropriate ornamentation—the Lord giveth and the Lord taketh away, that pattern integral in the lives of the saints and so fundamental to

Thérèse's condition of servitude. Consolation, for a little while anyway, would have to rest upon the certain knowledge that at least, in the most obvious and prosaic terms, her dream had come true; she had a brother who was a priest.

The chain of confirmations never was broken in the case of Bellière, as seminarian or priest, as rarely it was broken in any of the linkings of souls with Thérèse. When his correspondence with his chosen sister was finally under way, it was, though short-lived, very moving to Bellière. Just before he left France to enter the novitiate of the White Fathers in Algiers, he wrote Mother Gonzague, Prioress again, marveling over the qualities of Thérèse. "What a saint!" he exclaimed. The day of his departure was not without some significance, too: it was September 29, 1897, the day before Thérèse died.

Abbé Bellière was marked by his relationship with Thérèse in more than one way. It was not only a relationship of coincidences and near-coincidences, which in a burst of enthusiasm we may want to attribute to the intercession of Providence. It was a relationship much more significantly governed by temperamental coincidences, by similarities of struggles and strippings. When the Abbé came, finally, to write Thérèse in July of 1896, it was to narrate his temptations against the missionary vocation, his "storm," as Thérèse called it, when she was able, three months later, to speak of the temptations in the past tense. Like Thérèse, he felt temptations at the heart of his being, at the core of his faith. No slight imperfections for him, no trivial faults. He had to struggle against fundamental doubts about what he was doing in Africa as a novice and planning to do afterwards as a priest. Thérèse responded with prayers and sacrifices and letters of spiritual counsel designed, as she put it, not merely to make him an able and acceptable missionary, "but a *saint*, all aflame with love for God and for souls." And she asked for an equal and opposite grace through his intercession: "Obtain that love for me too, I beg, that I may help you in your apostolic labor. You know that a Carmelite who was not an apostle would be losing sight of the goal of her vocation and would cease to be a daughter of the Seraphic St. Teresa, who would have given a thousand lives to save a single soul."

Abbé Bellière found the necessary strength to survive his temptations, whether directly from Thérèse's words or indirectly from her prayers and sacrifices does not matter. It would not matter if one could prove that he found all the necessary sustenance for his vocation far from Thérèse, with no conscious or unconscious repairing to the resources she provided. The fact is that he was enough like her in temperament to react like her to the difficulties of the religious life. And it is also a fact that his life, like hers, was brief and ringed with suffering. He achieved his ordination with considerable peace and became a missionary of considerable skill. But he soon contracted sleeping sickness—not immediately recognized as such—and was sent back to his home in Normandy, not far from the seminary from which he had first written Thérèse, and not very far from the Carmel in Lisieux, to die at the age of thirty-three. However much or little we may conclude his life was shaped by his relationship with Thérèse, he himself thought it was closely tied to his intercessor's life and thought. When he read her autobiography, he wrote Mother Gonzague again, to attest to the ties. He felt, he told her, "the continual action" of Thérèse on his soul.

Thérèse herself was quite certain of her role as intercessor. She knew her prayers had power; there was never any question about that. She concluded her offices for Céline in the year 1895 by slipping a note, on the back of a picture of the Child Jesus cutting lilies, into one of her sandals on Christmas Night. The action was an adult version of the family's ancient custom which had ended with her Christmas conversion in 1886. The note was an affirmation of faith in prayer that she gave as her Carmelite Christmas gift to Céline the Carmelite. It begins with the quotation from Jesus (in Matthew 18:19-20) upon which so much of the strength of conviction of priests depends. Jesus is speaking to his disciples, saying, "I say to you, that if two of you shall consent upon earth, concerning anything whatsoever they shall ask, it shall be done to them by my Father who is in heaven. For where there are two or three gathered together in my name, there am I in the midst of them." Upon this certainty, Thérèse rests an additional prayer, begging God never to separate her from Céline or Céline from her. Keep your two lilies together to console you, she asks the Lord, "for the little love you find in this valley of tears, and may their petals glow with the same brilliance for all eternity and shed the same perfume when they bend towards you!"

It is characteristic of Thérèse's increasing boldness in the last years of her life to appropriate to herself and Céline as nuns the text in Matthew so long regarded as conferring sacramental powers upon priests, and especially those which permit them to make fundamental moral judgments, from a pronouncement of dogma by the Bishop of Rome to an act of absolution in the confessional. The text immediately preceding the one Thérèse quotes is the thundering definition, bare and precise: "Amen, I say to you, whatsoever you shall bind upon earth, shall be bound also in heaven: and whatsoever you shall loose upon earth, shall be loosed also in heaven." In more familiar language, this is to say that whatever the disciples forbid, the Lord will forbid; whatever they permit, the Lord will permit. And the Church has understood the role of the disciples to be shared with all those in the apostolic succession who have the necessary orders to bind and to loose, to forbid and to permit, that is to say, bishops and all other prelates and priests. The classical commentaries of the Church all give this interpretation. As St. Jerome puts it, "the sentence of man is ratified by the sentence of God." But the Fathers of the Church were not content with the legalistic reading alone. They heeded always St. Paul's injunction not to neglect the spirit of the law in their adherence to the letter. And so John Chrysostom says about Thérèse's text: "He did not say barely, *Where two or three are gathered together,* but added, *in my name,* as much to say, If any man look upon Me as the chief motive of his love to his neighbor, I will be with him, though his virtue be shown towards other men." Chrysostom is precise, too, in requiring that the prayer of Christ's religious must be in his name and for his purposes. Origen, the most imaginative of all commentators, says much the same thing, but with perhaps a deeper sense of what agreement means. He says, "our prayers are not granted because we do not agree together in all things upon earth, neither in doctrine, nor in conversation. For as in music, unless the voices are in time there is no pleasure to the hearer, so in the Church, unless they are united God is not pleased therein, nor does He hear their words." Jerome, finally, seeks a still richer modality of agreement in the individual. This is his spiritual paraphrase of the text: "where our spirit, soul, and body are in agreement, and have not within them conflicting wills, they shall obtain from my Father everything they shall ask; for none can doubt that that demand is good, where the body wills the same thing as the spirit."

248

This is Thérèse's transfiguring certainty: her body and her spirit will the same thing. She feels the force of her love inwardly and outwardly, in tangible ways and in ways altogether beyond touch or taste of the senses. All her poetry of this fiery year is shot through with this sort of feeling, carrying passion back and forth from the spirit to the flesh and the flesh to the spirit, making the ineffable somehow effable. She concludes her poem for Sister Marie of the Trinity, "My Heaven Here Below," with the familiar plea to be held in Jesus's flaming embrace. It is here below she asks for her embrace—and soon—

> Soon, from your adorable mouth,
> Give me that everlasting kiss!

For that embrace, for that kiss, she is content to strip herself of all other consolation, she says in the same poem. It is enough to know the mystery of Jesus in some inner radiance. But is it? The poem is about something quite open and tangible, after all, the Holy Face, which she calls her "only wealth." Hiding in its scarred furrows, she will be like Jesus himself, she says. And how will she be like him? The answer is in her plea that he mark her with his image so that she can draw all hearts to him. She wants nothing less than everything. She demands the deepest sensations of the spirit; she pleads for the physical marks of love to heighten her sensations.

Ultimately she would receive the physical marks of her love, the marks of suffering; she was very close in the winter of 1895–96 to those deep significations of requited love between such lovers. She dwelt constantly on the humanity of Jesus in her meditations; that was why she was so firmly fixed on the Holy Face and turned others to it as often as she could. There were marks on that face, marks that could be imitated, marks that should not be forgotten. No, inner radiance was not enough; there had also to be some outer glow, even if to the world it did not shine at all, but looked more like weariness, or boredom, or sickness, or distraction of some strange kind. She was following the advice of Jesus to St. Gertrude, as recorded by the thirteenth-century mystic in her book *The Herald of Divine Love*. In his appearances to her, Jesus reproached her, Gertrude says, for her too great devotion to works of the intellect: she was a learned woman, skillful in languages and in philosophy. Turn instead to me, was the Lord's counsel. Make your research "those of my words that breathe the most of love; copy them, and then guarding them like precious relics, be sure to read them over and over again." These, Gertrude says she was told by Jesus, are "the most precious relics of mine that remain on earth . . . the words of my love, the words that came from my tender heart."

Thérèse quotes the conversation of Gertrude and Jesus as an epigraph to a long series of verses on the tune of "*Rappelle-toi*"— "Remember thou"—written at the request of Céline. Céline had asked for a set of lines based on the familiar air, which should "remind" Jesus of all that had been sacrificed for him by Céline and by the other members of her family. Thérèse responded with a very long poem, thirty-three stanzas, in which she never referred to any sacrifice of Céline's or the family's. She addressed herself to "Jesus, My Beloved," whom she asked to remember signal events in his life, in which he made his humanity and his divinity manifest to men. Céline thought Thérèse's refusal even vaguely to advert to her own sacrifices or to those of the Martins was the result of an intention to give her "a little lesson" in humility. She compared herself to the Pharisee, in the parable of the Pharisee and the Publican, boasting of giving away a tenth of all his goods. She saw Thérèse as teaching self-abnegation so that she might live only for love and in love, and certainly the poem is a long series of reiterations of the size and stature of Jesus's deprivations, of Jesus's derelictions, of Jesus's loving gifts to man, which make man whatever he is and indicate how much more he might be. But one does not forget self entirely, as Céline suggests Thérèse teaches us to do in this poem. Self emerges richer, fuller, more loving, more loved, more itself, from the energetic memory exercises of "*Rappelle-toi.*" Self comes through self-purged, but no less, if one may be allowed to continue this play on words, no less itself, but rather far, far more. For what is purged—purified—is attachment to self, self-importance, self-gratification, but not self itself. One's identity is more pronounced than ever if one loses oneself in the love Thérèse outlines here as she cites the central events of Jesus's life, for by that great paradoxical doctrine of merit to which she was herself so attached, the more one gives freely away to Jesus, the more one receives back; the more one hides in him, the more one is exposed to him, and to be exposed to him is to be exposed to Being pure, to Being Itself, and thus to be enlarged far beyond one's original size. Then, one has a self worth claiming, when one has, as best one can, merged one's self with the Lord's Self.

Thérèse was fond of saying that she paid little attention to poetic form or rules of versification. She wanted no part of the little treatise on prosody that Marie of the Trinity brought with her to the Carmel in 1894. "I prefer not to know the rules," she told Sister Marie; "my poems are a burst of the heart, an inspiration." She wanted no part of the discipline of poetry if it meant subjugating the spirit to a rule of technique. "At that price," she said, "I would prefer to give up writing poetry altogether." But she did find ease in adapting her lines to familiar tunes and in "*Rappelle-toi*" she managed a complicated stanza with facility. Each nine-line strophe consists of four ten-syllable lines, two alexandrines, two verses of six syllables each, and a concluding four-syllable cadence. Each ends in *toi* or *moi*, in *thee* or *me*: the intimacy of her relationship with Jesus is never lost, even when she is merely detailing the events of his life on earth. For what she is saying in this complicated stanza is, Come, come to me; remember how eagerly I run to you and, please, run as swiftly and warmly and joyously to me. She says it many different ways, with plays on words that are obvious and plays on words that are subtle, with paraphrases of Jesus's own words and a constant reiteration of the symbol system of the Song of Songs. In one stanza, the twenty-second, much of the wit and worth of the poem seems to me to be concentrated. It is a handsome example of Thérèse's joining of the flesh and the spirit, of her love of verbal paradoxes as paradigms of metaphysical paradoxes. She was, she knew, wholly virginal and as a direct result most fertile. For if the soul, in her memorable coinage, could be properly *virginized*, then it would be truly fruitful, not at all sterile: it would bear endless generations of love. She was saying what others have understood, too, that chastity is not a synonym for celibacy, and that celibacy, all by itself, is not necessarily pure in the way that only the fiery embraces of love could make one pure—could *virginize* one's soul.

> *Ton sang, tes pleurs, cette source féconde*
> Virginisant *les calices des fleurs,*
> *Les a rendus capables, dès ce monde,*
> *De t'enfanter un grand nombre de coeurs.*

Je suis vierge, ô Jesus! Cependant, quel mystère!
En m'unissant à toi, des âmes je suis mère. . . .
Des virginales fleurs
Qui sauvent les pécheurs,
Oh! souviens-toi!

For once, I think, one must be punctilious in preserving the second-person singular pronoun of the French in translating this stanza. Thérèse made much of the way she addressed Jesus. He was distinctly "thou" and "thee" to her, in a time and place when the choice to *tu-toyer*, to use the second-person singular, was, if not momentous, at least something one did with great conscious-ness of what one was doing. Addressing a stranger, or even a well-known acquaintance who was not a very close friend, as *tu* was at worst insulting and at least bad manners. Children were properly addressed as *tu*, children and, Thérèse would have added, God.

Thy blood, thy tears, that fertile source
Virginizing the calyxes of flowers,
Has made them capable—right here on earth—
Of impregnating a huge number of hearts.
I am a virgin, O Jesus! But what a mystery this is!
In uniting with thee, I become the mother of souls. . . .
Of virginal flowers
That rescue sinners,
Oh! remember this!

The verses came pouring out in an abundance of feeling. There were thirty-three verses for Céline, to enjoin her to remember Christ's sacrifices rather than her own; a Christmas pageant for the community with twenty-six sets of verses begging the alms of charity from her Sisters in Carmel, and another pious drama, "The Flight into Egypt," to celebrate Mother Agnès's feast day in Janu-ary. The Christmas piece, "The Holy Little Beggar of Christmas-time," places an angel with the infant Jesus in her arms at stage center. She chants the marvel of the Incarnation, sets the babe in his manger and then turns to the community with a slip of paper for each of the Sisters. They draw their slips, one by one, each holding up her ticket before the angel, each singing her appro-priate song of love, asking gifts for Jesus, in clipped little verses, a throne of gold, milk, birds, roses, grapes, a smile, a toy, bread, cake, honey, etc. There were five tunes on which Thérèse based this pageant; there were six in the piece she wrote for Pauline. In this last, she mixed prose and verse to such emotional effect that she evoked her own tears; she found herself deeply moved at the time of the performance, whether because of the performance itself or her own words or the subject, we do not know. She was in a great state of excitement in any case. The day before the performance, on January 20, 1896, she presented Mother Agnès with the first pages of her memoirs, the opening chapters. Her fertility was unmistakable.

When, in February, Céline was professed, Thérèse had another rush of words to paper, and with the words drawings, illuminations in imitation of a parchment coat-of-arms. Every detail was chosen to bring alive the majesty of the occasion in terms of the central allegory of religious souls, the marriage of the human spirit and the divine. Once again, Thérèse sneaked her greeting into Céline's cell. There Céline found an oversized envelope with a drawing of the Holy Face affixed to it as a stamp. It was addressed

From the Knight Jesus
To my beloved Spouse
Geneviève of St. Teresa
Living on love upon the Mount of Carmel
Land of Exile

The imitation of parchment was as complete as Thérèse could make it, following the heraldic designs Céline had made for herself. But where Céline had used only pen and ink, Thérèse used paint for the double blazon over Céline's chosen motto, "Who loses wins." She carefully lettered all that followed, a Marriage Contract between Jesus and Céline. The titles were somewhat less elaborate than those she had worked out for the Heavenly Court in making her own wedding announcement. There was less humor and more serious doctrine here. Jesus, "the Eternal Word, the Only Son of God and of the Virgin Mary" weds "Céline, princess in exile, poor and without titles." He gives himself to her, he says, "under the name of Knight of Love, Suffering and Contempt." She is not yet ready to be received into her homeland with her permanent titles and wealth. Here, like her Lord, she must lead a hidden life, concealing the gifts he gives to her, freely allowing him to take back what he gives, if he wills, attaching herself to nothing, without human respect, without any

253

regard even for that which might raise her in her own esteem. It is the substance of the story of Patient Griselda, as narrated by Boccaccio and Petrarch and Chaucer, Griselda, that model of patience and obedience and love who remains faithful to her ignoble marquis of a husband, in spite of all the trials he sets her, through destitution and desertion and the loss of her children, all effected by her apparently stone-hearted spouse. Griselda was a "type" of Christ or the Church for her medieval chroniclers, a startling incarnation of the virtues, but not an impossible one. What she accomplished was, in greater or lesser degree, to be emulated; she was not, for all her miraculous patience, inimitable. What she did in the tales told of her, what Jesus did in the life lived by him on earth, what the saints do—all can be done again, with difficulty, but with joy and with charm, too. The marriage contract Thérèse draws up for Céline neglects none of the marvels of fidelity or of femininity. Sister Geneviève will bear her knight's absence with exemplary patience; he will be allowed to fight alone so "that he alone may have the glory of victory." And what will she have? She will be happy enough, wielding "only the sword of Love. Like a sweet melody, her voice will charm me in the midst of camps. The slightest sigh of love she utters will inflame my best troops with a wholly new ardor."

In the great tradition of all lovers, of all knights and of all knights' ladies, and in the consecrated tradition of Carmel, Céline will carry her lover's name with her, marked indelibly on her person: all Carmelites have a symbol to mark their clothing— Thérèse's was the Reed, Céline's was nothing less than the first three letters of Jesus's name, the Greek capitals IHS, that monogram which adorns so many of the vessels and vestments of Christianity. That "royal seal," Thérèse comments, as Jesus's spokesman in the contract, "will be the mark" of Céline's "allpower" over his heart. That monogram as her symbol and her hidden association with the Holy Face were dowry enough. The auguries were magnificent and Thérèse's writing glows with them. In fact, as it turned out, Céline did not have to wait until eternity to take possession of her permanent title. In 1916, her long association with the devotion to the Holy Face was recognized with the widespread reprinting of her drawing of the image that is to be seen in the Shroud of Turin and the simultaneous restoration to her of the key words of her first name in Carmel: she became Sister Geneviève of St. Thérèse and of the Holy Face.

As a quite tangible proof of her own intense joy on the occasion of Céline's profession, Thérèse gave to her the linen cloth in which she had caught the last tear of Mother Geneviève. With it, she sent a brief note written as if from the beloved foundress—"To you, my dearest Child, I give as a wedding present the *last tear* I shed in this land of exile. . . ." Nor was that all Thérèse did—the profession on February 23 and the veiling on March 17 required a set of verses—"Sweet Souvenir"—and a holy picture, bringing together Mary and the Child Jesus and another child and four little cherubim, a series of simple and clear emblems of beauty and of suffering and of endurance. It was still another way of signifying Thérèse's depth of emotion at the riches of family life that were being gathered round her in ever-deepening circles at Carmel.

How deep those circles were! The same day that Céline received the veil, Marie Guérin took the Carmelite habit with the name of Marie of the Eucharist. Four days later, Mother Gonzague was re-elected Prioress in place of Mother Agnès (Pauline) with, one gathers, a high degree of ill-feeling on the part of several supporters of each of the illustrious ladies. The election required seven ballots before Mother Gonzague was chosen. Thérèse, close as ever to Pauline, was also very close to Mother Gonzague. In spite of all the vigor with which the Prioress had established her rule over Thérèse in her early days at the Carmel, in spite of what seemed a sometimes grim, never gracious, and always clumsy manner in dealing with Thérèse, Mother Gonzague remained what her name insisted she should be in a community of Sisters, a mother, and even, as Thérèse calls her, a dear and a darling mother. She was not ever the evil genius that some of the biographers of Thérèse have made her out to be. She may even, on several occasions and in several ways, have been the presiding genius that Thérèse deserved, that Thérèse needed, for she managed to keep the peace, no matter how tremulously, in a frightfully difficult situation. For there she stood, there she ruled, installed again as Mother Prioress, a mother with double title to motherhood in the Lisieux Carmel, as favorite of a great many of the nuns and as the head of the family within the family, the four Martin girls and their cousin Marie.

Perhaps it was Mother Gonzague's fondness for her own family, amounting so often to the weak indulgence of her sister, the countess, and of her sister's grandchildren, and demanding of her community a like indulgence. Perhaps it was Mother Gonzague's laziness or timidity about facing the obvious conflict with Carmelite rule and tradition that the presence of so many members of one family represented. Perhaps it was her fear of Mother Agnès's disapproval or popularity. Or perhaps it was a recognition on her part of Thérèse's real stature, slow to come, not quite conscious at first, but real enough, finally, to emerge as still another family relationship, the one that assures Mother Marie de Gonzague of her own permanent titles in the history of high human achievement, in the history of sanctity. For the recognition did come. Mother Gonzague made Thérèse feel entirely at ease in her last years, her last months, her last days. The tribute Thérèse pays her in the opening pages of the third section of her autobiography, written just three months before she died, is a glowing witness to the Prioress's understanding handling of Thérèse, and more, to her love for this girl, this difficult girl, this thoughtful girl, this touching girl, this most gifted of her Sisters, this genius among nuns.

"*Mère bien-aimée,*" Thérèse begins each of the first two paragraphs addressed to Mother Gonzague, not just "Dear Mother," as it has been translated into English, and certainly not "Dear Reverend Mother," but literally, "well-beloved," or more idiomatically, "my beloved," or "darling." She is not gushing over her religious superior, but recording her very warm feeling for Mother Gonzague, who first encouraged her, when as a child she conceived the ambition to become a Carmelite, and who was now so straightforwardly continuing the trust of Mother Agnès in Thérèse's concluding task on earth, "to sing the mercies of the Lord." Thérèse quotes the first line of the eighty-eighth Psalm to define that task and sees herself as nothing less than another psalmist, with Mother Gonzague as the visible representation of the God who inspired both the writers of the Psalms and herself. Under the guidance of Mother Agnès she sang of the graces given the little flower in the springtime of her life. Under Mother Gonzague, she must "sing of the happiness of this very small flower now that the bashful rays of the dawn have given way to the burning heat of midday." She remembers with deep emotion that it was under this superior that she gave herself up entirely to

God, when she was professed. And she remembers with equally intense feeling that difficult day for Mother when she was re-elected Prioress, a day of tears for Mother Gonzague, but a joyful one in what it promised of her ultimate reward.

Is it enough to say, as some have done, that this is an example of Thérèse's great delicacy, this way of treating the sensitive issue of authority in the Carmel, the authority and the allegiance divided, at least in the minds of their supporters, between Mother Gonzague and Mother Agnès? I think we must be guided by the tribute to Mother Gonzague that follows, in which Thérèse explains that she thinks of her superior as more her mother than her prioress and begs to be excused for her childish simplicity in thinking of her this way. It is more than a show of comely rhetoric, for Thérèse goes on to defend the Prioress against all accusers and all accusations. Some of the Sisters say Mother Gonzague spoiled Thérèse always—not so, not so, as the first manuscript of her autobiography clearly reveals. No, Thérèse says, quite the contrary, I've always received the most stiff treatment from you, "*forte* et maternelle," strong and motherly. And then she goes on, as if to anticipate the accounts to come, in which Mother Gonzague will be cast as the villain, to express her gratitude for such treatment. The sensitive little plant that she was needed the invigorating waters of humiliation; without them it could not have taken root. And now, that treatment having achieved its aim, a new warmth is indicated, and *voilà!* Mother provides the necessary tenderness, the easy smiles, all the marks of confidence which she must have. For a year and a half now, Thérèse writes, Jesus has wanted this new treatment, and so, with that precision which makes Mother Gonzague so convincing a representative for the Lord, the treatment has been changing.

With what ease, then, Thérèse could settle down to her last year and a half on earth! She was herself the visible representation of love at the convent, the healing spirit that brought peace between the two hostile camps. She enjoyed the complete confidence of both mothers. Mother Gonzague early signaled her trust by continuing Thérèse in her post as associate mistress of novices, with all the duties of that key position in the community, in spite of the limited title. Mother Agnès raised no open signal and did not need to—she had never been very different in Thérèse's eyes,

257

even when she was her superior, from the sister who became her first little mother after Zélie's death.

Thérèse did need the reassurance that the succession of motherly figures in her life brought her. As she confides to Mother Gonzague in that remarkable succession of pages with which she begins the last section of her autobiography, she knew in the last years of her life with absolute certainty that she was not going to change in stature or character. Hers was the little way in every sense of the term—she would have to be content with remaining a little person, perhaps even becoming smaller than she had been. She looked then for a very little way, the shortest possible road to eternity, reasoning that her littleness could find such a short-cut and with a special ease in this era of inventions. We don't need stairs anymore—the rich, at least, always use an elevator. What elevator would lift her up to Jesus? She was too small to make the steep climb to perfection by herself. She consulted Scripture and found her answers, the triumphant chain of answers that, strung together, did just as she wanted, her spirit was elevated; she was lifted along the little way, through the short-cut, to her lover.

From Proverbs (9:4) she took her principle: "Whosoever is a little one, let him come to me." Running to obey that command, she found the support given to the smallest of all, the newly born baby: "As one whom the mother caresseth, so will I comfort you," she read in the book of Isaiah (66:13), and just above it, "You shall be carried at the breasts, and upon the knees. . . ." Thérèse croons her joy over these passages. "Ah!" she exclaims, "never were words sweeter than these, never more melodious. . . ." It is in the arms of Jesus that she will be lifted up to heaven. The road is clear. She knows her way, her little way. She has found her short-cut.

She muses that the road may be very short indeed. She meditates on two verses from the seventieth Psalm, "Thou hast taught me, O God, from my youth: and till now I will declare thy wonderful works. And unto old age and gray hairs. . . ." What does old age mean for her? Couldn't it be now, right now? Wasn't it possible that she was now in her old age? She realized that for the Lord of all being, two thousand years were no more than twenty, no more, really, than one day. Though she does not say so explicitly, she suggests in this way that she has some idea of the accelerated rate at which she has lived her life, that she knows that, like Mozart and Pushkin and a few other rare people, she has lived at double or triple the normal rate, so that at twenty-three she is a mature woman, a wise old woman, nearer, much nearer, seventy than thirty.

Beloved Mother, she hastens to reassure her superior, Beloved Mother, I am not anxious to leave you. All I want, all that means anything to me, is to do his desire, to give pleasure to him, to Jesus. Forgive me, forgive me, she begs, if I sadden you. You want me to go on doing here, near you, what some time ago you asked me to do, in the words of Jesus to Peter, "Feed my lambs." Can't I do that sweet task, that lovely and easy task, in heaven just as well as here? I am so small a person, the most insignificant of persons, too small to be burdened with a large-scale vanity. You told me, you were not afraid to tell me, that God would illuminate my soul, would give me in bursts of light the experience of years. I know such experiences, without being able to find the eloquent phrases for them; great things have been done in me, in my littleness, and the greatest is to know just how little I am beside the omnipotence of God.

Thérèse had many trials in these last months of her life. With each great moment, with each unmistakable impression of the presence of God, there came, almost like an answering antiphon of desolation to the amen of joy, a sense of deprivation, of being without her lover, without her love; without hope; without faith. But no matter how terrible this test of faith was—and it seemed often enough to touch bottom, to reach the depths of despair—it never altogether obscured the vision that came to her on the night of the second of April 1896, and the early morning of the third, the vision that came to her touch, to her taste, and finally to her eyes. It was Good Friday Eve. She went late to bed, at midnight, after a long vigil at the altar of repose. Hardly, she says, had she put her head on her pillow, when she felt a flood welling up in her, a warm flood bubbling up in her until it it reached her lips. "I did not know what it was, but I thought that perhaps I was going to die and my soul was filled with joy." It must be blood; she was fairly sure it was blood. The lamp was out and so, with her own strict asceticism, little enough in its way, but firm enough too, she stifled her natural curiosity and waited until morning to see what it was, to see what she had tasted and felt. When she awoke, her immediate thought, a feeling more than a thought, really, was that there was something delightful to learn about, good news. She stood up to the window and looked and there was the sign, the unmistakable stain of blood; she was not mistaken, she thought with pleasure. It was a "great consolation," no less, that Jesus, on the anniversary of his death, should echo the glorious words of his "first appeal," the words which announced his gladsome arrival, "Behold the bridegroom cometh. . . ." She heard the words; she felt them, she writes, "like a sweet and distant murmuring. . . ." She knew then, she must have known with the greatest certainty, that she would not have much longer to do her tasks here on earth, and it was not a difficult knowledge for her, not an insupportable one, but the best of news, the news for which she had waited most of her life.

THIRTEEN

*T*HE night following the first bloodletting, the night of Good Friday, brought the same welcome taste to Thérèse's lips. She had been allowed to spend the day in fasting, in spite of her confession of the night's events to Mother Gonzague. She had begged not to be dispensed from the austere Carmelite celebration of the sacred day and her wise superior had gone along with her on the assurance that she felt no pain. All day she thought about the nearness of paradise and her thoughts seemed fully confirmed when that night "Jesus gave" her, as she puts it, the same signal once again that her "entrance into heaven was not far off."

Thérèse rhapsodizes about the vision of eternity which her intense faith had erected in her at that time. Surely everybody believed as she did? How could there be anyone without such certainty as hers about the place itself? How could anyone miss that sense of clarity, of order, of an end reasonable and joyous, giving purpose to everything here below, straightening the furrows of a quizzical and querulous uncertainty with the simple tidy sweetness of heavenly certitude? Those who spoke against the vision, she thought, were denying their own inner beliefs, were denying themselves. And then suddenly, capsizingly, all at once, in a terrible flash of blackness, her own certainties were turned into doubts, her own affirmations became denials. In the cruelest of metamorphoses, her nighttime visions became daytime darkness. For every leap of light in the dark of night, there was an accompanying burst of darkness in the light of day. She woke, within a day, to volumes of darkness and doubt. She was no longer sure of what she believed. She was not sure of anything—suddenly—startlingly—terribly—not sure of anything except that she was not sure of anything.

Thérèse records those doubts that came all at once in the first days of April 1896 with the lucidity of a soul that knows all its experiences with absolute and thorough consciousness. Hers is the consciousness of the spirit that brings total recall. For in it she lives altogether alert to darkness, to blindness, to rejection, desolation, and near despair, as she also stays alive to every mark of hope, of consolation, of acceptance, of clearsightedness, of light. From childhood she had worked hard on her spiritual geography, had charted her course from world to world, knowing by intuition and instinct just where she was going and what it would be like when she arrived. This was banishment. That was home. And she had as firm a presentiment about its existence and how she would reach it as, she says, Christopher Columbus did of his new world. And now suddenly it has all disappeared into a dense fog of doubt, a mist dark and thick and horrifyingly alive with voices! Her doubt chatters to her. Her darkness has a loud and nagging theological voice. It mocks her in agonizing tones borrowed, she explains, from sinners. It addresses her intimately—no polite second-person plural when the darkness speaks: *"—Tu rêves la lumière, une patrie embaumée des plus suaves parfums, tu rêves. . . ."* You dream, you dream, you dream, you dream . . . of the light, of a paradise bathed in the most delicate fragrances, of permanent possession of the Creator of all these wonders. You dream, oh, how you dream, if you think of emerging someday from these mists that surround you! Go ahead, take comfort, rejoice in the death that will bring you, not what you hope for at all, but a greater darkness still, *la nuit de néant,* the night of annihilation, of nothing.

Beloved Mother, Thérèse writes to her prioress, I'm not at all sure you want to hear all of this confused and badly expressed thought of mine. I don't write to produce literature, she explains, but only under obedience. Literature? Well, it is a kind of literary form; she understands that. It resembles a fairy tale. But the fairy tale has all of a sudden turned into a frightened prayer. The fairy-tale imagery of her vision of heaven, blotted into darkness by all her doubts, has become a set of nervous ejaculations, of staccato seekings after peace, of obstinate reiterations of hope in the face of despair. She has had her prayers of tenderness and loving confidence. She has had her exquisite glimpses of perfection. She has had the light. Now she has the darkness and has it almost all the time. Now she must make her acts of faith in the dark. Now she must make the dark itself into an act of faith.

Nothing in the literature of the mystics detailing the torments of the so-called dark night of the soul is more eloquent of personal experience than the pages of Thérèse's autobiography in which she describes the settling of the darkness over her days. This is not the poetry of John of the Cross, in which the soul, cast in the role of the Bride in the Song of Songs, is purged, systematically, to meet its Bridegroom. And this is assuredly not the extensive sort of prose gloss on a poetic text that Saint John makes, showing the way one who is called to this sort of transfiguring experience can move stage by stage through a whole sequence, first of active and then of passive purifications, to become worthy of meeting Love in some sort of direct union. There is reflection here. There are many pauses, digressions, really, in which Thérèse attempts to make sense of her deep suffering, to explain it to herself, to explain it to Mother Gonzague, and to reconcile it in all its terrors with her joyous expectations of childhood, of girlhood, of the years in the convent, of the night just before and the night just before that, the two April nights in 1896, Good Friday Eve and Good Friday night, when heaven seemed to light on her shoulders and beckon to her with the utmost directness and clarity and certainty. There is all this and then there is something more: There is a superlative honesty, a bluntness of expression, a simplicity that makes her understandable to us today as no poetry, even such sublime poetry as John's, can ever quite be, and convincing as no systematic theological exposition of mystical states, even such extraordinarily brilliant theology as John's, can hope to be.

She apologizes several times for the quality of her writing. It is badly expressed, confused. It is as imperfect as an artist's rough sketch when compared to his model. She fears she may have blasphemed: "I am afraid I've said too much. . . ." She begs Jesus's pardon if she has done him any wrong—"He knows that even when I have nothing of the joy of the faith, I try to do its works. I think I've made more acts of faith in this last year than in all the rest of my life." She doesn't attempt a face-to-face meeting with her adversary—it would be cowardice to try to duel with him. She runs instead to Jesus, ready to shed her blood to the last drop to defend the fact of heaven. Too much suffering?

How can there be? "For is there a greater joy than this, of suffering for your love?" And if it is hidden suffering, ignored even by God himself, it will be enough if perhaps it can be used to obstruct one sin, just one sin against faith, or to make up for one.

"My Beloved Mother," she cries out, "I may seem to exaggerate my trials, especially if you judge by the sentiments I express in the little poems that I have been writing this year; I must seem to you a soul packed with consolations, a soul for whom the veil that hides the faith is nearly ripped away. . . . No, no, it isn't a veil, it's a wall that reaches right up through the skies and blindfolds the stars themselves. When I sing of the happiness of heaven, of possessing God forever, I feel no joy at all, I sing only what *I WANT TO BELIEVE*. Yes, sometimes, the tiniest bit of sunlight cuts through my darkness and for *an instant* the misery is suspended, but right afterward the memory of that moment of light, far from bringing me joy, makes the darkness seem thicker than ever."

Can she bear it? She can. Her trial by doubt has come at the right time. She is strong enough now. She will not be discouraged as she would have been at any earlier time. Now it is an acceptable purgation, weaning her from that natural satisfaction which her longings and her images of heaven have brought her. Nothing remains now to stop her soul from taking flight, she tells Mother Gonzague on June 9, 1897, the second anniversary of her Act of Oblation: "I have no other great desire in me except to go on loving until I die of love."

Undoubtedly it took weeks, months, for all of this to sort itself out in Thérèse's mind, perhaps the whole long period, as time is measured in Thérèse's life, from April 1896, when the first annihilating doubts assailed her, until June 1897, when she made her great confidences about them to Mother Gonzague. There were distractions, duties; as always, someone was around to see her, begging a poem to solemnize an occasion; there were letters to write, to felicitate Léonie on her feast day, April 11, St. Leo the Great's day, or to explain a stream of flowers on a young nun's bed, forget-me-nots, with which she was celebrating the profession of her favorite novice, Sister Marie of the Trinity. There were, as always, too, a few moments of grandeur, in which, no matter how terrible the darkness of the moment before or how depressing the mists inexorably to follow after, she was granted some further hint of an eternal ecstasy and was now, here and now, allowed, however briefly, a *soupçon* of exaltation.

One suspects that the growing weakness in her body contributed its share to her random ecstasies and periodic exaltations, as well as her bouts of depression. The tuberculosis that was making its way through her system with such stately persistence must have occasionally lost its awareness of the protocol of the blood, to flare up in an undignified fever or a far from stately cough. Thérèse was prepared to welcome these outbursts and to be consoled by them, because she found confirmation in them of her early great expectations—a shaft of light in the gloomy darkness. That was the conscious side of her experience, the joy she could know with her mind and feel with her body. There was also the euphoria that so often accompanies tuberculosis. Unquestionably from time to time she would surrender to that curious elation that is the occasional compensation for the ravages of tubercular fever and chill. But the really extraordinary relief from constant darkness and debilitation and gloom that she was several times vouchsafed cannot be diagnosed as wild lines on a fever chart or the mere chattering of an overnourished imagination. For what she was granted now, just a month and a few days after the terrors of darkness first descended, was foreknowledge of her approaching death, rather more precise than the presentiment that accompanied her first vomiting of blood and really a great deal more consoling in its detailed assuaging of her fears and uncertainties and little griefs.

It all came in a dream, the details of which she specified in the letter she wrote in September 1896 at the urgent request of her sister Marie, the shortest of the three parts of her autobiography, manuscript B. It was a Saturday night in May, the eve of the second Sunday in Mary's month, Thérèse calls it, and perhaps, she thinks, the anniversary of the great day of the Virgin's smile, when the statue of Mary came alive to her. This conjecture was close enough to the facts, since it was the second Sunday in May 1883 that the earlier event had occurred and there was only a difference of a few days, this Sunday being May 10, the earlier one May 13. Thérèse went to bed with the same depressed feeling with which she had been living for the past month: her sky, she says, was still filled with clouds. She had no dreams, she thought, to look forward to; dreams were not for her little soul.

But at dawn, after a fitful night, she did dream a remarkable dream, a moving one that brought more light than she would have thought possible a few hours before.

She found herself in a kind of gallery, one among several persons, but the others, except for her prioress, were at some distance from her and not altogether clear. Suddenly she became aware of three Carmelite nuns, fully veiled and mantled; they manifested themselves like spirits out of the wall or up from the floor. They had apparently come to see the Prioress. Thérèse knew at once where they had come from; she knew with certainty that they were from heaven. In the depths of her heart she cried out to herself, Oh, if I could see the face of just one of them! With the majesty of dream—or of heaven—in quick answer to Thérèse's prayer, the tallest of the Sisters moved towards her, uncovered her face and threw her veil over Thérèse, a symbolic gesture that Thérèse did not bother to interpret, but which clearly brought the two nuns, the living and the dead, into the same world, binding them together in timelessness, in certitude, and in love. Thérèse recognized the saintly figure immediately as Venerable Mother Anne of Jesus, the sixteenth-century member of St. Teresa's community at St. Joseph in Avila, who later brought the reformed Carmel to France and Holland. Thérèse had never had any particular devotion to Anne, had never made special requests of her, had hardly thought of her at all except as a historical figure who turned up from time to time in books or conversations about Carmel. But here she was, very much with her, a beautiful woman, of an unmistakable ghostliness, through whose presence an ineffably sweet light could be seen and felt.

Anne smiled at Thérèse and the smile breathed love at her; the look was unmistakable, unforgettable. Anne kissed Thérèse and the kisses lingered with Thérèse, a memory tactile and fully alive to her senses for months. She was at ease again, finally at ease, and found no difficulty in asking Anne questions. "O my Mother, I beg you, please tell me, will God leave me here much longer on earth? Will he come for me soon?" Anne's answer was clear enough: "Yes," she said, "soon, soon, I promise you." Thérèse then asked further, "Does God ask nothing more of me than my poor little works, my hopes, my desires? Is he satisfied with me?" Anne had smiled touchingly, tenderly, in response to the first question; now she showed an expression incomparably more ten-

266

der, Thérèse says, and with a tender caress accompanying her words, she said, "God asks nothing more of you at all. He is content, fully satisfied!" And then, before Thérèse could ask for special favors for her Sisters in Carmel, Anne gathered her up to her with the warmth and love of the sweetest of mothers, she says, and then, alas, it was all over: She woke up.

Thérèse felt buoyant as she had not for weeks and weeks. And she continued to feel the lightness and joy of this moment for months afterward. Unlike those instants of relief which only thickened the darkness when they subsided, this dream softened and sweetened everything for a long time to come.

The extraordinary graces of that moment did not erase the darkness, however. The mists continued around her, enveloping her days with the shabby certainty of an old theater curtain dropping its empty thuds across a hundred matinees. But now there were also memories of joy and a higher certitude that did not disappear with each nagging question about the afterlife and with each clumsy uncertainty about the operations of faith. After narrating the events of the dream, in her letter to Marie, Thérèse confides to her the pledges she had long ago made to Jesus, had continued to make, and would still be making for a long time to come, at every prick of the love she felt at such moments as this one. She feels overcome with an ambition to every vocation of love, to be a warrior, to be a prophet, to be a priest, an apostle, a doctor; to be every sort of martyr, a Crusader or one of the Pope's Zouaves, dying on the battlefield in defense of the Church. She feels with particular unction the vocation of the priest—to carry Jesus in her hands, to invoke him at will, to call him down from heaven. With what love she would bring him to souls! And yet at the same time, she admires and envies the humility of a St. Francis of Assisi and feels called upon to imitate his refusal of the sublime dignity of the priesthood. She wants to go all over, to be a missionary to every people in every part of the world, and not simply in her own lifetime, but from the beginning of time and until the end of time. She must give witness in every way, at every time. Martyrdom must be every martyrdom, all deaths, all cruelties, all sacrifices, in an endless offering of herself. She would be scourged and crucified with Jesus, flayed alive like St. Bartholomew, plunged in boiling oil like St. John, beheaded like Agnes and Cecilia. She would go to the stake like Joan of Arc, her ancient heroine, and like her would die murmuring the blessed name, O Jesus. . . .

These wild dreams, these tumultuous fantasies, do not seriously disturb her. They are the crescendos which bring her canticles of love to their moments of enormous but not shattering volume, only to give way, soon enough, to softer sounds, to whisperings, the gentle reflective meditations which answer her loud adventurous speculations. She finds in St. Paul, in the twelfth and thirteenth chapters of the First Letter to the Corinthians, the strong reminder that we can't all be prophets, doctors, apostles. Like the Magdalen looking for Jesus in the empty tomb, like the figure in John of the Cross who finds himself by digging deep into his own nothingness, Thérèse finds her heights in her depths, finds herself most where she esteems herself least. Love is all. Love is enough. Every vocation, every true vocation, is a vocation of love. That is the key to all. All the members of the body of the Church find their strength in this, the love that comes from the noblest and most necessary of the members of the mystical body: its heart, its heart that burns with love.

The ecstatic passage on love in the letter to Marie bursts with italics and capital letters. And still all the capital letters are not large enough for the word of love, for AMOUR, which must rise in the largest letters, well above all the others, as love must tower over everything else. Delirious with joy, she says, she cried out: "O Jesus, my Love . . . my *vocation*, I have finally found it, MY VOCATION, MY VOCATION IS LOVE!" But she has a further specification of this vocation, one which is quite consistent with her role as the smallest of things. Yes, she says, she has found her place in the Church, the place assigned her by God, "in the heart of the Church, of my Mother; I will be *Love*, and thus I will be everything, and thus my dream will be realized!!!"

But why, she asks herself, do I talk of a delirious joy? No, that's not the way to put it at all. She has found rest, the calm and peaceful ease that a navigator feels when he spies the beam of the lighthouse which is going to light his way into port. "O luminous lighthouse of love," she prays now, "I know how to come to you; I have found the secret, I know how to wrap myself in your flame." She is the flame, the holocaust, the burnt offering of love. She is as totally sacrificed as any offering in the time of the old law. But where a fear-dominated theocracy required that its victims be perfect of their kind, the law of love is content with such weak and imperfect creatures as Thérèse. Thus are the depths raised to the heights; thus is nothing made into all. In order to be fully satisfied, Love must lower itself as far as it can go, lower itself to the point of nothingness and so transform everything it infuses with its fires, even nothingness itself, so that everything, finally, may be on fire with love.

What follows, in Thérèse's account of her ecstatic meditation, is the familiar language of the Little Way. She speaks as a child, awed but not overwhelmed by her big brothers, the angels and the saints. For even if her glory is only reflected glory, it is enough. All she wants is love—to love Jesus and to show in as many ways as possible how much she loves him. She can scatter flowers about, even she, little child that she is; she can make the royal throne fragrant with their perfume, and can pipe in her high voice her canticle of love. She can pluck her flowers wherever she finds them, even among the longest and most cutting thorns: she is eager to make sacrifices for her love whenever and wherever she can, even that most demanding of sacrifices, the sacrifice of her dearest and deepest and most long-held dreams of heaven and eternal union. Let those dreams collapse, let those hopes disappear, if they must. She is up to the truth, up to knowing it all in all its wounding details, and in any case isn't it better to end this long and senseless martyrdom of hope, if her hope has no chance of being realized? Isn't it better? she answers herself very shrewdly. No, she says, no it has been enough to have had the dreams, the aspirations, the longings, to have held such lofty hopes. In her martyrdom of hope, in her madness of longing, she found more sweetness, she suspects, than she could have expected even in heaven—that is her rhetorical way of expressing the intensity of feeling her love let loose in her. Faced by the thought of losing the memory of those dreams, those longings, those hopes, she cries out in anguish: Let me have these things still, the delights of love; let me go on savoring the bittersweet delights of my martyrdom. "Jesus, Jesus, if just the desire to love you is so deeply pleasing, what must it be to possess you, really to enjoy your love?"

The concluding pages of Thérèse's letter to Marie have already turned up in this book, as inevitably they must whenever one contemplates Thérèsian doctrine or looks for some significant insight into her allegorical narrative. In those pages she becomes, in the central terms of her allegory, a chick, a fledgling; tutored by eagles, but alas, also quickly reduced to feeble twitterings and twitches; a contemplator of the heavenly sun, but also, sadly enough, a victim of the clouds, easily driven to sleep, a compulsive dozer; a wretched little soul, but the object of Jesus's affections; the feeblest and most minuscule of souls, and yet the recipient of great revelations. Thinking such thoughts, feeling such feelings, the darkness would be light enough for Thérèse, for in it she could find her most constant consolation, namely, that that love she venerated, incarnate Love, was most itself, was most loving, when it was most condescending, when it stooped as low as it could, when it reached down into nothingness and as at the beginning of all things made something out of nothing, fired nothingness with love and thus with being. Suffering was such a great consolation, littleness was so overwhelming a comfort, because there, at the far end of things, at the bottom of being, one could experience the deepest and the fullest expansion of God's love. There, on the edge of permanent darkness, light, when it finally reached one, had such healing strength and offered such glowing support as nothing one could experience in any other way. This is the force of the prayer which concludes the letter to Marie—"I entreat you," she cries out to Jesus, "I beg you to look down in mercy on great numbers of *little* souls. I beg you to choose an entire legion of *little* victims, of those worthy of your *LOVE!*"

Within a few weeks of the great dream of Mother Anne, Thérèse could feel once again the light at the edge of darkness, could hear once again an answer to her prayer for the least of beings, the most insignificant of her lover's clients. She was given her second missionary to look after and to pray for. Here was still another opportunity to be all things, to respond to all calls, to be in some fashion a part of a priest's vocation, with all its majestic fiats, and at the same time to recognize, in all its depths of abasement, her own littleness, like St. Francis's, humble but joyous in its humbleness.

Thérèse's second brother in the missions was Père Roulland, Adolphe-Jean-Louis-Eugène Roulland, of the Society of Foreign Missions of Paris. He was another Norman, born near Bayeux, and educated at the seminary of his missionary society in

Paris, destined for the Far East, like most of those ordained in this two-hundred-year-old congregation of secular priests. A month before ordination, he had asked Mother Gonzague, through a priest-friend, for someone in the Carmel to be his special intercessor, in the great tradition of the order. Mother Gonzague promptly selected Thérèse, the best, she told the seminarian, of her good ones, a dear little creature who belonged entirely to God. It was to be a hidden relationship—most delightful of relationships for Thérèse! Mother Gonzague asked her to keep her secret from everyone, from all her Sisters, from Mother Agnès even, and not to reveal the association even at those breathless moments for her, during the community's recreation periods, when letters from Père Roulland were to be sampled for the delectation of the Sisters; it would be enough to read from them without indicating the name of the nun to whom they had been written. And so when Thérèse sent Père Roulland gifts to signify their association and to bless his missionary activity in China, to which he was quickly off, she reminded him that she wanted no one but Jesus himself to know of their "union in the apostolate." It is this reminder that permits her to sign herself, as she will be happy she says "to style herself eternally, Your unworthy little sister in Jesus-Victim. . . ."

Thérèse didn't hesitate to ask for Père Roulland's intercession in exchange for hers, although not on a quid pro quo basis exactly. At the first instance of his exercise of his priestly power—"on the day when Jesus deigns *for the first time* to come down from Heaven *at your voice*"—she begged for a prayer for her too: "ask Him to inflame me with the *fire of His love* so that I may kindle that fire in hearts." And with a conventional phrase—"If I did not fear to seem overbold"—she asked to be remembered every day at the altar. Her gifts assured her, too, of being remembered daily at Père Roulland's altars, wherever he went. She sent him the altar linen he would need—corporal, purificator, and pall; the linen on which the Host and chalice rest at Mass, the linen used to dry the chalice and the priest-celebrant's fingers when they have been washed clean with wine after Communion, and that small piece of stiff linen which covers the chalice at Mass as protection against dust, insects, etc. She made at least the pall very much her own by decorating it for her spiritual brother with

271

paints, and "joyfully," she says, to remind him of his intercessor on Mount Carmel.

Thérèse was very happy to surround herself with things that reminded her of Père Roulland. "My Brother," she wrote him at the end of July, as he prepared to leave for the China missions, "I hope you will allow me from now on to call you by no other name, seeing that Jesus has deigned to unite us in the bonds of the apostolate. It is very sweet to think that from all eternity our Lord formed this union, which is to save Him souls, and that He created me to be your sister." As one so supernaturally close, she had a full share of mementi. Mother Gonzague had allowed her to keep her brother's photograph—a rare enough privilege, as Thérèse reminds him, since Carmelites are not allowed portraits of even their closest relations. But this was a spiritual relationship; it was consecrated and above any law designed to keep affections from being tied to this world. On the wall of the room in which she did most of her work, there was a map of the province in China to which Père Roulland was being sent, and in the Gospel which she carried around next to her heart was the young priest's ordination card, on which he had written, "Let us work together here below; in Heaven we shall share the reward." Thus the card itself was next to her heart. And what a good augury it was, she suggests, that when she thrust the card into her Gospel book, it should have fallen into the Gospel of Luke at the eighteenth chapter, leaning up against the twenty-ninth and thirtieth verses: "Amen, I say to you, there is no man that hath left house, or parents, or brethren, or wife, or children, for the kingdom of God's sake, who shall not receive much more in this present time, and in the world to come life everlasting."

For Père Roulland, Thérèse meditated on certain passages in the Bible, at particular length on verses in chapters 41 and 44 of Isaiah. She asked him for the principal dates in his life, so that she could unite herself to him with every precise particularity and therewith thank the Lord for the graces he had given the priest. This was only her second letter to him, but she felt no constraint about expressing her most intense feelings in it. Here, after all, was a finished priest, miraculously delivered into her hands; her other spiritual brother, young Bellière, was suspended between worlds in military service, and as she wrote Père Roulland three months later, he felt his conviction of vocation far less certainly after a year in the army. Darkness was all around her, but light too, signs of order in the universe, signs of the acceptance of her "poor little works," of her hopes, of her desires, just as Mother Anne had assured her in her dream. And so she ends her letter of July 30, 1896, in an ecstasy of blessed certainties: ". . . distance can never separate our souls, even death will only make our union closer. If I go to Heaven soon, I shall ask Jesus's permission to visit you in Su-Chuen and we shall continue our apostolate together. Meanwhile I shall always be united to you by prayer, and I ask our Lord never to let me be joyful when you are suffering. I would even wish that my Brother should always have joys and I trials, but perhaps that is selfish! . . . but no, because my only *weapon* is love and suffering, and you have the sword of the word and of apostolic labors."

Thérèse could bear to relinquish into the hands of Père Roulland all her vast ambitions as priest, prophet, doctor, warrior, and apostle as long as her share in the great multifaceted work of the missionary could be large, as large as her dreams and the fantastic correlation and coincidence of dates would permit. She received his list of dates on All Saints Day, November 1, 1896, and that same day sat down to work out the details of their fraternity under God in a long letter to him. There was, for example, the remarkable coincidence of September 8, 1890, the day of Thérèse's profession, on which she had prayed earnestly that she might some day have entrusted to her a priest's soul. On that day, in the Church of Our Lady of the Deliverance in Normandy, Adolphe Roulland, uncertain about his vocation and his acceptance at the seminary, was praying for some clear indication of his calling. There was an answer. All at once, he found himself; he knew he was for the priesthood; his vocation was clear. Thérèse had hesitated for a moment when Mother Gonzague proposed this intercessory relationship; her spiritual brother, her apostle, it seemed to her by then, was not to be found here below. But, she reflects in her long letter of November 1, she did not know after all that she had had a brother preparing for six years to become a missionary. Now the answers to her prayers had been granted in such abundance she could even believe that her greatest prayer for him, one which his humility probably prevented him from making himself, would come true: "Yes, I have the hope, that after *long years* spent in apostolic labors, having given Jesus love for love, life for life, you will also give Him *blood for blood.*" He could look forward, she thought, to the "incomparable favor" of martyrdom. In point of fact, he was not martyred, except in a manner of speaking: his own desires had to be sacrificed. He had hoped to spend his life in the missions and prayed and prayed and entreated Thérèse's prayers to keep him in the East, to spare him the cross of the seminary. He lost his hope—or perhaps the stronger set of prayers was answered in an unexpected way. He was brought back to Paris in 1909, first made Director of the Seminary and then Procurator, and ended his life, in 1934, as chaplain at a convent.

Signals had a way of being crossed between spiritual brother and sister. Thérèse had worked out an elaborate series of consecrations of Christmas Day prayers to coincide with his Mass at dawn, which was to be offered for her and for Mother Gonzague. He was not able to say that Mass, which Thérèse later learned, to her chagrin: "And I . . . had united myself with it in such happiness at that exact hour. Ah, all is uncertain here on earth!" There were, nonetheless, enough interweavings of feeling, and even of words, to carry everything warmly into the most satisfying exchanges of sentiment. Père Roulland called Thérèse his Moses in his All Saints Day letter; in a letter to Céline, four years earlier, Thérèse had put the same words in the mouth of Jesus, talking to those singularly devoted to him—". . . each one of you is my Moses praying on the mountain. . . ." Both the priest and the Carmelite liked to describe Jesus as the "divine prisoner of love." They had found little but ease in each other ever since the first exchange of letters and Père Roulland's Mass in the Carmelite Church on July 3, when the two had met across the grille. In commending shaky vocations to each other's prayers—a girl was entrusted by Father to Sister, Bellière was placed by Sister in Father's hands—they felt the surest confidence in their mutual strength.

Thérèse's letters to the Abbé Bellière in October and December 1896 were quite different from her outpourings to Père Roulland. This little brother needed counseling and cautioning and slow and thoughtful spiritual conversation. It was a year now since he had been assigned to Thérèse by Mother Agnès in October 1895, a year without any letter from her, but that was no more strange than the fact that he had waited almost that long before, as Thérèse put it, he showed any signs of life. He had acknowledged the association quickly enough, but then, except for the briefest notification that he was off to the army, he had not written until July 1896, when he had confessed how difficult his life was, how full of doubts and temptations. Now, finally, in October 1896, Thérèse answered him and tried to bring some peace to his discouraged soul. She quoted Scripture: "Blessed is the man that endures temptation" (from the Epistle of James, 1:12) and "He that has not been tried, what does he know?" (Ecclesiasticus 34:11). She added her own tough-minded commentary: "The fact is that when Jesus calls a man to guide and save multitudes of other souls, it is most necessary that He make him experience the temptations and trials of life." On the day after Christmas, Thérèse drove the point home again to Monsieur l'Abbé. "It is very consoling," she reminded him, "to remember that Jesus, the *God of Might*, knew our *weaknesses*, that He shuddered at sight of the bitter cup, the cup that earlier He had so ardently desired to drink." What could be less than beautiful about a condition so much like Jesus's? Suffering? "Was it not by suffering and dying that He redeemed the world?" An eagerness for martyrdom? ". . . the martyrdom of the heart is no less fruitful than the shedding of blood, and that first martyrdom is yours already."

Thérèse was writing the young seminarian—disturbed at his own temptations against his vocation, troubled at the then distant prospect of having to leave his family and friends behind for missionary duty, and yet anxious to give some heroic witness to his faith—out of a fullness of understanding. Her temptations were not exactly the same as his, except for that of martyrdom, which stretched its bloody fingers toward her with the same entrancing attraction as did every suggestion of quick delivery into the arms of her lord and lover. No, hers were not the identical doubts and disturbances and temptations, but they were close enough; they would do; they sprang from an all too steady darkness. Great favors—dream fantasies, one might call some of them; mystical intuitions, others—great favors relieved the austerity of *her* dark days. Surely there would be like graces for anyone else who could show enough trust? She wasn't necessary; of that she was sure. Jesus could speak directly to those who needed him, and she prayed fervently that he would do just that. But she remained necessary nonetheless to her clients, that growing group that now numbered novices, full-fledged nuns, her two spiritual brothers, and all the members of her family in and out of the convent. With great skill, she varied her tone for each of them. For Mother Gonzague, as a final assuagement for the raging spirits that plagued even so experienced and confident a soul as she for quite a while after her difficult re-election, Thérèse composed the "Legend of a very Little Lamb." It was a tale brilliantly designed for its medicinal effect upon her superior's troubled soul. It was also an explanation of the steady recourse of Thérèse's clients to her—then and now.

A lamb, a very small lamb, weeps because its beloved shepherdess weeps. A shepherd of shining beauty and "sweet majesty" appears, the divine Shepherd, Jesus himself, and taking the little lamb on his knees, gently discovers the source of its grief. He had given each flock, as he knew so well, the right to choose its own shepherdess. The last time the choice fell upon the lamb's beloved mistress it had taken "a sevenfold deliberation" before once again she was raised over her sheep. "Once you *wept* upon our earth," the lamb reminds the Shepherd; "do you not realize how the heart of my dearest shepherdess must suffer?" The explanation of the Good Shepherd, delivered at some length and in familiar phrases, is that the shepherdess's flock, *"dear to me among all,"* was being used as an instrument of sanctification. Yes, he knows he could speak to her directly and could swiftly remove all her trials from her; but this he does not want to do; she must have the Cross and must realize it comes from him, from heaven. Still the lamb persists: tell her this directly, do not leave her open to all the tales of falsehood to which she is exposed. No, the Shepherd explains, I leave this to you, her favorite; no, I will not give this duty to those more learned in the ways of the world—"Your shepherdess knows that it pleases Me *to hide My secrets* from the wise and prudent, she knows that I *reveal them to the little ones,* to the simple lambs whose white wool has taken no stain from the dust of the way . . . She will believe you . . . and if tears still flow from her eyes, those tears will no longer have the same bitterness, they will make her soul beautiful with the austere splendor of suffering loved and accepted with gratitude." Finally, the Shepherd explains that his shepherdess must not look to human support; she must gaze steadfastly at his wounds and must be content to be filled with him. But that does not mean that she should separate herself from creatures altogether or in any way look down upon their love or despise the world as a way of pilgrimage and sanctification. "To ascend, one must *place one's foot* upon the steps of creatures, and attach oneself to none but Me."

Thérèse, speaking as the lamb, does not only believe that the Shepherd's words are true, she *feels* their truth, all the more so when she is once again assured that she is not long to be delayed from "the joy of the fields of Heaven," even if she herself has put the words in her Shepherd's mouth. In her moments of light she is altogether free with her lover's person. She writes Léonie in the middle of summer in 1896, "Personally, I find perfection quite easy to practice because I have realized that all one has to do is take *Jesus by the heart*." She has been tutored by the example of little children who, when scolded by their mothers for their disobedience or their noisy fits, are smart enough not to sulk or scream in anticipation of punishment, but rather come with open arms and broad smiles to beseech a kiss and promise not to do it again. Of course, Thérèse comments, mothers know that their children will do it again, and not only again, but at the first possible opportunity, but that does not matter; as long as the offending child takes his mother *"by the heart,* he will not be punished."

We live now not under the law of fear but the law of love, the time of the Spouse who constantly makes "loving advances" to us, Thérèse reminds her sister. "How can we fear One 'who lets himself be held by a hair of our neck'?" she asks, quoting the Song of Songs. She sums up the principle: "It seems to me that if our *sacrifices* are hairs to hold Jesus prisoner, so are our *joys.* . . ." And this is so, she knows, she above all, even when the joys are very small and very few. She can share warmly Léonie's hope of death, Léonie's tender hope of death; for her at least as much as for her troubled sister, there is no longer anything on earth to care for, certainly nothing to hold her from the fields above. This is a sentiment Thérèse expresses to her other sisters, too. Her sister Marie is sad to learn, in September 1896, of Thérèse's "extraordinary desire for martyrdom," but she knows that the desire is a proof of Thérèse's love. "Yes," Marie writes Thérèse, with the greatness of her sadness evident enough, "love you do possess: but not I! You will never make me believe I can attain the desired goal, for I fear all that you love." That proves, beyond question, Marie thinks, that she does not love Jesus as Thérèse does. Thérèse may say she really *does* nothing, but she has *desires* of such dimension that they themselves are great works. "Oh," Marie cries to her godchild, "I was very close to weeping as I read lines which are not of earth, but an echo from the Heart of God. . . . May I tell you? I will: you are possessed by God: literally *possessed*, exactly as the wicked are by the devil."

Thérèse's answer to Marie's sweet anguish and holy envy is to attempt to sweeten it further and to transfigure the envy, to make her sister see how earnest her own disposition already is to be possessed. All that pleases Jesus in herself, Thérèse explains, is her love for her littleness, for her poverty; her blind hope in his mercy, and her trust, yes, beyond everything else, her trust. She is certain that Marie is ready to suffer, as she always is certain that those who drop their troubles at her feet are able and even eager to take on any pain. The point is, "if you want to feel joy in suffering, to be drawn to it, what you seek [and presumably will find] is your own consolation, for when one loves a thing, the pain vanishes." The essential ingredient is the longing to be a victim of love, which means to be quite content with one's weakness, one's lowliness, one's nothingness. Then, at the bottom of things, in that desolation which represents true poverty of spirit, love will find one, love will consume and transform one. This is the signal for Thérèse's anguish now: "Oh!" she cries out, "how I wish I could make you realize what I mean! . . . It is trust, and nothing but trust, that must bring us to Love. . . . Fear brings one only to Justice." She adds a footnote to her profound theology of love and fear: Fear brings us to "*strict justice* as it is shown to sinners, but that is not the *Justice* Jesus will have for those who love Him."

The final point of this graceful addendum to her great letter to Marie is an expansion of a famous text, those rich words which are at the center of the Mystery of Jesus as Pascal contemplates it in his *Pensées*. Jesus says to Pascal, "Console yourself. You would not be seeking me if you had not found me." Thérèse says to Marie, "I am sure that the good God would not give you the desire to be *possessed* by Him, by His *merciful Love*, if He did not have this favor in store for you [the free gift of Heaven]; or rather He has already given it to you since you are given over to

Him, since you *desire* to be consumed by *Him,* and the good God never gives desires that He cannot fulfill." It was a *final* point: it was the Charter of Thérèse's way of love, not a Magna Carta, not a great charter, but a little one. It was enough. It offered trust, for those who can trust. And it offered trust at the point at which trust seems altogether impossible, in suffering, in uncertainty, in the dark, the only point, really, at which such trust is important. It is enough to feel it to want it; it is enough to desire the love of God, if that desire, just the desire, is strong enough. For the desire is proof of the reality. You would not be seeking him, Thérèse assures her clients, if you had not already found him. Her assurance was as much for herself as for them. She could counsel trust in a time of uncertainty and darkness because she had herself found it then. She could tell others of the power of desire, tell others how much desire, just desire, really meant, for she knew herself.

FOURTEEN

*I*N the last months of her life, Thérèse spent much of her time—
perhaps most of it—in an extraordinarily intense self-examination. She dismembered her soul with the coolness and the precision and the detachment of a hospital pathologist performing an
autopsy. She took account of the failures and the successes of her
spiritual life with the courage and the maturity of an Augustine
reconsidering all his works, four years before his death, when he
made a great volume out of all his retractations and revisions,
and with the passion of the same saint making his Confessions.

"Let not those who read this book," Augustine warns, in the
Prologue of his *Retractations*, "imitate me in my errors, but rather
in my progress toward better things." Thérèse, for her part,
breathes a great amused sigh. "Alas!" she mock-mourns, "when I
think back to the time of my novitiate and realize how imperfect
I was! I laugh now when I think of how I carried on about such
little things. How good God has been to have made my soul grow
up, to have given it wings." No snares can trap her now, she
boasts, for as Scripture says, "a net is spread in vain before the
eyes of them that have wings" (Prov. 1:17). Later, no doubt, her
present imperfections will be clear enough to her, but now nothing amazes her, she writes to Mother Gonzague in her autobiography; now, no fussing over her realization that she is weakness
itself—"on the contrary, I glory in it and each day I look forward
to finding new imperfections in myself." Like St. Paul, she glories
only in her infirmities. Like Paul, she wants no one to see her as
anything but what she is, to hear in her anything more than is
really in her, to think of her as anything but what she herself
shows herself to be. Imperfection? Sin? Fair enough; foul enough.
The same book of Proverbs explains her situation: "Love covers a

multitude of sins" (10:12) and with what a great shelter her love and her lover have provided her!

The temptations against faith were as convulsive as ever. The dark days alternated with the light and sometimes threatened to extend their shadows over all. But Thérèse had been granted, even amid these terrors, a sufficiency of light. Her confidence, if not enough to blot out all temptation, was enough to permit her to convert every ugly visitation of fear and trembling into an occasion of love, and she had enough strength of conviction, in all her physical pain, amid all the tortures of religious doubt, to bring comfort to others, to her novices, to her cousins, to her aunt, to her sisters. When, in December 1896, Pauline showed herself shaken by her duties as Depositrix, the chief administrative officer of the convent, calling herself, in words long associated with a revered Sister of the Carmel at Tours, "little ass" and "little servant" of the Holy Family, Thérèse reminded her what a privilege it is to be the Child Jesus's donkey, and what a future such service presages: "He will prepare a *little* place for the *little* Mother in His Kingdom which is not of this world; and then, in His turn, He will *minister* to her." As a Christmas offering to Céline, a few days later, Thérèse extended a kind of consolation by proxy. In it she speaks for Mary, and in Mary's voice acknowledges the sad fact that Céline is gloomy, that Céline is suffering, that Céline anguishes. But for all the sadness, all the suffering and gloom and anguish, the Virgin has no glib consolation; she knows their value too well. "If you are willing to bear serenely the trial of being displeasing to yourself," she tells Céline, "you will be a pleasant place of shelter to me." That will bring no end to suffering, of course. It will still be an exile, this place of shelter. "But have no fear, the poorer you are, the more Jesus will love you. . . . He would rather see you striking your foot against the stones along the way by night, than walking in broad daylight along a road gemmed with flowers which could easily slow your advance."

Thérèse was shameless in her appeal from her own littleness and all the littlenesses of all the little people in the world to the largesse of the Lord. "I am a *poor grasshopper*," she wrote her aunt, when for the last time she was able to greet her on her aunt's feast day, in November 1896. Her songs were nothing better than a grasshopper's songs and really not songs to be heard by anyone else at all, for with such an unmelodious voice the grasshopper could sing only in the inner recesses of its heart. But for Mme. Guérin, says this clattery-voiced locust of a saint, "I shall sing my finest tune on the day of your feast, and I shall try to do it with a note so touching that all the saints, taking pity on my poverty, will give me treasures of grace that I shall be enchanted to present to you."

She was brazen in her constant appeals to the divine pity, the divine compassion, the divine love, which, as she understood divinity, was far more susceptible to appeals from the bottom of society than from the top, far more moved by poverty and misery and gloom than by riches and comfort and assurance, and always open to suffering, of whatever intensity, of whatever significance, no matter how slight, no matter how superficial, no matter how inconsequential. Suffering understands suffering. The greatest suffering that has ever been can understand with directness and in full detail the least suffering that is. No one has ever penetrated fully to the depths of the suffering of Jesus; it is, of necessity, hidden from men, even from those who do their utmost to associate themselves with it, to understand it, to share it; in their finitude, they cannot gather up infinite suffering, endless pain. But by the very token of their smallness, by their limitations, by their inability to imitate Christ Crucified or to become totally one with Jesus in his passion, they come closer to sharing it with him, to imitating him, to living with him. Hidden in their obscurity, despised for their smallness, rejected by all, even by themselves, they can grasp something of the nature of Christ's pain and know something of his glory. For here is their highest achievement, at the bottom of their sorrows. Here is their greatest openness to majesty, in their most hidden moments. Here is the most exquisite and privileged of pleasures, in that pain and suffering that no one else can understand or share but Jesus. What a special favor it is, she told Pauline, to have to follow Christ now that she is no longer Prioress, to follow him in a hidden way, to suffer in the obscure corners of the convent, to ascend Mount Carmel in darkness, with almost none looking on. "O Mother, how splendid is your lot!" she exults. "It is truly worthy of *you*, the favored one of our family, who show us the way, like the small swallow one always sees ahead of his companions, tracing in the air the path that is to lead them to their new homeland." Thérèse is pierced with love for her sister in her new hiddenness. She bursts with joy at being able to gather her into the fold of the little ones, the asses, the grasshoppers, the swallows. She signs this, her first letter of her last year, 1897, with a line swollen with love. "Oh!" she exclaims, "do realize the affection of your little girl"—underlining your five times—"who would love to say *so many, many* things to you!"

When doubts were not assailing her, Thérèse was full of premonitions about her approaching death. She lived buoyantly, in her moments of lightness and consolation, filled with images of the joyous world to come. Her poetry was simple, simpler than it had ever been before, a bare rendering in rhyme and easy cadence of soft, simple, tender prayer. For one of the Sisters, she composed five stanzas "To My Guardian Angel." It is a sketch for a last will and testament:

> I have nothing but my sacrifices,
> And my severe poverty:
> United with your pure delights,
> Offer them for me to the Trinity.

It is a commission. She is grateful, she tells her guardian spirit, for its tenderness to her, for its care in removing obstacles from her way, stones in the road. Good enough, but not enough. She wants a similar attention to be given to others. She directs her guardian to guard others; it is in anticipation of duties to come once she is gone, though she does not say so openly, and in the poem what she means can be gathered only by those few who have been made privy to her premonitions and those, surely much fewer, who have intercepted the direction of all her glances, the direction of her inmost being, in these last months. She makes her prayer public, now, but its deepest drift is hidden from most of those who hear it.

> O you who travel across space
> More swiftly than light,
> Fly often into my place,
> Close to those who are dear to me.
> With your wings, dry their tears.
> And sing, sing of Jesus's goodness,
> Sing of the charms of suffering,
> And very softly whisper my name.

In "My Peace and My Joy," written at the request of Pauline, Thérèse sings in place of her angel, sings in accents she clearly associates with the divine. There are some who look in vain for happiness, she begins her meditation in verse; but not she. Joy lives in her heart, she cries, joy, least ephemeral of flowers, endlessly, always, hers; like a rose in springtime, it smiles at her every day. Her joy is to love suffering; her joy is to remain hidden in shadow, always to hide herself, to abase herself. The poem is a small kenotic outpouring, to use the appropriate theological term for it. Thérèse is overwhelmed by the abasement of God, by kenosis, Jesus's great lowering of himself to achieve the human condition, and so she finds peace in contemplating that will which willed so enormous and so stubborn a stooping, and this is what she says, though not in exactly those words, in a quartet of handsome peaceful prayerful stanzas. Each is a double quatrain, following that most elementary and satisfying of rhyme schemes, a-b-a-b, c-d-c-d, clicking comforting sounds quickly into place, sounding the sounds of peace in the most ordinary of vocabularies, unpretentious, commonplace really, and yet to those who have followed Thérèse through her years of purgation and illumination deeply affecting. This is, I think, a fair sample. This is also, I think, a moving example of her exaltation of the commonplace, of her making extraordinary illuminations out of ordinary experiences, ordinary sounds, ordinary words:

> Ma paix, c'est de rester petite;
> Aussi, quand je tombe en chemin,
> Je puis me relever bien vite,
> Et Jésus me prend par la main.
> Alors, le comblant de caresses,
> Je lui dis qu'il est tout pour moi . . .
> Et je redouble de tendresses,
> Lorsqu'il se dérobe à ma foi.

> My peace is to stay small;
> And too, when I fall along the way,
> I can pick myself up very quickly,
> And Jesus takes me by the hand.
> Then, covering him with caresses,
> I tell him that he is all to me,
> And I redouble my displays of tenderness
> When he robs me of my faith.

This is a peace made of tears carefully hidden from her Sisters in the community. This is a peace which is a constant struggle to produce a chosen people for her lover, "*Afin d'enfanter des élus,*" in order to give birth to them, to the elect.

This poem of January 1897 is a fiery outburst of love once again and a tightly tenderly restrained show of docility at the same time. The blood coursing in the night, wetting her lips, streaking her pillow, gave hope of a quick end. The shadows of doubt, lengthening during the days, were a constant reminder of her littleness, of her need to suffer still more, to bend her will yet again, to will for herself whatever was willed above for her. She made a soft submission in her last stanza, a sweet resignation, but not without its fire:

> Willingly I will live for a long while yet,
> Lord, if it is your desire.
> I want to follow you up to heaven,
> If that would give you pleasure.
> *Love,* the fire of the fatherland,
> Consumes me on and on, unceasingly:
> In death or in life,
> *My only happiness is to love you!*

When she wrote to the family's old friend and her special bene-factor of those brief but blessed Roman days, Brother Simeon, it was as one dying old religious to another. He was nearly eighty-three and she was just twenty-four, as the world counts birthdays, but in her journeys in the roads she had aged not one year nor even two with each birthday, but something closer to three or four. She speaks to the Christian Brother as one intercessor to another. If you get there first, you who were so eloquent in our behalf with Pope Leo, please don't forget me: "if you have the good fortune to see Him before I do. . . . The one thing I beg you to ask for my soul is the grace to *love* Jesus and *make Him loved* as much as lies in my power." But what if she should die first? Why, then, simply enough, she will pray for him and his in-tentions and those dear to him, and of course she won't forget the Director of the College of St. Joseph in the wonderful Piazza di Spagna in her present prayers either. She felt, she said, a "pro-found gratitude" to him, in part, presumably, for his numerous intercessions at the Vatican for the Carmel of Lisieux, one of which was the occasion for this letter, but more importantly for his association with that great moment in her life when, for all the ambiguity of the Pope's words and the complications to follow back home, she felt herself on the edge of that straight way to eternity which Carmel was for her.

Thérèse was more and more open about her presentiments of death. Obviously, with the unmistakable symptoms of physical deterioration and the less certain, but far from obscure, signs of spiritual growth, Thérèse was convinced that her term on earth was just about to end. As is so often true in the religious life, the divisions of the Church year began to fall into place too in her calendar. Lent corresponded perfectly with her preparations for departure. She writes Abbé Bellière on the eve of "the hallowed forty-day silence" and seems full of joy at being closely associated with him in his priestly career. She invokes his help with what seems to be her first glimmer of understanding of her career—not here below, but in the time and in the place to come, to come soon. She says to him, Pray for me, as you have promised, pray every day, pray in these words, for they say everything I wish to have said: "Merciful Father, in the name of our sweet Jesus, and of the Virgin Mary and of the saints, inflame my sister with your Spirit of Love and grant her the grace to make you greatly loved." One would have no conviction of special plans for a life to come if the paragraph that follows this request were not so explicit. "You have promised to pray for me *all your life*," Thérèse reminds her brother, with a well-placed set of underlinings. "I am sure it will be longer than mine: and you are not allowed to sing with me: 'It is my hope, my exile will be short!' But neither are you allowed to forget your promise. If Our Lord takes me soon to Himself, I ask you to go on saying the same little prayer daily, for in heaven I shall want the same thing as on earth: to love Jesus and make men love Him. Monsieur l'Abbé, you must find me very strange. Perhaps you regret having a sister apparently so anxious to go off and enjoy eternal rest, leaving you to work on alone. . . . But you need not worry, the only thing I desire is the good God's will, and I confess that if I could no longer work for His glory in heaven, I should like exile better than the Homeland."

Her constant meditation, in darkness as in light, in the bright sun of certitude as in the gloomy shadows of doubt, was on the beckoning future. The Abbé would continue with his apostolate in the missions, she would continue with her life of prayer and love. In the middle of Lent, on March 19, she dashed off a note to Pauline: "Thank you, little Mother: Oh! yes, Jesus loves you. . . . And so do I! He gives you proofs of it daily, and I don't. . . . True, but when I am up there, my little arm will reach very far, and my little Mother will hear of it. . . ." This, most commentators on the life of Thérèse say, is perhaps the first presentiment on the part of the saint of her extraordinary posthumous career, but surely she had been saying as much for months and perhaps even longer, just as long as she had realized how powerful a weak little sister could be, as long as she had been working out her intercessory role, acting as both Beatrice and Dante in her version of the Divine Comedy.

Thérèse's view of her paradisial role was very much like that of Dante's in his *Commedia*, or of the troubadours, upon whose eloquent testimonies to the intercessory powers of their ladies Dante built his conception of Beatrice. The great lady, in this exalted view of the place of women in the world, was she who pleaded for her lover, she whose purity and sacrifice and suffering made an argument far more powerful in heaven than merely persuasive words could have been. For the troubadours and for Dante, for Petrarch and Chaucer and all the others who followed their noble lead, the great lady was great because of her closeness to the Virgin. She was the most exact analogue to Mary they could find. In her vulnerability to suffering and her willingness to accept it, not only without complaint but with something like active joy, she emulated Mary at the foot of the Cross. If her depth of insight and breadth of equipment were large enough, she did not have to wait for the cross; she anticipated its torments and accepted them. She stood up to pain, if not always with ease, at least never with a noisy anguish. And she found herself able to face the last great pain, death, the pain for which all other pains are rehearsals and overtures, with dignity and even with delight. She was not a stoic. She was not a masochist. She did not revel in sickness for its own sake or discover a sensual pleasure in physical suffering. She was recollected in the face of death, with a whole life of recollection behind her, seeing life as the servant of death and looking to death, as she had to life, as a conveyance to "that magic country," as Thérèse describes paradise in a letter in March 1897 to Père Roulland, "where they convey what is in their mind without writing or even speech."

Thérèse needed no Dante, no troubadour, to salute her virtues or to serenade her in quest of her intercession. She was her own serenader. If she required tribute, she could herself construct it and deliver it, and it would never seem excessive to those who understood her or her species of great lady, for it was never a single tribute; the triumph, such as it was, was not hers alone. If her achievement was anything, if it was anyone's, it was her Lord's, and there was never any greater delight for her, or any-one like her, than in acknowledging the true hero, the true con-queror, whose virtue alone made virtue possible. Furthermore, since the triumph was really a triumph of littleness and weakness, of poverty and emptiness and deformity, who could criticize such boasting? who could deprecate such praise, even though it was praise of self alongside tribute to God?

In these last months, packed with purgatorial suffering and filled out with illuminating bursts of understanding, Thérèse was eager to tell everybody what she had found out in her long short life; she was writing the last pages of her own Imitation of Christ, an addendum to the great fourteenth-century work. As she did so often, she took many passages from the original *Imitation,* as for example in her March letter to Père Roulland, when she filled out her customary description of paradise with a quotation from the second book of the *Imitation:* "When you find suffering sweet and love it for the love of Jesus Christ, you have found Paradise upon earth." To this, she added her own comment: "That is, in fact, the Paradise of the Missionary and the Carmelite; the joy the worldly seek from pleasure is a fleeting shadow, but our joy, sought and savored in labor and suffering, is a most sweet reality, a foretaste of the bliss of heaven." She really identified herself with the missionary; if her Lord doesn't come soon and snatch her up to the Carmel of heaven, she tells Père Roulland, she will just get up and go one day soon to the newly established Carmel at Hanoi. She still has an urge to the missionary life. Intercessor and missionary—there is no conflict; they are the same calling; they both call to others to come and join them; they both intercede with infinite justice to the limits of their finite love in order to bring as many as possible up with them. Thérèse wanted to save souls at any cost, by any means, by every means. In this same great letter to Père Roulland she echoes Teresa of Avila to her nuns: "What care I if I stay in Purgatory till the end of the world, if I save a single soul by my prayers." Thérèse's antiphonal response is in the same key: "I want to save souls and forget self for them; I want to save them even after my death. . . ." And so, she explains to her brother in China, please don't ask God to deliver me from the purgatorial fires; say, instead, "My God, permit my sister to go on making you loved."

All this talk of heaven, all this thought of paradise, all this planning for eternity, far from turning Thérèse sour or even very sober, left her lightheaded and full of laughter. Père Roulland's visiting card, lettered in Chinese characters, delighted her; she turned it every side up, trying to find its compass points—"I am like a child trying to read a book upside down." And Father's irascible Chinese cook, who bashed in his saucepan, and Father's "holy gaiety" in telling his story, lead her to one of her choicest parables. The story is a true one, to illustrate the fact that the Carmel, like Father's part of China, is a foreign land where the most simple, ordinary customs and procedures are unknown. One of the Carmel's benefactors had given the Sisters a *little* lobster as a present—the italics are Thérèse's. It was bound up in a packing case, altogether a rare sight in the convent, but not entirely outside Sister Cook's culinary knowledge. She knew the animal had to be cooked alive in boiling water. This she did, grieving loudly at the cruel treatment of an innocent creature. "The innocent creature was apparently asleep and let itself be handled without protest; but the moment it felt the heat, its mildness turned to fury. It knew its innocence and, without so much as a by-your-leave, leaped out onto the kitchen floor, for its soft-hearted executioner had not yet put the lid on the pot." Sister Cook ran after the lobster with a pair of tongs. Sister Cook was quite vanquished by Brother Lobster. She ran off to Reverend Mother and gave it as her opinion that Brother L. was clearly possessed. "Her face was even more expressive than her words (poor creature, a moment ago so mild, so innocent, now possessed! Truly you can't trust the praise of 'creatures'!)." Mother broke into laughter at hearing "the judge demanding justice." She did more; she went to the kitchen, grabbed the lobster, like the fine resolute superior she was. The lobster, "not having made a vow of obedience, offered some resistance," but Mother held firm, threw it into "its prison and went off after closing the door—that is, the lid—tight. In the evening at recreation the whole Community laughed till the tears ran at the little lobster possessed by the devil, and next day everyone was able to enjoy a *mouthful.* . . ."

Thérèse says "everyone" enjoyed a mouthful. It would be more exact to say everyone but Thérèse. Her illness had reached the point where swallowing food was a particular difficulty. Her Lent was more austere than even the full black fast prescribed as of old for the Carmels of the reform, though it was not quite precisely observed at Lisieux. She was beginning to follow a daily pattern of temperatures, with a high fever attacking her in the afternoon at three o'clock with dreadful regularity. She was very, very sick. But her gaiety, her holy gaiety, was unquenchable. It was no wonder, with such a point and counterpoint of suffering and laughter, that she found herself so much moved by the life of Blessed Théophane Vénard that she had read at Père Roulland's suggestion. Here was a splendid martyr, nearly a contemporary—he was born in 1829 and died in 1861—and a Frenchman and a person easily susceptible to illness and a missionary and a victim of the Chinese in West Tonkin, not far from Père Roulland's station, and still a very happy man, at his most outwardly gay in his last days, even though in prison awaiting execution.

Théophane Vénard was the victim of a decree against Christian missionaries promulgated in Tonkin not long after his arrival there. Priests and bishops lived in caves, hid in the great woods, and, if they were extraordinarily courageous, did their work as religious at night. Father Théophane was not content with night-time activity, and though he was ill most of this time, began to go out by day to minister to the sick and the dying, to baptize, to perform all the duties of his station. In November 1860, he was caught by the Chinese, who had been led to him by a man who had pretended friendship to the priest. The Chinese expected one betrayal to lead to another: they demanded that Father Vénard renounce his faith. He refused and so the mandarin before whom he was tried sentenced him to death. Until his beheading, two months later, he lived as a captive in a cage. From there, he wrote letters full of joyous expectation of heaven. "Though in chains," his bishop wrote of him, "he is as gay as a little bird." To his father, Théophane wrote, "A slight sabre cut will separate my head from my body, like the spring flower which the Master of the garden gathers for His pleasure. We are all flowers planted on this earth, which God plucks in His own good time, some a little sooner, some a little later." He expressed the hope that he would meet his father in Paradise—"I, poor little moth, go first." When he finally did go to his death, it was with softness and ease. To those around him who jeered, he smiled; to the executioner, who offered a speedy beheading in return for the gift of his clothing, he replied, "The longer it lasts, the better. . . ." He sang psalms and chanted hymns and apparently walked comfortably to his death.

Thérèse needed no special invitation to write a poem for the "angelic martyr," as she called him, whom even the seraphim aspire to serve. Unable, she says, to mingle her voice with the blessed on the other side, at least she would like to take up her instrument and sing his praises here below. The floral metaphor so beloved of both Théophane and Thérèse is nicely turned to use in her seven-stanza poem: for Jesus, she tells Théophane, your poetic soul made flowers burgeon at every moment. She celebrates with almost audible awe the martyr's savoring of suffering in his very last moments, when he refused any curtailing of the pain of execution. Gathered by the Master of the garden for his pleasure, this wide-open flower has leaped beyond its exile forever, to be admired by the blessed, its fragrance to be breathed by the Virgin herself. She asks his aid, now—

> For sinners, I should like now, here below,
> To fight, to suffer, to give my blood, my tears.
> Protect me; come, support me, hold me up.
> For them, ceaselessly making war, I want
> To take the kingdom of God by assault. . . .

She asks his support for afterwards, for the life to come—

> Oh, if only I were a spring flower
> That the Lord wanted to pluck soon!
> Come, come down from heaven at my last hour,
> I entreat you, O blessed martyr!
> Out of your love for virginal flames,
> Come inflame me here in this mortal abode. . . .

Once again in this poem she expresses her willingness to come or to stay at the Lord's invitation. She cherishes "*cette plage infidèle*," that infidel shore, which Théophane loved so much; she would fly to it immediately if Jesus asked it of her. And equally she would leap up to heaven—the implication is clear and leads her to her last stanza in which she asks to be plucked as a spring flower. The point is, as she says just before turning into a flower again, that there is only one consuming interest for her in all the vastness of the universe, and that is that her works, her little sufferings, will make God loved to the edge of the seas and beyond.

More and more, Thérèse was feeling the physical suffering of her eaten insides. The decay within, however, for all its cramping clamors, never could claim full control of Thérèse's spirits. She remained cheerful, and in her cheerfulness was eager to help others whose spirits were sagging, such as that poor frayed soul, Sister Marie of St. Joseph, who will be forever famous for having burdened Thérèse with her neurotic chattering and clattering in the late winter of 1897, when Thérèse was falling heavily into the grip of her illness. In a series of sparkling little notes, Thérèse commiserated with Sister Marie, carried on a gay exchange of sobriquets—she called the mournful older nun "Little Brother" and "Small Boy" and "Little Child" and played at being her "enchanted" friend. No matter how trivial Little Brother's complaints, Thérèse gave them dignity with her answers. Do not lower yourself to a fight with pebbles and small stones as your weapons, she tells her sorrowing friend; your armament must be love. Don't be intimidated by the ordinary difficulties of life. We will work cheerfully together on the mending of the Sisters' torn linen, the work that we must do, she promises Sister Marie. If you are frightened of the night, she tells the Small Boy, don't look; close your eyes, *willingly* make the sacrifice that is demanded of you and just "wait for sleep to come!" Is this a terrible demand? No, not at all; it is not too much to be asked to close one's eyes and to be told not "to struggle with the chimeras of the night. . . . No, it is not too much, and the Small Boy is going to let himself go, believe that he is in Jesus's arms, be content with not seeing Him and leave far behind the sterile fear that he is unfaithful (a fear that goes with childhood)." None of this is to make small of Sister Marie's fears or to show any impatience with them. Thérèse makes the most solemn, if brief, assurances of her agreement about the harshness of this life, but it is a harshness, she points out in a subtle way, matched with love: "The most pain-filled, the most LOVE-FILLED martyrdom is ours, since it is seen by Jesus alone." And then she offers Sister Marie the profoundest hope of all for an undistinguished religious. This martyrdom will never be made known to anyone here on earth, "but when the Lamb opens the *book of life,* what a surprise for the Court of heaven to hear, along with the names of missionaries and martyrs, the names of poor little children who have never done anything outstanding." It is no great surprise that with Thérèse dancing such attendance upon her gloom-filled companion of the needle it was not long before Sister Marie was, if not cured, at least willing to say that she had stopped worrying about herself. With the special bounty that her kind of neurotic always finds, she was able soon enough to start worrying again, however, this time about Thérèse, for she had learned that her great good companion was very sick.

In her deep and joyous concentration upon littleness, Thérèse assumed a whole series of poses in which diminutive size and a humble station should combine to secure the indulgence and protection of heaven. Some of her impulsive translation of these poses into notes and letters may seem coy to the reader who scans her words as quickly as Thérèse wrote them, or if not coy, then sentimental and surely not very important. That would be, I think, a superficial judgment and even a dangerous one. For to miss the importance of Thérèse's spirituality as she translates it on the run is to miss the enormous vitality of her doctrine and its applicability to a life lived as most modern life must be lived on the run. To miss the way Thérèse applies her way of littleness and weakness and humble disposition to the trivia of her life—the nagging little irritations, the constant minor vexations, the creepy-crawly afflictions—is to miss her genius for dealing with the human condition as it generally and inevitably must irritate and vex and afflict us all. To miss it is to fail to understand how one can lift oneself above the tiny despondencies that far more than any one great terror lead one to despair. To turn away from it is to turn away from the most graceful way offered us in our time to cope with our time.

Thérèse had many opportunities to apply her way of littleness and weakness and humble disposition in the face of great disappointment. For example, she speculated much about the possibility of going to the missions, and to China in particular. She shared her speculation with Mother Gonzague. And that woman, at this point in her vocation as a religious superior really quite superior, assured Thérèse that she had the special gift for that sort of exile all right, but, she told her daughter, it was a gift not likely to be used. For "that," Thérèse explains to Père Roulland, "the scabbard has to be as strong as the sword and perhaps (thinks our Mother) the scabbard would be thrown into the sea before it ever got to Tonkin." This comment leads to a fine bittersweet meditation on the difficult nature of the union of body and soul. "As a matter of fact," she muses, "it's no great convenience to be composed of a body and a soul! Miserable Brother Ass, as St. Francis of Assisi called the body, often hinders his noble sister and pervents her from darting off where she would." But Thérèse is no Jansenist, any more than her father or mother were, superficial readers of the annals of the Martins to the contrary notwithstanding. So she continues on the subject of Brother Ass, her body: "Still, I won't abuse him, for all his faults; he is still good for something, he helps his companion to get to heaven, and"—vital addition, not to be skipped over in a hasty reading—"gets there himself." Her writings are not filled with the language of theology, but she is a sound theologian; she knows the logic of her faith, perhaps as much by the grace of intuition as by the intellectual concentration of scholastic exercises. The union to which she looks forward is total. Her heaven has physical dimension; it is not merely a spiritual state, however free of the aches and anxieties of the flesh it may be.

The unconcern Thérèse affects in the face of her mounting pain is the unconcern of a child. All the deliberate exercises she has practiced now take command. She is firm in the face of her annihilating illness, eager somehow to continue to work for her Lord, for her love and for his love for others, even if her efforts can only be fumbling and furtive, the efforts of a poor misshapen Brother Ass, the abortive flights of a dying sparrow, the movements of a crippled religious that must seem as untutored to the world as those of a handicapped child. But how wonderful it is to be a child, she tells Sister Marie in one of her little notes: "How marvelous a thing is a child missionary and warrior!" To drive her point home, she identifies herself with her "brothers in heaven, the Holy Innocents," in eleven stanzas of a poem positively pulsating with happy emotion. Some of the pulsation is in the form of the poem itself, eight-line stanzas, in which stately long alexandrines alternate with terse four-syllable lines. But it is her own intense feeling that gives the poem its most affecting movement. She stands in a kind of contemplative rapture before the Innocents, caught up without understanding or responsibility or choice in the world's furies of hatred and vengeance and destructive force. She delights in the reception of these victims of Herod, victims who had no way at all of abating or deserving their fate, offerings chosen by evil itself, one might say, to swell the ranks of eternal goodness. Their beauty, as Thérèse contemplates it, is a kind of allegory of all the beauty of eternity. For they arrived, infants of one day, before the immense riches of paradise and came to know them before knowing anything of our bitter sorrows. They came to their victory without combat, without preparation; *parvenus à la gloire,* Thérèse describes them. She sees them in conventional enough images—golden-curled, shining jewels that charm heaven itself; playfellows of the angels, with a childish audacity that gives pleasure to the Lord. But conventional or not, she sees them and sees them clear and bold in outline before her, her model, a mold from which she seeks a stamp here below. Let me carry your likeness here, she pleads; give me "the virtues of childhood," for I find, she says, that "Your candor, your perfect abandon, your sweet and amiable innocence charm my heart." She is herself daring enough to offer herself, with all her joys and sorrows, as an addition to the heavenly host of the innocents —"Among these Innocents, I demand a place. . . ."

Thérèse's longings for heaven do not for more than a moment diminish the pleasure she feels in being able to offer up her suffering to assuage the miseries of others. She wants to increase, if that were possible, the love of God for all the poor and hapless souls in creation, and to bring them to find love in their misery as she has, to discover joy in their joylessness and pleasure in their pain. But that sort of exchange is not enough. In her eagerness to offer everything, to make every possible little hidden sacrifice, she examines all the avenues of love that were exposed when she opened her heart wide to the Lord's *"new commandment."* She means, she tells Mother Gonzague, the admonition to love one's enemies and pray for those who persecute one. Suppose there are no enemies in Carmel, after all there are sympathies and preferences; one inevitably is drawn more to one Sister than to another. Invariably one finds oneself making long detours to avoid the other one so that without her realizing it she becomes your persecutor. Well, then, there you are, *that's* the one Jesus says you must pray for, all the more if she seems not to like you either. It's no achievement, as Jesus says, to love those who love you; even sinners love those who love them. Nor is it enough just to love this unfortunate Sister; you must really prove your love by giving and giving of yourself, and giving not only what is fun to give, a gift, say, that one thinks up as a charming surprise, but also what the other one asks for and doesn't necessarily think of as a gift at all. One must give even when the request is made rudely and one's pride is hurt by the rudeness of the demand. And remember, there is no achievement in first scolding your rude friend and explaining, with a fullness of rhetorical detail, the nature of her offense before you do what she has asked, which is probably a trifle in itself which you could do in a twentieth of the time it takes to assert your imaginary rights.

There are tougher things still, which this tough-minded saint has worked into her way of the world. There is, for example, the still more difficult kind of giving involved in letting others take one's things without demanding them back. Of course, it only *seems* more difficult. *Of course?* Well, it is natural enough for one who has opened her heart wide and watched it being consumed in the fires of love. When that has happened, she says, it is sheer joy to travel the roads of the new commandment, singing the new song of love. And isn't she right, really, however sticky this language may seem to those of us who have spoken the harsh words of modern speech so long? Do any of us really want to refuse anything to those we love? Are we, any of us, really uncomfortable when those we love keep what we have merely loaned to them or when they take our things heedlessly? Oh, we may not be entirely free of irritation or annoyance; neither, we can be sure, was Thérèse, or she would not have stressed this whole pattern of behavior so strongly. But love conquers petty irritations and turns annoyances upside down, making warmth where there was coldness and ease where there was awkwardness and dissolving everything in the floods of feeling that overwhelm the lover, any lover, every lover, the lover of children, the lover of adults, the lover of God, and especially that greatly gifted lover who loves everyone and everything because he loves God.

Thérèse argues that hers is a special case. She really has no great problems of this kind because she has taken a vow of poverty and nothing that anybody asks for from her or even takes from her belongs to her anyway. But there are some hard moments, when the things one has to work with have been all messed up by somebody else—paints and paintbrushes, for instance—or when something one needs to do one's work with has simply been taken away by some Sister, for whatever reason. What then? A beggar's role, a beggar's disposition. Never mind the shattered patience. Just hold your hand out like a beggar and hope for the best—and do not be amazed if you are refused; nobody owes you anything.

This way lies peace. There is no joy like that which comes with poverty of spirit, and—as Thérèse understood so let us understand it—with poverty of body as well. They go happily together —so give the man who begs you for your suit your overcoat as well, just as Jesus advised. Now, stripped of these garments, free of all pretenses, forgetting your precious rights, you're in great shape to walk a long hard distance, or even to run. Once again the Lord's admonition comes to Thérèse's mind—if you are required to walk a mile by an importunate friend, go two miles with him—but go of your own free will! It is not enough to give people what they ask for; we must do more, much more, and do it with an air of enjoyment, of being pleased, really, to have had the opportunity. No reluctance must be in it: when something of yours is taken, you must look as if you wanted nothing so much as to be rid of it. None of this is to say that Thérèse did these things easily or even well, she assures Mother Gonzague, but even just thinking of doing them and wanting to do them brings an ineffable peace.

Thérèse is full of this sort of giving as she writes these late lines to her superior, because her Sisters in Carmel have been so full of such actions. They have so surrounded her with attentions, have positively leaped to such tasks, have extended their journeys by such long distances, that she barely has time to do any writing. They always have good talk for her, always have objects to offer around which she can construct poems; they have so much of everything but that silence and inattention for which Thérèse yearns so that she can stop opening and shutting "that famous

notebook," as she calls her autobiography. She's lucky if she can
get in ten lines without interruption. If nothing else, someone
comes along to commiserate with her on the fatigue she must
be feeling from writing so much!

In her constant and acute analysis of herself in these last
months, nothing preoccupied her so much as the apparatus of
charity which she was giving her life to learn and to transmit to
others. It wasn't enough, she concluded, just to love your neighbor as yourself. Jesus's new commandment, the one he gave the
apostles, was to love one another as he loved them. That is the
real love of neighbor, to love as Jesus loved. And so Thérèse
must love with the love of Jesus in her and look at others always
through and with such a love. Defects that one notices so easily
in others have a history after all. Who knows how often a Sister
has conquered her faults in the past, how hard she has fought to
overcome her defects, and how much, out of humility, she has
hidden her struggles and her conquests? Furthermore, what
seems a fault on the surface may in fact have been an act of virtue; it depends on the intention, doesn't it? When she is con-
fronted by such defects in a Sister, Thérèse says, then she starts
to think of all the goodness in the nun, all her good acts in the
past, all her good intentions. It's just not a good idea to make
judgments. Furthermore, it works both ways: what the world
judges in any of us as a virtue may in reality be a defect. Thérèse
had enough experience of that sort of misjudgment. Fortunately
for her system of values, she kept her sense of humor whenever
that sort of incident occurred.

There was, for example, that time near Christmas when some
nuns were needed to open the big door so that trees could be
brought in for the Crib. The sub-Prioress indicated that Thérèse
or another Sister who was doing needlework with her in the recreation room was to go. Thérèse thought the other Sister would
like bringing in the trees, so she was deliberately slow about finishing her work. The result was that she was judged much too slow
and perhaps even selfish. If that's the way it must be, then good
enough. It's an excellent way to cauterize one's vanity and to remind one how unimportant is human respect, which is so easily
misled by appearances into making wrong judgments.

Thérèse didn't mean to boast about her achievements, but
neither did she intend to underrate them. She had conquered

some of the worst, the most immediate and dubious, of her judgment-making impulses. And at least once, she was willing to boast, she had managed wonderfully well to overcome her aversion for a particular Sister, who seemed to have a particular knack for irritating her with every characteristic of her personality. Her words, her manners, everything, all, seemed *très désagréable*, nothing less than offensive to Thérèse. But she was clearly a holy nun who must have been *très agréable* to God. Thérèse, then, went through all the reasoning that she had rehearsed so many times for such situations and determined on a firm strategy: she would treat the holy nun as if she loved no one more. She prayed for her every time she met her, crying all her good qualities to heaven, looking deep down inside her to find what would be really pleasing to God about this holy terror. She did every act of kindness she could think of for her; whenever in response to something this nun said a brusque word or a cutting answer came to mind she smiled instead and changed the drift of the conversation. When things got too bad, Thérèse simply ran away. The result of all this was that the nun ended by thinking Thérèse did indeed find her *très agréable*. She once asked Thérèse, "What attracts you so in me? Why do you smile so every time you see me?" The answer should have been, "It is Jesus, Jesus hidden deep down inside you who attracts me, Jesus who makes everything bitter turn sweet," but that is hardly a winning answer, even for a holy religious—It's not you but Christ in you that draws me to you! Thérèse answered that she smiled because she was happy to see the nun—"Of course," she told Mother Gonzague, "I didn't add that the happiness was altogether spiritual."

When in great doubt about her own strength in a tense situation, Thérèse's habit was to run for her life; there was no more certain way to avoid a fight. When a young Sister intercepted Thérèse trying to return some keys to Mother Gonzague's room at a time when Mother was sleeping off a bronchial attack, a small wrangle ensued over who should put them back in the office. Both of them, who liked each other a good deal, meant well; both wanted to spare the ailing Superior any noise. It was Thérèse's duty to return the keys, as she delicately reminded the other nun. Let me do it, the young nun insisted—and the great vocal concern of the two not to wake up Mother ended, of course, by fully wakening her. Thérèse knew at once that if she stayed to defend herself she would become shrill, or show great impatience, or at least seem to. So she ran from the battle, "without drum or trumpet," she says, leaving the unhappy young Sister to continue with her great denunciation—like Camilla's imprecations against Rome in Corneille's *Horace,* Thérèse adds.

Running away was only a last resort for Thérèse. She knew all sorts of other ways to deal with the difficulties of living in close quarters with a community of women. On the rare occasions she said *no,* she said it so graciously as to make a refusal into something even more pleasant than compliance with a request. She learned to be able to accept meaningless verbal formulas which this sort of life—any life in any kind of community, really—demands. When someone asked if she could borrow something or could have some service of Thérèse, with the understanding that she would perform one in return, Thérèse knew that the loan of time or energy might very well not be repaid and came, I think, to accept each failure of repayment or exchange as just that sort of rich experience Jesus had promised to those who could lend without any hope of return. After a while, she came to accept just as easily those extraordinary appropriations of ideas and bright turns of phrase, without even the grace of a verbal excuse, to which Thérèse, like all who are gifted with words and insights, had to accustom herself. She had come to realize, in the great stock-taking of the last months, that whatever wit or wisdom she managed was not her own, anyway. Like the title to worldly goods which she gave up when she entered Carmel, her words, her thoughts, and her ideas were to be shared in common. Anything of quality in what she said was certainly an infused grace; why shouldn't the community take as much of her thinking for its own as it wanted? She acknowledged her great joy in any perceptions that came to her, but also recognized that she was only a donkey carrying relics of great worth, a creature being used for an end far more worthy than any creature in herself could ever be.

Thérèse was practicing acts of charity as carefully as she could long before those final months of exacting appraisal, but it was during that intense self-examination that she was able to see what her accomplishment really was and to set it down in her autobiographical notebooks in remarkably unembarrassed and unembarrassing detail. She remembered the way she used to take charge of old Sister St. Peter after evening prayers, when the infirmarians were too busy to attend to the ailing ancient. She did it so well that it became a habit with the old nun to wave her hourglass at Thérèse, the unmistakable signal to get going. It was a nuisance for Thérèse in the beginning, with all sorts of fussy details to get straight for a fussy old Sister. She had to grab Sister St. Peter by her waistband or else she fell down. She had to walk just so slowly with her or else she grumbled; just so fast, or else she complained about that too. One had to sit her up in the refectory, adjust her sleeves, and leave her poised for her bread. Thérèse noticed one day that the nun's mangled old hands were not up to fixing her bread for herself and so, without being asked, she did this little extra service for her, too. Suddenly, in a burst of grace, Thérèse's cutting of the bread for her won something like the proper gratitude from Sister St. Peter. This was a mercy shown Thérèse, as Thérèse saw it, this whole tortuous action; it was decidedly not her own charity that motivated her. One vivid winter night's experience framed that mercy clearly in her mind. It was cold and dark; the setting was the familiar bleak one; the work of mercy was the same old one for Sister St. Peter, but suddenly something strange happened, something strange and wonderful. Thérèse heard, as from a distance, the sound of a sweet musical instrument; it was such that it conjured up in her mind a handsomely illuminated drawing room, filled with elegant young girls and a worldly chatter that fitted their costumes and the setting. Then, says Thérèse, she looked down at the poor sick old nun she was tending. Instead of a musical sound she heard groans and there, in place of the elegant setting, she saw the bare bricks of Carmel, just visible in a faint light.

It was a transfiguring experience for Thérèse. She says that for a thousand years of the world's great feasts she would not give up those ten minutes of her life, those ten minutes of pushing and pulling Sister St. Peter along. The light of truth within that she suddenly felt had no worldly equivalent that she knew about. If Jesus himself had been given into her care in place of the old nun, she could not have performed, she says, with better grace. If one moment's break in the midst of our world of suffering and struggle can light up our lives with so much happiness, she muses, can lift us so far beyond the happiness of earth, what marvels will we see and have in heaven?

Acts of love did not always produce such transfiguration, Thérèse admits, but ever since her first days in religion, Jesus had made it possible for her to feel the sweetness of his presence in the souls of those closest to him. No, it wasn't always easy, but there were ways of dealing with the difficulties, ways that have become famous over the years among Thérèse's friends and clients. When, for example, a nun who occupied the place in front of Thérèse at evening prayers began her nightly serenade, clicking her finger-nails against her teeth, Thérèse almost invariably began to suffer, to sweat and to shake with irritation. She simply could not forget the sound; her sensitive ear repeated and magnified every click. But somehow peace and joy would have to come. How? By deliberately listening to the clicking cadences rather than by trying to tune them out; by listening as if to a "ravishing concert," and so she did and so all her prayer ("which wasn't the prayer of *quiet*") was passed in offering the concert to Jesus.

To match her sensitive ears, Thérèse, like most of the rest of us, had an equal aversion to bring splashed with dirty laundry water, a shower with which one Sister managed to splatter Thérèse when they were both doing laundry duty. It was simple, really: all one had to do was beat the linen against the broad ledge of the tub with a flat stick and after a little while one could splash almost anyone nearby in the face. Thérèse's first instinct, like anyone else's, was to jump back. But then she thought better of it. Here was a new kind of holy water with which to be sprinkled; could she turn down such a "treasure"? Thérèse hid her irritation carefully and concentrated on developing a taste for dirty water in the face, which she did so well that she soon volunteered for more of this splendid duty.

"You see, beloved Mother, that I am a *very little soul* who can offer God only *very little things*," Thérèse sums up. And so she spent her time looking for very little things to offer, and finding them. In fact, she found them with such ease, after a while, that almost too great a peace descended upon her, as she saw things. Though she was not up to any great open display of heroism, she thought, surely such repose would not long be satisfactory for any of those concerned, for herself, for her lover, or really for any of those whom she loved. And so it was not. The trials of faith came and more trials that threaded together every bit of her, body and soul, soul and body, in stitches of pain. "Without changing my way," she wrote, "He sent me the trial that mixed a salutary bitterness with all my joys."

FIFTEEN

THÉRÈSE spent the end of her life as she had the beginning, surrounded by members of her family. Though depleted by the deaths of her father and mother and the absence of Léonie, the family was larger than ever, swollen to a huge number by the devoted nuns around Thérèse. Almost every member of the community was deeply concerned as the signs of Thérèse's illness became more and more alarming, almost everyone, even those who were not altogether convinced of the seriousness of her condition, and even those others who gave it out that the blood-letting, the fever, and the great weakness were not things to be upset about, because they themselves were so upset about them they could not face them. Céline was in constant attendance as second infirmarian; she slept in an adjoining cell and never left her sister except for the hours of the Divine Office, which had to be prayed in community, and for the occasional care of other sick nuns, which was also her responsibility. And when she left, on almost every occasion Pauline replaced her. The two Maries, the oldest of the family, Sister Marie of the Sacred Heart, and that dearest of cousins, Sister Marie of the Eucharist, stopped in at the infirmary with increasing frequency—but then everybody did, within the limits imposed by work and good sense.

Pauline was particularly determined to show good sense. Not a drop of Thérèse's suffering must be wasted; none of her precious last words must be lost. From early in April, at the end of Lent, when it became apparent that Thérèse was dying, or at least might be, Pauline began to note down the more significant comments, until, on May 1, she was dating them. Using her golden-wisdom standard of value, she soon found herself taking down nearly every word that Thérèse pumped up slowly, wryly, smilingly, wittily, wisely to her lips.

One should not have an image of Thérèse spending those last months, from May to September, in a lingering splendor, attended by her worshipful community of Sisters. She did not die like Dumas's Camille, or her prototype, the famous courtesan Marie Duplessis, in a great agonized burst of misery, at stage center, with every step of the way prepared for perfectly, dramatically. For quite a while her drama had to be contained within her, as she executed the sad silly tasks prescribed for her by a medicine almost as sorely diseased as her own body. She had, for example, to take walks in the convent garden: that was the duty assigned to her by the first infirmarian. When, in a note, Pauline asked her please to hold open "a bare quarter-hour's conversation" for her, "in spite of your vagabond walks," Thérèse scribbled in reply on the back of the note, quoting from an old song the Martins used to sing together, "I must 'keep walking till my last moment— that is what will end my torment'—like the poor Wandering Jew."

Another of the constant demeanings of these days was the application of a burning needle to Thérèse's back by the bemused doctor who hoped in that way to cauterize—that is, to make callous—the wasted tissue of the dying nun. One day Céline counted more than five hundred such applications, during which time the only thing that was made callous was the doctor, and he was already callous enough. While Thérèse stood, leaning helplessly against a table, he burned away with his needle, all the while keeping up a sprightly conversation of banalities with Mother Gonzague. At the end of the treatment, Thérèse made her trembling way to her cell, to sit down in exhaustion on the edge of the canvas and straw paillasse which passed for a mattress in Carmel. She was certainly in no shape to lie down. All she could do was hold still, or as close to still as she could hold herself, continuing, perhaps, the large-scale offering for others that she told Céline she had to make of these sessions, and dwelling, as she almost always did on such occasions, on the suffering of the martyrs.

It was a shared martyrdom, Thérèse's. Céline herself had to administer the needle at times, by the doctor's orders. If Thérèse had not also ordered her to do so, she probably could not herself have gone through the ordeal. When once Céline wanted to forget the hideous duty, Thérèse reminded her that Mother Gonzague would be unhappy if she did so, for the Superior was a great believer in those *frictions*, especially on the back. And then the doctor would come and demand to know why his orders were not being followed. Well, maybe a one-day postponement, but that's all. There is a great poignancy in the remark Thérèse made to Pauline when Pauline showed her a photograph of herself: "Yes, but . . ." she said, "that's only the *envelope;* when shall we see the *letter?* Oh, how I would like to see the letter!" Brother Ass, her body, was not in high favor in those debilitating days. There was not much pleasure in contemplating it.

Thérèse was really being eaten alive. The tuberculosis in her lungs had been joined by an intestinal extension and development of the same grave disease. Gangrene had begun to set in and her body was starting to show those great ulcerated wounds which were all the more painful to endure as she wasted away into the terrible leanness of advanced tuberculars. But no matter how bad the state of her body, nor how frequent the shadows of doubt— and they continued to come, shadows amid the shadows, right up to the end—no matter what her misery, she worked hard at being a comfort to all those who came to comfort her.

With Céline, Thérèse returned often to the language and to the scenes and events of their childhood. She made a point of calling herself Monsieur Toto, as she had occasionally done years earlier, when she and Céline had played a storybook game together. She called Céline Mademoiselle Lili, Toto's older sister. The names were drawn from a story they had read over together in an illustrated children's book at Les Buissonnets. She also called Céline *Pauvre, Pauvre* (Poor, Poor Little One), a name drawn from another children's story, and fell happily back on *bo-bonne,* meaning Little Servant, as still another way of addressing Céline. At her weakest moments, it was much easier for her to say *bo-bonne* than Céline's name in religion, or to address her by the equally proper title of Sister Second Infirmarian. In the convent she would not call her Céline, in spite of the dearness to her of that name, so dear, Céline explains, that Thérèse would never suffer a calendar around her that did not take due note of the feast of St. Céline on October 21. Her family was very close to Thérèse and she saw nothing wrong in having her sisters with her as much as possible. As she so often reminded her sisters, her place in heaven would be with those little saints who had always retained their great love for their family, and not with those great ones who had cut themselves off from their families in their desire for perfection. Nonetheless, she observed the rule in the little things that protected it from decay, such little things as the use of religious names, and when she first called Céline *bo-bonne* she asked permission before using it, very humbly, Céline records. Little things were, in the last days as in all her years in religion, important things.

The name *bo-bonne* was at the core of a story Thérèse liked to gloss and comment on at some length in conversation with Céline. It came from an examination of a holy card which showed a little boy and a little girl at the edge of a precipice, with their guardian angel standing in protection over them. The boy was lightly dressed, free of all restraint except the hand of his sister; she, however, was weighed down with a large bouquet while she was bending down to gather up some more flowers. Thérèse improvised around the picture a dialogue between a *demoiselle*— she liked the chivalric tone of the word—of great riches, and her poor sick little brother. In his illness, he said to his sister, "Throw all your riches into the fire, for all they do is worry you. Then you will become my *bo-bonne,* rejecting your title of *demoiselle,* and I, when I get to the enchanted land where soon I am going, I will come back for you, because you will have become poor like me, without worrying about tomorrow." The *demoiselle* was convinced by his words. She threw away her wealth, became his *bo-bonne,* free of torment, and was in her turn gathered up to heaven, the enchanted land where God is King and the Blessed Virgin is Queen and the *bo-bonne* and her brother could live forever, Thérèse concluded, in the lap of the Lord.

Her conversation, her letters, her meditations were all full of death, packed with images of the enchanted land to come, laced with longer and longer contemplation of the influence she might have after death and the use to which her present suffering and the suffering she caused others by her illness could be put. She was certain that death was to come soon, but it was like the cake that was always being promised to a child. "They show it to him from a distance. Then, when he comes near to take it, they pull it away!" She found nothing grisly about this coming great event or any of its appurtenances. When a box of artificial lilies that had been ordered for her bier arrived at the convent, she demanded to see them. She exclaimed in great joy, Céline says, "They're for me!" And later she showed equal interest in the candle that was to be placed beside her coffin. "When the Thief comes to take me," she said to the nuns around her, "put the candle in my hand, but don't bother with the candlestick, it's too ugly!"

She was quite specific about the money that was to be spent on decorations for her coffin. She did not want wreaths such as those that had been used for Mother Geneviève, the foundress. Use the money instead, she suggested, to rescue some poor little Negroes from slavery. "Say then that that's what will give me pleasure." She even had names for a couple of the freed slaves: "I should like a little Théophane and a little Marie-Thérèse." As for her grave, when that subject came up because of discussion of a new piece of ground for the Carmel in the cemetery at Lisieux, she said that her place of burial was of very little concern to her. What difference could it make then, after death? She had a joking reference to finish the subject, which perhaps did not amuse all her listeners. "There are missionaries who are buried in the stomachs of cannibals, after all, and there are martyrs whose cemeteries are the bodies of ferocious animals!"

She was made to think about the shortness of her life by Pauline, who told her of one old Sister in their community who believed that a long life of faithful service to God was "more meritorious and more profitable to souls" than a brief one. Thérèse did not agree. "Did you notice," she asked Pauline, "in the reading in refectory the letter written to the mother of St. Aloysius Gonzaga in which it is said that he would not have become more learned or more saintly, even if he had lived to the age of Noah?" No, she said, age is not the point. It won't matter whether I am cured or not, whether I live or die, or when I go. "Age is nothing in the eyes of God," and in any case, Thérèse had reached the point in her spirituality where she was bound to stay always the same age: "I shall so order my life as always to remain *a little child*, even if I live a very long time."

Over and over again, she repeated to her Sisters the formulas of self-abandonment. She refused to dwell at any length upon the possibilities of purgatory, except as a means of saving other souls, in which case it was a splendid subject for contemplation and quite agreeable to discuss. She was not able, however, to spin out any time schedule for her last days on earth or for her first days after departing this world. She was abandoned to the will of Providence, she said, and so bold in her open affirmation of this abandonment that many, ever since that affirmation was made public in the memoirs of her sisters, in her own letters, and in the proceedings that attended her beatification and canonization, have been just as openly repelled. Religious, female religious in particular, have often expressed themselves as uncomfortable with such assurance, which reaches its peak in the several brief, blunt asseverations of Thérèse that she never knowingly withheld anything from God, that she always did what he asked. Imagine knowing his will to begin with! And imagine the self-confidence that permits you to say you have always done what he asked!

This is the essence of Thérèse, however attractive or unattractive one may find it. Even in the depths of her doubts, she was still impelled by a desire to do the will of God and to abandon herself to that will, even when it seemed to be the will of God to abandon her. It was never a love of suffering for its own sake that moved her to her constant prayer to do God's will, never a reveling in the tortures that afflicted her body and her soul. "I have had a very great capacity for suffering," she told Céline, "and a very poor one for rejoicing. I cannot long sustain joy. Joy seems to take away all my appetite—so much so that when I suffer a great deal I eat enough for four people! I am just the opposite of everybody." Of course she wasn't just the opposite of everybody; the psychologists' casebooks are full of people whose appetites increase with worry and pain. But in the special place she gave suffering in her life she was surely a rare person, though again not unique. Love was the motivating force in her high endurance of suffering, a force many others, and women in particular, have known well, though perhaps not so many for love of God directly, without human intermediary. "I desire neither suffering nor death," she explained to her sister, the second infirmarian, "and yet I cherish both. Today, abandonment alone is my guide. I can ask for nothing else with fervor except the perfect accomplishment of God's will in my soul." It was an abandonment in which only her own confidence could sustain her; there were very few other consolations and almost no assurances to contradict or even attenuate her doubts. She compared her condition in these last months, so sunk in doubt and temptations against faith, to one of two little children sitting together in silence. Sometimes, Thérèse said, she turned and said some little thing to Jesus, "but he doesn't answer me. No doubt he's asleep."

The great sadness of these words, spoken to Céline near the end of Thérèse's life, is that they were spoken right after Communion one morning.

Abandonment was not a literary exercise for Thérèse; it was a genuine and a total emptying of self, which she had made two years before in her solemn Act of Oblation and which she was continuing to make right to the bittersweet end, with that toughness of soul which she had achieved with her own kind of cauterization, her genius for translating every sting, no matter how trivial, into a purposeful burning of the fiery love to which she had abandoned herself. On the second anniversary of the Act, on June 9, 1897, she told Pauline that she was very happy. Had the trials of her soul passed, were the doubts and temptations gone? "No, but it's as if something were suspended. The hideous serpents don't hiss in my ears any longer." That did not mean that she had found a perfect balance in her illness, but she was relaxed even a little more than usual amid the misunderstandings and misapprehensions and clumsy judgments around her. The community thought she was getting better—she let the nuns go on thinking so. The nuns showed great skill in turning the facts upside down. She was at peace when, after she stood up, they all insisted she was very sick, and remained calm when the same good Sisters insisted she was recovering, even though she could not stand up without somebody's help.

In all the intense activity, all the talk, all the pain, Thérèse somehow remained recollected. Her answers to all sorts of questions, about her faith, about her temptations, about her expectations for the next world and her schedule of departure remained lucid, informative (insofar as she could offer information), instructive, entertaining, wise. She was able to talk on this way, to answer on and on and on, because of her peace in the face of death and because of her faith in the face of doubt, because she had yielded so completely to her love for a God whose justice and mercy seemed to her all one, united in a love that defined and determined everything that was divine. Of course in a simple being, in Being itself, all must be one. But Thérèse was not reasoning merely theologically. Her logic was founded upon love, hers and God's. This is what she tried to explain, with logic, yes, but more important, with feeling, with love itself, as she wrote Père Roulland at the beginning of May, to answer his doubts about his immediate entry into heaven if his life should be taken, like Théophane Vénard's, by the "infidels." Thérèse's statement to Father Roulland was definitive as an expression of her understanding of divine justice. It satisfied her enough so that when, in July, after completing work on her autobiographical manuscript, she suddenly remembered that she had hardly said two words in it on the subject of justice, she told Pauline that if she wanted to know her thinking on the theme, she would find it in one of her letters to Père Roulland.

She starts by making a scholastic point. Yes, she knows that "one must be pure to appear before the God of holiness. . . ." But the same God is "infinitely just" and that infinite justice, "which terrifies so many souls," is the foundation of her joy and of her trust. Why? "To be just means not only to exercise severity in punishing the guilty, but also to recognize right intentions and to reward virtue." She hopes for just as much from God's justice as from God's mercy, and she quotes Psalm 102 in support of her hope, zigzagging back and forth from the eighth to the fourteenth to the thirteenth verses: "The Lord is compassionate and merciful, long-suffering and plenteous in mercy. For he knows our frame. He remembers that we are dust. As a father has compassion on his children, so has the Lord compassion on them that fear him!" These are consoling words to Thérèse. How, she asks her missionary brother in China, with such a directive from the "Prophet-King," can one doubt what God's response will be to those who have left everything for him, who have sacrificed all for him, put family and country and everything else behind them in order "to make him known and loved," and who also willingly offer their lives for him? How can we doubt, she asks, that he "will open the gates of His Kingdom to his children"?

While she is at it, she deals with the problem of purgatory, with dispatch, with clarity, with ease, in spite of her own fear that she has used such "a lot of phrases to express my thought, or rather to manage not to express it. . . ." The essential question is the one that is aroused by Père Roulland's letter, in which he explains that, if he is put to death by the brigands, she, Thérèse, will have to get him out of purgatory so that he can go ahead and wait for her in heaven. "How can [God] purify in the flames of Purgatory souls [already] consumed in the fires of divine love?" Thérèse asks in reply. "Of course no human life is free from faults; only the immaculate Virgin presents herself in absolute purity before God's Majesty. What a joy to remember that she is our Mother! Since she loves us and knows our weakness, what have we to fear?" In sum, the reasoning goes thus: since "all missionaries are *martyrs* by desire and will . . . in consequence, not one should go to Purgatory. If, at the moment they appear before God, some traces of human weakness remain in their souls, the Blessed Virgin obtains for them the grace to make an act of perfect love, and then gives them the palm and the crown they have so truly merited." And that's that. Q.E.D.

Thérèse could not quite say with Blessed Claude de la Colombière, whom she very much admired, "All my confidence is in my confidence," because there were moments when her faith trembled and her confidence was tortured by doubt. But her confidence in God's justice-mercy-love never entirely deserted her, even when the exact terms of the afterlife and the precise structure of the divine ordering of things seemed altogether impossible to understand. For no matter how hazy her comprehension became under the attacks of an obscuring doubt, she could always say as she said to Père Roulland, "my way is all trust and love; I don't understand souls who are afraid of so loving a Friend." She had a point to make which every writer of spiritual books, every retreat master, every conductor of days of recollection, every director of souls, every confessor should ponder long. "Sometimes, when I read spiritual treatises," she says to Père Roulland with an almost audible sigh, "in which perfection is shown with a thousand obstacles in the way and a host of illusions round about it, my poor little mind grows very soon weary. I close the learned book, which leaves my head muddled and my heart parched, and I take the Holy Scripture. Then all seems luminous, a single word opens up infinite horizons to my soul, perfection seems easy. . . ." Then, she remembers her essential confidence, her own special way, which could be and should be everyone's: "I see that it is enough to realize one's nothingness, and give ourself wholly, like a child, into the arms of the good God."

The closer she came to death, the less concerned she was to have any visible signs of her high calling or any significant consolations at all. "Don't be astonished if I do not appear to you after my death and if you do not see any remarkable sign of my happiness," she told Pauline in June. "You must remember that it is in the spirit of my *little way* to wish to see nothing." She asked her sisters not to worry about the suffering she might have to endure at her death and the fact that with it there might be no sign of happiness. She reminded them of the agony of the death of Jesus, a true victim of love; clearly, with all the signs of victimhood that she was receiving, that was her only significant consolation, her only visible sign of high calling. She could barely swallow any food. The hemorrhages were increasing, until by early July they were coming two and three times a day. Her prayers were accompanied by physical pain and anticipations of the death agony that several times might just as well have been the agony itself. Her side ached intolerably, and when it let up there was always the possibility of such a set of interior doubts as she expressed at the end of June, one day, when she said to Pauline, "My soul is quite in exile; heaven is shut against me, and on earth, trials. . . ." No, she said dryly, "to die of love, is not to die in ecstasy."

In spite of all the misery, she was not low in spirits. She caught glimpses, she said, of her lover, as if he were looking at her through the lattices mentioned in the Song of Songs (2:9). She looked forward to a closer and closer glimpse, to final encirclement in his arms; she rejoiced, she said, at the approach of each bloodletting. She had spent a long time preparing to abandon herself to that utter trust that is expressed in the words of Job's prayer, "Although he should kill me, I will trust in him" (13:15); now she could do so. She remembered the piercing dart of fire she had received when she made her Act of Offering and while the same sensation did not come again, she was obviously moved in something like the same way when she looked, at first with fascination and then with joy, at the shrinking of her body. "I have already become a skeleton," she marveled; "and that pleases me!"

In June, she promised a shower of roses after her death, that emblem of her intercession that became such a fixation for so many thousands of her clients for so many years that they looked for her roses as a sign of divine intervention as delightful and as certain as the scarlet pimpernel that promised rescue for the victims of the French Revolution in Baroness Orczy's fanciful novels. In July she promised a great many graces for all those who had been good to her, so many for Pauline that she would not be able to make use of them all. "There will be much," she said, "to make you rejoice." She felt assured of the tenderness of God's judgment; once again she asserted her happy willingness to take the pains of purgatory if they were a means of saving souls. For that purpose, she could, like the three Hebrew children in Daniel's book, sing canticles of love in the fiery furnace. Purgatory, perhaps; damnation was impossible, for "Little children do not damn themselves!" And no matter what the condition of her body at death, no matter what ugliness should show on her face in the contortions of death, everyone was to remember that soon afterward she would be all smiles. She would die in some less than ceremonial way, in a way fitting her littleness, not after Communion, not with any splendor that others like her, little souls following the little way, could not emulate. She meditated much on the power of one little spark to set a whole phalanx of candles ablaze, delighting in the fact that one obscure soul could "produce great lights in the Church . . . Doctors and Martyrs." How many times she had thought, she said, that perhaps all of her graces had come through the prayers of some little soul who had demanded them of God for her, a little soul she would not know, it might be, until heaven.

She had recourse to some of her own poetry in these long painful July days. She spoke aloud some of the lines from "*Rappelle-toi*," and perhaps inspired by the sight of the statue of the Virgin of the Smile, which had been brought to her in the infirmary, she recited the sixteenth stanza of her last poem of any significance, the twenty-five-stanza "Why I Love You, Mary," written at the request of her sister Marie, in May, Mary's month. The poem, written in simple rhyming alexandrines, is not, I think, one of Thérèse's more compelling efforts. But it does hold some vivid pictures of Mary, emphasizing her nobility in suffering, and in the last stanza it works in some felicitous references to Mary's beneficences to her, and to her early enrollment in sodality of the *Enfants de Marie*, the Children of Mary. "You, who smiled at me in the morning of my life," she says in that last stanza, "Come smile at me again . . . Mother, now it is nighttime."

The burden of the sixteenth verse, which Thérèse recited aloud in July, is suffering, suffering sweetly accepted and offered up to love:

314

Since the Son of God has willed that his Mother
Should feel the depths of night, the anguish of the heart,
Isn't it a good thing to suffer much on earth?
Yes, to suffer for love, that's the purest happiness!
All that he has given me, all, Jesus may take away.
Tell him not to worry about me, not ever;
He can hide himself as he wishes; I'm quite happy to wait for him
Till the break of day, without cringing, in full joy.

Her offering of her life to her Lord is that of a child, trusting, simple, without any terror, without any diminishing of the pleasure she had had in earlier years in contemplating the end of exile, the arrival in heaven, beatitude. In one of her loveliest flights, she describes herself and others like her as they would be when they entered the Communion of Saints: "With the virgins, we shall be like virgins; with the doctors, like doctors; with the martyrs, like martyrs, because all the saints are our relations; but those who have followed the way of spiritual childhood will always retain the charms of childhood."

Over and over again in July and August and September she was asked how she felt about her approaching death, whether she feared it, whether she would be unhappy to recover or more unhappy to die. And over and over again she answered that she would be happy as long as she was doing God's will. That she kept her temper in all of this was remarkable. Her sisters, who were the most clamorous with their questions, seemed to be anxious to keep something like a precise record of her interior dispositions and especially her disposition for death, looking, apparently, for the most minute changes of emphasis or outlook, but not often getting them. The one change that did come was the gradual shift of emphasis from the suffering in this world to the joys to come in the next, but not so much the joys for Thérèse herself as those she would be able, from a paradisial vantage point, to confer on those here below. Will she look down from that high point? No, she said, "I will *come* down." She had no long concentrated periods of thought or feeling about heaven, she explained, but just one great expectation that stirred her heart—"that's the love that I shall receive and the love I shall be able to give. I am thinking about all the good that I should like to do after my death—getting little children baptized, helping priests and missionaries, the whole Church. . . ." Then there were the famous words of July 17, "I feel that my mission is about

315

to begin, my mission of making others love God as I love him, of giving my little way to souls. . . . Yes, *I want to spend my heaven doing good on earth.* That's not impossible, since from the midst of the beatific vision itself the angels watch over us."

The italicized words have become Thérèse's identifying motto. All the cures, the changes of heart, the deepenings of faith, the strengthenings of heart, the toughenings of minds which seem in all fairness to be attributable in some way or another to her are witness to the central place of this dedication in the huge population all over the world that considers itself blessed by her. She promised to teach the method of her little way. She offered as her own understanding of beatitude an extension of what she had already known and practiced on earth—it was all a matter of love: "To love, to be loved, and to return to earth to make Love better loved!"

It was with her concentration on love that she fought the exhausting attacks of her illness. She could not, as she understood the logic of love, be anything but confident, and that logic, as much of the heart as of the head, spared her some of the more tormenting fantasies and illusions that usually accompany the fever and bloodletting of her kind of tubercular and gangrenous death. If she thought, in the words of John of the Cross that she quoted to Pauline, of breaking "the web of this sweet encounter," she also dwelt much on the wounding that is reported in the Song of Songs (5:7), where the keepers of the walls strike the Bride and take away her veil. They will tell the Bride, Thérèse explains in her deathbed gloss of the Song, where her Dearly Beloved has gone, *if* she asks humbly enough, but if she makes her demands out of the desire to be admired herself, then she can look forward only to trouble and to the loss of simplicity of heart. She will not then be performing those exercises of love that John of the Cross recommends as vital to the breaking of the web; her course will not then be quickly finished; her face-to-face encounter with God will then be very much delayed. All of which is Thérèse's moderately obscure way of explaining her deep desire to stay humble, to remain content with her suffering, and not to be disturbed at any delay in her departure, not in any way to be demanding. Her aim was not to hold on to herself through any sort of stoicism, which could so easily lead to self-admiration, but to rest content in her suffering through sheer sweetness of love, that love which she could so richly give, she thought, because she had been so richly endowed with it, and which it was all the more important to give now, at what looked like the end, and without any special consolation to make the giving easier.

Thérèse had dispensed with all books. Her source of wisdom had to come now from what she remembered of the books, of the words of the Office, of Scripture. The Gospels were always close at hand and while she was working on the last pages of her auto-biography, from June 3 to July 10, she couldn't help having recourse to those passages from the Old Testament and from the saints, especially the Carmelite saints, that seemed best to instruct her speculations about prayer, about her relations with her novices, and her intercessory role in the lives of her two missionary brothers. The spirit throughout these passages is the spirit of abandonment, which certainly she had in part, at least, deepened and strengthened through her reading of John of the Cross and of Teresa of Avila, and which she always thought about, as she almost always had, in terms of the Bride and Bridegroom relationship of the Song of Songs. Because that relationship was so deeply engraved on her consciousness and in her subconscious, she had quick and easy recourse to its language and its spirit when she came to sum up her life and spirituality at the end of the autobiography. She needed no complex set of instructions, she explains there, to deal with all the intercessory and supervisory duties which had been entrusted to her. She doesn't have to draw up a long list of prayers, this one for one novice, this one for another, one for Abbé Bellière and another for Père Roulland. Everything she has is for everyone. She does not have to divide her prayers any more than she has to divide her affections. In this, she makes clear, she simply follows the example of God, who does not parcel out his love in fractions, a little for this one, a little for that. He gives without measure whatever she asks of him. And what she asks she asks for all those who have a name in her prayers and all those who do not, for the community, for the missionary brothers, for missionaries everywhere, for priests and religious everywhere, and for the Pope's intentions, which, after all, she reasons, embrace the whole universe.

Her method is simple enough, she explains—simple prayers, the simplest prayers; if nothing else comes to mind, then just the

Our Father and the Hail Mary. And, as she makes abundantly clear, the simplest and most useful prayer for her is not the prayer that is said in community, not the rosary, but rather the most direct inclination of the heart, a simple glance tossed heavenward, "a cry of gratitude and love from the depths of despondency or from the heights of joy. . . ." It is, she sums up, "something of grandeur, something supernatural, which opens out my soul and unites me to Jesus." Some pages after writing these words, she makes the point again. No long lists for her; if she tried to work out all the needs of her brothers and sisters, the days would be much too short and she would be sure to forget something important. No, she says, "for simple souls, complicated methods are unnecessary." Because she is one of the simple ones, she tells us, one morning after she finished making her thanksgiving, Jesus gave her a simple method to accomplish her mission: "He made me understand that line of the Song, *'DRAW ME: WE WILL RUN after the fragrance of your perfumes.'*" She goes on with the same typographical intensity: "O Jesus, it isn't even necessary to say, *'In drawing me to you, take also all those whom I love!'* That simple phrase, *'Draw me,'* is enough."

The comment that follows is a handsome example of the kind of meditation one gathers Thérèse was making in these last days of hers on earth, the kind she had been making for some time. "Lord," she says, "I understand that when a soul allows itself to be captivated by *the intoxicating fragrance of your perfumes,* it cannot simply follow after you all by itself, alone, for all those whom it loves come running with it. And this happens without effort or constraint, as the inevitable result of your attraction. In the same way, a great flood of waters rushing to the sea draws after it all that it has met on its way. And so, O my Jesus, the soul that plunges into the boundless ocean of your love draws with it all its treasures, everything it possesses. And you know, Lord, that I have no other treasures or possessions than the souls that you have been pleased to unite with mine. . . ." Those treasures, those possessions, those souls, embolden Thérèse to make over to herself, in her own voice, the prayer Jesus addressed to his Father in heaven after his final discourse to his disciples at the Last Supper. She prays in the words of the seventeenth chapter of John, from the fourth to the twenty-fourth verses, with considerable skipping and adaptation. She knows her last evening on earth is not far off. She dares this employment of Jesus's words, not to identify herself with him, but to make her imitation as close as finitude and devotion will permit. The omissions are as interesting as the words she keeps. I will try to indicate both.

"I have glorified you on earth; I have accomplished the work you gave me to do," she begins. She skips the fifth verse—"And now glorify me, O Father, with yourself, with the glory which I had, before the world was, with you"—for obvious reasons: she is not Christ, nor does she pretend to be; that is not what union accomplishes. She then repeats fairly exactly the sixth, seventh, and eighth verses: "I have manifested your name to the men whom you have given me . . . yours they were and to me you gave them . . . [she omits here, significantly, I think, the words "and they have kept your word"; she makes no claims for others, but simply commends them to the love of God] Now they have known that all things which you have given me are from you: Because the words which you gave me I have given to them, and they have received them . . . and they have believed that you sent me." She repeats the ninth verse, but without the words in italics: "I pray *for them: I pray not for the world but* for them whom you have given me because they are yours." She omits the tenth verse, in which Jesus speaks of being glorified in the world, and then skips about from the eleventh to the thirteenth to the fifteenth and sixteenth verses, and finishes with the twentieth and the twenty-fourth verses changed about to fit her smallness, which, it must be remembered, is, all the way through, substituted for the grandeur of Jesus. The alterations do no mayhem to the original text; they simply share Thérèse's love with all whom she loves; they associate her goodness with what she assumes must be the goodness of all those she loves and with the source and end of all goodness. This is the way the two prayers read from the eleventh verse on:

JOHN 17:11–24	THÉRÈSE
11. And now I am not in the world, and these are in the world, and I come to you. Holy Father, keep them in your name whom you have given me. that they may be one as we also are one.	11. And now I am not in the world, and these are in the world, and I come to you. Holy Father, keep them in your name whom you have given me.

12. While I was with them I kept them in your name. Those whom you gave me have I kept, and none of them is lost, but the son of perdition, that the Scripture may be fulfilled.

13. And now I come to you; and these things I speak in the world, that they may have my joy filled in themselves.

14. I have given them your word and the world has hated them, because they are not of the world as I also am not of the world.

15. I pray not that you should take them out of the world, but that you should keep them from evil.

16. They are not of the world, as I also am not of the world.

17. Sanctify them in truth. Your word is truth.

18. As you have sent me into the world, I also have sent them into the world.

19. And for them do I sanctify myself, that they also may be sanctified in truth.

20. And not for them only do I pray, but for them also who through their word shall believe in me.

21. That they all may be one, as you Father, in me, and I in you; that they also may be one in us; that the world may believe that you have sent me.

22. And the glory which you have given me, I have given to them, that they may be one as we also are one.

13. And now I come to you; and it is so that the joy that comes from you may be perfect in them that I speak these things in the world.

15. I pray not that you should take them out of the world, but that you should keep them from evil.

16. They are not of the world, as I also am not of the world.

20. And not for them only do I pray, but for them also who will believe in you because of what they hear of you.

23. I in them and you in me; that they may be made perfect in one, and the world may know that you have sent me, and have loved them, as you have also loved me.

24. Father, I will that where I am they also whom you have given me may be with me; that they may see my glory which you have given me, because you have loved me before the creation of the world.

24. Father, I will that where I am they also whom you have given me may be with me, and that the world may know that you have loved them as you have loved me.

Thérèse's further commentary on her variations on Jesus's prayer is a subsidiary prayer in itself. She asks to be excused for any brashness in this undertaking, and explains that when she asks that those she has loved, those whom the Lord has given over to her care, may be with her in the same place, it is not to deny them higher degrees of glory than she may merit. She is simply asking, like Thomas More, that someday they all may meet merrily in heaven. The Lord knows that she has never wanted anything except to love, has never had any ambitions for a greater glory than that. That leads her in turn, by way of a tribute to the fulfillment she feels in God's love, even here on earth, and a clarification of her relationship to missionaries—she doesn't pretend to teach them; she's not that proud—to a further explication of her use of that great signifying text from the Song of Songs, "Draw me: we will run after you. . . ." It is with this noble exegetical task that she brings her manuscript to an end.

The last words of the autobiography should have been tortured ones. They were written in the infirmary, to which Thérèse was moved on July 8, at a time of great physical pain. The community was desolate, Marie Guérin wrote to her father on the day of Thérèse's move downstairs—tears, sobs, every mark of misery was to be seen and heard in the convent. The sign of the sad event was everywhere. Mother Agnès was "admirable," Marie wrote, in her show "of courage, of resignation." And Mother Gonzague was splendid in her show of maternal concern for everyone else, she who was suffering, according to Marie, "the greatest of sorrows, for Sister Thérèse of the Child Jesus was her greatest treasure." Marie's own sorrow burst across the paper in a flood of verbal tears: "Oh, my dear little Father, I don't know how to say it—we feel crushed, overwhelmed; we cannot believe in the misfortune that threatens us . . . no, we cannot believe that the good God will take our Angel. . . ." But the convent's Angel was, as Marie sadly noted, "ripe for heaven." She was busy with ultimate thoughts, happy with them, and with the last words of her manuscript, and the last days of her life on earth, with the last things.

"Darling Mother," Thérèse wrote in those radiant last pages, "I think it's necessary to give you some explications of the passage from the Song of Songs"—that is, the *Draw me* passage. She was not content with what she had written earlier. Now she wanted to associate the words from the Song with some more choice words, from Jesus, inevitably, and once again from John's Gospel. "No one," she quotes from John 6:44, "can come to me, unless MY FATHER, who has sent me, draw him." Needless to say, the capitals are Thérèse's. And so is the good cheer hers, and the confidence in God's abundant grace. What Jesus teaches in this theology of "drawing," she says, is that all we have to do, to have whatever we should have opened to us, is to knock; to find, but to seek; to receive, but to offer ourselves humbly; to get anything, but to ask in the name of her lover. That, obviously, is why the Holy Spirit, before the birth of Jesus, spoke those prophetic words, "Draw me. . . ."

And what do those words mean? What is it to be drawn but "to be united intimately with the object that has captivated our heart? If fire and iron could reason, a piece of iron might say to the fire, 'Draw me to you,' and wouldn't that prove that it wants to be penetrated and infused with the burning fire until it has become one with it?" This, says Thérèse to Mother Gonzague, is her prayer: "I ask Jesus to draw me into the flames of his love, to unite me so completely with him that he will live and act in me." She knows that the more the flames of love surround and embrace her heart with fire, the more she must say, "Draw me. . . ." And the more she finds herself drawn and enflamed, the more all those around her will be drawn and enflamed, for even she, "poor little useless piece of iron" that she is if she wanders any distance from the fires of God, is magnetic. No soul that has been enkindled by love can help enkindling in its turn; like the Magdalen sitting at the feet of Jesus, merely listening to his sweet and fiery words, she cannot help but give something to oth-

322

ers, cannot help giving a great deal, really, far more than the Marthas of this world, for all the virtues of those hard humble workers who torment themselves with their sense of duty.

Prayer, unworried and calm prayer, that is the great duty and the great joy that Thérèse sets down in the last two paragraphs of her book. In the midst of Martha's *inquiétude,* she shifts from pen to pencil, in the manuscript, to inscribe her doctrine, in gray but still remarkably firm letters. She invokes the examples of those illustrious friends of God who have chosen the Magdalen's way—Paul, Augustine, John of the Cross, Thomas Aquinas, Francis, Dominic. She uses a metaphor taken from Archimedes: "Give me a lever, a fulcrum, and I will lift up the world." Archimedes wasn't granted his request: he didn't ask the right person—Jesus —and he wanted to raise merely the earth. But the saints know better. To them God gives the true fulcrum, himself, and the proper lever, prayer, the prayer that sets a heart on fire with love; with those implements, they really do lift up the whole world.

The lever and fulcrum, though real enough in effect, are rhetorical. The perfumes of the last paragraph surely go beyond rhetoric and into physical reality, for they come from that great reality to which Thérèse dedicated all her rhetoric, to which she had attained even before the cruel tortures of her tubercular passion. These are the fragrances of the Bridegroom, of her beloved Jesus. After his ascension what was left for those who yearned for him but those "traces" that he left behind, those luminous traces, those exquisite fragrances? One can doubt, if one is skeptical about mystics in general or about Thérèse in particular, that she is speaking more than metaphorically when she tells us she has but to open the Gospels to breathe the perfumes which the life of Jesus exudes and which draw her inexorably in the right direction. Thérèse has not had much to say about the ravishing of her senses, neither the senses of the body nor the senses of the soul. She makes little or nothing of the precise data of her religious experiences. But clearly she goes beyond rhetorical devices in these last large words of hers. The fragrance is Jesus's, and the fragrance is hers, as she goes with the great scent, following it into the places of the last followers of Jesus, the places at the rear, the places of the last who shall be first (though she does not make any such claim for herself), the places of those who will not press and push their way forward into the front ranks (which she does say clearly and happily enough). Her exemplars are the publican —not the Pharisee; Mary Magdalen—not Martha. And full of the fragrance of that love which has now certainly penetrated all of her, infused all of her, from head to toe, from lung to bowel, she proclaims herself the Magdalen's special client: "especially," she says, "will I imitate the example of the Magdalen, her astonish- ing—or rather, her loving—brazenness that charms the heart of Jesus and that seduces my own heart. Yes, I know for a fact, that even if I had on my conscience all the sins it is possible to com- mit, I would run, my heart overwhelmed with contrition, to throw myself into the arms of Jesus, for I know how much he loves the prodigal child who comes running back to him." No, she says in that last remarkable sentence of her story, "It is not because God, in his *prepossessing* mercy, has preserved my soul from mor- tal sin that I leap up to him with all confidence and all love."

A few days before Thérèse died, Céline saw her preparing for that confident leap, for that last loving run into Jesus's arms. Thérèse's hands were joined in the classical position of prayer; her eyes were lifted up. "What are you doing!" Céline asked in that awkward rhetoric in which loving members of a family in- dulge themselves when they want to scold their loved ones—as if it were not clear what Thérèse was doing. "You must try to sleep!" Thérèse answered, "I can't; I'm suffering too much. So I'm praying. . . ." "And what are you saying to Jesus?" "I'm say- ing nothing to him; I am just loving him." That, over and over again, is the burden of Thérèse's last conversations, of her last prayers, her last writings, her last languishing looks at those who came in such unrelenting numbers to share the great lady's dying days with her, to be in at the glorious kill. What should she say to all her well-wishers, all those patently good women who crowded in on her with all their goodness effulgent in their faces, all their dedication blossoming in their gestures of help and pos- tures of hope? "How are you?" they would ask. Could she tell them exactly how she was? "I am dying" was the logical response, and she gave it, in more or less those precise words, as often as possible. "Do you like it?" "Well, it isn't exactly a picnic," she replied, in a remarkably imaginative set of ways, if not in quite those words, varying the theme and the tone as best she could.

"Do you want to die?" "Yes." "Will you be unhappy if you do not die?" "No." "How do you feel?" "I am dying. Pray for me."

Who knows how much she believed in the details of her last forecasts and prognoses or how much she invented answers and predictions to still the silly questions and convert into sense the conventional phrases of those who were determined to share all her sighs, all her tears, all her sufferings, all her death with her? Certainly, she did begin to work out the geography and history of her future reign in some detail, and certainly the conversations with her flock of well-wishers took on a richer turn as a result. She promised that to those who would in future years read her autobiography much of herself would be revealed; thus far, that might simply be delicate irony. She also thought those pages would do "much good"; that was surely not meant to be ironic, but it would be a fair appraisal of the sentiments culled from Scripture and the saints with which the book is full. When she added that she knows for sure that "everybody" will love her, she was not joking; there was no edge to her tone now. She knew, she said several times, that she would come back; for the present, enough of this suffering; she would like to go. More and more she looked toward heaven; literally, she raised up her eyes, but not because she was always thrusting herself up with confidence. She made that clear to Pauline after her sister Marie had commented on her loving upward glance: No, she explained, it wasn't the "true heaven" that had drawn her glance, but rather the skies. Heaven itself seemed far from her. And yet, love did surround her; that she knew. If love imbued and informed everything she did, wasn't any glance of hers really directed toward heaven, *lovingly* thrust up through the skies and beyond them? Such meditations lightened some of the torture and some of the doubt that still assailed her in the hot days of August and the sticky days of September.

She had to hold onto those interior consolations as much as possible; her exterior life was as full as that of some reigning queen of the Paris salons. When, on July 30, she received the last sacraments, Extreme Unction and the Viaticum, she barely had time to recollect herself before several nuns had crowded in upon her. She remembered, she told Pauline afterward, how crowds followed Jesus when he tried to retire into his solitude and she was content to follow him too in the sweetness she showed the nuns.

325

It was about the same time that she wryly quoted Alphonsus Liguori's definition of charity to Céline: "Charity consists in bearing with those who are unbearable."

She kept her sense of humor. In the middle of a conversation with another nun about Thérèse, Céline sighed, "I shall never be able to live without her." Thérèse, overhearing her, seized on the last two words—*sans elle,* in French—and turned them into an engaging pun based on a happy coincidence of pronunciation: "Well, then, I shall bring you *deux ailes,*" two wings. In actual fact, she was endowed with no visions of wings; the angels did not hover about her imagination at all and when a nun promised her an escort of angels to receive her at her death, she said dryly, "All those images do me no good at all. Nothing nourishes me but the truth. That's why I've never wanted visions. You can't see heaven and angels on earth as they really are—I much prefer to wait until after my death for that." She would not pretend to great ecstasies either. She was suffering, and by the middle of August wanted it made perfectly clear that she was. Transports and joys did exist for her, but *"au fond de mon âme seulement,"* only in the depths of her soul. It would not encourage many, she believed firmly, even in those days, perhaps all the more in those days, if they believed that she had not suffered much.

The suffering reduced her at times to silence, or occasionally, very rarely, to a plaintive comment, as, for example, that she would not have believed such intense suffering was possible, that one had to experience it to believe it. Her last letters barely touch on her pain, however, except for that sad outburst to Céline on August 3: "O my God, how kind You are to the little victim of Your merciful Love! Now even when You add bodily suffering to my soul's anguish, I cannot say 'The sorrows of death surrounded me' [Ps. 17:5]; but I cry out in my gratitude 'I have gone down into the valley of the shadow of death, yet will I fear no evil, for You, Lord, are with me' [Ps. 22:4]!" The same psalm from which she drew her last line to Céline, that most celebrated of psalms in the King James version—"The Lord is my shepherd; I shall not want. . . ."—was the basis of a long letter to Father Pichon into which she put, she told her Sisters, her "whole soul." It was destroyed, sadly enough, like all the rest of her correspondence with Father Pichon, but at least we know what the texture of the letter was—full of hope and trust, with a particularly hopeful indication of the good she might be able to work here below after her death.

Thérèse was, some might think, immoderately full of her plans for the afterlife. But this was basic doctrine for her. In heaven, she believed, love is all and love is active. She explained to Abbé Bellière in her last letter to him, on August 10, that the great compassion of those in heaven for the misery of the earth-dwellers must motivate in them a sense of protection for all of us here below and an unceasing prayer. Every one of the blessed in heaven, after all, was once a weak earthling, a committer of faults, a struggler, a laggard. That memory and the infinite mercy of the Lord in which, inexorably, they now dwell must make them loving, compassionate, and merciful.

To her Little Brother, the Abbé, she has willed, she tells him, the reliquary she was given on the day of her Clothing, the last picture painted by her, and a small worn crucifix which she has had since it was given to her at the age of thirteen. She has touched it to everything of value in that great touching expedition of hers through Italy. She has kissed it and fondled it for the last time; now he can add his fondlings and kisses to hers.

Thérèse was distributing her favors with as much largesse as her Carmelite station permitted. To Léonie, whose last communication to her was a coverlet that she herself had made for Thérèse, the dying nun wrote, "I am *touched beyond all bounds* by your eagerness to give me pleasure," and she told her too that she would offer her Communion for her the next day. Just which Communion this was we shall never know; the letter is not dated. We know that it was not Thérèse's last Communion, which was on August 19, for that was offered for Hyacinthe Loyson, the ex-Jesuit, in the hope that he would find his way back to God's favor, at least as far as a blessed death.

On the twenty-third birthday of that great favorite of hers, Sister Marie of the Trinity, Thérèse dispatched a little picture of the Holy Family to the girl, with a few words on the back to mark the date and the occasion and one earnest hope: "May your life be all humility and love, that you may soon come where I am going, into the arms of Jesus!" That done, only one piece of writing remained for Thérèse. On September 8, the day celebrated in the Church as the Virgin's birthday, she wrote her last lines on the back of the photograph of Our Lady of Victories to which she had fastened the little white flower her father gave her on May 29, 1887, the day she announced her Carmelite ambitions. Now, three weeks and a day before her death, she wrote, "Mary, if I were the Queen of Heaven, and you were Thérèse, I should want to be Thérèse so that you might be the Queen of Heaven!!!"

The Virgin's birthday was the anniversary of Thérèse's profession and it was celebrated, fittingly, by a nun who brought her a bouquet of wildflowers, and by a robin who bounced in through the infirmary window and perched on Thérèse's bed. She was grateful for these *délicatesses* of a good God and she said so, but she also explained that however rich her outward life, within she was always under trial. But still, she added, there was peace as well. Always, in her dying days, she conducted this dialogue with herself. If she complained or in any way noted a limitation in the world around her—in the world of her Sisters, in the world of statesmen, in any part of the world—she almost invariably answered the complaint with a compliment. When she cried out in anguish to Céline, "I suffer, I suffer!" she remembered just a few breaths later to comment, "Whenever I cry, 'I suffer,' you must reply, 'So much the better.' I haven't the strength to say so myself, so you must make clear what I'm thinking." She tried, she told Pauline, to remain cheerful, but she did not always succeed, not even with Pauline, as for example when her Little Mother thought to interest her on September 3 with news of the great reception given the Russian Tsar in France. "Oh," Thérèse said in effect, "who cares?" Her exact words were "Ah, all that doesn't dazzle me! Speak to me of God, of the examples of the saints, of all that is true. . . ." She was equally disdainful of an illustrated book that a novice brought her on September 11, hoping its stories and pictures would amuse her. "How could you think this book would interest me?" she asked the unhappy girl. "I am too close to my eternity to want to distract myself with nonsense."

Flowers, on the other hand, elicted happiness, joy, and warm words. A bunch of violets—"Ah, the perfume of violets!" A rose —"In September, little Thérèse still lets the petals of the spring rose fall upon Jesus," she exclaimed and she held the flower so its petals could fall upon the wounded figure on the cross. What's more, she offered the rose petals as more than mere emblems —"Gather these petals with care, my little sisters," she said;

"they will serve to give pleasure later on; don't let even one be lost." They were saved and, according to the annals of the Carmel at Lisieux, an old man was cured of cancer of the tongue with one of the petals in 1910 at the hospital of the Little Sisters of the Poor in Lisieux, one of the hundreds of cures with which Thérèse was associated in the years right after her death.

She held her temper well at the end, even when she was plagued with the same old questions about how she was feeling, and the same old long faces, and noisy tears, and silent sobs, the multiple expressions of individual and community grief. "Around the sick," she did caution the Sisters, "one must be gay! One must not grieve like those who are without hope. You will end by making me regret life." The Sisters mocked her, with some gaiety, one hopes, explaining they were sure she could not regret life. "That's true," Thérèse admitted. "I said that only to frighten you!" She was serious, however, about wanting no more pity, no more praise for her patience, no more foolish talk about the great ascension or assumption to come. When it was predicted by the Sisters that she would go to heaven amid seraphim, she answered with calm wit, "If I do, I shall not imitate them. *They all cover themselves with their wings in the presence of the Lord* [Isaiah 6]. As for me, I shall take care not to cover myself with my wings."

The last few days were days of terrible suffering broken by radiant moments, long minutes of open smiles and sweet humor, and a great last burst of strength with which to face the crescendo of pain which was growing louder and louder within her. She managed to hold on against the torture of near-suffocation brought on by a Sister who was standing too close a guard over her and leaning too hard against her bed. Forced to explain what had disturbed her breathing so terribly, Thérèse finally admitted that it had been her rather too zealous friend. Her great friends all seemed to be failing her. "The air of earth is failing me!" she cried out two days before she died; "When will God give me the air of heaven?" But that same night, she and Céline, who was with her for much of the evening, heard the soft singing of a turtledove in the convent garden, and then, says Céline, a fluttering of wings like the sound a bird makes when it comes to a sudden stop on a perch somewhere. Inevitably, the lovely sounds suggested to Céline and Thérèse the famous lines of the second chapter of the Song of Songs: "Arise, make haste, my love, my dove, my beautiful one, and come. For winter is now past, the rain is over and gone. The flowers have appeared in our land, the time of pruning is come: the voice of the turtle is heard in our land."

When her breathing became so fitful on the eve of her death that she seemed within moments of expiration, she worried about just what was happening to her and about her skill to deal with it. "Is this the agony?" she asked, and then, "How shall I go about dying? I am never going to know how to die!" The air of a flustered middle-aged hostess that this seems to give her is not entirely wrong. For her the proper manner at death was more important than any other show of decorum which might be expected of her. Carmelites practice all their religious lives for this moment: each Carmelite keeps a skull in her cell which sets early in her career the image of death in her skull; the writings of their saints are fitted out with many exercises of preparation for death; their careers are, in fact, a series of approaches, variously profound and elegant, to death—and the life that follows. In the deepest sense of the word, it can be said, I think, that the death of a Carmelite has style. Perhaps Thérèse felt she was inadequate to these last monumental moments because her life had been so completely dedicated to the minuscule, but in her conduct at the end she gave enormous stature to the little way she had chosen; once again, she made the minuscule seem monumental and by her few words and actions dwarfed the large motions and pretentious verbiage of some more famous deathbed scenes.

On Thérèse's last full night on earth, Pauline read to her the Office of St. Michael and the prayers for the dying, in French. At the reference to the devils, Pauline reports, Thérèse gestured in a childish way, as if to scare the demons, and with a smile cried out, "Oh! Oh!" The sweetness of this repudiation of the black spirits makes one wonder about the strength of conviction she brought to the two or three earlier assertions of diabolic visitations in her illness. One does not doubt that she said the words attributed to her, but one may question, I think, the implication that Thérèse felt seriously threatened by anything demonic. Neither hell nor purgatory held any great dread for her—except as others might be menaced by them; she made that quite clear on several occasions when she was being catechized about herself and the afterlife.

On the morning of September 29, she asked Mother Gonzague about her death—"Is it today?" When the Prioress said yes and Thérèse's sisters exclaimed that God was very happy this day, Thérèse nodded her agreement—"I too," she said. Five other remarks of hers were recorded on this day. She said out of her mixture of joy and suffering, "If I should die right now, what happiness!" In the afternoon, she said she was "utterly spent. Pray for me. If you only knew . . ." When Céline asked for a last word, a word of adieu, Thérèse managed, "I have said all . . . all is accomplished! It is love alone that matters." After Matins, she again evinced her readiness for death: "Yes, my God; yes, my God. I desire everything, all." When the Prioress asked her whether her suffering was atrocious, she said, "No, Mother, not atrocious, but it is a great deal, a great deal. . . . I can just about bear it." She wanted to bear it alone, to be left to herself for the rest of the night, but Mother Gonzague would not agree to it and her sisters Céline and Marie were given the last watch between them.

Thérèse was in torment, exhausted, sensible of her suffering much of the time, and resigned to it. She invoked the help of the Virgin in the simplest of prayers—"Come to my aid," she said. She exclaimed over the terror of the death agony—"If this is the agony, what must death be like? Oh, Mother, I assure you the chalice is full to overflowing." At three o'clock in the afternoon, she stretched out her arms in the form of the cross; the moment was marked by the convent bell, like the ringing of bells that accompanies the consecrations of the Mass. Thérèse's great offering was now in its last stages. Her oblation was as much on the surface as within, and perhaps as deeply scarring to those who watched as to her who was being watched. At five o'clock, after several indications of violent pain, she fixed her face in a tender smile, and with her crucifix grasped firmly in her hands, she gave the community, now gathered around her, a beatific image of peace and love. It was not for long. Her last agony was ugly, angry, tortured. Her chest rattled in death; her feet were freezing cold while her head and face were encased in perspiration. Her body shook. She made weak little cries, moanings of misery, involuntary sounds of pain, Pauline thought, not noises of apprehension. For a moment shortly before the end, when Céline brought the relief of a little piece of ice to her parched lips, Thérèse once more smiled, a smile of such relief, such joy, such sweetness, bestowed directly upon Céline, that everyone took it for the most ardent farewell and all rejoiced in it.

Then came the Angelus bell. It was six o'clock. Thérèse lifted her eyes to the statue of the Virgin, the Virgin of the Smile. A long slow hour passed and then came the seven o'clock bell. Mother Gonzague dismissed the community, thinking the final moments were still some time off. Thérèse looked up at the Prioress. "Oh, Mother," she said, "isn't this the agony? Am I not going to die?" Mother Gonzague suggested that the agony might take some hours to run its course. "*Eh bien,*" Thérèse resigned herself; if it must be this way, let it be. "*Allons, allons,*" she sighed. "Oh, I do not wish to suffer any less." Then she looked down at her crucifix and said, with some pauses between her words, "Oh. . . . I love him! . . . My God! . . . I . . . love . . . you. . . ." Those were her last words, those words that said everything for her, those words she had said so often, those words that meant so much to her. She sank back on her pillow, her head falling a little to the right. But she was not yet dead. There was time to call the community back and for the Sisters to arrange themselves, kneeling, around the bed. Then, all of a sudden, she raised herself enough to fix her eyes on a place just beyond the statue of the Virgin. Her look was transfixed, transfigured, for just about the time, according to both Céline and Pauline, required to intone a slow Credo. Thus she died, on a lingering Amen.

In mid-July, two and a half months before Thérèse died, M. Guérin wrote his daughter Marie at the Carmel to tell her how moved he was by the example of Thérèse, lying there, awaiting her death with joy. He was all admiration for her, he said. Her supernatural wisdom and her intimate knowledge of the mysteries of divine love elicited the most profound respect in him. Her courage too—no, he decided, it was not courage. For as with St. Paul, when one has penetrated the divine mysteries so far, it is not remarkable that one wants to break one's ties with earth. "What instruction she gives us, that little girl," he exclaimed, "and how I am going to engrave in my memory everything she did and said, to try and reproduce it on the day of my death! I march toward that day with large steps; I descend rapidly along the downward slope of the years. What are ten years, or even twenty years? For all of that, after such a long life, I will not have the baggage of that child with which to present myself to God." Who would? Who would have as much as "that little girl . . . that child. . . ."? Who else has had so long a childhood? Who else was so old at birth and so young at death?

SIXTEEN

*N*OTHING in the history of the modern Church matches the impact of Thérèse after her death, upon believers and non-believers, upon the credulous and the skeptical, except perhaps the effect of John XXIII in the last years of his pontificate and immediately after his death. She who had been an obscure nun in a Norman convent of negligible importance, she who had so prized her hidden life, was suddenly the center of attention the whole world over. In the open corridors of monasteries and the cloistered quadrangles of convents, in hospital wards and school common rooms, in vestries and sacristies, in homes and offices, wherever Christians gathered, her name became a commonplace. There was marveling over the miracles that so quickly became associated with her. There was mocking astonishment at the ease with which so many seemed to be taken in. There was joy in her wisdom, even as it was revealed in the mottled pages of the *Story of a Soul* as edited by Pauline and a Premonstratensian Prior, Père Godefroy Madelaine. There was suffering, caused by the sticky style of that much-scarred autobiographical manuscript and the even stickier style of those who first wrote about Thérèse. There was much praying, great hope, an endless confiding in the young nun who promised so much and, startlingly, seemed to deliver even more than she promised. There was much deprecation, learned, witty, ironic, urbane, of Thérèse, of her admirers, of her artists, who seemed determined to immortalize her in the most bulbous and blearily painted effigies made since it was first discovered that almost any kind of ugliness could be stiffened into semipermanence in plaster of Paris. There was all of this. There still is. And it looks as if there always will be. It all started with the publication on September 30, 1898, exactly a year after Thérèse's death, of two thousand copies of the autobiography, and it

334

has never stopped; not with beatification in 1923; not with canonization in 1925; not with the extension of her feast to the universal Church; not with her astonishing aggrandizement of titles and benefices, as co-patron of all the missions and missionaries of the Church with St. Francis Xavier, as secondary patron of France, along with Joan of Arc; not with the entrusting to her of the cause of Soviet Russia's recovery for Christianity or any of the other causes, variously desperate and resolute, which have been delivered with such obvious and open relief into her hands.

The efficient cause of everything was the book. And how efficient it was, how much more than even Pauline and Céline and Marie had in their most sanguine moments dreamed it might be. It was an irregularity, really, to send the autobiography around, fittingly irregular for Thérèse. Normally, after the death of a Carmelite nun, a monograph is circulated to the religious houses of the order, briefly narrating the facts of life of the nun, her striking virtues—there are always striking virtues—and her ups and downs in her last illness, if she has departed this life in anything like a dramatic fashion. The point of the monograph is not to indulge in spiritual histrionics, however hard it may be to read it aloud without heaving bosom and trembling gesture; it is to elicit prayers for the nun among her Sisters and to recommend her, whenever possible, as a model for imitation. What better, then, for Thérèse than her own words, which, though some editing seemed quite in order to Mother Gonzague and to Pauline, clearly were remarkable words likely to draw warm responses. Warm responses? They were frenzied! All over the world the Carmels vied with each other in praise of the autobiography. Translations began to appear, as fast as permission could be granted by the Lisieux Carmel and the work could be completed, and the permissions were so often competed for that it took some considerable sorting out to make a decision. The first translation, for example, was made into Polish, but before that could be done a choice had to be made among requests to do the work by a countess in Cracow, a Polish Jesuit, and a religious at a Carmel in Polish Galicia, and even before the Galician Carmelites, the chosen instruments, completed their work, a professor at the University of Cracow began to translate the book into English. What is particularly remarkable about all of this is the speed with which the requests came in, the decisions were made, and the work completed: the official Polish translation was finished and was being printed before the end of 1901. Before the beginning of the First World War, there were editions in Italian, Dutch, Portuguese, Russian, Spanish, Breton, Chinese, and translations had been begun into languages far outside the central tongues, such as Armenian, Maltese, Georgian, and not only the languages themselves but dialect variations within them.

By the time of Thérèse's canonization, in 1925, the sales of the somewhat expanded edition of the *Story of a Soul* that Pauline and Father Madelaine had edited were approaching the half-million mark, more than two million copies of an abridged version of the book had been sold, and the number of languages into which it had been translated was thirty-five. Relics attached to pictures and wrapped in sachets and holy cards made up of pictures of Thérèse and quotations from her had sold in numbers just under fifty million and several thousand pages of the volumes called *Shower of Roses* had been detailing all the favors granted and petitions answered by the clients of Thérèse since 1902. By 1925, there was little question among millions in and out of the Church that Thérèse was an incomparable intercessor. She had cured dread cases of tuberculosis, of cancer, of almost every known deformation and pollution of the body; she had relieved all sorts of oppression of the mind and the spirit; she had brought relief to the poor, saved families from destitution, brought whole convents back from bankruptcy or near-bankruptcy. The documents seemed to prove her intercession in every case. Clearly, for both the beatification and the canonization processes, there had been an embarrassment of miracles. The only difficulty for the postulators of her cause was to choose the most telling. Why, out of the annals of her deeds on the battlefields of the 1914–18 war alone, an enormous volume of miraculous intercession could be written.

Need one be credulous to accept these stories at face value? Was it simply a massive wave of self-hypnosis that cured so many of their physical and mental and spiritual illnesses? Can the seemingly miraculous recoveries from cancer and tuberculosis be explained by remissions the full nature of which medicine has not yet been able to understand but which in time will be susceptible of simple scientific explication? These questions will trouble some more than others, as some find themselves particularly irked by all the rosy rhetoric that attends the Thérèsian miracle—the rose petals at the foot of the bed of the happy beneficiary of Thérèse's intercession; the constant aroma of roses, even within sealed envelopes, opened some months or years after being put away in, say, that least rosy of environments, a cashbox. A rose is not a rose is not a rose in this world; it is simply a sign that St. Thérèse has called.

There is no doubt about the high place of roses in Thérèse's own life, especially at the end of her life, no question that she took great comfort from their color and form and fragrance as earlier she had enjoyed the shape and the scent of lilies and asters and the whole natural world around Les Buissonnets. It is a matter of clear fact that she suggested that the nuns gather one of the petals that dropped from one of the bunches of roses with which Mother Gonzague saw to it that she was consoled in her last days, gather it and keep it for later use. And equally, it is beyond dispute that the petal had, whether because of supernatural powers or the powers of suggestion, a curative effect upon the very ill and the grossly suffering.

One can, if one wants, see all of this as signifying nothing more than Thérèse's great trust in God's presence in the natural world, *his* natural world. But if one interprets Thérèse's roses this way, one must allow for the power of her philosophy of nature, in which she sees God's presence as so constant and so easily invoked that some form of assuagement of grief or pain can be achieved by anyone. It is this conviction, perhaps, which her autobiography and her confidences and counsels and reminiscences on her sickbed and the meditations and reflections contained in her letters made so contagious after her death. If one is content to accept her philosophy of nature as her means of intercession in people's lives all over the world, good enough. It has the requisite dignity, it seems to me, to explain the extraordinarily intense confidence placed in her by all sorts of people, both well educated and illiterate, both those long accustomed to devout religious exercises and those with only the most rudimentary instruction in the language and procedures of the faithful, both those easily and quickly commanded and those long stubborn in their refusal to accept anyone's lead in anything.

However Thérèse's clients came—and come—to her, by reluctant intellectual conviction or eager credulity, they always end

337

by following in some manner her way, her little way. They humble themselves before a power larger than any other in the world, larger than any merely worldly power. They make a complete submission of themselves. They admit to a trust, a confidence, that nothing can shake, not all the evidence of their own suffering, not all the arguments of the world of reason around them, not all the helplessness or hopelessness of their doctors, whether they are doctors of the soul or of the mind or of the body. Like Thérèse in the terrible darkness of her own doubts, they cling somehow, anyhow, to this trust. They offer their suffering in sacrifice, sometimes blindly, with no particular end in view, sometimes for a special cause—for someone sicker than they, for the missions, for an oppressed minority, for the beleaguered majority—and always, if one can trust the records where they are detailed enough to offer these things of interior disposition at some length, that their cure may enable them to bring some hope or love to others. Thérèse's intercession does not seem to interest the utterly selfish, or if it does, it is only that it may in time surprise the selflessness in the selfish, that concern for others that suddenly leaps alive in persons who have made a positive faith of their self-centeredness.

The miracles that Rome chose to accept for Thérèse's beatification and canonization, after the grueling scrutiny to which all such evidence is submitted, were not unnaturally of people close to the Church. Two of the four were of religious; one was a seminarian. The records of their efforts to end or somehow to appease their sufferings were easily accessible to the supporters of her cause and to the Congregation of Rites. The fourth cure, of a Belgian laywoman, had a brief association with Lourdes, where very careful documentation is kept; that added to the plausibility of this case. The seminarian, Charles Anne of Lisieux, was not merely confident in his demands; he was peremptory. He had tried a novena of prayers to Our Lady of Lourdes to cure the pulmonary tuberculosis which was clearly going to kill him unless it was arrested immediately. Nothing had happened. He began one in 1906 to Thérèse, saying of his enrollment in the seminary, "I did not come here to die; I came to work for God. You must heal me." With those words, he fell asleep. When he awoke, his fever had gone down, the cavity in his right lung had disappeared; it was clear that he had been cured and only the briefest recovery period would be necessary. He went on, with no further difficulties, to become a priest.

The women of the beatification and canonization documents offer similarly dramatic transformations. Sister Louise of St. Germain, of the Daughters of the Cross at Ustaritz in southern France, was almost dead in the fall of 1916, of what seemed to be an incurable ulcer. She was required to make two novenas to Thérèse, in 1915 and 1916, before, according to her testimony, Thérèse appeared to her and promised a cure, and before, according to the doctors' witness, she was brought back to complete health, with no apparent medical explanation for the change. Sister Gabriella, a religious of Parma in Italy, was not only completely healed of tuberculosis of the spine, in June 1923, but of arthritis as well, as a result of prayers to Thérèse. Marie Pellemans was a Belgian girl, with a cruel pulmonary tuberculosis with intestinal complications, who had tried Lourdes in vain. In March 1923 she found her recovery at the tomb of Thérèse in Lisieux in a sudden burst of good health while kneeling with a group of pilgrims with whom she had come to the hallowed spot.

The supporters of the cause of Thérèse were also very much impressed, among a host of tales of such miraculous interventions, by the story of some events of 1910 and 1911 at a poor Carmelite convent in the town of Gallipoli in southern Italy, built on a little rocky island joined to the mainland by a small bridge of arches. The convent was a poor enough place in a poor enough area, a speck on the heel of the Italian boot, kept clean and warm by the waters and sweet breezes of the Gulf of Taranto, but still so poor that the Prioress of the convent, Mother Carmela, went to sleep each night trembling in fear of the demands of her creditors. On January 15, according to the Prioress, Thérèse interrupted her sleep with a few words and more money, putting enough in the convent cashbox to pay off the bills and leave something more for some unaccustomed ease. What is more, Thérèse continued to make contributions on each succeeding month, according to testimony given by the Prioress in September of 1910, once making up for the loss of some money on the part of the Bishop of Gallipoli, who had intended the lost funds for the convent. Three times in this period Thérèse appeared to Mother Carmela again. The last time, on the fifth of September, the eve of the exhumation of Thérèse's body, "after having spoken . . . as she always did of the spiritual welfare of the community," says the Prioress, "she announced to me that 'only her bones' would be found." And indeed only bones were found when Thérèse's body was exhumed in Lisieux on September 6, but bones, say those who were there, that produced an unmistakable fragrance.

However striking these events may have been, there was a more unmistakably Thérèsian note to subsequent events in Gallipoli, a tonality at once mischievous, serious, and directed to support Thérèsian spirituality. The Bishop of Nardo, a small diocese near Gallipoli, had been moved by the words Mother Carmela said that Thérèse spoke to her on the first appearance in January. The Prioress had supposed the apparition to be of the Virgin and had addressed her as such—"O my Holy Mother." "No," the nun replied to her, "I am not our Holy Mother, I am the Servant of God, Sister Thérèse of Lisieux. Today in Heaven and on earth we celebrate the feast of the Holy Name of Jesus." Still the Prioress could say no more than "O my Mother." But when, after the money had been put into the cashbox, the visitor made ready to leave, Mother Carmela managed a few more words: "Wait," she said, "you might mistake the way." With a smile, the young nun answered, "No, no, my way is sure and I am not mistaken in following it." The Bishop of Nardo had some money he had been given as a general offering, to do with as he liked. In December 1910 he placed it in an envelope with one of his visiting cards on which he had written

IN MEMORIAM

"MY WAY IS SURE; I AM NOT MISTAKEN."

Sister Teresa of the Child Jesus to Sister Maria-
Carmela at Gallipoli; January 16, 1910.
"Pray for me daily that God may
have mercy on me."

He wrote "In Memoriam" on the outside of the envelope as well, then placed it in another stronger envelope with a double lining and sealed it in wax on which he stamped his episcopal arms. He then required that the double envelope be placed in the convent cashbox, to be opened on the anniversary of Thérèse's first appearance to Mother Carmela, on January 16, 1911. When this was done, in the Bishop's presence, everything was found as he had arranged it—the envelope within the envelope, with his own writing on it and his card and his money inside. But in addition to his money, some 500 lire, there was an additional 300 lire, in the form of two 100-lire and two 50-lire notes, one of which had an unmistakable fragrance of roses about it. Since there was no indication of any tampering with the envelopes, with the wax or the gummed seals or anything else, and there was every evidence of supernatural intervention, with Thérèse's calling card—attar of roses—attached, to the Bishop, the Prioress, and the postulators of Thérèse's cause, the conclusion was unavoidable. Said the Bishop, this is the way Thérèse confirms the point of her words, "My way is sure."

One is tempted to dismiss stories like this one—and there are a great many others like it—as the silly imaginings of credulous religious. It is easy, after all, to think one is smelling a rose; there is nothing rare about the fragrance, especially in climes like southern Italy. But what about the increases in money? Was that the work of a mischievous friend? Did the Bishop simply not realize how much money he was putting in the box? Was the Prioress equally absent-minded about how much money the convent still had? Whatever the explanation, the convent was rescued from near bankruptcy and starvation, by the real or imagined intervention of Thérèse. Her figure was captivating enough, in genuine apparition or dream fantasy, to bring release from worry and to move a prince of the Church to act like a prince, perhaps more like one than he had intended. One way or the other, it was a sure way.

Thérèse's way seemed sure as no other to those whose prayers for her intervention were answered by cures. Rarely, however, did the cures come without suffering. When in 1907 a lay Sister at the Carmel of Nîmes in France was cured of double lobar pneumonia by what was presumed to be Thérèse's intercession, it was not until near suffocation had set in and the poor Sister was almost dead. Tuberculars, the cancerous, the severely ulcerated—all were allowed their share of misery in the Thérèsian way, terrible bloodlettings, eviscerating fevers, the hellish pains of peritonitis, the stiffening terrors of paralysis, agonies of all kinds. Those who invoked Thérèse's aid could expect peace and calm for sure, at least intermittently, and perhaps a miraculous healing as well, but not without their full experience of suffering. That was her way.

She knew no other on earth; she was apparently not going to unfold any other from heaven.

Those who followed Thérèse as far as the convent, right up to her own enclosure at Lisieux, were given the full treatment. The young Breton woman who became Sister Marie-Ange of the Child Jesus had changed almost every texture of her life in becoming a Carmelite. She had been a haughty person, patronizing to "the good Sisters," altogether worldly in her interests. When she read Thérèse's book, she felt overwhelmed by the spirit of the little way and went to apply for admission to the Lisieux Carmel, as so many other young women who had been deeply moved by the book were doing. She was accepted and she made everything about herself acceptable to the community until she was elected Prioress. But hers was a short reign, eighteen months to be exact. Her emulation of Thérèse was complete unto tuberculosis and she died in 1909 of the then almost always incurable disease. She promised, before her death, to "spend" her "heaven in helping my little Thérèse."

Mother Marie-Ange became one of a series of celebrated followers of Thérèse at Lisieux. Another was Mother Isabelle of the Sacred Heart, who was sub-Prioress when she died in 1914, at what might be thought to be an advanced age for one of Thérèse's great imitators, thirty-three. She achieved a considerable fame among Thérèsians for model performance as mistress of novices and for her own poetry, especially a long poem of meditations on her great devotion, the Divine Tenderness. A third Carmelite at Lisieux often coupled with Mother Marie-Ange and Mother Isabelle was Sister Thérèse of the Eucharist, the former Countess de la Tour d'Auvergne, who succeeded Mother Isabelle as sub-Prioress. Thérèse in name, Thérèsian in quality, her particular shining virtue was to keep her virtues hidden by behaving at all times the way she thought the community's sainted Thérèse would have in the same circumstances.

These were Thérèse's special clients, the admirers of hidden strength, the softly selfless, the short-lived, the trustful—all those who eventually found that plenitude of confidence that turns suffering into joy and even the most trivial difficulty a possible occasion for heroic virtue. This is not to say that they indulged in the histrionics with which the obituary monographs of the Carmels sometimes make their deeds noisy. It is no great trust in God and no trustworthy confidence in a spirituality that is always calling attention to itself. The figures of Thérèsian virtue are not self-proclaiming; they have to be sought out among the shadows. If ever they leap at one it is almost always because their one besetting openness is their eagerness to credit their source. Cured by Thérèse's intercession of haughtiness or a running sore, relieved because of her mediation of the tensions of the world or the terrible debilitations of cancer or tuberculosis, it is to Thérèse that they want to call the world's attention. It is as if they want to make up for whatever neglect she may have suffered in her life on earth, or, as in the case of missionaries, who like to cite her great appeal to non-Christian cultures, to give her the far-ranging career in the outposts of the Church of which she had dreamed.

No series of testimonies to the power of Thérèse's intervention was more stubborn or more eloquent than that given by French soldiers in the First World War. The French books written about Thérèse in the 1920s almost invariably contain some tale or other about a soldier who was despondent without his relic of Thérèse, nearly in despair, and returned to joy when he could go out to battle with a new memento of the saint. French planes were named after her; several regiments were placed en bloc under her protection. Swords and military decorations still give witness on the walls of the Carmelite chapel at Lisieux to the support soldiers felt they received when they prayed to Thérèse. A well-known aviator in the first war, who later became a celebrated missionary in New Guinea, Père Bourjade, credited Thérèse with several spectacular rescues. In the British army, an infantry corporal, Francis Coyle, who was a great distributor of pictures and relics of Thérèse, found himself in a devastating barrage of artillery fire, cried out a fervent "Save us!" to Thérèse and, according to his testimony, was saved in spite of a rain of shrapnel that left eleven holes in his uniform: he had been protected by a pocket-knife and a purse filled with nine copper pennies, several of which, like the knife, were twisted and torn by shrapnel hits.

The stories of miraculous aid go on, into the Second World War, into the battles of independence being fought by and for new nations in Africa and Asia, just as the sales of the *Story of a Soul* go on, into the millions, now in the fresh words of Thérèse, scrubbed clean of the well-intentioned but senseless revisions of Pauline. But the real miracle of this extraordinary success of

343

Thérèse's with generation after generation of the twentieth century is less dramatic than the medical kind, less startling than the battlefield variety, and more lasting than either. Céline felt it necessary to warn that many readers of the autobiography "never see the Cross hidden beneath the flowers." That, I think, is no longer so true. Thérèse has brought the miracle of Christian realism to the modern world, has given to so many so firm a sense of the presence of God—in flowers, in people, in every aspect of created being—that they have gone beyond the flowery fragrances, attractive as they are, to the wounds beneath and have found them at least not unattractive. Free of the sticky carapace of the first version of her story, she now speaks boldly, clearly, enthusiastically to her followers, and with a simple clean virility that almost nullifies the ugly art and the saccharine hagiography that always cluster around truth and beauty. These forces, among the most powerful that evil has ever found with which to attack goodness, will not now or ever be entirely vanquished by a Thérèse. But they will be significantly reduced in strength by such realism as Thérèse's, in which, by word and by example, divine presence, human presence, all created presence, is so unmistakably summoned forth. For what Thérèse achieves in such a confrontation of persons with persons is reconciliation with the human condition. Here, she says, here is man, weak, wasteful, full of sorrow, full of suffering, languishing in exile, and yet worthy of trust and of hope, for whether through merit or not he has in all his weakness and misery the support of divinity. See man for what he is, good and bad, she says, see him and accept him; accept yourself as you have been accepted by your maker. Accept it all, she says, even the darkness, the doubt, the weariness, the depression, the collapse of spirits; accept it not by denying any of it, but by facing it and facing it with the most powerful and the most enduring of human resources, with a trusting, a confident love. This is what, somehow, she makes convincing. This is her miracle. This is her cure, her cure of souls. This is why, long after her beatification and her canonization, her cause is still espoused by so many.

THE IMITATION OF THÉRÈSE

*M*OST saints, for most people, are remote figures. Almost by definition they are superhuman, of an entirely different order of being from the rest of us. When we petition them to intercede for us in the courts of heaven, it is because they have direct access to a world entirely beyond us. When we invoke them as examples, it is as examples of the heroic ideal, much larger than life, however much we may aspire to it in this life. Saints are for other saints to imitate.

Not so Thérèse. The shadow she casts is, if anything, smaller than life. Her genius was to find a way little enough for the littlest of us. One does not have to be a saint to imitate Thérèse; it is enough just to be alive. And yet what she offers has majesty, has elegance, has all the marks of the true thing. The point is that she sees the human condition realistically, sees how high it can reach at the same time that she sees how low it can descend. Like Pascal and Pascal's teacher Augustine and Augustine's teacher Paul, she sees man as portent and prodigy, as chaos and contradiction, as glory and as off-scouring of the universe. Unlike that great line of thinkers, of which she is surely a part, she speaks a humble language; her rhetoric is middle-class; her images are not beyond the experience or understanding of the television audience. She speaks to us in this time; she speaks to the mass. And yet, no matter how bourgeois her accents may become, the intellectual is not at any point insulted, demeaned, or left outside either her discussion or her world. There is room, too, ample room, in her considerations for the dandy, the gangster, the whore, the bum, the banker, for the captains and the corporals, for the foot soldiers and the firers of missiles from supersonic planes, for in the mass to which she addresses herself she always sees the individual and sees him as he really is, idiosyncratic, full

345

of his own queernesses, full of his own joys, full of his own sorrows, full of his own talents, fully expressive of his own identity, no matter how much he may also be a member of a class or profession. A nun clicks her teeth in a senseless counterpoint to plainchant. Another is a habitual scold. Still another spreads water all about her every time she does the laundry, liberally sprinkling all her companions with the wet dirt. And all about there are Sisters quick to misunderstand or slow to understand, fussing happily or fussing unhappily about one, filling the life that was intended for God with silliness, with nuisances, with the nagging noises of the humdrum, the noises which most of us are condemned to hear most of the time. Amid this terrible plenitude of ordinariness, Thérèse finds contentment, finds ease, and even finds God. Here, in this design for mediocrity, she discovers a love as immense as anything ever dreamt or pursued by Tristram and Iseult, or Antony and Cleopatra, or the great lovers of the Hollywood pantheon, a greater love really, for it endures, not to be ended by any accident of history, by any drug, or by any last-reel histrionics.

Thérèse is a modern saint; Thérèse is our saint. She offers us our world, not any other, and in it, as it really is, a vision of order and peace and beauty that can be fully accomplished by the least of us, perhaps can be accomplished best by the least of us. It is a vision that is clear and open, that starts in littleness and ends in littleness, but that even at its most minuscule, when it seems no larger than an object viewed through the wrong end of a telescope, has about it an unmistakable grandeur.

Paradox is inevitably the hallmark of the Thérèsian vision. It is a Christian vision. Eternal life still comes through death; the land here below is still a land of exile. But exile has its own rich fruits —and flowers—in the Thérèsian vision, and not simply the fruits of anticipation. Best of all, these fruits seem to come most frequently when everything is upside down, when we are at the bottom of our resources and the world seems most hopeless. Love is the key to everything; suffering is the basic challenge to love, and at the same time the greatest opportunity to practice love.

Driven nearly mad by loneliness or by physical or mental illness, kicked around by people or things or both, we have—in this vision of the world—a greater chance for peace and joy than ever before, a more certain means of order in our lives than we could

346

otherwise ever have known. This is how we begin: with a loving acceptance of reality, with all its difficulties and paradoxes. This is where we make our submission. This is the opening move in that remarkable scheme of conduct which can best be called, I think, *The Imitation of Thérèse.*

Qui sequitur me . . . *"He who follows Me shall not walk in darkness,* says the Lord." Thus Thomas à Kempis opens his *Imitation of Christ,* quoting Jesus speaking to the scribes and Pharisees, who had just brought to him the woman taken in adultery, the woman whom he refused to condemn. Thérèse's *Imitation,* in effect, opens the same way. For Thérèse's light was Jesus too, and her life was a long following in the darkness after him and his light. She followed the opening advices of the *Imitation* as literally as she could: she said over and over again, in her own words as well as in those of Thomas à Kempis, "let it be our chief business to meditate upon the life of Jesus Christ." She believed with all her body and soul and heart and mind that his teaching "excels all the teachings of the saints" and that "if a man have his spirit he shall find therein a hidden manna." It is best, then, in any attempt to follow Thérèse to follow her exactly in this, to keep before one always the image of Jesus, the person of Jesus, his counsels, his commandments, his way in all its windings and turnings, but most of all that part of his way that leads to the Cross, for in the democracy of suffering which is Thérèse's everyone's suffering takes on meaning and stature especially in this, that in some measure it participates in Jesus's suffering.

Thérèse's great confidence in the procedures of love sprang from her great love of Jesus, which even in her darkest days she never relinquished. We may not find it possible to match that love or even to come close to it. We can, however, develop enough confidence in the procedures themselves to move us far along her way. We may not be able to give ourselves with such a totality of giving, surrendering everything as she did, will, intellect, the very blood in her veins; that does not mean we cannot give at all. If we come to see, through a close examination of her way, the majesty of this little way of love, the dignity that is in ourselves and others, if only it is sought for and appealed to, the nobility that every created being has simply by being, then ineluctably our confidence will mount too and we will swell all around us the ranks of love and bring, if only in the tiny exchanges of the day, peace and comfort and love. The tiny exchanges make up most of the day, after all; great tumultuous events are rare in most people's lives and even they, one comes to recognize, are only different in degree from the little happenings with which our days are filled. A headache may be our best rehearsal for a major illness. A stubbed toe may prepare us perfectly for a broken leg. Every sign of affection, the least tenderness, is an overture to love.

From the beginning of her life in Carmel, Thérèse never tires of telling us, she found suffering and found it possible to accept it, to draw it to her and hug it with joy and with love. It was through the cross that she knew she would win souls, and the more crosses that came her way the more she rejoiced, for in the crosses, which is to say in the suffering, she found the appropriate means for her great end, a loving means toward eternal love. None of this is to say that she made a public display of her suffering. It was only at the end of her life, in her dying moments really, that she confessed that she had been cold almost every minute of her life in Carmel, deathly cold as it turned out, shivering night after night and even day after day, in that damp cloister, in that damp cell, in that exquisite environment for the tubercle bacilli, perhaps the finest culture for that particular set of bacteria to be found in northern France. No, the flower of her suffering was not to be revealed to the world, except in the pages of her autobiography after her death. The "fragrance," as she calls it, the great aroma of her suffering, was for Jesus alone, and even when she records it in the *Story of a Soul* she does so only as part of the documentation of her life and to encourage others to do the same, to offer themselves and their fragrances to their common lover, to their common lord.

But what, one may properly ask, if one does not feel the same devotion to Jesus? What if the figure of Christ on the cross, for all its drama and nobility and poignancy, does not elicit such a response as Thérèse's? What if one cannot bring oneself to search in all things for the presence of Christ? What if one lives, insofar as Christ is the light in all things, in utter darkness? How then does one imitate Thérèse? Does one, can one, in fact, follow her at all? The answer is, I think, that one can imitate Thérèse very well indeed, though some of the motivation and much of the inspiration will be lacking. Suffering is what makes the whole world

348

kin in Thérèse's understanding of human experience and suffering continues to exist with or without devotion to Jesus Christ; and what makes suffering bearable is love.

Suffering *is* an essential ingredient of life, and along with it some sort of acceptance of it, even if it falls very far short of Thérèse's joyous welcome. Thérèse held out great hope for the power of love as a conqueror of hate and tyranny and all the sniveling, snarling little miseries with which men afflict each other. But she realistically faced the fact that earth is not paradise. Nothing that science has conceived or concluded since her time on earth would, I think, change this certainty of conviction of hers; all the sorry political and economic history of the twentieth century would only confirm it. We take the first steps in our following after Thérèse if we can accept our suffering, or indeed any part of our suffering, with love. It may be that, to begin with, we find we can take only the slightest physical pain with something like Thérèsian acceptance, or perhaps not even that; perhaps it is only an occasional insult that we can bear, a nasty word intended for us, or for others, that until then we had not been able to endure. If we find we can endure anything that earlier we had found unendurable, we have moved along the tender little way of Thérèse of Lisieux, we have begun our Imitation.

This must be as clear as possible. I am talking about very little things indeed. We may for years have found ourselves irritated by chalk rubbed the wrong way up a blackboard or by the feeling that seems to shoot all through our bodies when by mischance we bite on a piece of tin foil. We may have our own tooth-clicking friends or associates, our own inveterate whistlers whose quarter-tone-flat assaults on pop tunes or patriotic airs drive us up the wall. It may be somebody's clamorous taste for garlic, which is evident after each trip to an Italian or French restaurant, or somebody else's great whiffs of sickly cigar smoke, blown with all deliberate speed right into our shrinking faces and up our noses. It may be the bump a friend or spouse invariably takes with too much speed, as we drive down our street, bouncing us against the roof of the car or just shoving around an internal organ or two. Or it may be the acerb remark that spouse or friend makes as we take the bumps too readily in stride when we drive. Worse than any of these it may be somebody's constant nagging or regular nastiness that galls us, a laconic insulter or a garrulous scold full of words of deprecation. Or it may not be anything that happens regularly at all; it may be only the occasional real or seeming insult, the joke about our looks or our clothing, the jibe about our tastes in food or art or literature that stings so much it brings tears to our eyes. If any of these very, very little things annoy us to the point of great anger or pain or that sort of pricking loss of self-respect that actually diminishes our capacity to go on living, then we have excellent materials for the Thérèsian spiritual exercises. If we have not yet begun the Imitation, then we should begin now. We have all the requirements except perhaps the will to follow the little way where it logically leads.

If we follow Thérèse, we must make every attempt to welcome these occasions of minor misery that so quickly become major. Without becoming masochistic about the miseries, as many babies do when they learn to compensate for the deprivation of their mothers' milk or their comfortable cribs by taking pleasure in the loss, we must turn to them as useful opportunities to develop our resistance to tiny tortures and minuscule misfortunes. That does not mean a course of wandering around schoolrooms in search of those freshly minted pieces of chalk that produce the most spine-bruising screeches or a steady diet of candies that come wrapped in tin foil. It does not indicate a haunting of the homes or offices of tooth-clickers or a laying in wait for off-key whistlers. It does not involve screwing up our faces under the mouths of garlic collectors or finding seats in trains or restaurants as close as possible to the smokers of the largest and smelliest and wettest stogies. It does mean shutting up in the face of such smells, in the hearing of such sounds, in the feeling of such sensations, and not just shutting up, but putting on as pleasant an expression as possible in place of that so-called "involuntary grimace" with which we have hitherto told the world what was happening to us. It means taking the bumps without complaint, if not with the joyous laughter that once at least in our lives we were probably able to muster for a ride on a roller coaster. It means resisting the exquisitely cutting remark, the positively Oscar-Wildean thrust with which we were about to lay low our bump-loving friend or spouse. On the great battlefield of nagging and nastiness, it means a constant retreat from involvement in the battle: no feinting or parrying, not even the passive resistance of long-suffering looks so that everybody around us can see how well we take our martyrdom. The only witness that counts in this encounter is the witness within; we may know what is happening, but nobody else should.

And so it must go, remark for remark, wound for wound, whether it is our looks or our words or our tastes or any other aspect of our lives and persons that is under attack. In the Thérèsian combat, the central weapon is cheerful acceptance, no matter how intense the attack. Strategic retreat is always acceptable. The avoidance of the situation, or of the person, or of the opportunity for the assault is also often right and proper but it must not be such a plotting of avoidance and withdrawal that one becomes a recluse, turning from any real meeting with people or environments new to one for fear of the wounds that may come, the insults, intended or not, the possible diminishing of our self-respect. Living always involves such threats to our ease. The answer to the threats is neither to turn away from all encounters which may bring on misery nor to answer misery with misery, threat with threat. In Thérèse's book, every sting we receive from others, every discomfort brought to us by others, every break in our composure, is an opportunity to help others compose themselves, to bring others comfort, to assuage their hurts and palliate their miseries.

The little tortures are an excellent introduction to the Imitation of Thérèse. They expose us to ourselves, revealing to us our significant weaknesses, our points of most immediate, if not greatest, vulnerability. If in this self-exposure we develop sufficient self-control to keep from exposing ourselves to others in our great little weaknesses, then we have worked ourselves into something like the right condition for the full-scale Imitation. The method here is not prescribed. Thérèse did not work out an orderly set of exercises, but her life, her autobiography, her letters, and her confidences to her sisters, especially in the last months of her life, suggest something like a logical procedure for those who would follow after her in the most practical of all spiritualities. She starts with a finish: she sees a clear end: union with love: the final meeting with Jesus that transcends time and in so doing redeems time, making every moment spent on the way to that final meeting a moment replete with justice and mercy and love, giving reason to the least rational of human experiences, righting all wrongs, explaining all iniquities, making sense of nonsense and order of disorder. Toward that glorious end she begins her pilgrimage with

her own reordering of the world around her, assuaging griefs by
her own good cheer, arresting suffering in others by her uncom-
plaining shouldering of her own suffering, taking every little opportunity offered her as a way of expressing love and especially
those splendid chances afforded by the pettinesses and shabbi-
nesses of others. It is this reordering that we parallel with our
cheerful acceptance of jarring sounds and tastes and smells, with
our warmth in the face of coldness, with our easy tolerance of the
alternately scabrous and frivolous attacks on our persons with
which our days inevitably must be full if they are human days.
We may lack Thérèse's fullness of inspiration. We probably do
not look forward with such eagerness or openness to the embrace of our lord and maker in a life after this life, even the most
reverent of us, even the most determinedly spiritual. We may utterly lack any clear end in view, but if we can see the justice of
Thérèse's way of dealing with little ills and littler annoyances and
irritations, if we can turn each of these gnatlike bites into something like a signification of love, then we have accomplished our
own share of the reordering of the world, we have enlarged love's
holding in the world, we have increased in some way or another
love itself.

After these opening exercises, Thérèse moved more deeply into
herself. She had found a way of dealing with others, which she
rehearsed two or three times before she entered Carmel—with her
mother, with her father, with her sisters, with her aunt and uncle
and cousins, with her companions and teachers at school. After
each set of exercises, each tentative exploration of the little way,
she began another set of exercises, another and deeper exploration, leading further and further into herself. She developed, as
everybody who makes any progress in the spiritual life must
develop, her own kind of self-examination, never altogether
systematic, never apparently altogether clear as to purpose, and
yet marvelously functional in her life in the way that such interior
conversation always is with those who are greatly gifted of spirit.
The famous Christmas conversion would never have occurred if
she had not earlier developed the ability to meditate quickly and
easily upon everything that happened to her or around her. She
responded almost immediately to her father's deprecation of the
old Christmas custom in the Martin household of leaving shoes
out to be filled with presents; she did not respond instinctively;

she did not respond either carelessly or thoughtlessly. When she made her way downstairs, it was with every deliberate thought. She knew just what she was doing. She had leaped years ahead, matured in a few seconds, it appeared. She had in fact conferred with herself, as by that time she had become used to doing, found a way of dealing with her father's complaint and adopted it.

Thérèse followed approximately the same procedure at the time of her devastating childhood illness. Whatever the force of the intervention of the statue of the Virgin of the Smile, whether it was strictly speaking miraculous or not, it required an equal and opposite response from Thérèse to be more than just a momentary recovery. As it happened, the recovery was permanent and the cure was more than just a cure of body, it was a cure of soul as well. As earlier there had been violent convulsions in her whole being, turning her away from any sort of bodily or spiritual or mental peace, now there were great turns in the opposite direction, convulsive in their own way, that established a lifelong serenity in her. It was not a peace that overrode everything else, but it was a resource deep down inside her with which she could meet the shrinking of her body and even the wasting away of her faith in the terrible dark doubts of her last year. It was not a resource that came all at once, with a smile from her father's old statue. It was at the deep end of a spiral of interior conversation, that dialogue to which even as a child she had so often had recourse, and which she would come back to again and again. And so we must, too, if we are to follow her. It is essential to Thérèsian spirituality. It is a constant counterpoint to the other exercises of the little way.

Here, too, in the development of an interior conversation in the manner of Thérèse, there is something like an order of things, but never so systematic a procedure that one must go to sleep with certain prayers on one's lips or particular images in one's mind. This is not like the "You are there!" school of spirituality which insists upon your matching every moment in your interior life with a mystery of the rosary, an incident in the life of Jesus or of Mary or of the Holy Family. With Thérèse one can be tired when one is tired, alert when one is alert, verbal when one is brimful of words, wordless when only pictures come to mind, and altogether blank if a commanding vacuity has taken over. As in the other exercises you constantly adjust to other people, so in this sequence, you adjust to you, to what you are, to who you are, and to what and who you are at any given moment.

All of this may sound hit-or-miss. It is not, though it allows for every variegation of personality and change of temperament. Thérèse moved in an unmistakable line from great self-consciousness to less and less awareness of herself in these conversations with herself, until finally she could say with absolute certainty that she was no longer talking to herself but to Jesus within her. But the self-consciousness had to come first. She had to plunge into herself with the most eager concerns for herself. She had, in fact, to become a counter and measurer, sorting out all her good deeds in the way her sisters had taught her, clicking off prayers and good thoughts and tender loving care of others and every other kindness that she had demonstrated with the precision of an old hand measuring Hail Mary's and Our Father's on the rosary beads. There may be natural-born saints, though outside of myth and legend there doesn't seem to be any good evidence for them. In any case, Thérèse was not one. She had to learn the drill just as methodically as she had to learn her numbers and her grammar and her history. If it came to her fairly easily, rather more like learning to ride a bicycle than like learning to play the violin, it did not come with such grace that she could quickly relinquish the proud joy she felt in adding up the good deeds and sweet thoughts. No one else should feel chagrined, then, at the large gusts of pride that sweep over one as one accomplishes a kindness. The first sort of interior conversation that follows upon the successful performance of Thérèse's kind of goodness is self-congratulation, warm self-congratulation. Required not to let anyone else know what one has done by the basic terms of the exercise, one must turn somewhere for acknowledgment of the accomplishment. To whom else than oneself? To whom better?

It would be a mistake, I think, to attempt to skip this stage of the inward life. The very childlikeness of the procedure is a guarantee of its fitting place in Thérèsian spirituality. Either way one feels little—because one takes pride in doing good or because one counts each small achievement like notches on a Western gunslinger's pistol or like Hercules marking off each of his titanic labors. It is a little person's way of doing things. With Thérèse one starts very little and as one progresses becomes smaller and smaller. But this is the smallness of simplicity, that simplicity

354

which at their best children constantly, wonderfully demonstrate, that simplicity which at our best brings us closer and closer to the nature of love, to the nature of being, to the nature of God. It is a world outside dissembling and pretension that we inhabit then. It is the truest of worlds for all of us, the world within us, where we face ourselves as we really are, with all our imperfections, with all our perfections, with all our sense of failure, with all our pride of success, and where, having known failure so often, we necessarily, at first anyhow, greet each success with tremendous enthusiasm. Chalk one up for our side! Against very great odds, against the very nature of the world, against our own nature, we have been sweet—thoughtful—kind—full of praise for others—silent about our own accomplishments—stolid in the face of nastiness—cheerful in the face of nagging—charming in the face of pain. How much do we exaggerate, after all, when we compare our accomplishment with the great gun of the old West who cleaned out a nest of villains from a terrorized town or with any one of the feats of Hercules? If it is an exaggeration, it is an allowable one, and even, perhaps, if you read Thérèse as I do, a genuinely necessary one.

The point of this counting and measuring stage of interiority is that one gets to know oneself a great deal better as a result of it. We discover in this process how much we depend upon the acknowledgment of others, their plaudits, their open praise, their encouragement. We may find that we cannot accept anything about ourselves, literally anything, unless it has found acceptance with others, either because we imitate exactly what they do, or because they tell us that what we are doing is acceptable—good —superb, some positive adjective of approval. We are almost bound to discover how rankling it is to have only ourselves as guarantors and approvers of our own actions—at first, anyway. It is here that measuring and counting becomes a rich and subtle mode of interior discourse, because here we begin to dig deep into the motivation of our actions, here we find our real as against our confessed beliefs, here we find ourselves. And here, if we follow each group of good deeds with a substantial colloquy with ourselves, we may eventually find ourselves acceptable to ourselves, and without need for any confirmation from anyone else outside ourselves. And then, having found ourselves somehow acceptable to ourselves, we may, following the quite simple sort of interior conversation which was Thérèse's, come to find ourselves somehow worthy of love, the love of others, the love of ourselves. I mean find *ourselves* when I say ourselves, not some extravagant version made up to suit the fantasies in which most of us think about love most of the time, but the real selves, with all the physical moles and mental moles and spiritual moles showing, with birthmarks and lifemarks, with marks of suffering and marks of joy, with all the record of ourselves that we reveal, not only to others but to ourselves. When we can see that that curious agglomeration of characteristics becomes character and that character, almost any character that is real character, is in some measure lovable, then we have reached a high level of achievement indeed. Then we may be ready really to love others, for then, in the noble terms of Jesus's commandment, we may be able to love our neighbors as we love ourselves.

What starts out, then, as a preoccupation with ourselves ends by becoming the most selfless of loves, ends by becoming love. And so it was with Thérèse. Thrown more and more into herself by all the early events of her life—by her mother's death, by her sisters' departure for the Carmel, by her great convulsive illness, by the apparent frustration of her own Carmelite ambitions—she made her way more and more out of herself. She did so by finding herself with such fullness and certainty that she could then give herself with fullness and certainty in love. She had something to give. When earlier she looked eagerly for hiding places and longed for nothing so much as to be overlooked, it was not out of devotion to God or to love, or at least not altogether; there was in the urge to be forgotten something of fear and timidity, and something of self-centeredness as well, I think. But when in her convent years she came to follow the ways of hiddenness, it was clearly because of a profound determination to merge herself with the object of her love, to suffer with him, to rejoice with him, to be despised with him, to be as much as anyone of us can be all things with him. Anyone who has ever loved anyone intensely— child, adult, parent, friend, wife, husband—will recognize the urge in Thérèse to give everything she had, to give everything she was, to the one she loved. Even if we cannot match the intensity of Thérèse's love, we can make large progress in her direction by developing in ourselves such a concentration upon the giving and receiving of love that we come to live always in its shadow, that

356

we come to be in some measure, at all times, a part of love. All this comes, almost inevitably, when we start the Imitation of Thérèse and persevere, even if with something less than brilliance. The certain marks of progress will be evident in the interior life, when we move, as inexorably we will move, from counting the marks of our own achievement to seeking opportunities to give marks to others' achievement, when we become content simply with the fact of love, noting all the time how remarkable a fact it is—people do love, people are lovable; amid all the misery and malice of mankind, in the midst of all the futility and the frustration, the tyranny and the torture, men and women still come together in love, children still produce their beatific smiles, tenderness and affection continue to exist in spite of all the good reasons why they should not.

In the late years of her life, Thérèse marveled much at love as a fact. If the mere desire of love, she meditated, was so extraordinarily sweet that words could not describe it, imagine what joy there must be in the possession and enjoyment of it forever, in eternity! It was a meditation, it or a hundred corollary meditations, that stayed with her in all the tasks of the conventual day. She washed, she tidied, she sewed, she walked about the garden, she sat in repose in the chapel—and she contemplated the fact of love, the fact that love was, that love is, that love would always be. The simple formulations of the Our Father and the Hail Mary were enough to gather her feelings of love together and to bring tears to her eyes. "How sweet it is to call God our Father!" she exclaimed to one of her novices who found her sewing in her cell one day but obviously doing more than sewing, so tender, so far away was the expression on her face. She had been thinking about the meaning of the words of the Lord's Prayer.

One real danger to our own meditations upon love, in this following after Thérèse, is the natural tendency in all of us to sentimentality. It is easy to mistake surface impressions for profound ones in the contemplation of love, to be caught up in all those pleasing but essentially superficial externals that the advertising agencies have for so long depended upon to break down our defenses—a baby or an animal or a young woman of great charm or beauty, drawn or painted or photographed in a setting designed to show off the charm or beauty to best advantage, or a woodland or meadow scene, reproduced with all the irregularities removed, without any ruffling of the dirt or disturbance of the grass, with every flower the right height and the right color, the others having been carefully airbrushed out. If one comes to believe strongly enough in these signs of beauty or charm as the real things, one comes, inevitably, to find the real thing sadly wanting. Flowers do not grow in perfect line with each other, even when they are planned and planted by a master nurseryman. Dirt does ruffle; grass is easily kicked about, bent, scarred, burned, and weeds keep turning up in the most carefully sown lawns. Not all babies are magazine or picture-book babies; only a small portion of young women possess the necessary set of proportions to sell beer or perfume or cigarettes or deodorants or detergents, even after they have been worked on by the armies of technicians who can push, pull, add, subtract, pluck, tease, paint in or paint out beauty. Some animals are mongrels; only a few, even of the oh, so carefully bred, can be shining examples of their species. If love were to be confined to the best of breed or the most shrewdly made up, how little love there would be in the world. If we were to confine our concentration upon love to the mere signs of love, how superficial our love would be and how quickly dissipated. We must start with superficialities, making all our normal little exchanges with other people, even the most trivial of them, into loving ones, but we must not expect in these exchanges to find any significant revelation of persons, except insofar as our own acts of loving kindness elicit in others the kind of meditation that we are trying to develop in ourselves. We certainly cannot depend upon anything we do arousing such a chain of reactions in them, so that, conscious or unconscious of our motivation, they come somehow to parallel our activity and to reveal all that is lovable in them as we hope in some way to show, at least to ourselves, those qualities in us which are lovable. No, we must dig deep into our friendships; we must contemplate with some of the same fervor Thérèse brought to the Our Father and the Hail Mary, even if all we are contemplating is a mongrel dog, or a strange-looking female cousin thrice removed. We must go well below surfaces to avoid being caught up in surfaces. We must avoid like the plague the terrible distortions of sentimentality or its ugly blood relative, hardness of heart. In so doing, however, we must not be quick to call sentimental all manifestations of intense feeling, whether for a mongrel dog, a strange-looking female

358

cousin, or Jesus Christ. Nor must we diagnose hardness of heart, in ourselves or in others, because the language or look of admiration comes slowly or reluctantly to the surface. It should be enough that it comes to the surface.

It is vital not to stop at surfaces in our relationships. We must guard against mere sentimentality. But in our probing to establish the deepest possible level of love and friendship we must be equally on guard against ascribing every sort of dubious motive to others, whether it be hardness of heart or selfishness or bad faith, a perverted desire to lead or an equally twisted need to be led. If anyone elicits anything approaching love in us—and sooner or later in the Thérèsian Imitation everyone will—then that is enough to go on. There is only one appropriate response—love and let *the other* do as he wills. It is not weak to do so. It is no sign of sentimentality to open our arms to those who open their arms to us. It is only sentimentality when the sign is all we want, the look of love, the language of love, the shining surface, with none of the claims that follow after, with no responsibility, no commitment, no continuing involvement.

Thérèse's genius was to recognize what depths were concealed in the signs of love that she found all around her. She saw that a harsh word could be a clumsy manifestation of affection. She recognized in nervous habits and unruly dispositions the sputtering noises of sick but not unloving hearts. She came to know as she performed her little exercises of tenderness that insofar as sick hearts could be repaired, she had the tools. If we, in reading her, are foolish enough to stop at the signs of tenderness, and to be affronted by their occasional stickiness or stuffiness or girlish exaggeration, then we will be guilty of almost every possible sin against the Thérèsian canon. We will ourselves have stopped at surfaces and we will have judged by surfaces. We will have failed to answer an irritation with affection and understanding. We will not have paused to think with any thoroughness about the possible meaning of her sometimes ornate manner. We will have turned unlovingly from one of the great displays of love of the modern world.

It is difficult for many to see how the life of a nun far removed from the world may be instructive for the lives of laymen deeply involved in the world. It should not be if we have learned that crucial lesson of Thérèse's that everything and everyone in the world can teach us something of love, and especially those things and persons that force us out of ourselves by way of some humbling reconsideration of ourselves. We need not look up to Thérèse because of her religious vocation; we must not look down upon her because of it. If we go to her, we go to one of those who are remarkably wise in human relations, an elder in the courts of love, who was extraordinarily well tutored by her elders, and who left in word and example an incomparable course of spiritual exercises, though one not quite methodical in shape or structure—and therefore endlessly flexible and more capable of wide application than any rigid method. Her choice of a Carmelite convent as the place in which to pursue her researches into the wisdom of love makes as much sense as the selection of a great technological institute by those who want to do research in nuclear physics or the choice of a manuscript collection such as that of the British Museum or the Bodleian at Oxford for those who have humanistic studies in mind. As a specialist, she went to specialists, to impart her learning, to gather theirs, and to leave us the fruit of both.

INDEX

Agnes, St., 129, 267
Agnès of Jesus, Sister, 46, 48, 86,
  127, 129, 172, 101, 105, 110.
  See also Martin, Pauline
Albertus Magnus (Albert the
  Great), 6
Aloysius Gonzaga, St., 308
Alphonsus Liguori, St., 91–92,
  326
Anne, Charles, 338
Anne of Jesus, Ven. Mother, 266–
  67, 270, 273
Anthony, St., 128
Archimedes, 323
Arminjon, Abbé, 119, 150, 165–
  69
Augustine, St., 167–68, 184, 232,
  280, 323, 345
Augustine of St. Thérèse, Sister,
  137

Balthasar, Hans Urs von, 104–6,
  122, 141
Beevers, John, 48
Bellière, Abbé Maurice-Barthé-
  lemy, 244–46, 272, 274, 286,
  317, 327
Belloc, Hilaire and Louise, 72
Benjamin Minor (by Richard of
  St. Victor), 235
Bernadette Soubirous, St., 6–8,
  31, 41–43
Bernard, St., 5, 18, 141
Bernini, 236
Bérulle, Pierre de, 229

Bishop of Bayeux. *See* Hugonin,
  Msgr.
Bishop of Gallipoli, 339–40
Bishop of Nardo, 340–41
Boccaccio, 254
Bonaventure, St., 6, 167
Books on St. Thérèse, viii, 11,
  16, 50–52, 82, 195, 236, 309,
  336, 343. *See also Conseils et
  Souvenirs; Heroic Sanctity and
  Insanity; Hidden Face; Inte-
  rior Carmel; Love Is My Vo-
  cation; Search for St. Thérèse;
  Shower of Roses; Story of a
  Family*
Bouix, Marcel, 196
Bourjade, Pere, 343
Brewster, Sir Davis, 227
Bunyan, John, 54

Camus, Albert, 53
Carmela, Sister Maria, 339–41
Carmelite rule, 140, 146, 195,
  201, 212, 214, 266, 272, 290,
  330, 335
Carmelite spirituality, 182, 195,
  207, 246, 330. *See also* John of
  the Cross; Teresa; Thérèse
Carmelite tradition, 254, 271
Catherine, St., 128, 158, 218
Chateaubriand, François-René
  de, 13–16
Chaucer, 254, 287
Clarkson, Tom, 236
Claude de la Colombière,
  Blessed, 204, 312

Martin, Céline (cont'd)
118–19, 121, 123–34, 136,
138, 142–44, 146–52, 154–56,
162–63, 166–67, 169–70, 174–
77, 195–204, 206, 208–16,
218–20, 223–24, 226, 228,
240, 247–48, 250, 252–55,
274, 281, 304–7, 309, 324,
326, 328–29, 331–32, 344;
memoirs of Thérèse, 195, 309;
paintings, 177; relationship
with Thérèse, 84, 87, 89, 97,
99, 111, 113; travels, 123–33,
163; vocation to Carmel, 121,
136, 149, 174, 176, 196, 200–
1, 204, 206, 208, 210–16, 218–
20, 223–24, 226, 228, 253–55,
306–7
Martin, Hélène (sister of Thérèse), 23, 26, 28, 115
Martin, Joseph (two brothers of
Thérèse), 23, 24, 28, 115
Martin, Léonie (sister of Thérèse; Sister Thérèse-Dosithée
of the Visitation), 17, 20, 23,
26, 35, 38–40, 44, 56, 65, 74,
80–81, 84–85, 87, 90, 99, 102,
113, 115, 121, 135–36, 146–
49, 163, 175–76, 199, 202–4,
208, 213, 219, 238–41, 264,
277, 304, 327; death, 238; vocation to the Poor Clares, 115,
204; vocation to the Visitation,
121, 135–36, 163, 199, 202–4,
208, 219, 238–40
Martin, Louis (Thérèse's father),
13–22, 24, 26–27, 29, 35–36,
43, 45, 47–51, 54, 58–61, 65–
67, 69–74, 80–81, 84–87, 89–
90, 99, 101, 113–16, 118–19,
121, 123–33, 138–39, 143–50,
155–56, 163–65, 170, 175–
204, 208–10, 328; illness and
death, 121, 143–50, 163, 175–
204, 208–9; literary tastes, 14–
15, 18, 59–60
Martin, Marie (Thérèse's oldest
sister and godmother), 17, 25,

29, 33, 35–38, 40–41, 44–46,
48–49, 56–58, 61–66, 69–71,
80–81, 84–90, 97, 99, 101,
107, 111, 113–15, 120, 125,
129, 135, 137, 139–40, 146,
155, 170, 177, 201–2, 206–9,
240, 265, 267–69, 277–78,
304, 314, 325, 331, 335, 356;
entry into Carmel, 114–15,
120, 140, 356; relationship
with Thérèse, 58, 88, 111,
113–14, 120, 125
Martin, Mélanie-Thérèse (sister
of Thérèse), 23, 26–27, 115
Martin, Pauline (sister of Thérèse; Sister Agnès of Jesus in
Carmel), v, 3, 17–18, 22, 23,
29, 31, 35–42, 44, 46, 48, 50,
56–59, 61, 64–70, 72–74, 76–
79, 84, 87–89, 91, 95–96, 99–
100, 113–14, 120–22, 125,
129, 131, 135, 137–39, 145–
48, 150, 152, 154–55, 170,
172, 177, 182, 185, 195, 201–
2, 205–6, 211, 214, 218–19,
225, 228, 236–37, 240, 244–
45, 252, 255–56, 258, 281–82,
284, 287, 304–6, 308, 310–13,
316, 325, 328, 330–32, 334–
36, 343, 356; "adoption" as
Thérèse's mother, 46, 58, 67,
258; editing of Thérèse's manuscripts, v, 334–36, 343; guidance and training of Thérèse,
65, 67–69, 72–74, 76–77, 95–
96, 125, 172, 256; entry into
Carmel, 76–79, 84, 91, 120,
122, 138, 219, 356; term as
Prioress, 46, 182, 185, 202,
205, 244–45, 252, 255, 282
Martin, Thérèse. See Thérèse,
Saint
Martin, Zélie Guérin (Thérèse's
mother), 12–13, 18, 21–47,
54, 59, 67–68, 75, 80, 83, 88–
90, 114, 125, 131, 146, 154,
164, 170, 185, 203, 238–39,
356; death, 239, 356; letters

Poor Clares, 115, 204
Pope, the, 7–8, 28–29, 39, 120, 124–26, 129–31, 285–86, 317. *See also* John XXIII; Leo XIII; Pius X; Pius XI
Pranzini, 118–19
Prayer, types of, 193–94; efficacy of, 247–48. *See also* Devotions; Mysticism; Thérèse
Prioress of Carmel, 46, 77, 86, 133, 136–37, 141, 178–82, 186, 188, 191. *See also* Agnès, Mother (Martin, Pauline); Geneviève, Mother; Gonzague, Mother; Marie-Ange, Mother
Prou, Father Alexis, 172
Proust, Marcel, 51
Proverbs, Book of, 68, 280
Psalms, 219, 235, 258, 311, 326
Purgatory, 288–89, 294–95, 302, 306, 314–16, 321, 325–27, 329
Pushkin, 259

Quietism, 15, 196

Racine, 15, 196
Raymond Pennafort, St., 157
Religious life, characteristics and difficulties of, 187–88, 195, 201–2, 228, 247, 286. *See also* Devotions; Prayer; Scruples; Spiritual life
Renan, 51
Reverony, M. (Vicar-General of Bayeux), 130–31, 133
Richard of St. Victor, 235
Rimbaud, Arthur, 160, 162
Robert Bellarmine, St., 167
Robo, Father Étienne, 80–82, 88, 90
Rohrbach, Father Peter-Thomas, 50–51, 81
Rosary, 95–96, 193–94, 318, 354
Roulland, Père Adolphe-Jean-Louis-Eugène, 270–74, 287–89, 294, 310–12, 317

Sacred Heart, 5–8, 43, 233
St. Joseph of Jesus, Sister, 173
St. Peter, Sister, 301
Saints, 1–2, 4–10, 12, 17, 29–30, 45, 51, 63, 82, 128–29, 158, 160, 162, 226, 236, 245, 306, 315–17, 323, 328, 345, 354; characteristics of, 236, 345; communion of, 226, 315; families of, 29–30; hagiography, 12, 29, 45; in 20th century, 5–9. *See also* individual saints listed by first names
Scripture, 321–22. *See also* Epistles; Gospels; Old Testament; Thérèse, love of *and* Quotations from
Scruples, 86, 91–92, 152
Search for St. Thérèse, 50
Sevigné, Mme. de, 56
Sheed, Frank, ix
Shower of Roses, 336
Shroud of Turin, 254
Simeon, Brother, 131, 155, 285
Sodality, 314
Song of Songs, 99–100, 118, 154, 159, 200, 203, 251, 263, 277, 313, 316–17, 321–22, 330
Spiritual life (*see* Thérèse); spiritual direction, 92, 140–41; spiritual writers, 13–14, 59, 72, 166–67, 233, 312. *See also* Arminjon; Balthasar; *Cloud of Unknowing;* Guéranger; *Imitation of Christ; L'Année Liturgique;* Maistre; Thérèse, books read by
Stein, Edith, 120
Story of a Family, 11
Story of a Soul. See Thérèse, autobiography
Strabo, Walafrid, 95
Suarez, 167
Surin, Father Joseph, 196–97, 229

Taille, Rose (Martins' wet nurse), 24–25, 29

367